DECOLONIZING MEMORY

Jill Jarvis

DECOLONIZING MEMORY

Algeria and the
Politics of Testimony

Duke University Press
Durham and London
2021

© 2021 DUKE UNIVERSITY PRESS
All rights reserved
Designed by Courtney Leigh Richardson
Typeset in Huronia Pro and Helvetica Lt Std by typesetter, Inc.

Library of Congress Cataloging-in-Publication Data
Names: Jarvis, Jill, [date] author.
Title: Decolonizing memory: Algeria and the politics of testimony / Jill Jarvis.
Description: Durham: Duke University Press, 2021. | Includes bibliographical references and index.
Identifiers: LCCN 2020032094 (print)
LCCN 2020032095 (ebook)
ISBN 9781478011965 (hardcover)
ISBN 9781478014102 (paperback)
ISBN 9781478021414 (ebook)
Subjects: LCSH: Collective memory and literature—Algeria. | Collective memory—Political aspects—Algeria. | Literature and history—Algeria. | Politics and literature—Algeria. | African literature (French)—History and criticism. | French literature—Algeria—History and criticism. | Imperialism in literature.
Classification: LCC PN56.C618 J378 2021 (print) | LCC PN56.C618 (ebook) | DDC 840.9/965—dc23
LC record available at https://lccn.loc.gov/2020032094
LC ebook record available at https://lccn.loc.gov/2020032095

Cover art: Illustration based on "XIII planches/poètes (a genealogy a constellation)," by Samira Negrouche.

IN MEMORIAM

Yamina Mechakra
(1949–2013)

Assia Djebar
(1936–2015)

Fadwa Saïdi
(1983–2016)

Marcel Bois
(1925–2018)

Gisèle Halimi
(1927–2020)

Contents

Acknowledgments ix

Introduction. THE FUTURE OF MEMORY 1

1   REMNANTS OF MUSLIMS 27
2   UNTRANSLATABLE JUSTICE 63
3   MOURNING REVOLT 98
4   OPEN ELEGY 141

Conclusion. PRISONS WITHOUT WALLS 168

Notes 197
Bibliography 255
Index 267

Acknowledgments

Though it can feel like a solitary process, one does not write a book alone. I was able to see this one through because I was held up by the solidarity, friendship, encouragement, criticism, advice, and care of the following people.

At Princeton, I learned much from Ben Baer's keen insight, nimble intellect, and precise questions. Simon Gikandi's rare wisdom and perspective helped me to cultivate critical courage. Nick Nesbitt was a vital interlocutor and consistent ally. Early drafts of material that found its way into this book benefited immensely from conversations with Gayatri Chakravorty Spivak, Madeleine Dobie, Ann Smock, Emily Apter, Jeffrey Stout, Cornel West, Sandra Bermann, Wendy Belcher, Lital Levy, Susana Draper, and Michael Wood. I am indebted to Eileen Reeves and Valerie Kanka in Princeton's Department of Comparative Literature for moral and tactical support. Bella Brodzki at Sarah Lawrence College pointed me toward this path before I could see it for myself. Thank you.

Now, I am wildly fortunate to work alongside such generous, smart, and kind colleagues in Yale's French Department. In particular, my heartfelt thanks to Alice Kaplan, Christopher Miller, Maurice Samuels, and Pierre Saint-Amand for reading—and rereading!—this manuscript at crucial junctures. Agnès Bolton has done the needful and infinitely more. I am grateful to my undergraduate and graduate students at Yale; their insights into these materials have indelibly changed my own ways of reading and thinking about them. I am also indebted to brilliant and hospitable colleagues and friends whose paths I first crossed in Algeria, especially at les Glycines centre d'études diocésan in Algiers and at the

Centre d'études maghrébines en Algérie in Oran. My deep gratitude to Guillaume Michel, the late Henri Teissier, the late Marcel Bois, Brahim Rouabah, Karim Ouaras, Robert Parks, Nassim Balla, Afifa Bererhi, Nacéra Khiat, Lamis Saïdi, Miloud Yabrir, Samira Negrouche, Djamel Hachi, Jim House, Elizabeth Perego, Samuel Anderson, Sami Everett, Naoual Belakhdar, and Pauline Poupart.

Elizabeth Ault at Duke University Press is an inspired and impeccable editor. I am immensely grateful to her and to the two anonymous readers whose astute feedback helped me to clarify every aspect of this book. My admiration and gratitude to Walid Bouchakour and Doyle Calhoun for their very fine attention to stylistic and linguistic details of the manuscript, and to Neil Belakhdar for his sharp-eyed expertise.

Research for this project has been supported by the American Institute for Maghrib Studies, the Princeton Institute for International and Regional Studies, the Yale Whitney Humanities Center Griswold Faculty Research Fund, the Frederick W. Hilles Publication Fund of Yale University, the Junior Faculty Manuscript Colloquium fund from Yale Faculty of Arts and Sciences, and the Yale MacMillan Center.

A thousand thanks to those who have buoyed my spirits, asked the right questions, offered refuge and sustenance, and celebrated with me at milestones throughout this long marathon: Cate Reilly, Francisco Robles, Brahim El Guabli, Kameron Collins, Gavin Arnall, Melissa Gonzalez, Jill Richards, Marta Figlerowicz, Cajetan Iheka, Sunny Xiang, Robin Dembroff, Morgane Cadieu, Christophe Schuwey, Melissa Febos, Shelly Oria, Cara Gardner, Jeannette Zimmer, Jesse Newman, Erin Blankeny, Wanjiru Kamau-Rutenberg, Marie Constance Hountondji, Kanchuka Dharmasiri, and Yemisi Damisah. And to Fadwa Saïdi, a beloved friend and gifted teacher of Arabic who left this world too soon.

Finally, thank you to my family for providing me with both the freedom and the love necessary to sustain me through this work—including the nonhumans, Otis and Eliot, who have sat so faithfully beside my desk from beginning to end, watching over every word.

Introduction

The Future of Memory

Literature is not evidence, but an instrument for imaginative training. —Gayatri Spivak

L'Algérie coloniale championne du monde du rendre-invisible: on n'avait même pas besoin d'apartheid: on pouvait se promener au milieu de la foule algérienne sans les voir.

Colonial Algeria, world champion of making-invisible: we didn't even need apartheid: we could walk around surrounded by Algerian crowds without seeing them. —Hélène Cixous

...*musulmans* (le vocable inscrivait l'exclusivité dans laquelle la société coloniale nous avait tenus depuis 1830 et les différents décrets qui avaient annoncé la décrépitude dans laquelle nous devions être maintenus: *Français-Musulmans, disaient les uns, musulmans à part entière, disaient les autres, sans qu'aucune de ces deux appellations puisse nous fournir l'illusion de quelque disponibilité juridique*) ...

...*musulmans* (the term registered the exclusive state in which colonial society had held us since 1830 and the various legal decrees announcing the decrepitude in which we were to be kept: *French-Muslims, said some, fully Muslim, said others, while neither of these two names could give us the illusion of any legal access*) ... —Nabile Farès

Seeing Ghosts

In the last epigraph above—from *Mémoire de l'Absent* (1974) by novelist Nabile Farès—a parenthetical clause disrupts the syntax of a sentence. As if muttering commentary on the italicized word *musulmans*, this interjection opens space on the page to veer away from the narrative present. A reader is slyly confronted by the complaint that Algeria under French occupation was ground zero of a uniquely strange juridical regime whose afterlife has indelibly shaped the present order—or rather, disorder—of the novel's world.[1] Like Farès, many of Algeria's writers have found themselves in the difficult bind of trying to make perceptible what has been forcibly disappeared, and of sounding out what cannot yet be heard. *Decolonizing Memory* tracks their literary responses to a historiographic impasse: how to see or to hear what history has rendered ghostly?[2] As the digression in Farès's text seems almost to whisper, the magnitude of the legal violence exercised by the French to colonize and occupy Algeria is such that *only* aesthetic works, in particular, literature, have been able to register its enduring effects.

Above all, *Decolonizing Memory* is a defense of literature's unexpected, disruptive, and surreptitious power to make ghosts perceptible, and to make possible what state violence has rendered nearly unimaginable. I chart a literary constellation whose center is Algeria.[3] Foregrounding the ways that texts speak to one another across time and between languages, I explore anarchival forms of literary expression that unsettle and elude official discourses of both the French and Algerian states in ways that not only rewrite the colonial past, but also make it possible to envision decolonized futures. While I am indebted to scholarship that has established the myriad ways in which Algeria's independence war indelibly shaped French political and intellectual life as well as anglophone literary and critical theory, the focus of my inquiry lies elsewhere. By taking Algeria to be an important nexus of aesthetic innovation and theoretical contestation rather than a periphery legible only in relation to the former imperial metropole, and by highlighting the profoundly multilingual and heterogeneous character of Algerian writing, this book contributes to expanding decolonial approaches to African memory. Through a critical practice grounded in close reading across languages and informed by research conducted in Algeria, I aim to help shift the spatial, temporal, and linguistic frameworks that have to this point organized aesthetic and theoretical studies of testimony around Euro-American reference points. Maghrebi and African literatures *already* "theorize from below," presenting an opportunity to radically retrain our political imaginations.[4]

From its legal annexation to France in the mid-nineteenth century until Algeria's national independence in 1962, Algérie française was founded on a juridical distinction drawn between French citizen (*citoyen*) and French noncitizen subject (*sujet*).[5] Soon after the French invaded the Ottoman Regency of Algiers, a military directive (September 1830) declared the seized territory a blank slate on which to write French law. A directive issued the following month (October 1830) revised this claim to recognize the limited jurisdiction of what the French called *musulman* and *israélite* civil codes. These categories and codes evolved over time to facilitate state-sponsored violence whose destructive impact has not been fully calculated or worked through.[6]

In her *Le trauma colonial: Une enquête sur les effets psychiques et politiques contemporains de l'oppression coloniale en Algérie* (2018), Karima Lazali cites details from recent demographic studies done by Kamel Kateb in collaboration with historians Abderrahmane Bouchène, Jean-Pierre Peyroulou, Ouanassa Siari Tengour, and Sylvie Thénault that attempt to count Algerian victims of French state violence. Lazali underscores that during four decades of French colonizing war to break Algerian resistance (1830–75), *nearly one third* of Algeria's indigenous population was exterminated. That is, between the massacres, military razzias, epidemics, and famines that took place during these decades of military rule, nearly one million out of almost three million estimated inhabitants of Algeria were killed.[7]

My guiding claim is that literature provides what demographic data, historical facts, and legal trials cannot in terms of attesting to and accounting for this loss. This legally orchestrated mass murder has never been the focus of a legal trial or state-sponsored reconciliation process like those held to reckon with the Shoah, or more recently in South Africa after apartheid and in Rwanda after genocide. As Lazali also points out, studies of the enduring psychological impact of the calculated erasure that forcibly made and kept Algeria French—the destruction of entire tribes, lineages, patronyms, toponyms, languages, worlds—do not yet exist, with the exception of Frantz Fanon's works, which he composed before French occupation ended in 1962. The explicitly nonrestorative power of literary representation does not retrieve or recuperate; it does not provide verifiable evidence. It does, however, register the traces of the disappeared in ways that provoke disturbance, unsettlement, pain, anger, and movement.

Decolonization tends to be the framework for narrating histories of Algérie française and what came in its wake. But, as scholars like Todd Shepard and Françoise Vergès have pointed out, this can be a deceptive frame that freezes settler colonial violence into a story about the past. Drawing insight from Shepard and Vergès, I take the terms *decolonization* and *postcolonial* to be invented—not neutral or natural—temporal categories with consequences for political imagination. In its unsettling and disturbing way, literature can help to set memory and imagination free from the temporal and spatial frames that underwrite the *ongoing* coloniality of power.

The multilingual, genre-defying literary works at the heart of my inquiry test and stretch testimonial practices beyond such frames. These literary experiments in testimony, as I read them, move in what Lia Brozgal has called an *anarchival* relationship to the language of the nation-state and its laws.[8] Transforming Derrida's adjective *anarchivic* into a noun (*anarchive*), Brozgal underscores the ambivalent and contestatory relationship of anarchival aesthetic works to state-controlled archives: "the anarchive is not located in any single text," she writes, "but rather designates a set of works that evince an archival function and that, together, produce an epistemological system in oppositional relationship to an official archive."[9] The anarchival movement facilitated by writing, publishing, translating, circulating, and interpreting literature in Algeria has created clandestine space not only to protect and preserve threatened historical memory, but also to nurture political resistance and rebellion.

The peculiar legal history of French-colonized Algeria casts the relationship of testimony to law in a troubled light. This history has also been narrated in ways that render rebellion illegitimate or invisible. In 1848, the constitution of the French Second Republic legally annexed Algeria to France, carved it into three French departments (Constantine, Alger, Oran) and a southern territory, and affirmed a consequential distinction between *les citoyens français* (bearers of full citizenship rights) and *les sujets français* (bearers of extremely limited or no political rights, subject to military conscription, forced labor, and a separate disciplinary system) in order to facilitate wide-scale dispossession and occupation of Algeria's profitable, arable land. As the French military invaded south into the Sahara during the mid-nineteenth century,[10] the initial premise of political assimilation was institutionalized with the 1865 "Sénatus-Consulte on the Status of Persons and Naturalization in Algeria," which further classified les sujets français as either *indigènes israélites* or *indigènes musulmans*. A few years later, the Crémieux Decree (1870) extended French citizenship to most (but not all)[11] of the thirty thousand "indigènes israélites" living in Algérie française but reserved the ambiguous status of sujet for those millions of inhabitants designated as "indigènes musulmans," legally considered to be "Muslim" French subjects, but not citizens.[12]

The French category of the "musulman" subject had little to do with the religious practices and commitments of those it supposedly described and much to do with placing a vast population of noncitizens at a precarious legal threshold.[13] The noncitizen "indigène musulman" juridical status persisted under different names until beyond World War II, while Algeria's Jewish inhabitants abruptly lost and regained French citizenship under the Vichy regime between 1940 and 1943.[14] Jacques Derrida, who left Algiers for the first time in 1949 at age eighteen, refers to this complicated situation as "the most extraordinary history of citizenship in Algeria, which has to my knowledge no equivalent, *stricto sensu*, in the world."[15] In her "Lettre à Zohra Drif" (1999), Hélène Cixous remembers her adolescence in colonized Algiers where she was one of few Jews among even fewer Muslim "indigène" students enrolled at the prestigious Lycée Fromentin in 1947. "Colonial Algeria, world champion of making-invisible: we didn't even need apartheid: we could walk around surrounded by Algerian crowds *without seeing them*."[16]

In recent years, scholars have elucidated the myriad ways in which the peculiar legal "exceptions" that governed Algérie française created defining fissures in the very institutions of modern citizenship and democracy, as well as in the concept of modernity itself.[17] The invented category of colonized person classified as a French national but not a citizen technically lasted until 1948, but the French ways of perceiving Algerians—and of *not* seeing them, as Cixous describes—that this category both reflected and engendered have lasted much longer, under different names and configurations.

Beginning in the 1880s, a chaotic jumble of legal decrees, circulars, and rulings were gathered together and formalized as a body of law called the Code de l'indigénat. This overtly discriminatory code outlined a separate penal system along with a list of infractions classified as punishable crimes *only* when committed by the majority of Algeria's population classified as "indigène."[18] Special infractions included such acts as behaving disrespectfully toward an agent of authority; refusing to furnish topographical information demanded by agents of French authority; living alone in an isolated place outside the *mechta* (small village); gathering for religious festivals without authorization; begging outside the *douar* ("duwār," a larger village; this became a term for French administrative divisions), even for the sick or disabled, except in authorized cases; giving asylum to undocumented vagabonds; burial outside the specified areas or at a depth less than what has been determined appropriate; and shooting weapons without authorization during festivals.

In his study of this dark side of French law, tellingly subtitled *Anatomie d'un "monstre" juridique*, Olivier Le Cour Grandmaison calls the code a "juridical anarchy" and underscores the extreme and unprecedented nature of this legal experiment in the history of French empire.[19] Historian Sylvie Thénault has studied the relationship of the Code de l'indigénat to the expanding network of prisons, detention centers, and concentration camps that was indispensable to the French conquest and administration of Algeria from the nineteenth century through the long war waged against Algerian resistance during the mid-twentieth century (1945–62). "With the *indigénat*," Thénault argues, "colonial violence was inscribed into law. Legitimized, it was made banal."[20]

Dictating from his hospital bed in Bethesda in late 1961 as the anticolonial uprising in Algeria raged to its end without him, Frantz Fanon observed the magnitude of French legal violence with prescient acuity. "The colonial regime draws its legitimacy from force," he writes near the conclusion of his essay on violence in *Les damnés de la terre*, "and at no point does it try to dissemble this order of things."[21] Fanon was not convinced that legal independence for Algeria would resolve the damage already done by the force of French law. He outlined the tragic "misadventures" that would befall any decolonization process entrusted to a national bourgeoisie already poised to take up the relay of state power in Algeria, as had happened in other recently liberated African states.[22] He also observed the French state's effort to make disappear its own long-standing politics of extermination, and raised serious questions about relying on any future nation-state as a framework for genuinely decolonial justice.

Near the conclusion of the chapter "De la violence," Fanon accents the calculated, arithmetic character of a "disparition" that entails both the legal erasure and actual killing of human beings: "This line of reasoning that so arithmetically foretells the disappearance of colonized people," he writes, "does not shock the colonized with moral indignation."[23] Fanon initially depicts this "disappearance" from the viewpoint of the French occupier, to whom mass murder appears as an instrumental, unsurprising, even necessary part of civilizing progress: "And when, prescribing specific methods, the colonizer asks each member of the oppressing minority to take down 30 or 100 indigènes, he sees that no one is outraged and that ultimately the whole problem is to determine whether this can be done all at once or in stages."[24]

Such reasoning "does not surprise the colonized either," Fanon emphasizes—though for different reasons.[25] From the standpoint of colonized Algerians that Fanon assumes in this passage, such violence is not shocking or surprising because at no point was it hidden or secret. Algerians targeted by French law were never blind to its brutality. They never mistook the occupier's law to be a humanizing or civilizing force, or regarded such terror as "progress." Having seen French law in action from the start, Fanon points out, the colonized know well that the law was never meant to protect those whom it identifies for calculated destruction and erasure.

Fanon's observation about the nature of colonizing law appeared less obvious to French citizens who were not its targets but its beneficiaries. Just before resigning from his civil post at the Blida psychiatric hospital to join the Front de libération nationale (FLN) in 1956, Fanon had written a short "Letter to a Frenchman" designed to shock a well-meaning French citizen of Algeria out of his own blindness to the legally orchestrated disappearance of Algerians taking place all around him. In the letter, Fanon gestures to spectral human figures vanishing into the desert landscape: "Unseen Arabs. Ignored Arabs. Arabs passed over in silence. Arabs vanished, hidden. Arabs repudiated every day, transformed into Saharan scenery. And you are on the side of those: who have never shaken an Arab's hand. Never shared coffee."[26]

Fanon had already diagnosed this problem many years before he composed *Les damnés de la terre* in 1961 or resigned from his post at Blida in 1956. In fact, analyzing a French propensity for creating "Muslim," "North African," and "Arab" ghosts[27] is the central preoccupation of Fanon's first published essay, "Le 'syndrome nord-africain'" ("The 'North African Syndrome'"), which appeared in print just before *Peau noire, masques blancs*. In a February 1952 issue of the journal *L'esprit*, Fanon focused on the condition of North African workers in France.[28] He had just completed his medical residency in Lyon, where he had treated many of these workers in his clinic. Fanon raises pointed questions about the Algerians hidden in plain sight in the French city, where their status as human seems to recede beneath a torrent of racist epithets: "Who are they really, these creatures who dissimulate themselves, who are dissimulated by the social truth behind attributes like *bicot, bounioule, arabe, raton, sidi, mon z'ami?*"[29]

As the quotation marks in its title immediately signal, the essay mimics the etiological protocols of a scientific medical paper in order to subvert its diagnostic norms. What opens sounding much like a case study transforms itself into a cutting indictment and a justice plaint. At the essay's conclusion, Fanon shifts abruptly to direct address, demanding of his French reader: "How, how, this man that you reify by systematically calling him Mohammed, whom you reconstruct or rather dissolve on the basis of an idea—an idea that you know to be disgusting (you know perfectly well that you're robbing him of something, that something for which not so very long ago you were willing to give up everything, even your life), well then! *this man*—don't you get the sense that you are draining him of his very substance?"[30] Here, Fanon's parenthetical aside pinpoints the irony that the very "humanity" that so many French citizens had been willing to die in order to protect from Nazi destruction just six years earlier is what the idea and the institutions of Algérie française are designed to strip from men (*cet homme-ci*) whom the same French citizens routinely treat as interchangeable, disposable "Mohammeds."

The essay concludes by appealing to a sense of justice that transcends French law. Fanon sounds the keywords of French republicanism—"Rights, Duties, Citizenship, Equality, how nice!"[31]—to underscore the precarious status of colonized subjects to whom such promises never really applied: "The North African on the doorstep [*seuil*] of the French Nation—which is, they say, his own nation—experiences in the political realm, at the level of citizenship, an imbroglio that no one wants to face."[32] He exposes a founding paradox: France had promised to the "indigènes musulmans" a place in a modern republic of equality and rights where, by legal design, "there is absolutely no place for them."[33]

A decade later, just before he died in 1961, Fanon underscored the point he had long been making about the vanishing force of this legal imbroglio. In "De la violence" he narrates from a standpoint close to those living under French occupation in Algeria: "[The colonized] notice on the spot that all of these discourses about the equality of human beings that are spewed one after another cannot mask this banality which makes it so that seven Frenchmen killed or wounded at Sakamody Pass ignite the indignation of civilized consciences whereas the sacking of the *douar* of Guergour, the *dechra* of Djerah, and the massacring of the very populations who had caused the ambush count for nothing at all."[34] In this scene, Algerians see plainly that while French deaths exacted during an ambush at Sakamody Pass count as precisely seven, the multitude of lives lost in massacres in the villages of Guergour and Djerah *comptent pour du beurre*; that is, they do not count at all. Such discrepancies in colonial record keeping also have made it difficult for historians to accurately count Algerian deaths. In Fanon's analysis, Algerians see right through French discourses about human rights and equality because they recognize the banal truth that their own lives do not count as human before French law, so that killing any number of Algerians never quite adds up to the crime of murder under French-colonized jurisdiction: "Soon it will be seven years of crimes in Algeria," adds Fanon, "and not a single Frenchman has been tried [*traduit*] before a court of justice for the murder of a single Algerian."[35]

The French idiom *traduire en justice* (literally, to translate into justice) in Fanon's sentence can be glossed in English in a number of ways—to bring to justice, to prosecute, to call someone before a tribunal—but none of these translations does justice to the verb *traduire* at the heart of the idiom. In French, legal prosecution is etymologically linked to the act of translating. In Algérie française, Fanon observes, killings only count as murder when the victim is a French citizen; justice for Algerian victims simply does not translate or compute. This impasse points to an intractable decalage in the French state's legal order, and to the state's self-authorized power to decide which human lives to protect and which to dispose of in the name of "justice."

For this reason, Fanon adds, "these commissions do not exist in the eyes of the colonized."[36] Algerians are not confused about the status of their own lives in Fanon's account. Rather, they see clearly that French law itself has mistaken its own power to confer or confiscate human status, and to calculate the value of lives. This authority is not legitimate in the eyes of Algerians—hence the revolutionary situation, whose outcome Fanon would not live to see.

Decolonizing Memory

The kinds of blind spots that Fanon noticed in 1961 have since played a role in shaping the story of Algeria's independence war and its afterlife, and continue to limit what can be seen about the Algerian present and future. Algeria's eight-year war to end French occupation—described by Fanon in 1959 as "the most hallucinatory war ever waged to break colonial domination"—was the longest and most violent anticolonial uprising of the twentieth century.[37] The conflict transformed political, social, intellectual, and aesthetic domains on both sides of the Mediterranean and created waves across the decolonizing Global South. It became both an inspiration and a cautionary tale for audiences as divergent as the Black Panthers—who had offices in Algiers provided by the FLN during the 1960s—*and* intelligence strategists at the Pentagon and West Point who were preparing for military invasions and occupations in Iraq and Afghanistan after September 11, 2001.

This complicated history is difficult to fully fathom not only because of how differently it has unfolded in postcolonial France and Algeria, but also because what Todd Shepard has called the French *invention of decolonization* has played such a powerful role in shaping the way that the war's history has been narrated. Shepard argues that *decolonization* was invented in France as a temporal category—the inexorable step "after" colonialism in a progressive liberal teleology—precisely in order to exorcise Algeria from France after 130 years of their profound entanglement.[38] The implications of this exorcism become evident in the forms of collective forgetting and blindness that Karima Lazali points out in her study of colonial trauma. Nonexistent archives and lacunae in historiographic and psychoanalytic studies further reflect the French state's concerted effort to distance itself from its own long-standing politics of disappearance, a politics that the Algerian state has taken up and honed for its own purposes since 1962.[39]

In the wake of national independence in 1962, Algeria became viewed by millions across the African continent and diaspora as an effervescent beacon of liberation. Algiers, its capital city, was known as the capital of the Third World, a "Mecca of revolutionaries" where emancipatory ideas and practices could be forged.[40] This radical promise and hope appeared to die a swift death in subsequent decades. By 1988, Algerian citizens protesting against the government were attacked on the streets of their once-revolutionary capital city by state security and police forces. This repression, often referred to as *octobre noir*, marked a dramatic rupture for many Algerians, who were stunned and traumatized to see their own state turn its weapons against the people it had so recently been founded to protect.

For many Algerians, the date October 1988 now names the unofficial start of a devastating and brutal war on civilians that unfolded throughout the 1990s. Its official start is more often taken to be 1991, when the government canceled parliamentary elections that would have given the Front islamique du salut (FIS) a ruling majority and ended the single-party rule of the FLN. This more recent war, often called *la décennie noire* (the black decade, in Arabic *al-'ashriyya al-saudā'*) or *snīn al-irhāb* (the years of terror) transformed Algeria into an apparent crucible for the failures of decolonization, a dramatic theater for a supposed battle between modern democracy and antimodern Islamists, *and* a key ally on the Maghreb front of the U.S.-led global war on terror. Beginning in 1999, President Abdelaziz Bouteflika's government passed a series of laws that both legislated a formal end to this conflict and more deeply entrenched government authority to justify unlimited exercise of force in the name of "fighting terrorists."

Since February 2019, a massive people's revolt against Bouteflika's regime has been underway in Algeria, a movement (*ḥirāk*, in Arabic) that continues to unfold in the early months of 2020, although its course is being changed by the global pandemic that began in March 2020.[41] To observers persuaded by the version of decolonization invented by France, this peaceful uprising might look like a potential step forward in a teleological progression that has been best modeled by European democracies. However, the dignity revolution (*thawrat al-karāma*) taking place in Algeria cannot be described as simply a popular revolt against the dictator of a failed African state or another episode in a so-called Arab Spring. Such tropes and terms reflect distorting Eurocentric assumptions.[42] Seen from the standpoint of the people who have put their bodies on the streets every week for the past year, this movement is a much more radical and powerful collective dispute with the cartographic and temporal frames that underwrite the coloniality of power itself. If we take seriously what many of the protestors themselves are saying, the *Ḥirāk is* the unfinished liberation war.[43]

On the French side, knowledge of the anticolonial war seemed to arrive belatedly in public discourse and historiography after a long period of traumatized amnesia, and it remains a charged and contentious topic in France now. As Benjamin Stora pointed out in his influential book *La gangrène et l'oubli: La mémoire de la guerre d'Algérie* (1991), for decades the French government referred to the war as anything *but* a war—*évènements, opérations de police, actions de maintien de l'ordre, opération de rétablissement de la paix civile, entreprise de pacification, le drame algérien*—because to call it a war would tacitly recognize Algerian sovereignty. It was not until 1999 that the French National Assembly adopted a law formally recognizing that an event called *la guerre d'Algérie* had taken place. It was not until September 2018 that a French head of state acknowledged the systematic nature of the violence done to Algerians and their allies during that war when President Emmanuel Macron made a public declaration announcing the French government's responsibility for the disappearance, torture, and murder of Maurice Audin in Algiers in 1957.[44]

The work to overcome official disavowal and silence is far from finished in France, as Macron declared. One of the motivations driving this ongoing *travail de mémoire* (memory work), in the French president's words, is to help heal a nation scarred by its recent colonial past: "The Republic cannot... minimize or excuse the crimes and atrocities committed by either side during this conflict. France still bears scars, some of them not fully closed."[45] That said, it remains impossible to classify *as* crime the violence that was exercised by the French in Algeria for well over a century prior to the intense counterrevolutionary war waged by France between 1954 and 1962. For instance, outraged furor swept through the French media after Macron stated, during a visit that he made to Algiers while he was a presidential candidate in February 2017, that the colonization of Algeria had constituted a "crime against humanity."[46]

In Algeria, on the other hand, the independence war has always been called a revolution, *thawra* in Arabic. Algeria's second constitution names it "one of the greatest epics in history to have marked the resurrection of the peoples of the Third World."[47] In Algeria it is common and not the least bit controversial to refer to French colonization as a genocide—it would be provocative, in fact, to deny this. There, the revolutionary narrative is openly and ritually celebrated as the birth of a sovereign nation emerging from the night of colonial terror. This sanctified revolutionary epic serves both as a symbolic touchstone for consecrating state power (the Algerian government has been ruled since 1962 by the party that claims the mantle of the revolutionary vanguard, the FLN) and as a symbolic resource for staging resistance against the government and the oligarchs in and beyond Algeria monopolizing the nation's oil wealth. Reworking the revolutionary story has long been a contestatory strategy for groups disputing state power and calculated dispossession in Algeria. This includes Islamists critical of the state during the 1990s as well as those millions of citizens who recently have taken to the streets armed with banners, posters, slogans, songs, images, and chants that tap into collective revolutionary memory as a resistant practice of generating new political possibilities.

Since Stora published his study of the war's memorial afterlife in the early 1990s, literary scholars and historians of postcolonial France and Algeria have explored how official national discourse and popular memories on both sides of the Mediterranean have been shaped by lacunae, disavowal, amnesia, blind spots, and ongoing acts of silencing and forgetting.[48] They have analyzed the state-sponsored torture whose exposure so shocked and transformed French public opinion about imperialism during the late 1950s and 1960s, and they have brought to light long-obscured instances of state violence such as the police massacre of Algerian protestors that took place in the heart of Paris in October 1961. In 2010, Michael Rothberg, Debarati Sanyal, and Max Silverman together edited a volume of *Yale French Studies* entitled *Nœuds de mémoire: Multidirectional Memory in Postwar French and Francophone Culture*. This collective project reignited questions of cultural memory by pivoting from Pierre Nora's massive, multivolume *Lieux de mémoire* project—started in 1986, and itself characterized by an amnesiac relationship to French empire, as the editors of the *Yale French Studies* volume point out—in order to "probe the points of contact between the memories and legacies of genocide, colonialism, and slavery in a world defined both by decolonization and the aftermath of the Shoah."[49]

Over recent decades, a growing body of memory studies scholarship has illuminated the ways in which Algerian decolonization constitutively shaped "postwar" French cultural memory and political institutions, and also has demonstrated that the force of Algeria's anticolonial revolt lives on in what the Anglo-American academy has inherited in translation as poststructuralist and thus postcolonial theory.[50] In short, it has become impossible to seriously study French history, literature, philosophy, politics, cultural memory, or experiences of World War II without also seriously considering French empire. It has also become increasingly salient to understand "France" itself not as a self-contained nation that happened to once possess overseas colonies that it has now shed, but rather as an inherently imperial territory whose institutions and ideas (equality, liberty, fraternity) were forged through *and remain unthinkable apart from* centuries of transatlantic slave trade, colonizing war, and settler occupation. As Gary Wilder has aptly put this point, modern France was never not an imperial nation-state, although it is the character of constituent state violence to train us not to see this fact.[51] France remains constitutively haunted by the empire that it has tried both to exorcise and atone for.

While such scholarship has done much to highlight and to redress the amnesia that France's swift "decolonization" has helped to institutionalize, other scholars point out that the forms of political decolonization that were established in France in the mid-twentieth century *still* facilitate blindness and amnesia concerning the true historical scope and ongoing intensity of French state violence and racism. For instance, Françoise Vergès extends Todd Shepard's argument in her recent book *Le ventre des femmes: Capitalisme, racialisation, féminisme* (2017) to argue that the French invention of decolonization that took hold during the decades after 1945 produced a mutilated understanding of both cartography and history that continues to reinforce the *coloniality of power* in the present.⁵² "Postcoloniality," as Vergès defines it, "designates a period that opens the moment that France presents herself as liberated from her colonial empire. It does not indicate a temporality, but a politics."⁵³

Until this point, postcolonial francophone memory, testimony, and trauma studies have been largely oriented by cartographies, textualities, and temporalities that implicitly center French experiences and narratives of decolonization, even when critiquing these narratives. For instance, the interpretive pattern of forgetting, remembering, acknowledging, and working through the traumatic exorcism of Algeria from France has simply never been a shared framework. This pattern does not play out in comparable ways on the Algerian side of that complex rift, where blindness to French state brutality was never a real option. Likewise, the "multidirectional" memory paradigm has reflected a critical orientation in which wide-ranging vectors appear to lead back toward the French metropole, so that the "tangled knots" of memory that come into clearest focus also tend to be those located within or indelibly connected to French cultural spaces and public spheres, while aesthetic works addressed to other audiences or in Algerian and African languages other than French have largely fallen outside the scope of consideration.⁵⁴ The linguistic partitions and assumptions that have tacitly endured in francophone literary studies scholarship replicate a colonialist enterprise. It is time to collectively expand reference points both by moving beyond French materials and by recognizing French as an Algerian language that is not intrinsically preoccupied with (or tormented by) France.

My study also takes a cue from the art historian Hannah Feldman by amplifying her point that the term *postwar* itself is not a neutral or shared reference. In *From a Nation Torn: Decolonizing Art and Representation in France, 1945–1962* (2014), Feldman argues that the widely accepted term by which scholars name the period "after 1945" institutionalizes European experience of World War II and elides the fact that the very same years were also a time of escalating anticolonial resistance and colonial repression. The term further eclipses more than a century of colonizing massacre and indigenous resistance underway in Algeria *prior* to 1945. From an Algerian standpoint, the date May 8, 1945, does not signify a triumph over fascism but rather its brutal escalation; it does not name a moment of liberation but rather a series of attacks and repressions carried out on Algerian civilians by French colonial authorities and *pied noir* settlers, also known as the Sétif, Guelma, and Kherrata massacres. For Algerians, the date May 1945 marks the start of the armed resistance that would become a long decolonizing war to break French rule.⁵⁵

In *The Invention of Decolonization,* Todd Shepard further points out that the radical questions raised by theorists of decolonization such as Fanon and Aimé

Césaire remain unanswered. That is, the version of political "decolonization" that fundamentally transformed France after 1962 also enabled the French to avoid facing more thorny and unsettling questions concerning the "paradoxes, limits, and incoherencies of Western universalism, as well as the violence it required and thus produced."[56] Both Shepard and Vergès demonstrate that French "postcoloniality" has made it possible to elide such questions in ways that have exacerbated rather than addressed ongoing practices of state violence, xenophobia, and racism in France.

These unsettling decolonial questions are at the heart of the literary texts that I bring together in this book. I understand *decolonial* in the way that Vergès defines it, as a term that names "the struggle to deconstruct the coloniality of power."[57] In other words, "decolonizing" is not a process that has already happened to bring us all into a shared "postcolonial" time and space. The present participle in my book's title names an ongoing struggle that concerns whether there will *be* a future, and for whom.[58] Literature, I argue, creates and protects indispensable space for *present* struggles against the coloniality of power.

In other words, a central claim of this book is that the radical decolonial questions like those raised by Fanon and Césaire, highlighted by Shepard, and taken up by Vergès did not in fact die out during decades of political decolonization and postcolonial amnesia. Such questions may have gone underground, but they have been kept alive thanks in no small part to Algerian activists, workers, artists, writers, and theorists working in the face of considerable and ongoing repression. Over four chapters and a conclusion, I explore how works by some of these writers sound out demands for justice that cannot be articulated within existing legal frameworks. At the juncture where aesthetic imagination confronts juridical reason, the capacity of literary representation to complicate and contest reality comes to light. These texts are not documents of past events, but traces of a dynamic, collective, open-ended process oriented to the future.[59]

Finally, this book highlights the indispensable value of aesthetic study in a disciplinary space that has tended to be the domain of social scientists. In the wake of both Algeria's "dark decade" of the 1990s and the "war on terror" launched after September 11, 2001, historians and sociologists such as Sylvie Thénault, Jim House, Neil MacMaster, Marnia Lazreg, Malika Rahal, Muriam Haleh Davis, James McDougall, Walid Benkhaled, and Natalya Vince have undertaken important studies that contextualize the violence exercised during Algeria's independence war within a more expansive picture of colonizing violence. They have also identified in this conflict a recessed prehistory of contemporary counterterror practices.[60] Their research has made Algeria's modern history speak meaningfully to global movements[61] and has connected the history of French empire and its long afterlife to other imperialist projects in and beyond Africa. Very recently, scholars have begun to substantively evaluate the ongoing impact of the 1990s war, as Karima Lazali and Tristan Leperlier do in fields adjacent to and deeply informed by literary study (psychoanalysis and sociology, respectively).[62] I draw on Leperlier's detailed, data-rich overview of the politics of literary production in Algeria during the 1990s, and am inspired by Lazali's turn to fiction as a way to supplement the lacunae in historiographic and psychoanalytic studies.

These vital projects are shaped by nuanced attention to the specificity and heterogeneity of Algerian cultural spaces, yet they also leave open the question of literature's transformative and disruptive capacity. I turn directly to literature in search of alternative interpretive and theoretical frames, and practice close textual analysis to highlight the seditious play of signification within a given text. In Algeria, acts of critical dissidence and textual sedition have long taken place in more than one language, and not just French or Arabic. Furthermore, French is now an Algerian language with an Algerian literary genealogy, shaped through intertextual and translational contact with Arabic and Tamazight literatures both spoken and written. *Decolonizing Memory* is an exploratory lexicon that brings together multilingual texts that I read in ways that test and expand the limits of testimonial forms. Reading across and between languages wherever possible—French, Arabic, Darija, Kabyle, Chaouia—permits me to make a case for how literature creates space for material that has been ghosted through acts of legal and linguistic violence. Read closely, these translingual texts pose resolute challenges to a long-standing ideological schema that continues to reinscribe reductive political divisions along linguistic lines in contemporary Algeria, a schema that has too often served the interests of abusive power.[63]

Following a loose chronology, *Decolonizing Memory* weaves together close readings of literary fiction with analyses of theoretical, juridical, visual, and activist texts concerning disappearance, detainment, torture, and genocide that have circulated within and beyond Algeria in the wake of both the national independence war (1954–62) and the (un)civil war (1988–99). Neither of these wars is truly over yet. My book's temporal sense therefore departs from an established trend in both historical and literary scholarship that narrates Algeria's modern history as a tragedy in three separate phases: colonization, decolonizing war, and civil war.[64] By contrast, I foreground the ways in which literary texts register out-of-joint temporal scansions to help see continuities between periods of violence that have been framed as discrete and discontinuous, and to help to articulate connections between myriad sites of violence beyond Algeria's borders. I linger over the impasses and disjunctions brought to light by this anarchival network of literary texts to demonstrate how Algerian writers have transformed the genre of testimony in ways that both defy imposed linguistic partitions and dispute the authority of the modern nation-state to serve as ultimate arbiter of justice.

Hearing Voices

Literature offers something other than evidence; it can be, as Gayatri Spivak tells us, an instrument for imaginative training, capable of moving at precisely those points where historiographical and legal genres reach an impasse. Here, works by Frantz Fanon and Assia Djebar permit me to bring to the fore this surreptitious and disruptive capacity of literary representation to loose memory and imagination from received temporal and spatial frames. Djebar's novel *L'amour, la fantasia* even works as "instrument" in an acoustical sense, like a vessel resonating with the unsettling demands of ghosts.

In his description of colonial law, Fanon enacts a point of view shift. From the vantage point of any "indigène musulman" living under occupation in Fanon's picture, French law never looked the least bit neutral or just: "He had always known that his encounters with the colonizer would take place inside a rigged system," writes Fanon. "The colonized loses no time in lamentations and almost never seeks that justice be done for him within the colonial framework."[65]

The absence of lamentation does not, of course, suggest that Algerians do not experience grief and pain; it means that they know it is futile to address their complaints and injuries to French judges and courts. In the series of clinical case studies appended to *Les damnés de la terre* in a section entitled "Guerre coloniale et troubles mentaux" ("Colonial War and Mental Disorders"), Fanon describes the disfiguring violence inflicted by the French colonial regime in Algeria without hyperbole as "a true apocalypse" and "a real genocide."[66] He had, of course, read Aimé Césaire's *Discours sur le colonialisme*.[67] He had also spent several years working in a psychiatric hospital in Blida, and thus witnessed firsthand the pathologies wrought by settler colonial violence.

The final text included in the appendix is not a clinical case study but an essay entitled "De l'impulsivité criminelle du Nord-Africain à la guerre de Libération nationale" ("From the North African's Criminal Impulsiveness to the National Liberation War") whose title and tone recall those of Fanon's first published essay "Le 'syndrome nord-africain'" (1952). Much as the earlier essay had done to the genre of French medical diagnosis, "De l'impulsivité criminelle du Nord-Africain" outlines a psychiatric theory elaborated by French magistrates, professors, police, lawyers, journalists, and doctors, in order to subvert and denounce it: "The Algerian, they all maintained, is a born criminal."[68]

Fanon outlines the colonial theory of Algerian criminality, citing evidence from reams of scientific studies produced by faculty at the University of Algiers: Algerians kill frequently, savagely, and for no reason. They love death, and submit to it willingly. Fanon parodies the anti-Muslim racism on which the legal and penal order of Algérie française depends—"These magistrates, these police officers, these doctors all dissertate quite seriously about the relationship between the Muslim soul and blood."[69] He exposes the French doctrine of Algerian criminality as a lie that renders the "indigène musulman" legally disposable. He also mimics the solemn pronouncements of a French judge in his legal chambers in Algiers in 1956, who sees what he takes to be "aggression in purest form" (*agressivité à l'état pur*) manifested by the Algerian rebels' supposed affinity for the military "fantasia" as a spectacle of bloodthirsty fanaticism.[70] The French judge cannot see what Fanon does: a political act of armed resistance to colonial terror.[71] Fanon notes that the apparent willingness of Algerians to die has nothing to do with their being fanatical Muslims, but is rather a sign of revolt and protective solidarity in the face of unlivable conditions: "The Algerian combatant has a particular way of fighting and dying," writes Fanon, "and no allusion to Islam or to the promised Paradise can explain this selfless generosity when what is at stake is protecting one's people and shielding one's brothers."[72]

At the essay's conclusion, Fanon abruptly shifts the temporal and spatial frames in order to clarify his central argument that Algerians' psychic dysfunction and distress are not "the consequence of an arrangement of the nervous system, nor of a congenital disturbance [*originalité caractérielle*] but the direct product of the colonial situation."[73] To illustrate his claim, Fanon interrupts the narrative present—the last months of anticolonial war—to splice in a series of past scenes of war.

First, the point of view zooms out and pans back to swiftly survey more than a century of colonial war and dispossession that had created unlivable circumstances for the "indigène musulman." Fanon writes: "Exposed daily to attempted murder: famine, eviction from his unpaid room, his mother's dessicated breasts, skeletal children, closed-down construction sites, the unemployed hanging around the foreman like crows—the indigène comes to view his own neighbor as an implacable enemy.... Yes, during the colonial period in Algeria and elsewhere, one might do a lot of things to get a kilo of semolina. One might even kill several people. *We need imagination to understand such things. Or memory.*"[74]

After dramatically widening the historical frame, Fanon brings into sharp focus a specific camp scene. At a glance, this description reads like a direct citation of harrowing descriptions from testimonies of survivors of the Nazi camps such as those offered by Primo Levi and Elie Wiesel—accounts that, by 1961,

Fanon had almost certainly heard of or read.[75] "In the concentration camps," writes Fanon, "men killed each other over scraps of bread."[76] Then Fanon's point of view shifts to first person, specifying that the camp scene he envisions is not located in Nazi Germany but rather in French-occupied North Africa in 1944: "I remember a horrible scene," Fanon writes. "It was in Oran, in 1944."[77]

Fanon recounts in detail what he remembers witnessing outside a military camp in Oran in 1944, where he was stationed as a soldier in the Free French Forces waiting to embark from North Africa to launch operations against the Axis powers and Vichy-occupied France: "From the camp where we awaited departure, soldiers tossed scraps of bread to little Algerian children who fought each other over them with rage and hate. Veterinarians might shed light on such problems by recalling the well-known 'pecking order' observed in poultry yards. The corn distributed is in fact a target of relentless competition. Certain birds—the strong ones—devour all the feed while the less aggressive grow visibly thinner. Every colony tends to become an immense poultry yard, an immense concentration camp where the only law is that of the knife."[78] Fanon's geographic and temporal shifts create a haunted transposition that not only moves the carceral conditions of the concentration camp to the colonized terrain of Algeria, but dramatically alters cartographical scale.

In Fanon's picture, colonized territory appears as an immense concentration camp where the law is a weapon used to destroy those at the bottom of its brutal pecking order. Children end up ravaging each other over a scrap of bread tossed their way by French soldiers, like desperate birds in a poultry yard. This transposition disrupts Eurocentric postwar chronologies, so that Nazi camps are not a model for understanding the colony, but the other way around. Thus, in Fanon's splicing, the hallucinatory war of 1954–62 appears within a longer historical memory of state violence. This reoriented perspective *also* imbues Nazi horror with alternate historical meaning: "Not so long ago," Fanon writes in 1961, "Nazism transformed all of Europe into a true colony."[79]

Karima Lazali, who is a psychiatrist currently practicing in both Algiers and Paris, points out that Fanon's is still one of the only clinical and theoretical studies that exist to analyze the effect of this politics of mass extermination on Algerians. Lazali dwells especially on the practice of *enfumades*, which were deliberate asphyxiations of entire tribes carried out by orders of generals such as Pelissier, Bugeaud, and Saint-Arnaud as the French military invasion moved beyond Algiers: "Saint-Arnaud himself went on to asphyxiate [*enfumer*] entire tribes," writes Lazali, "nearly eight hundred people in a single cave. The descriptions of children, women, elderly people, and men convulsing from smoke inhalation are unbearable."[80]

Such images are unbearable, but they are also true. As Lazali illustrates by weaving together psychoanalytic theory, historiography, and literary readings in her study, existing categories are not sufficient to register the psychic and political effects of the human destruction carried out to colonize Algeria. As Fanon pointed out, "*we need imagination to understand such things. Or memory.*" This quality of imagination and memory is best cultivated by way of literature, as the distinctively literary quality of Fanon's generically disruptive writing itself attests. On this point, Lazali offers critical inspiration: "Literature tries to write the blanks [*les blancs*] and the unthinkables [*les impensés*] of history. Above all, literature points the reader toward that shuttling movement [*dynamique incessante*] between the text and its invisible margins."[81]

The "enfumades" ordered by Pelissier and carried out by Saint-Arnaud during the colonizing wars of 1845 constitutively haunt what is perhaps Assia Djebar's most well-known novel, *L'amour, la fantasia* (1985). This novel features a historian narrator—like the writer Djebar herself—who grapples with the tactical and ethical problem of how to write, in a language inherited from the colonizer, a history of those who have been violently blanked out of historical record. Their only traces in the material archive appear in General Pelissier's diaries, which record his descriptions of the terrible massacre authorized by him. By manipulating aesthetic form to generate haunting sonic effects, Djebar's novel reckons with the paradox of subaltern testimony that has also long preoccupied subaltern studies of historiographers and literary theorists—how to write the history of those who leave no traces of their own in the archive?[82]

L'amour, la fantasia translates Gayatri Spivak's famous question into literary form by taking up the archival documents penned by the very person who massacred Djebar's ancestors as her only available starting point for writing about them. What is required of a writer-narrator whose own story must confront the "difficult task of rewriting its own conditions of impossibility as the conditions of its possibility"?[83] *L'amour, la fantasia* answers not by restoring lost testimony that provides access to what has been forcibly and violently erased, but with an act of literary haunting that moves in other ways. As Spivak insists and Djebar's poetics reveal, *subalternity* does not point to something or someone to be recovered, but rather to a structural mechanism that one ought instead think about how to abolish.[84] As Avery Gordon has written, it is in the act of submitting to a haunting that we recognize the urgency of this kind of ghostly call for justice—a demand that something else be done, something different than before.

This novel's part 1 ("La prise de la ville ou L'amour s'écrit") and part 2 ("Les cris de la fantasia") juxtapose intimate first-person narrative with dramatic scenes from the history of French colonization in Algeria reconstructed from archival records, while part 3 ("Les voix ensevelies") knits the colloquial oral histories of women involved in the 1954–62 anticolonial war with the narrator's own meditations on the painful contingencies of her writing task. The sections of the novel that concern textual transmission and archival excavation are perpetually interrupted by sections whose titles signal an abiding concern for the colloquial Arabic and Tamazight lacunae in the scriptural French and Arabic archive, often denoting indecipherable or nonsignifying forms of human language: "Clameur," "L'aphasie amoureuse," "Murmures," "Chuchotements," "Le cri dans le rêve," "Soliloque," four meditations entitled "Corps enlacés," and "Tzarl'rit."[85]

Djebar's is not a work of testimony that gives unmediated access to obscured voices, but a haunted and haunting testimonial poetics that invite the reader into a different kind of interpretive practice. Djebar's narrator-historiographer cites her peculiar debt to a multilingual sheaf of texts produced throughout the history of imperial conquest that predates the French arrival in Algiers in 1830, drawing epigraphs from Eugène Fromentin, Barchou de Penhoën, Ibn Khaldoun, Saint Augustine, and Ludwig von Beethoven, as well as a series of French-Arabic dictionaries. Each citation at once transcribes and attests to the untranslatability of spoken forms of Arabic and Tamazight, a sonorous wordplay that articulates the oral with the textual *and* that highlights their trace-structure, so that voices only signify under the sign of their effacement. Djebar's sonorous poetics refuse to sustain any illusion of direct or unmediated access to the *cris* within her *écrits* by consistently framing the embedded discursiveness of their transmission, which is also an act of erasure.

The sonic qualities of Djebar's text reveal an imbrication of the aesthetic and deadly: *fantasia* is a military cavalry exercise (a French description of an event performed by Algerian horseback riders) as well as a musical form (taken up by Beethoven).[86] The term *tzarl'rit*, which Djebar cites from an Arabic-French dictionary, invokes what is mutilated by the French writers of dictionaries, given that tzarl'rit is a transcribed approximation of a trilling cry that is not Arabic at all.[87] A musical network of rhymes and homophones begins to sound from the text's opening epigraph, which is from Eugène Fromentin's *Une année dans le Sahel* (1859), and which conveys a scene of violence that is not visible, but audible.

At first there is just one cry: "Il y eut un cri déchirant—je l'entends encore au moment où je t'écris," but this multiplies: "puis des clameurs, puis un tumulte..." (There was a searing cry—I still hear it as I write to you—then clamors, then a tumult...) The novel's second epigraph is from Barchou de Penhoën's *Expédition d'Afrique* (1835). This also conveys "cris" and footsteps arriving from somewhere unseen: "L'expérience était venue à nos sentinelles: elles commençait à savoir distinguer du pas et du cri de l'Arabe, ceux des bête fauves errant autour du camp dans les ténèbres." (Our sentries learned from experience: they began to be able to distinguish from the footstep and the cry of the Arab those of the wild animals lurking in the shadows around the camp.)

The "cris" in these epigraphs accumulate and amplify in homophones on the novel's next pages, generating the effect of a subterranean clamor that becomes detectible especially when the text is read aloud: *les cris, je t'écris, tes cris, l'amour s'écrit, ses cris*. It is as if ghosts are rustling and whispering from between the lines and pages of the written text with this accumulation of homophones. Such stylistic devices enact a phonic and graphic haunting that cannot be reduced to a purely aesthetic quality. What is the status of the disembodied "cris" that seem to echo throughout Djebar's text?

An answer to this question arrives in a section of the novel which reconstructs the scene of Pélissier's 1845 asphyxiation of the Beni Menacer tribe. Immediately preceding the chapter is a brief passage entitled "Biffure" that falls on an unnumbered page in the text, as if it does not quite belong. A narrator descends into a cave as if searching for petroglyphs, or listening for the sounds of tormented ghosts: "To read this writing, I must contort my body, plunge my face into shadow, scan the rock or chalk vault above me, allow the immemorial whispers to resurface, blood-stained geology. What magma of sounds is rotting there, what stench of petrification emanates from it? I grope about, my sense of smell unsettled, my ears open like mollusks, in the flood of ancient pain. Alone, bare-faced, without a veil, I confront images of the dark... Out of the wells of past centuries, how to face the sounds of the past?"[88] Her body contorted and her bared face plunged into darkness, the writer descends into an ancient and echoing cave that is also a tomb stinking of putrid corpses.

This fragment alerts the reader to what will be exposed in the following section, "Femmes, enfants, bœufs couchés dans les grottes" ("Women, children, oxen asleep in the caves"), which describes in detail an extermination that took place in 1845, when an entire tribe—claimed by the narrator as her ancestral clan—was asphyxiated inside a mountain cave in which they had taken refuge from Pélissier's troops. The historian-narrator draws these details from Pélissier's own written descriptions, preserved in the French colonial archive; she envisions the charred corpses of women, children, and cows dragged from the smoldering cave to be exposed to the bright sunlight where Pélissier surveyed them.

She expresses profoundly conflicted gratitude to the French *bourreau-greffier* (butcher-scribe) whose writing is the only archival trace she can read to construct any memory of this massacre. She does not attempt to imagine the corpses back to life, but the sounds of their silenced screams weave through her French text, easily missed, but imminently detectible if sounded out by a reader. The literary text does not provide access to these lost kin. It does not offer healing or reparation. It is a prayer to be haunted that extends an invitation to the reader: to submit to becoming a vessel for anguished, indecipherable voices that arrive, insistent and disturbing, from another place and another time—like ghosts.

L'amour, la fantasia concludes with a different scene of violence described in detail by the French explorer-painter Eugène Fromentin in his Saharan notebooks. The narrator recounts to her kinswoman, Lla Zohra, a story about the murder of two young women, *naylettes*, violated in a desert tent by French soldiers. *Naylettes* is a French deformation of the tribal name Oualed Naïl; in Arabic "nā'ilāt" could designate women from this tribe, while the French suffix "-ette" inflects the word with casual misogyny. Djebar's narrator tells the horrible tale: a sympathetic French lieutenant arrived late at the murder scene to find the French soldiers leaving, their bayonets bloody and hands filled with stolen jewelry. Fatma was already dead and Mériem mutilated and dying, the button of her executioner-rapist's military uniform clasped in her stiffening fingers. The reader is offered no imagined reconstruction of either Mériem's or Fatma's voices. The details mark a point of fade-out in the historical record, like a vanishing trail of footprints—a trace that effaces even as it discloses. The novel's concluding chapter, "Air de Nay," extends this reflection on the mutilated "naylettes." Here, Fromentin offers a gruesome detail in the description of a woman's severed hand, as Djebar writes: "He offers me an unexpected hand, that of an unknown woman that he could never draw."[89] In turn, Djebar transcribes the sinister detail of an anonymous Algerian woman's severed hand, which Fromentin noticed, picked up, and then tossed back onto the dusty road he was traveling through the Algerian Sahel.

Djebar inscribes that mutilated appendage into her text with a desire not just to grasp it, but to bring it back to life: "Plus tard, je me saisis de cette main vivante, main de la mutilation et du souvenir et je tente de lui faire porter le 'qalam'" ("Later, I seize this living hand, hand of mutilation and of memory, and I try to make it take up the 'qalam'").[90] Here, the "hand of mutilation and memory" is *alive*, as if after the passage of time the severed hand might be restored to life in the act of writing. Djebar's "seizing" the severed hand conveys an ambivalent desire to suture and restore what has been mutilated and dismembered, as if to perform a resurrection or an act of necromancy.

Yet the word *qalam* stands resistant, a transliterated Arabic word set apart by guillemets. In evoking the name of the Arabic writing instrument, the text gestures to another vast archive of written histories of the Sahel and Sahara.

The agency registered by the clause "je tente de lui faire porter le 'qalam'" is not that of the narrator. Her desire is not to deliver the "qalam" to an immobilized hand, nor is it to write with the "qalam" on the severed hand's behalf. The narrator's vision is to touch a living hand, and her desire is to make *it* pick up the "qalam" to write on its own, and in a language other than French. This desire for a miraculous grafting offers a paradoxical, morbid vision of transmitting a story that cannot be retrieved.

The narrator's desire to make an anonymous, severed hand pick up a writing instrument remains unfulfilled by Djebar's novel, which concludes on the following page. Yet her closing image also offers a vision of future testimony, gesturing to a time in which a violently dismembered hand is grafted onto a living body with a beating heart in order to write what has not yet been written. As a metonym for discursive participation, this reanimated hand gestures to a future in which what was called "subaltern," violently scored out of history and inaccessible to memory, might become capable not only of writing and speaking on its own behalf but also of being heard as authoritative.

Itinerary

Chapter 1, "Remnants of Muslims," reframes the problem of subaltern testimony by juxtaposing Zahia Rahmani's *Moze* (2003) and *"Musulman" roman* (2005) with Giorgio Agamben's theoretical reflection on the enigmatic figure of the "Muselmann" as it appeared in the Nazi camps in 1945. Rahmani's literary works redress Agamben's consequential blind spot by bringing to light—and by putting on fictional trial—a repressed history of French colonial violence that produced an army of ghosts called "musulmans" in Algérie française, where the term long functioned as a founding juridical category of empire. Rahmani contemplates the bizarre and entangled histories of Muslim and Jewish citizenship under French law in colonized Algeria and considers the postcolonial afterlife and grim future of such laws. Furthermore, her vernacular Kabyle-Arabic literary history of modern Algeria and Abrahamic scriptural tradition features the shadowy figure of the fugitive slave Hagar alongside that of a ghostly "drowned Muslim" to highlight precisely what Agamben's theoretical reflection on testimony misses, namely, that the laws of nation-states do not have power to confirm or to deny human status, and that what is *most* human is that which lies beyond the reach of law.

Chapter 2, "Untranslatable Justice," explores the censored and clandestine testimonies circulated by Algerian and French anticolonial activists during the late years of Algeria's decolonizing war in order to sound out the unexpected call of the literary that inheres in the narrative genre of the legal plaint. Quasi-legal texts like *La gangrène* (1959), *Nuremberg pour l'Algérie* (1961), and *Djamila Boupacha* (1962) are constituted by an irreducible tension in their framing as legal testimony. This generic impasse generates a series of haunting literary effects that bring to view a dispute over what kinds of voices and speaking can be heard as legitimate justice claims, and that also open space outside existing legal and linguistic frameworks for other kinds of plaints to be heard. Given the terms of legal amnesty established by the Évian Accords that ended Algeria's independence war—and despite the formal recognition of state-sanctioned torture that was issued in late 2018 by the current French president, Emmanuel Macron—the justice demands sounded by these recessed testimonies have not yet been answered.

Chapter 3, "Mourning Revolt," moves squarely into the time and space of postindependence Algeria to explore a model of spectral justice that is oriented by a literary perspective noticeably disinterested in the European metropole. Here, I consider how Yamina Mechakra's two novels *La grotte éclatée* (1979) and *Arris* (1999) explode the state-sanctioned limits of historical testimony by transfiguring the politically charged Arabic term *shahīd* (martyr/witness). Mechakra's linked novels, published at either end of the period that began with Boumédiène's long presidency (1965–76) and ended with Bouteflika's much longer one (1999–2019), sanctify as grievable—and claim as kin—those who are most abject, banished, and dispossessed in Algeria's history. Moreover, Mechakra's French is marked by the haunting presence of the Chaouia language in ways that compel a reader to dwell on losses and disappearances that state policies attempted to erase, especially during and after the violence that took place in Algeria in the 1980s and 1990s.

Chapter 4, "Open Elegy," points out that the 1990s war on civilians remains unresolved despite amnesty laws instituted by Bouteflika's presidential decrees in 1999 and 2005. In light of these laws, I explore the elegiac form of Waciny Laredj's controversial Arabic-language novel *Sayyidat al-maqām* (1993), translated into French by Marcel Bois as *Les ailes de la reine* (2009). Analyzing the novel in connection with its central intertexts, especially *Alf layla wa-layla* (*The Thousand and One Nights*) and Fadhma Aïth Mansour Amrouche's French-Kabyle *Histoire de ma vie* (1968), counters a myth of intractable language and cultural conflict in postcolonial Algeria to show that Arabic, Tamazight, and French literary spaces are connected in translational practice. Laredj elaborates a poetics of testimony that make of the literary text a sanctuary for the ghosted material targeted by amnesty law for destruction. This translingual haunting creates modes of address not reducible to those plaints destined for public legal tribunals. It also anticipates the heterogeneous and alternative forms of testimony that have resounded throughout Algerian cities and streets in a grassroots vernacular "symbolic revolution" that has confronted and disrupted the ruling political order there since February 2019.

The conclusion, "Prisons without Walls," brings together works by two writers who were shaken and transformed when they witnessed the military repression of popular protests that took place in Algiers during October 1988—the novelist Assia Djebar and the poet Samira Negrouche. Whereas Djebar's poem "Raïs, Bentalha" (1998) tracks a writer's submission to the ghosts of the 1990s massacres and disappearances, Negrouche charts collective movement beyond mourning and paralysis by calling for testimony that has not yet been written. Here, my book's different lines of argument about the spectral force of "musulman" testimony come together to show how literature continues to hold open unauthorized spaces capable of registering the justice demands of those who are most invisible and silenced both in and beyond postcolonial Algeria.

Remnants of Muslims

A crush. A surge. Muslims. Skeletons. Skeletons. You do not see them. Just as you do not see the paper but the words written on it. —Ka-Tzetnik

Ironical Names

Giorgio Agamben's formulations of *the state of exception* and *bare life* have become touchstones for analyzing sovereign violence and biopolitics, yet it seems to have escaped note that Agamben's use of these terms depends on a peculiar oversight. While Agamben's Eurocentrism has been redressed by scholars such as Achille Mbembe, Ranjana Khanna, Michael Rothberg, and Sylvie Thénault, even his most careful readers do not comment on Agamben's treatment of the word that he takes from Primo Levi as the key to understanding politics and ethics after World War II.[1]

In *Homo Sacer: Sovereign Power and Bare Life* (1995), Agamben designates the Nazi concentration camp as the "new biopolitical nomos of the modern" and singles out an epithet that it seems to him has previously appeared only in texts written by or about survivors of the camps: "Now imagine the most extreme figure of the camp inhabitant," Agamben urges in the final passages of *Homo Sacer*. "Primo Levi has described the person who in camp jargon was called 'the Muslim,' *der Muselmann*—a being from whom humiliation, horror, and fear had so taken away all consciousness and all personality as to make him absolutely apathetic (hence the ironical name given to him)."[2]

FIGURE 1.1. Aldo Carpi, "Inmates," 1945. From the Ghetto Fighters House Museum archives.

Agamben's parenthetical "hence the ironical name" communicates but does not resolve anxiety about applying a variation of the Arabic word *muslim* to such radically dehumanized Jewish men. The logic of Agamben's "hence" is opaque at best. The "irony" to which he refers is surely the renaming of "Jew" as "Muslim." His diction implies either that he considers the association between absolute apathy and Muslims to be self-evident or that he assumes that such an association would have appeared self-evident to those who assigned the epithet. Calling this substitution "ironic" also suggests that a defining antagonism distinguishes "Jew" from "Muslim."

While these associations and distinctions invite careful reflection, neither in *Homo Sacer* nor in his subsequent study of testimony, *Remnants of Auschwitz: The Witness and the Archive* (1998), does Agamben demonstrate such reflection, nor does he clarify what is "ironic" about such a substitution.[3] Agamben's silence is not incidental or idiosyncratic, but a consequential silencing. The *Homo Sacer* project relies on his ignoring this particular "irony" so that he can appropriate the term *musulman* as a proper name for the lost witnesses to the Shoah and master image of "bare life," and as the key figure for thinking about the limits of testimony under conditions of extreme state violence.

Agamben's thesis that Auschwitz was a site of unprecedented biopolitical experimentation where "the most absolute *conditio inhumana* ever to appear on earth was realized" requires this spectral image of the "Muselmann," which he describes as a limit of a radically new kind.[4] Here, Agamben shares Hannah Arendt's understanding of Auschwitz as a final step in the Nazi state's murder of juridical personhood. In Agamben's account, systematic stripping of legal protections reduces "Jew" to bare life called "Muselmann," a term that Agamben takes up to designate "not so much a limit between life and death ... [but] the threshold between the human and the inhuman" (RA 55). This threshold orients Agamben's argument about the paradoxical relationship between modern state violence and testimony: "In Auschwitz," he writes, "ethics begins precisely at the point where the *Muselmann*, the 'complete witness,' makes it forever impossible to distinguish between man and non-man" (RA 47).

What Levi's text leaves opaque and uncertain, Agamben clarifies, defines, and hyperbolizes so that the "Muselmann" appears in *Remnants of Auschwitz* sheared of its many other semantic valences. In Agamben's argument, the Italian word *musulmano* designates an ontological rather than historical condition of unwitnessable life whose status *as* human was threatened and destroyed by the power of the state. By positioning this "musulman" (as it appears in French and English) as key to the "hidden matrix and *nomos* of the political space in which we still live," Agamben also obscures a colonial genealogy of the relationship between sovereign violence and testimony.[5]

The enigmatic appearance of the word *Muselmann/musulman* in the Nazi camps invites reckoning with a historical articulation that Agamben's rewriting of Levi effaces, an articulation that I trace in this chapter by turning to literary fiction that undertakes precisely such reckoning. Agamben is not the first or only writer to use this term, but no other writer so elevates the "musulman" as a theoretical exemplar, and few have attained Agamben's authoritative status and critical appeal.[6] That is, Agamben participates in a long chain of transmission whose omissions his work has helped to amplify and institutionalize. He did not invent this word, nor is he the first to remark on its disturbing function in the Nazi camps. The term has quietly sedimented in trauma, testimony, and memory studies. It was spoken by the famous survivor, novelist, and witness Ka-Tzetnik just before he fainted while testifying at the Eichmann trial in Jerusalem in a moment famously documented by Hannah Arendt and analyzed by many theorists of testimony, including Agamben.[7] It has entered dictionaries and encyclopedias; it has found new life on the pages of modern Israeli literature in Hebrew, Yiddish, and English; and it serves a defining if unacknowledged function in studies of state violence informed and inspired by Agamben's work. In a critical study of what he calls this "most visible and invisible of words," Gil Anidjar observes that although any reader familiar with Holocaust literature published since 1945 has read, heard, and repeated the term *Muselmann, musulman,* or *muslim* as a name for the most dehumanized victims of the Nazi camps, few appear to *see* this "unreadable" name, let alone to comment on its full semantic range, "its particular status, invisible yet everywhere."[8]

To a reader familiar with the institutions of French empire, where the term's function in juridical taxonomies both prefigured and coincided with its appearance in the deranged jargon of Auschwitz, the impact of the epithet *musulman* as a name for the Nazis' most abject victims is disorienting to say the least. Agamben's own narrow sense of the word *musulman* is made available to him in part by Levi's own limited understanding of the term. Though he has ample opportunity not to be parochial, Agamben amplifies Levi's opacities and omissions. According to Agamben (via Levi), the word *musulman* was an epithet used by inmates of the Nazi death camps to refer to the most abject among them, those who had abandoned all hope of survival and lurked at the bottom of the camp's brutal hierarchy; it was the mark of a distinction drawn by prisoners to distance themselves from the not-quite-living inmates doomed for extermination. While the semantic availability of a colonial juridical category as an epithet for the most abject victims of Nazi violence in 1944 might have prompted

Agamben to explore affinities between Nazi and French colonial violence, he does not. Despite his keen interest in juridical categories (*homo sacer, testis, supertes, spondeo*), Agamben nowhere acknowledges that the use of the epithet *musulman* at Auschwitz coincided with its simultaneous function as a juridical category of exception long experimented with by the French in Algeria.

Taking Agamben's text as a case study and starting point, I build on the work of scholars such as Hannah Feldman and Abdelmajid Hannoum who object to writing "postwar" histories that treat 1945 as a decisive break only by leaving European colonial violence—in particular, French state terror against North Africans—outside the historical and epistemological frames.[9] In the introduction to *From a Nation Torn: Decolonizing Art and Representation in France 1945 to 1962* (2014), Feldman highlights Algeria's peculiar status as "a litmus test for the turn to extra-juridical means to implement and develop political invisibility."[10] This insight shapes her study of the ghostly status of Algerians as political agents in French visual culture during the period between 1945 and 1962, the period that is typically described by scholars as *postwar*. However, as Feldman insists, apparently descriptive terms like *postwar* or *between the two wars* are not neutral. Rather, they are Eurocentric temporal demarcations that "reflect how the elision of subaltern agendas has been naturalized within histories of modernity and the disciplinary structures upon which they depend."[11]

From the perspective of millions in French-colonized North Africa, "May 8, 1945" registers something very different than it does for most white Europeans. This charged proper name marks a symbolic rupture point—not a liberation from repressive totalitarianism ("Victory in Europe Day") but rather its intensification and dramatic escalation ("Sétif"). For Algerians, the date May 8, 1945, also signals a critical turning point in organizing resistance that would culminate in a sustained war for Algeria's independence from France.[12] From this widely shared standpoint, Algeria's anticolonial revolt effectively began on the day that the Nazi camps were liberated; May 8, 1945, marked the dramatic intensification of totalitarian state violence, not its end.

My aim is neither to produce a comprehensive genealogy of the epithet *musulman* nor to solve the problem of its unsettling appearance at Auschwitz,[13] but rather to highlight the occluded colonial context to Agamben's master category in order to provide a better account of testimony's structural paradoxes and its recessed possibilities. Agamben uses the term *Muselmann* to name an ontological condition of life exposed to the dehumanizing power of the state. This formula, frequently reiterated by Agamben, also implicitly assumes overlap between juridical personhood and human status. Other writers have pointed out that this confluence is not ontological, but rather a historical articulation that cannot be understood separately from European colonizing projects. Samera Esmeir provides one such account in her historical study of the colonizing operations of modern law in Egypt. Counter to historical analyses of state violence such as those developed by Hannah Arendt and Giorgio Agamben, Esmeir's *Juridical Humanity: A Colonial History* (2012) traces not the murder but the *birth* of the juridical person in the exercise of colonizing law. As modern positive law systematically supplanted shariʻa in an effort to "juridically humanize the colonized" in Egypt, Esmeir argues, "humanity" *itself* came to be thought of as something that European law had power to confer or to confiscate.[14] A version of this metanarrative is also implicit in Agamben's study of the radically dehumanized "Muselmann," an argument which silently binds human life to the power of the modern nation-state in ways that preempt challenging the law's authority to decide what is human at all.

Thus, while the application of a word like *Muslim* to the predominantly Jewish victims of Nazi genocide is provocative, the question pertinent to my own inquiry is not "why *this* name?"[15] My goal is not to salvage usable strands of Agamben's theorizing for application to non-European scenes; I do not aim to resolve "the conundrum of Agamben's absent colonial consciousness," nor to explain his "inability to think the colonial encounter as biopolitical event."[16] Instead, by turning to literary texts that directly engage the Algerian context that is so noticeably blanked out of Agamben's historical imagination, I am building a case for how literature creates openings to challenge precisely this power to confirm or deny human status that has for so long been entrusted to the law.

In addition to tracing a colonial history of juridical personhood, Samera Esmeir also raises an important question that falls beyond the scope of her study: "Is it not possible," she asks near the end of her book's introduction, "to conceive of a human who lives outside the protection of the law and in the midst of violence?"[17] She further cautions that it "takes a particular kind of rebellion, not just any rebellion, to break these chains" that bind the human to the power of the law.[18] The anarchival relationship of literature to the language and institutions of the nation-state creates ways to imagine a human who lives outside the terms established by law. This is the very premise, for instance, of Zahia Rahmani's fiction. By holding open discursive space for ongoing contestation with the colonizing force of law, literary texts can open up a protected and surreptitious site for disputing the juridical framing of humanity in ways that foment rather than neutralize rebellion against the authority of the state.

As the title of her novel *"Musulman" roman* makes immediately clear, Rahmani does not shy away from the historical ironies that Agamben avoids. Rahmani's autofictional texts *Moze* (2003) and *"Musulman" roman* (2005; translated by Matt

Reeck as *"Muslim": A Novel* in 2019) are the only published works I am aware of that undertake direct investigation of the Algerian colonial history that created the "indigène musulman" alongside direct reflection on the epithet's strange appearance in the Nazi camps in 1945. In fact, Agamben's work is an implicit intertext for Rahmani. Her literary texts challenge and augment his consequential blind spot in many different ways—perhaps most dramatically by staging a fictional trial whose star witness demands justice for the centuries of state lawfare that created an army of half-living zombies called "musulmans" in Algérie française.

Rahmani's literary experiment with testimony provides a model for a theory of justice that is not so tangled up with the idiom of the state. Unlike Agamben, Rahmani contemplates the bizarre equivocations of Muslim *and* Jewish citizenship in and around 1945. She also constructs a vernacular literary history of modern Algeria and of the multilingual transmissions of Abrahamic scriptural tradition across North Africa, a nuanced historical vision so starkly absent from Agamben's theoretical ruminations. Rahmani's counterhistory features the fugitive figure of the banished slave Hagar alongside fleeting remnants of "drowned" Muslims, a juxtaposition with insurrectionary implications. Among other things, this poses a resolute challenge to accounts of the law that conflate what is *actually* human with what is recognized by law *as* human to sound out demands for justice that question rather than confirm the state's power.

Ciphering Levi's Secrets

In *Remnants of Auschwitz* (*Quel che resta di Auschwitz,* in the original Italian), Agamben answers the invitation he had posed at the conclusion of *Homo Sacer* by recasting Levi's "absolutely apathetic" figure of the "Muselmann" as "the perfect cipher" of the Nazi death camps (HS 185; RA 55). Agamben understands the camp as site of an unprecedented biopolitical experiment made available to critical rumination by a figure that marks for him the very "impossibility of seeing" (RA 54). This spectral form slips from the edges of all frames in Agamben's account, a "faceless center" and "central non-place" that defies perception and representation (RA 52).

The "Muselmann" appears in no photographs, Agamben notes, although he detects its image in sketches drawn by memory by Mauthausen-Gusen survivor Aldo Carpi and in about twenty seconds of footage from an English film shot just after the liberation of a concentration camp that Agamben identifies as Bergen-Belsen in 1945.[19] The harrowing footage of mass graves and fields of corpses, Agamben observes, was shot in order to document Nazi atrocities for the public and as evidence for future legal trials, but these are not the frames that attract his attention. Agamben describes another sequence in detail:

> At one point, however, the camera lingers almost by accident on what seem to be living people, a group of prisoners crouched on the ground or wandering on foot like ghosts. It lasts only a few seconds, but it is still long enough for the spectator to realize that they are either *Muselmänner* who have survived by some miracle or, at least, prisoners very close to the state of the *Muselmänner*. With the exception of Carpi's drawings, which he did from memory, this is perhaps the sole image of the *Muselmänner* we have.[20] Nevertheless, the same cameraman who had until then patiently lingered over naked bodies, over the terrible "dolls" dismembered and stacked one on top of another, could not bear the sight of these half-living beings; he immediately began once again to show the cadavers. As Elias Canetti has noted, a heap of dead bodies is an ancient spectacle, one which has often satisfied the powerful. But the sight of the Muselmänner is *an absolutely new phenomenon, unbearable to human eyes*. (RA 51; my emphasis)

Agamben's study repeatedly underscores both the novelty and inscrutability of the "Muselmänner" phenomenon. He cites Carpi's complaint—"No one wants camp scenes and figures; no one wants to see the Muselmann" (RA 50)—and draws from Levi and Hannah Arendt, among many others, to refine his point that the apparition of half-living ghosts called "Muselmänner" at Auschwitz and Bergen-Belsen heralded not the mass murder of human beings but rather a new mode of administrative state violence that produced bodies so stripped of political status and human identity that their elimination could not be properly called murder or even death: "In Auschwitz, people did not die; rather, corpses were produced" (RA 72).

Agamben cordons off Auschwitz as exemplary in this sense: "There is a point at which human beings ... cease to be human. This point is the *Muselmann*, and the camp is his *exemplary* site" (RA 55; my emphasis). "This ... is the *particular* horror that the *Muselmann* brings to the camp and *that the camp brings to the world*" (RA 70; my emphasis). Wherever this thesis repeats in *Remnants of Auschwitz*, the "Muselmann/musulman" is its key: "Before being a death camp, Auschwitz is the site of an experiment that remains unthought today, an experiment beyond life and death in which the Jew is transformed into a *Muselmann* and the human being into a nonhuman. And we will not understand what Auschwitz is if we do not first understand who or what the *Muselmann* is—if we do not learn to gaze with him upon the Gorgon" (RA 52). Agamben treats this aporetic figure as cipher, in the sense of both "secret code" and "absence." Speculating that the

Nuremberg (1945–46) and Eichmann (1961–62) trials were "responsible for the conceptual confusion that, for decades, has made it impossible to think through Auschwitz" (RA 19), Agamben claims this absent witness as key to understanding what is new about such violence: "If we give the name 'Levi's paradox' to the statement 'the Muselmann is the complete witness,'" he writes, "then understanding Auschwitz—if such a thing is possible—will coincide with understanding the sense and nonsense of this paradox" (RA 82). Whereas Levi's text leaves the status of the "Muselmann" uncertain, Agamben reformulates its ambiguity as master key to the paradox of modernity.

Agamben's formulation of "Levi's paradox" amplifies particular aspects of Levi's account. Levi first mentioned the "Muselmann" in his memoir of incarceration at the Buna-Monowitze Lager (one of forty-four Auschwitz satellite camps), translated by Stuart Woolf as *Survival in Auschwitz* yet first published as *Se questo è un uomo* (*If This Is a Man*) in 1947.[21] Levi's only reference to the "musulman" in this book appears in a chapter titled "The Drowned and the Saved" in which Levi describes the brutal hierarchy among camp prisoners: "But in the Lager things are different," writes Levi. "Here the struggle to survive is without respite, because everyone is desperately and ferociously alone. If some Null Achtzehn vacillates, he will find no one to extend a helping hand; on the contrary, someone will knock him aside, because it is in no one's interest that there be one more 'mussulman'" (SA 62).

The Simon and Schuster English translation of Levi's text inserts a footnote at this point in the text; the Crane Books edition inserts the footnote into Levi's own prose as a parenthetical explanation. It reads: "(This word 'Muselmann,' I do not know why, was used by the old ones of the camp to describe the weak, the inept, those doomed to selection.)"[22] The word appears once more in the subsequent paragraph: "Whosoever does not know how to become an 'Organisator,' 'Kombinator,' 'Prominent' (the savage eloquence of these words!) soon becomes a 'musselman'" (SA 63). The English editions vary their spellings of the word; in the Italian it appears as *mussulmano*, at first enclosed by guillemets and then without. Levi's text leaves diffuse the status and significance of the term. While this orthographic, typographic, and semiotic variability suggests instability and uncertainty, Agamben makes its very instability signify.

Levi's *The Drowned and the Saved*—the last of his many texts, published the year before his own suicide in 1987 and translated in 1988—is preoccupied by the problem posed by the "musulman" for the practices of testimony and historiography, a problem that Agamben presents as central to the testimonial paradox at stake in *Remnants of Auschwitz*. Levi describes a narrative conundrum that took him four decades to see clearly: "One can today definitely affirm that the history of the Lagers has been written almost exclusively by those who, like myself, never fathomed them to the bottom," he writes. "Those who did so did not return, for their capacity for observation was paralyzed by suffering and incomprehension."[23] In a section of his text concerning language in the camps, Levi again cites the word: "Common to all Lagers," he writes, "was the term 'Muselmann,' 'Muslim,' given to the irreversibly exhausted, worn-out prisoner close to death" (DS 98). Nowhere does Levi speculate about the origin of the term, although he does register that he remains unpersuaded by the usual reasons given for its use: "Two explanations for it have been advanced, neither very convincing: fatalism; and the head bandages that could resemble a turban" (DS 98). Agamben reads *The Drowned and the Saved* as haunted by this lacuna. His citations from Levi both emphasize the spectral quality of Levi's memory and echo his own description of the "ghosts" filmed at Bergen-Belsen: "They crowd my memory with their faceless presence," writes Levi, cited by Agamben, "and if I could enclose all the evil of our time in one image, I would choose this image which is familiar to me: an emaciated man, with head dropped and shoulders curved, on whose face and in whose eyes not a trace of thought is to be seen" (DS 90; quoted in RA 44).

Agamben's portrait of the "musulman" as cipher is surely informed by his reading of Levi's preface to *The Drowned and the Saved*, which explicitly mentions an "army of ghosts" as both the great absence and the great secret of the Nazi camps. Levi's preface begins with a discussion of the testimonial and historiographic aporia deliberately plotted and carried out by the Nazi regime and integral to its logic. He offers a compelling account of the Third Reich's concerted (if failed) effort to destroy material evidence of its crime, especially in 1944 with the imminent end of the war in sight. Agamben transcribes Levi's own full citation of Simon Wiesenthal's *The Murderers Are among Us*, transmitting the cynical admonition of SS soldiers to camp prisoners in the final days of the war:

> However this war may end, we have won the war against you; none of you will be left to bear witness, but even if someone were to survive, the world will not believe him. There will perhaps be suspicions, discussions, research by historians, but there will be no certainties, because we will destroy the evidence together with you. And even if some proof should remain and some of you survive, people will say that the events you describe are too monstrous to be believed: they will say that they are the exaggerations of Allied propaganda and will believe us, who will deny everything, and not you. We will be the ones to dictate the history of the Lagers. (DS 11–12; quoted in RA 157)

As Levi notes, the Nazis blew up the Auschwitz gas chambers and ovens, but left visible ruins; they razed the Warsaw ghetto to the ground, but historians dug deeper; they burned the Lager archives and forced prisoners to exhume mass graves, to burn the corpses on pyres and to crush human bones to dust—yet material evidence remained to be read by future historians, collected and preserved as testament held up to prevent such atrocities from recurring.

In their systematic fabrication of a future absence, the SS also undertook what Levi calls "the murderous and apparently insane transfers [of prisoners] with which the history of the Nazi camps came to an end during the first months of 1945: the survivors of Maidanek to Auschwitz, those of Buchenwald to Bergen-Belsen, the women of Ravensbrück to Schwerin" (DS 14). Levi pinpoints the inherent logic of these "apparently insane" transfers: "The SS command posts and the security services then took the greatest care to ensure that no witnesses survived" (DS 14). Many exhausted prisoners died in this way just before liberation, yet their physical extermination wasn't the purpose of the death marches, according to Levi: "It did not matter that they might die along the way; what really mattered was that *they should not tell their story*" (DS 14; my emphasis).

The problem identified by Levi is that the multitude of still-living prisoners represented an army of future witnesses to the crimes of the Third Reich. Because their potential testimonies posed a threat to the authority of that state to control the production of history, all trace of these inmates had to be made to vanish—much like the physical gas chambers, the incriminating human remains, and the camp archives. Levi contemplates the nature of this threat posed to the Nazi regime by the inhabitants of its camps: "In fact, after having functioned as centers of political terror, then as death factories, and subsequently (or simultaneously) as immense, ever renewed reservoirs of slave labor, the Lagers had become dangerous for a moribund Germany because they contained *the secret of the Lagers themselves, the greatest crime in the history of humanity*. The army of ghosts that still vegetated in them was composed of *Geheimnisträger*, the bearers of secrets who must be disposed of" (DS 14; my emphasis). Mass murder is not the "secret of the camps" that appears to concern Levi here. As Agamben notes, Levi does not fixate on the spectacle of mass graves and corpses that emerged from the camps at the end of the war; the crime that concerns him appears to be not what the camps made visible so much as what they were designed to obscure. The passage above suggests that material evidence did not threaten "moribund Germany" nearly so much as the yet-to-be-killed "army of ghosts" whose reservoir of labor power had been extracted but whose undead bodies still "vegetated" within the walls of the camps. Levi calls this population of ghosts *Geheimnisträger,* and glosses the word—a German compound of *Geheimnis* (mystery, secret) and *Träger* (bearer, pillar, beam, truss, repository, porter)—as "bearers of secrets." *Geheimnisträger* denotes a person with security clearance who is entrusted with official secrets of state, a sense affirmed by Levi's suggestion that the prisoners were killed on death marches in 1944 precisely because their marginally living bodies were material evidence that could expose the great secret of the state's mass-produced administrative murder. Agamben completes the semantic link loosely suggested by Levi's preface, fusing "musulman" with *Geheimnisträger* in his formulation of the paradox of this absent witness, which creates a structuring lacuna at the heart of the genre of testimony.

Remnants of Auschwitz depicts Agamben as reader and rewriter of Levi: "And Levi," writes Agamben, "who bears witness to the drowned, speaking in their stead, is the cartographer of this new *terra ethica*, the implacable land-surveyor of *Muselmannland*" (RA 69). Citations culled from Levi's two texts riddle Agamben's own sentences as he embellishes and transforms Levi's formulations, so that in Agamben's account he stands beside Levi as surveyor and cartographer of an unknown territory inhabited by "musulman" ghosts. "One of the paraphrases by which Levi designates the *Muselmann* is 'he who has seen the Gorgon,'" writes Agamben, or: "As always, it is Levi who finds the most just and, at the same time, the most terrible formula: 'One hesitates,' he writes, 'to call their death death'" (RA 53, 70). In places, entire pages of *Remnants of Auschwitz* are dedicated to extended citations from Levi (see RA 33–34, 44). On these pages, the word *Muselmann* frequently appears untranslated and italicized (*muselmann*) in the English translation of Agamben's text, and either in citations or between quotation marks in the original Italian ("musulmano") and the French ("musulman"). However, as Agamben gradually familiarizes the reader with this word, it also appears in the text stripped (if inconsistently) of these distinguishing typographic markers; that is, Agamben domesticates and naturalizes the word as a proper name.[24] The passage in which Agamben first introduces this word to his own text clearly illustrates the process of lexical assimilation at work in his reading of Levi. He channels Levi, repeating and transposing Levi's title ("The Drowned and the Saved") and phrasings into his own theoretical scheme: "The 'true' witnesses, the 'complete witnesses,' are those who did not bear witness and could not bear witness. *They are those who 'touched bottom': the Muslims, the drowned.* The survivors speak in their stead, by proxy, as pseudo-witnesses; they bear witness to a missing testimony" (RA 34; my emphasis). This transposition is even more evident in the Italian, where Levi's "I sommersi e i salvati" is reinvented by Agamben's "i musulmani, i sommersi."

Agamben's treatment of the term *musulman* is especially peculiar in contrast to the philological attention he affords each of the other terms in the critical lexicon of *Remnants of Auschwitz*. The text's first chapter opens with a series of etymological studies of words such as *witness, martyr, testimony, responsibility, holocaust,* and *euphemism*. With reference to the inadequacy of the testimony on display at the Eichmann and Nuremberg trials, Agamben notes that two Latin nouns translate as "witness": *testis* names the "person who, in a trial or lawsuit between two rival parties is in the position of the third party," while *superteste* "designates a person who has lived through something, who has experienced an event from beginning to end and can therefore bear witness to it" (RA 17). Agamben designates Levi a paradigmatic witness in both senses (RA 17). He also introduces the term *spondeo*, a Latin verb that is the source of the juridical and ethical term *responsibility*, and discusses the Greek term *martis*, cautioning that "what happened in the camps has little to do with martyrdom" and pointing out that the concepts of martyrdom and witnessing are etymologically linked in Greek (RA 21, 26–27).

Agamben devotes several pages to tracing the semantic migration of the "incorrect term" *holocaust* (from the Latin *holocaustum*, "completely burned"), which he rejects for its gradually acquired meaning of "supreme sacrifice in the sphere of a complete devotion to sacred and superior motives" and for its long history as a polemic against the Jews (RA 31). "Not only does the term imply an unacceptable equation between crematoria and altars," he writes, "it also constitutes a semantic heredity that is from its inception anti-Semitic, which is why we will never make use of the term" (RA 31). Agamben likewise rejects the "unspeakable" character of Auschwitz on the grounds that *euphemein* describes a form of sacral worship, so that "to say that Auschwitz is 'unsayable' or 'incomprehensible' is equivalent to *euphemein*, to adoring in silence, as one does with a god" (RA 33). The chapter concludes by contemplating the indecipherable syllables "*mass-klo, matisklo*" spoken by the child Hurbinek in Auschwitz (see RA 37–39), and by introducing the "musulman" motif, which is also the title and central problematic of the text's second chapter. This chapter's opening sentence signals Agamben's ambition: "The untestifiable has a name" (RA 41).

Given his assiduous attention to every other term in his lexicon, it is striking that Agamben offers no etymological or historical information about the word *musulman* beyond its function in the jargon of the Lagers. Given that he dedicates an entire chapter to defining and explicating the word, including a brief discussion of "the uncertainty as to the semantic and disciplinary field in which the term should be situated," this omission is even more strange (RA 45–46). A skimming glance at the word's etymology provides a rough feel for its temporal and geographic migration from Arabic (*muslim, musalmānī*) and Persian (*musulmān*) through Ottoman Turkish (*müslūmān, müsılmān*), Turkish (*müslüman*), postclassical

Latin (*musulmanus*; 1588), Italian (*mussulmano*; 1557), Middle French (*mussulman*; 1553), French (*musulman*; 1562), Spanish (*musulman*; eighteenth century), Dutch (*muzelman*; 1622), German (*Muselman, Muselmann, Musulmann*; seventeenth century), Swedish (*musulman*; 1658), and English (*mussulman*), and gives a sense of the magnitude of this particular lacuna in Agamben's account.[25] No trace of this history appears anywhere in *Remnants of Auschwitz*, nor does mention of the term's use outside Nazi Germany during the mid-twentieth century. The term enshrined as foundational is presented by Agamben as if it lacks etymology or history. The distinct but dubious impression fostered by *Remnants of Auschwitz* is that a limit case for absolute subjection called something like "muslim" appeared in the modern world at Auschwitz between 1939 and 1945.

The text's second chapter puzzles briefly over the origins of the "ironical name." Agamben notes that the epithet was specific to Auschwitz—Mauthausen inmates called the most abject among them "swimmers," he writes, while at Neuengame they were "camels," at Dachau "cretins," at Buchenwald "tired sheikhs," and at Ravensbrück "Muselweiber," or female "Muslims" (RA 44).[26] He singles out "musulman" from this suggestive cluster and makes an effort to explain its selection as an epithet by noting that "the most likely explanation of the term" derives from the "literal meaning of the Arabic word muslim: one who submits unconditionally to the will of God" (RA 45). This is not an explanation. It is a racist trope that merely repeats the tautology of Agamben's earlier "hence" without clarifying why a body bent in extreme abjection and suffering might prompt the word *musulman* in the imaginations of the prisoners who generated and transmitted the epithet. Agamben's gloss of the Arabic word *muslim* is disconcerting not just for its reductive Orientalism, but because Agamben here appears to endorse the very notion of sanctified sacrifice and submission that, as he points out, qualifies *holocaust* as anti-Semitic. Agamben unequivocally rejects *holocaust* ("we will never make use of the term"; RA 45) yet permits "musulman" to pass without comparable scrutiny, instead consecrating it as the central category of his analysis of modern European state violence.

As the "musulman" is resignified by *Remnants of Auschwitz* as "the 'complete witness'" who "makes it forever impossible to distinguish between man and non-man" (RA 47), the disturbing rhetorical impact of the word's double-sounding either intensifies or dulls with repetition depending on how readily a reader accepts Agamben's theoretical and rhetorical tactics. Agamben appears to recognize just one of the myriad ironies that inhere in his use of the enigmatic and troubled word: "In any case," he writes, "it is certain that, with a kind of ferocious irony, the Jews knew that they would not die at Auschwitz as Jews" (RA 45). Rather, they would die as "Muslims."

The motifs that emerge in the second chapter of *Remnants of Auschwitz* call attention to ironies that Agamben does not explore. He introduces the figure of the "musulman" via a series of long citations transcribed from texts by not only Primo Levi, but also Elie Wiesel, Jean Améry, Aldo Carpi, Zdzisław Ryn and Stanisław Kłodziński, and Wolfgang Sofsky. All of these commentators respond to the persistent question (why *that* word?) by citing Orientalist tropes and images: Améry notes that the "Muslim" "no longer had room in his consciousness for the contrasts of good or bad, noble or base, intellectual or unintellectual" (quoted in RA 41); Carpi calls them "mummy-men, the living dead" (quoted in RA 41); Ryn and Kłodziński write that the "Muslim didn't defend himself. With the first kick, he folded in two, and after a few more he was dead" (quoted in RA 42), and further explain that "seeing them from afar, one had the impression of seeing Arabs praying. This image was the origin of the term used at Auschwitz for people dying of malnutrition" (quoted in RA 43). Agamben also cites the *Encyclopaedia Judaica*, which offers: "Used mainly at Auschwitz, the term appears to derive from the typical attitude of certain deportees, that is, staying crouched on the ground, legs bent in the Oriental fashion, faces rigid as masks" (quoted in RA 45). He cites Wolfgang Sofsky's citation of Marsalek's association of "the typical movements of the *Muselmänner*, the swaying motions of the upper part of the body, with Islamic rituals" (quoted in RA 45). Agamben summarizes these observations: "We have seen that to be between life and death is one of the traits constantly attributed to the *Muselmann*, the 'walking corpse' par excellence. Confronted with his disfigured face, his 'Oriental' agony, the survivors hesitate to attribute to him even the mere dignity of the living" (RA 70). Agamben does not interrogate what exactly is "Oriental" about such agony, abjection, and lack of dignity; he offers no critical reflection on the European Orientalism at play in the construction of the "musulman" both by camp inmates and by writers and historians of the Shoah. While the ready ease of such associations suggests that the word *musulman already* signified not-quite-living or not-quite-human when it assumed its new status as a camp epithet, Agamben repeats this equation without questioning it.

Thomas Keneally's Booker Prize–winning novel *Schindler's Ark* (1982) (later adapted as the Academy Award–winning 1993 feature film *Schindler's List*) comes closer to invoking specific historical experiences rather than ahistorical clichés, but Agamben does not cite this example: "The term was camp jargon," writes Keneally, "based on people's memory of newsreels of famine in Muslim countries, for a prisoner who had crossed the borderline that separated the ravenous living from the good-as-dead."[27] It is not impossible that some prisoners of Nazi camps had seen images or knew something about the famine that had devastated the Kabyle region of Algeria in 1939, but Agamben does not allude to "famine in Muslim countries" in his discussion.[28] He draws a tight geographic and temporal circle around this figure of "bare life" about which he underscores two points: first, that ethics and politics begin only once "we" come to understand "who or what the *Muselmann* is" (RA 52), and second, that the production of the "Muselmann" was a radically unprecedented phenomenon that transformed "our" modernity "after" the catastrophe of World War II. If this condition was so unprecedented, as Agamben insists, why should an epithet be so ready at hand to name it? Agamben does not follow these semantic clues, silencing rather than sounding out these historical resonances.

Despite his insistence on the unprecedented status of the Nazi genocide, Agamben's descriptions routinely point to precedents that he does not explore. For example, in the concluding chapter of *Homo Sacer*, titled "The Camp as 'Nomos' of the Modern," Agamben briefly mentions the colonial history of the concentration camp, noting that the first such institutions were built either by the Spanish in Cuba in 1896 or by the English during the Boer Wars (HS 166). Agamben does not examine these cases, but leaves them in the margin and footnotes of his study.[29] Likewise, when Agamben claims that Hitler had formulated, in 1937, "an extreme biopolitical concept for the first time" (RA 85) by instituting the principle of *volkloser Raum* (a space emptied of people), he writes sentences like the following without commenting on the evident parallels to techniques of settler colonization: "Hitler's 'peopleless space' instead designates a fundamental biopolitical intensity... that can persist in every space and through which people pass into populations and populations pass into Muselmanner. *Volkloser Raum*, in other words, names the driving force of the camp understood as a biopolitical machine that, once established in a determinate geographical space, transforms it into an absolute biopolitical space" (RA 86). Strategically isolating the case of Hitler's Germany, Agamben theorizes "muselmannization" as a systematic stripping of legal subjectivity and crossed thresholds that mark degrees of banishment from political and social community. The production of the "Muselmann," as Agamben describes it, marks the orchestrated death of juridical personhood. He hyperbolizes and ontologizes Levi's descriptions of the "Muselmann," transforming this word into a sanctified name for the secret of modernity that he makes the principle object of theoretical reflection:

> If, in the jargon of Nazi bureaucracy, whoever participated in the "Final Solution" was called a *Geheimnisträger*, a keeper of secrets, the *Muselmann* is the absolutely unwitnessable, invisible ark of biopower. Invisible because empty, because the Muselmann is nothing other than the *volkloser Raum*,

the space empty of people at the center of the camp that, in separating all life from itself, marks the point in which the citizen passes into the *Staatsangehoriger* of non-Aryan descent, the non-Aryan into the Jew, the Jew into the deportee, and, finally, the deported Jew beyond himself into the *Muselmann*, that is, into a bare, unassignable and unwitnessable life. (RA 156–57)

Even as the word *Muselmann* emerges in Agamben's prose stripped of its medieval and premodern history and severed from its precedent and coincident significance in French legal taxonomies and cartographic practices, it retains a troubling doubleness, as if it is haunted by what Agamben's belated making-visible leaves so utterly out of sight.

Agamben's sentences become difficult to read without detecting the ghosted colonial heredity of the term *Muselmann/musulman*. A condition of "unwitnessable" bare life—identified by him as the threshold where human becomes indistinguishable from nonhuman, where the state exercises its power to determine life that can be sacrificed from that which can simply be terminated—already had a name available to Auschwitz prisoners in 1944 that appears so natural to Agamben in 1998 that he does not even mention, let alone investigate, its colonial history. This enigmatic word is the central critical category in *Remnants of Auschwitz* and an object of sustained ethical and political reflection for Agamben, yet his reformulation of "Levi's paradox" relies on a semantic sleight that renders the category "musulman" visible at Auschwitz by ignoring its coincident function in Algiers or Aïn el-Bey. His theoretical appropriation of the term propagates a historiographic conundrum produced by colonial violence and maintained by postcolonial amnesia that continues to determine what can appear to whom as a recognizable subject of historical knowledge and ethical reflection—and what cannot appear.

"The Muslims, the Drowned"

There is something strange about the first instance in *Remnants of Auschwitz* in which the "ironical name" appears assimilated, translated, and stripped of typographic instability to signify as a proper name: "The 'true' witnesses, the 'complete' witnesses," writes Agamben, "are those who did not bear witness and who could not bear witness. They are those who 'touched bottom': the Muslims, the drowned" (RA 34).

This claim follows Agamben's discussion of the "conceptual confusion" that he sees generated by the post-Holocaust legal trials at Nuremberg and in particular

FIGURE 1.2. Jean Texier, "Ici on noie les algériens," October 1961, Paris. From the Mémoires d'humanité archives départementales de la Seine-Saint-Denis.

in the trial "in Jerusalem in 1961 that ended with the hanging of Eichmann" for his complicity in Nazi crimes against humanity (RA 19). Given the coincidence of the timing, this is a truly ironic instance in which to fully naturalize the appropriated word *musulman*. The trial that began after Adolf Eichmann was extradited from Argentina by Israeli intelligence in May 1960 and concluded with his execution in Jerusalem on June 1, 1962, serves a defining function for Agamben, as it does for many historians of the Nazi genocide and theorists of testimony, including Annette Wieviorka and Shoshana Felman. The Eichmann proceedings gave Holocaust survivors a platform to narrate their suffering to the world from the witness stand at the Jerusalem House of Justice, and this trial gave the new state an opportunity to exact vengeance, if not justice, for the Nazis' victims.[30] Observing the profound inadequacy of this process to the catastrophe for which it sought to account, Agamben reiterates his case: the absolute witnesses to the crimes of the Third Reich could never take the stand in Jerusalem in 1961. This is a point that Agamben appears to share with that trial's most famous witness, the camp survivor and writer Yechiel Dinur ("Ka-Tzetnik 135633"), who referred to the "Muselmanner" of Auschwitz just before fainting in the courtroom and whose depiction of these haunting figures in his 1961 novel *Moni: A Novel of*

Auschwitz underscores their mute illegibility: "A crush. A surge. Muslims. Skeletons. Skeletons. You do not see them. Just as you do not see the paper but the words written on it."[31]

Agamben argues that the foreclosure of *these* drowned "Muslim" witnesses—the camp victims lost to history and rendered absent before the law—itself signals the unprecedented magnitude of the Nazi crime. Had Agamben traced the epithet's other life as a juridical category of French empire or contemplated legacies of May 1945 from the perspective of those living under legal settler colonization at the time of Auschwitz, he might have revised his thesis or at least reconsidered using this particular metaphor to describe drowned "Muslims." At precisely the moment in 1961 that Ka-Tzetnik narrated his account from the witness stand at the House of Justice in Jerusalem, the French state was also waging the last brutal campaign of its long counterrevolutionary war to defend the idea and the institutions of Algérie française. On October 17, 1961—as witnesses continued to take the stand to testify in Jerusalem, as construction got underway for the memorial to the martyrs of the deportation on Île de la Cité in the middle of the Seine—around twenty thousand unarmed Algerian men, women, and children took to the Paris streets to protest a curfew that had been imposed by police commander Maurice Papon on only Algerian residents of the city, and soon thereafter an "invisible" police massacre of Muslims took place in public streets and squares and metro stations across the city of light.[32]

The text of Papon's curfew order targeted Algerian residents of Paris with shifting variations of the old colonial category, banning "travailleurs musulmans algériens," "français musulmans," or "français musulmans d'Algérie" from public space after 8:30 in the evening.[33] In reaction to the massive nonviolent demonstration organized to contest this racist curfew, the Paris police attacked Algerian protestors where they gathered on the *grands boulevards* and metro stations in the heart of the city. Police chased, beat, arrested, loaded demonstrators onto buses, and confined them to stadiums in the banlieues, where many were killed, and many others deported.

Throughout Paris, police threw battered and broken Algerian bodies into the Seine. Drowned corpses floated to the river's surface for days—in the calculated absence of official record or acknowledgment of these murders, the image of drowned bodies floating in the Seine has become a powerful metonym for the occulted massacre. This is reflected by the title of Anne Tristan's collection of photographs *Le silence du fleuve* (*The River's Silence*; 1991),[34] as well as by the iconic photograph taken by Jean Texier depicting the graffito scrawled beside the Seine in the shadow of the Louvre, just east of the pont des Arts, which reads: "Ici on noie les Algériens" (Here we drown Algerians).[35] Had Agamben registered contemporaneous uses of the term *musulman* by the French police as he reflected on the structuring aporia at the heart of testimony being spoken at Jerusalem, then surely he would not refer to Auschwitz's "Muslims" as "the drowned" without reckoning with a host of other terrible ironies.

The police murder of Algerian demonstrators on the streets of Paris on October 17, 1961, is one of the most contested instances of state violence in modern French history, but this colonial massacre was neither exceptional nor without precedent in the history of French empire. Due in part to a police-ordered media blackout imposed by Maurice Papon, the repression appeared to go deliberately unrecorded at the time. This does not mean that witnesses to and victims of this violence were incapable of testifying, of course—Jacques Panijel's 1962 documentary film *Octobre à Paris* (*October in Paris*) contains several recorded interviews with survivors. Rather, the apparent "absence" of an archive demonstrates that the French political and legal infrastructure failed to create a framework in which Algerian testimonies could or would be publicly heard in any way comparable to what was taking place so visibly and audibly in Jerusalem at the same time.

A number of texts concerned with documenting the October 1961 police massacre were published, or almost published, before the 1990s, yet most of these were censored, seized upon publication, circulated clandestinely, or published outside France, notably by the FLN news organ *El Moudjahid*.[36] The massacre did not become a subject for academic historiography until the mid-1990s, when the state-controlled archive was finally opened and when historians Jim House and Neil MacMaster began research for their monumental study *Paris 1961: Algerians, State Terror, and Memory* (2006).[37] House and MacMaster point out that October 17, 1961, was by far the most violent state repression of an unarmed demonstration ever to take place in mainland France—and that more people died in Paris that day than died at Tiananmen Square in 1989—yet that the event has also been subject to such historiographic delay and official disavowal that until surprisingly recently it was relegated to the margins and footnotes of histories of state violence in the twentieth century, if it was mentioned at all.

Scholarly histories of October 17, 1961, did not begin to be written until the 1990s, ironically because the state archives were at last opened in response to demand surrounding Maurice Papon's *earlier* role in ordering the deportation of 1,560 Jews to Nazi death camps between 1942 and 1944—a crime for which he went to trial and was convicted of complicity in genocide in 1998. By now, there is a considerable and still-growing repertoire of both critical and aesthetic works concerning October 17, 1961. Lia Brozgal has analyzed how, in the absence of an accessible historical archive, aesthetic works played an indispensable role in creating the history and contesting official silence concerning the occulted massacre.³⁸ However, as the historians House and MacMaster also point out, "October 1961" was also only one among numerous such massacres directed by the French military and police against "musulmans d'Algérie." This particular violence became controversial in France not for its magnitude or because it was unprecedented but because of its location in the heart of Paris rather than on the streets, in the mountain villages, or in the desert prison camps of Algeria where such systematic terror had long been practiced, and not in secret.³⁹

A conspicuous irony here is not that certain Nazi victims, most of them Jewish, were reduced to juridically dead "Muslims" at Auschwitz, but that Agamben's attention to this apparently inscrutable camp figure blinds him to the other histories of administrative state violence that the word discloses. The problem is not simply that Agamben fails to include colonial scenes and images in his frame, but that he does not see the colonial imagery already spliced into that frame. The haunting epithet links Nazi with European imperial violence with uncanny acuity. However, as Agamben founds his ethics on the site where "Jews" were transformed into the ambiguously human figures that he readily accepts "Muslims" *already were*, certain victims come to appear (even as they "drown") in place of those whose absence or drowning never gains the status of an ethical or political problem. Agamben's theoretical appropriation of the "musulman" reinforces a limit that determines certain lives grievable and certain cases exemplary—a rhetorical gesture with discomfiting proximity to what Frantz Fanon described, concerning French lawfare conducted in Algeria in 1961, as "this reasoning that so arithmetically foresees the disappearance of colonized people."⁴⁰

Agamben's claim may be more apt than he appears to know: the absent witnesses to the horror of state violence in the twentieth century may indeed be those "drowned" "Muslims" who cannot testify within existing political and juridical frameworks. Agamben's own theoretical account of the structural paradox at the heart of the genre of testimony is troubled by remnants of other "Muslims" that enter his study of modern state violence only under the sign of assiduous erasure. If such "Muslims" appear absent from Agamben's picture, surely this is not because they cannot speak, but rather because he cannot hear or see them.

Armies of Ghosts

Zahia Rahmani's literary project hinges on a different testimonial paradox than does Agamben's theoretical one, namely: a banished witness is speaking loudly and clearly, but is anyone actually listening? In particular, *"Musulman" roman* (2005) appears designed to explore the problems posed for testimony by the untranslatable word in its title without reinforcing the violence of the word's peculiar force as a founding juridical category of French empire. This becomes more apparent if Rahmani's 2005 novel is set alongside the other two literary works that she published in quick succession during the years that the global war on terror gathered force after September 11, 2001: *Moze* (2003) and *France, récit d'une enfance* (2006; translated by Lara Vergnaud as *France: Story of a Childhood* in 2016).

Together, the three novels, a loose trilogy, read like movements in a shared quest—literature searching for a way to write history other than as it has turned out. In *Moze*, the narrator casts her father's suicide as a tragic culmination of the bizarre history of French citizenship in colonized Algeria. While the narrator of *Moze* reckons with a father's suicide and that of *France* speaks directly to her dying mother, the narrator of *"Musulman" roman* does both and more. Notably, wherever the word *musulman* appears throughout Rahmani's writing, it is always enclosed by quotation marks (unless she is referring to practicing believers), and it is frequently capitalized like a German noun. This typography preserves the word's unsettling and inassimilable quality; it highlights its status as imposition, fabrication, epithet, and citation. Not once does Rahmani naturalize or neutralize the term. By this refusal, she summons its repressed ghosts and sets the singular experiences of her parents and herself within a much more expansive historical frame.

It is often noted that Rahmani's writing hews close to the autobiographical; her genre-defying trio of works is often described as autofictional. She was born in Algiers in 1962, a few months after Algeria's formal independence from French rule; her mother was Kabyle, and her father, accused of being a harki (an Algerian conscripted to fight on the side of the French military against Algerian revolutionaries), narrowly escaped the retributive massacres and purges that took place with national independence because he was temporarily imprisoned in a camp in the Sahara.[41] He sought political asylum in France, where Rahmani joined him five years later and eventually became a citizen—and also where her father committed suicide by drowning himself in November 1991, a month before the cancelled presidential elections now widely taken to mark the start of Algeria's deeply uncivil war.

Notably, Rahmani's three-part literary staging of this history opens with a scene of drowning. Rather, *Moze* begins with a series of lines and verses that appear on three unnumbered pages that fall before the prologue, dated November 11, 1991. The prologue describes a suicide by drowning in forensic detail. However, the text begins before this beginning. Its first printed line is an epigraph from Elias Canetti, whom Agamben had cited in *Remnants of Muslims*:

"L'unique bien qui soit resté à l'homme: libérer la honte" (The only good that is left to man: liberating shame).[42]

After the epigraph we turn to find three printed lines surrounded by the blank space of an otherwise empty page. The speaker makes a statement, followed by a request:

Je me souviens.
Écris que tu te souviens.
Que tu t'en souviens.

I remember. / Write that you remember. / That you remember it.[43]

This sounds like a request to remember something in particular—but what? On the following page, another verse appears, also adrift on a blank page, also composed in the first person. The lines might be read as a continuation of the opening lines, or as a response to their speaker's request and thereby a shift from monologue to dialogue. This second verse sketches a scene. It could be anywhere, at any time. The details—iron beds, a steely aircraft hangar, jingling military music—convey a speaker's fragmented memory ("Je me souviens") of what appears to be a detention, and an imminent deportation:

Je me souviens de mon lit en fer,
de tous ces lits de fer,
du hangar gris,
de la petite musique militaire.

I remember my iron bed, / all those iron beds, / the gray hangar, / the strains of military music.[44]

When the first-person speaker moves to intimate second-person address on the following page, it becomes jarringly clear that she has been speaking to a ghost, or to a corpse. Someone has just died: "You died on a Monday. Thursday, they brought your coffin to the house. It was closed. Because your body had been opened and cut up, we saw only your face behind a porthole."[45]

This face appears in a coffin window as if through the porthole of a sunken ship, "floating in white silk and seaweeds."[46] White silk evokes an Islamic mourning shroud, traditionally white linen or cotton wrapped around a body before burial. The surreal wisps of algae suggest death by drowning. In other words, *Moze* opens with the haunting image of a Muslim, drowned.

Rahmani's literary subversion of Agamben's theoretical project is subtle but it is sure. It runs throughout her three literary texts, especially the first two, which are my focus in this chapter. In some instances, Rahmani simply composes with the ghosted material that slips beyond the edges of Agamben's frame, and in others she explicitly corrects Agamben's oversights, assumptions, and hyperboles. Furthermore, from the opening line "I remember," Rahmani begins to articulate a dispute with the testimonial frameworks that have organized collective memory and collective justice in the late half of the twentieth century.

Rahmani knows about the epithet's disturbing appearance in the Nazi death camps.[47] The narrator of *"Musulman" roman* sets the scene of this terrible discovery: "I knew about the Name from the age of ten," when she lived with her family in a small town in northern France.[48] Forbidden to watch French television by her tyrannical and tormented father—"He never seemed alive. You could say that he was the living dead"—she does so in secret, and happens to discover there Alain Resnais's short documentary film *Night and Fog* (1956).[49]

Resnais's controversial film, which Rahmani does not describe in detail, includes footage of the abandoned Auschwitz and Majdanek camps, of prisoners who had inhabited the camps, of the gas chambers and the dead. It also depicts the convoys of trains that arrived at the camps filled with deportees from France, scenes that had been censored from the version of the film that a young Rahmani might have watched on French television in the late 1960s.[50]

The narrator of *"Musulman" roman* registers how stunned she was—a recently arrived Algerian political refugee in France—to learn of the horror of deportations and genocide that had so recently taken place with the silent complicity of so many French citizens. The word *Musulman* does not actually appear at this point in Rahmani's prose, which describes how the young narrator first learns of its unsettling function as an epithet in the Nazi death camps. A strategic gap at this point in Rahmani's prose summons enigmatic and overlapping histories of extreme violence and dispossession. She writes: "The film *Night and Fog* said, There were six million men and women killed. Killed because they were..." There is simply an ellipsis here. "They had just one Name," she writes. "One Name."[51]

The absence of the implied word (the Name, "Musulman") holds open typographic space that provokes disquieting uncertainty. By refusing to resolve the Name's instability and uncertainty, Rahmani allows for a counterhistory of kinship and shared suffering between Muslims and Jews to emerge in her own account—the kind of nuanced vernacular history that Agamben's cordoning off of Auschwitz as an unprecedented and exemplary site for ontological crime completely eschews.

Rahmani's sentences are also replete with implicit but clear allusions to Agamben and to Primo Levi, yet Rahmani also semantically and conceptually repatriates the "musulman" back to Algeria where it was born as a category of colonizing law. *Remnants of Auschwitz* had opened with the image of an "absolutely apathetic" crowd of "drowned" prisoners in the Nazi camps, an image that haunts Agamben by way of the Bergen-Belsen documentary footage and of Levi's own disturbing memory of the camps, which Agamben cites: "They crowd my memory with their faceless presence... and if I could enclose all the evil in our time in one image, I would choose this image which is familiar to me: an emaciated man, with head dropped and shoulders curved, on whose face and in whose eyes not a trace of thought is to be seen" (*DS* 90; quoted in *RA* 44).

The faceless presence of abject Muslims crowds Rahmani's memory too, but in *Moze* the drowned face of a broken man is first the unbearable gaze of her own dead father: "This unbearable gaze, this extreme face of guilt, I want to get rid of it. And yet I don't want to prove him innocent. What about this sin? The one I carry, one that is not my own and which I cannot absolve? How does one escape an assumed guilt alone?"[52] Rahmani, echoing Agamben and Levi, hesitates to call her father's death a *death*, because he had long been dead even when he was alive: "It happened on November 11th," she writes. "But it arrived long before. Even alive, he was dead."[53] She depicts her father's suicide as the ritual act of a soldier already ghosted, simply returning to join the ranks of the spectral army to which he already belongs: "Moze was an auxiliary in the French army. He rejoined his comrades-in-arms on November 11th, 1991. At 8:30 a.m., he was seen saluting the monument to the victims of the Great War. At 9:15, two hunters found him drowned, floating in the communal pond. His glasses and his hat were nearby."[54] After recounting the forensic details of Moze's suicide by drowning, Rahmani's narrative begins to shuttle rapidly between personal and collective histories to cast her father's own pariah status as a harki soldier—"marked as an outcast, a worthless being, some kind of man [*une espèce d'homme*]"—as the touchstone for an obscured counterhistory of violent modernity that encompasses but is not epitomized by the Nazi camps: "This man concerns history."[55]

Both *Moze* and *"Musulman" roman* are concerned with writing the recessed history that the "musulman" and "harki" concern. In her autofictional texts, it is Rahmani (as first-person narrator) "who bears witness to the drowned, speaking in their stead," and who stands as "the cartographer of this new *terra ethica*, the implacable land-surveyor of *Muselmannland*" (Agamben on Levi; *RA* 69). At no point does Rahmani depict Moze as anything other than *homme*, a human man, despite what French lawfare does to him ("désigne *comme*... une espèce d'homme"). "What his own tongue couldn't manage to name," she writes of her mute harki father, "was an entire system that allowed the French state to create an army of deadsoldiers [*soldatmorts*] without ever worrying that they were human men."[56]

In history as Rahmani writes it, the suicide of an already dead *soldatmort* (deadsoldier) in northern France in 1991 must be framed by the spectacular tragedy of Algérie française that began in the nineteenth century. She charts a history of the nominally French "indigènes-musulmans" conscripted by law—as provided by the sénatus-consulte of 1845—to serve as fodder for French wars. Rahmani frequently ventriloquizes the voice of the law or the state ("à la guerrrrrrrre soldatmort" [off to warrrrrrr deadsoldier])[57] as she reconstructs the obscured genealogy of this category of person lost in an ontological abyss between *l'ignoré-français-indigène-arabe* (ignored-french-native-arab) and *père-soldatmort-faux-français-traître* (father-deadsoldier-fake-french-traitor).

Rahmani's calquing and ventriloquizing of the French state's subconscious often sounds like a sarcastic twist on Agamben's solemn theorizing ("people did not die; rather, corpses were produced"); for instance: "Moze wasn't killed,... arrested, tortured, locked up, sold, displaced, hidden away, sold, displaced,... locked up, transferred, beaten, bartered, ransomed, imprisoned, tortured, hidden away, displaced, beaten, ransomed."[58] In Rahmani's narrative shuttling and splicing, her abused father appears to be one fleeting shadow among "thousands of lost bodies."[59] He became a shadow of a person, his dignity assaulted by forced conscription into an army of ghosts called "musulmans indigènes."

The monologues, dialogues, and diatribes that *Moze* comprises stage a series of testimonies on behalf of a ghostly multitude of Algerians like her father, erased from history by their subjection to an imposed name and legal status. This is the same condition to which the imprisoned narrator of *"Musulman" roman* abruptly finds herself subjected "yet again" ("I became, yet again, 'Musulman'").[60] When this narrator surveys the camp scene in which she finds herself, she peers out the window of her prison cell, beyond the barbed wire, to witness a scene that closely resembles those described by Agamben and Levi: "I looked farther, out beyond the barbed wire. There was the other camp. For the men. All seated, dark gazes lowered to the ground."[61] She notices crowds of imprisoned men whose bodies are bent as if in prayer and submission: "I watch the mass of kneeling bodies. Nothing seems to disturb it. The desert is powerful."[62]

The narrator's gaze lingers on the lowered faces of the "musulman" prisoners in the men's camp beyond the barbed wire of her own prison. She observes their downcast eyes, their folded forms, but detects there precisely what Agamben claims had been stripped away: dignity and humanity. Agamben had explained that the "most likely explanation of the term" derives from the "literal meaning of the Arabic word muslim: 'one who submits unconditionally to the will of God'" (RA 45). Rahmani rejects this equation outright: "Nothing in that gaze suggests that they submit to their condition."[63] In *Moze*, too, the narrator observes resistance and dignity in the broken postures of suffering bodies such as her father's, and she rejects the reductive Orientalism shared by Agamben with Elie Wiesel, Jean Améry, Aldo Carpi, Zdziław Ryn and Stanisław Kłodziński, and Wolfgang Sofsky: "His fatalism?" she scoffs. "That nonchalance *is his resistance*."[64]

In faces frozen in fear and bodies broken by suffering, Rahmani reads not a lack of human dignity but its epitome—opacity and resistance: "In their faces I could read it," she writes. "These faces didn't reveal an absence of existence, no—this is a face foreign to interestedness [*étranger à l'intérêt*]. A refusal of interest borne by the face, borne only by the dignity of the face. The kneeling body does not undo this face."[65] In the blank inscrutability where Agamben identified the "point at which human beings cease to be human," Rahmani detects what is most human: "His only real possession lies in this slowness; his human dignity is lodged in it, much like it was said of slaves in the cotton fields, slower, always slower."[66]

The faces of Rahmani's fellow inmates are not empty or absent simply because they do not make themselves available to invasive critical scrutiny. Agamben looks at the "musulman" prisoner and sees the absence of human dignity in that blank inscrutable face, an emptied abyss. Rahmani deftly connects this viewpoint to the cartographic gaze of the French military, which had surveyed the desert to see there only a space emptied of people, ready to be occupied and civilized: "Yes, this desert world just like his empty and uncultured soul! So the armed men who controlled the camp said to themselves. In this desert we will find nothing. Everything here is untouched. They couldn't even manage to cultivate their land!"[67]

Rahmani's direct channeling of the inner monologue of French military officers invading the Sahara also implicitly sets the ideology of Algérie française next to Hitler's concept of volkloser Raum—that is, the idea of a space emptied of people, which Agamben had identified as "the driving force of the camp understood as a biopolitical machine that, once established in a determinate geographical space, transforms it into an absolute biopolitical space" (RA 86). Rahmani deftly rewrites the camp scene in a way that slyly juxtaposes Agamben's gaze to that of the soldiers holding the machine guns in the desert prison where her story takes place: "Or so they told themselves, those men carrying the guns in this camp."[68] Rahmani's fictional reframing is thus also an indictment of Agamben's theoretical imperialism.

Acting Out Justice

The narrator of *Moze* speaks in multiple tongues but has two driving desires: first, to put the French nation-state on trial for its disavowed crimes, and second, to repatriate and bury a body that the Algerian nation-state has banished. The book's prologue ("11 novembre") and first section ("I. LA MORT") recast Moze's suicide as a form of *social death* a century and a half in the making.[69] Its second act ("II. LA SÉPULTURE: Les filles de Moze retournent dans le pays de leur père" [Moze's Daughters Return to Their Father's Country]) stages a theatrical dialogue between the narrator and her sister, who have just arrived in Algiers in late 1991. Its third act ("III. JUSTICE: La fille de Moze est reçue par la commission nationale de réparation" [Moze's Daughter Is Received before the National Reparations Committee]) stages a trial in which the justice demanded by "la fille de Moze" is not at all the kind of justice that the French magistrates at this hearing have in mind.

"II. LA SÉPULTURE" unfolds as dialogue. Moze's two daughters, one of whom is Rahmani's first-person narrator, have come to Algiers to file paperwork for authorization to repatriate and bury their father's remains in his homeland, but the Algerian authorities have forbidden such rites for harkis, who are considered enemies of the state and even have their remains banished from the nation's soil. Besides, it is 1991; the Algerian authorities are also rather preoccupied with the shadows and corpses of a newly turbulent time.[70]

Two voices speak a dialogue that recalls that between Antigone and her sister Ismene—the sisters are concerned with burying kin who have been banished by law. One asks questions; the other answers, digressing into historical diatribes effused with a righteous sense of justice. Among their first concerns is how to bury their father's body to rid themselves of his unquiet ghost: "I owe him nothing. But he owes it to *me* to leave me alone, to get out of my head, he owes it to me to move on. He owes it to me to never come back [*ne plus revenir*]. I came back here to shake him!"[71]

Yet harkis, despised traitors without citizenship or burial rights, cannot by law be interred. This poses a tactical problem for daughters desperate to be relieved of a potential revenant. One sister questions; the other responds:

—How do you instate the dignity of someone who does not exist?
—Take him back to the dead.
—Does a "musulman" come back from the dead?
—It is written that men die and are reborn.
—Rumours are brewing. It is better that he does not come back.[72]

Her sister's questions about Muslim dignity and "musulman" fatalism provoke increasingly intransigent historical monologues from the narrator. Here, she outlines centuries of French settler colonization and slavery in a single diatribe:

Muslims have been scorned. They have been killed in so great a number and so freely throughout past decades that it seems they were good for nothing except being exploited and domesticated for the needs of the moment. The ones in North Africa were exploited by way of struggles, thefts, sequestrations. Then, and by the thousands, by means of privations, epidemics, and famines. Some of them were even put on display at fairs. Those who fled conscription, or refused to serve the French flag, were sent to the penal colony or shot. There were those on the front lines in 1914 and those who, recruited as a labor force after the war, were already-finished men. Surviving the dire straits of colonialism required the dereliction of colonized men. Colonial *omertà* stems from this shame. That of having to admit to a total absence of humanity.[73]

She traces a picture of regime-made catastrophe that produced the slave, the "indigène musulman," the "musulman français," the "harki." There are centuries distilled into these lines, myriad settings sketched in sentences (massacres, imprisonments, colonial exhibitions, epidemics, famines, military conscription, forced labor), and a straightforward diagnosis of the shame enforcing a code of silence concerning these crimes, which she does not here call genocide: "Colonial *omertà* stems from this shame. That of having to admit to a total absence of humanity." As she sees it, the French are paralyzed by shame over the abject absence of their *own* humanity.

The more immediate battle over Moze's burial, however, has a different antagonist. Concerning harkis, the sister says, the Algerian authorities are beginning to talk about indemnity. The narrator's sense of justice is not appeased by such talk: "Don't you see that so long as we are talking about compensation, we aren't talking about the massacres?"[74] Concerning the truth of these massacres, the sister is skeptical, given that no one knows the number conscripted by the French or killed after the French departed: "You want a colloquium, a symposium, an international conference with archival photos? . . . The truth will be impossible."[75] To this provocation, the narrator replies with a torrent of numbers:

> They piss us off with their numbers! 20,000 deaths? 30,000; 90,000; 100,000; 130,000 harkis gunned down! Or lynched or burned? 150,000; 180,000 deadsoldiers ignored? 200,000; 250,000; 300,000; 400,000 enlisted! 600,000; 900,000 even? 1,000,000; 2,000,000; 5,000,000, more, more still! All the contracts had service numbers and these documents are archived. We know their names. They should tell us the names of the disappeared! They should give them to us, the names! Hand them over![76]

Edging up to the significant threshold *six million*, she demands that the national archives be opened and the names of the disappeared "soldatmorts ignorés" be handed over, every single one.

This scene in Algiers is abruptly interrupted by the arrival of an official letter from the French government summoning the narrator back to France to testify in a reparation commission: "French Republic—National Reparation Commission—Summons to testify."[77] She is dubious, but her sister urges her to go and speak in Moze's place.[78] She remains unconvinced: "And talk to them about what?" Her sister answers: "About those who remain [*De ceux qui restent*]."[79] The narrator decides to testify on behalf of *ceux qui restent* of the army of soldatmorts, those "living corpses" (*des cadavres vivants*) whose bodies she cannot bury and whose disturbing ghosts she cannot shake.[80]

Act III, "JUSTICE," is also staged as scene of address. This act takes place inside a courtroom, and it unfolds more as diatribe than dialogue. The French commissioners presume that our narrator has come there as summoned to speak on behalf of her dead father; they wish to make financial reparation for his suffering. However, from the moment that she is ordered to speak, it becomes clear that this witness is not going to adhere to the commission's rules:

> —COME FORWARD!
> So begins the act of justice.
> I am in a large space facing a high wall. I hear *come forward* and I know that I will say what I want to say. Everything I intend to say I am going to say it.[81]

The hearing is held in this large room with the witness facing a high wall atop which the commissioners sit so that she cannot see their faces, only hear their voices. She begins by swearing to tell the whole truth, but the disembodied voice of a commissioner interrupts from on high to inform her that this is a commission and not a tribunal: "Our aim is to collect your testimony about your father, and to do it in a transparent and equitable way. You are not required to swear by oath."[82]

While the faceless French commissioners insist they have convened a hearing that requires only the facts about her father's suicide, Rahmani's unruly desire for truth and justice breaks this frame to transform the hearing into something else. Her testimony flies beyond the protocols of the court. She veers off script, naming the real crime about which she wishes to testify: "Moze was an Algerian. A *musulman d'origine algérienne* according to the going terms. France, conquering and grateful, loving her lands, her ancestors and her power, made him into a *Français musulman d'Algérie*. So that's what he became."[83]

Disregarding the objections and pleas of the commissioners ("That war is over, says the president"),[84] Rahmani's belligerent witness brings the paradoxical history of French citizenship into court. The commissioners try to steer her testimony into a form that they can control, but the witness dodges and swerves. She opens discussion of an unfinished war that they wish desperately to close: "The history we are concerned with is not yet over [*n'est pas close*]," she tells them. "Everything is raw [*vif*]. One must act."[85]

The narrator's testimony pushes the generic and procedural limits set by the court and its magistrates. Against the protests of her interlocutors, she lodges a plaint, names a crime, accuses the criminal, provides evidence, and demands justice. She insists that the French commissioners' offer of reparation does not fit the magnitude of the paradoxical crime committed by the French state. She demands reckoning on the order of Nuremberg and Jerusalem; they are offering merely cash. Concerning reparation, she asks: "Can you ask forgiveness from the person from whom you demanded a betrayal?"[86] Concerning herself, she points out that her own citizenship is a wound: "I have been disfigured. A misunderstanding makes my nationality precarious, fragile. There is a hollow pit [*trou*] in my citizenship and it is difficult to live."[87] Then she moves to the real gist of her legal plaint: "My father bore the ambiguity of this century: ignominious humanity. The ignominious humanity of this century! We were given over because we were nothing! Arabs, Muslims [*Des Arabes, des musulmans*]. We were used to cover up an army's flight! A carpet of dead bodies as a souvenir."[88] Rahmani's narrator further specifies that the ambiguous, dishonored humanity shouldered by "Arabes" and "musulmans" was fabricated by French laws. She names the Crémieux Decree of 1870 that gave Jews citizenship to pit them against Muslims, and Pétain's 1940 law that transformed Algeria's Jews *back* into "indigènes," a status that they once again found themselves sharing with their "musulman" kin.[89] About this crime of terrorizing lawfare she is unequivocal. She calls it alternately a "a concentration-camp tactic [*technique*]"; "the pulverization carried out by colonial policy"; and: "A politics of separation. This country's Algerian policy was founded on this principle. It was narrow, racist, and cowardly.... And this world is that of *la France!*"[90]

An army of conscripted Algerians went to war for a racist state that claimed to have conquered Nazi terror in 1945 but was itself already criminal.[91] The witness considers such historical facts self-evident and a distraction from her primary accusation ("We should stop asking if there was torture. Of course there was. Rapes? In great number. Battered men? Too many").[92] What concerns her most is the unpardonable crime of systematically transforming men like her father into traitors willing to murder their own kin; she likens Moze to a *Sonderkommando* of French making, an analogy that the president of the commission finds absolutely intolerable.[93] Being compared to Nazis is too much for the French magistrates.

This analogy escalates the magistrates' attempts to tame the unruly witness in their courtroom. The disembodied voices object, variously: Now you are not testifying about your father, you are making plaints and accusations against *us*! We cannot hear this kind of testimony in this kind of court; if you want a tribunal you must make formal accusation! And besides, your father's situation is as much Algeria's fault as it is ours; we are not free to intervene in a sovereign state's business now! Her argument is about the profundity of a legal violation of what was *already* human long before French law arrived, but the agitated judges listening to her speak cannot or will not hear what she is trying to say.

The witness points out that no legal offices exist in which to lodge such a plaint, and so she must simply make her plaint and her demand before them. She turns their reparation hearing into a one-woman tribunal bent on bringing all of French empire to justice for a crime against the human dignity of millions of men like her father: "I accuse the French people of abandoning me," she announces, speaking in terms that echo Zola's accusation during the Dreyfus affair: "I accuse this country of killing my father. So there's the accusation. As for the plaint, it is missing the charge, office, and legal proceedings that should formally issue it.... So I speak the plaint to you. It's done. There! And the tribunal? Same. Here we are."[94]

As this dispute escalates, it becomes clear that the witness speaks not to get reparation or pardon but to fulfill a testimonial responsibility: "I must, however, lodge this plaint not to rehabilitate or to exonerate him but to express the meaning of this duty to witness of which I am the inheritor."[95] She knows exactly what this duty requires; she knows what needs to be said, and addresses the lawmakers directly with her exhortation: "You do justice. You are the judges and the law. If France's dignity is harmed by this request, you will figure out the argument to spare it from ridicule. This country created that man. And it is up to you, magistrates of the world, to outlaw its existence forever. Not one more man will be so banned! Not one! Let us imagine that no law, no policy can justify such a man. Never again! Never again shall any man be banned."[96] As she exhorts her interlocutors to abolish the condition of banishment itself—"What must be condemned in Moze's condemnation is that which allowed his existence at all"[97]— her sentences loosen and transform. They fill up the page, as exclamations and injunctions, spoken in the subjunctive like a plea or prayer about what else could be, if only the French code of debilitating silence and shame could be broken:

> It needs to be said. It is true that something serious took place in this country. It needs to be written. We need to talk, talk about what happened. Speak with those who lived it. Speak these things with them to quell the

violence, speak so that speech can exercise its rights, speak so that the face can exist, speak so that tears can finally fall, speak so that man no longer kills, speak so that contempt ceases, speak so that men reconcile, speak so that weapons are melted down, speak so that the song is no longer so dark, speak for all these women...[98]

At the conclusion of this impassioned monologue, the narrator looks up to discover that she is "alone here to tell them that my people are dying from having believed in this lie. The Republic..."[99] The commission has disappeared, as illusory as the promises of the French Republic itself. She is talking, but no one is listening. The narrator finds herself back in the paradoxical position of speaking truth that cannot yet be heard, and of pleading for justice alone in an empty room.

Am I Not One of the Disappeared?

"Musulman" roman picks up and runs with a question about testimony that *Moze* leaves wide open: A virtuosic witness is speaking the full truth and nothing but the truth but can anyone hear her? In Rahmani's second text the human condition that Moze's narrator had denounced ("Never again! Never again shall any man be banned!") becomes her own serious problem.

The story begins and ends in a prison camp in an unspecified desert. It is narrated by a prisoner alone in a solitary cell. This might be anywhere, though the desert setting and title of the book's last chapter ("Desert Storm") are suggestive. In the present-tense scenes that bookend the narrative, this prisoner has been stripped of her history. She has no nation. Her identification papers have been lost, as has her proper name. She wears an orange jumpsuit; she waits; she observes; she remembers; she speaks, but who is listening to what she says? Captured while wandering alone in the desert, she finds herself detained, interrogated, and condemned by the epithet she thought she had escaped: "Musulman." Because she cannot explain herself in terms that allay her interrogators' suspicions, she is presumed to be a terrorist and held in a state of indefinite detention.

Rahmani's banished prisoner is not alone. She is in solitary confinement but surrounded by multitudes of other detainees also condemned, like her, by the enigmatic name *Musulman*. Their numbers grow by the day. None of them is meant to be seen or heard from again. "And if they all disappeared?" she asks, and continues: "But haven't they already disappeared? Disappeared. Am I not one of the 'disappeared'? I have a body. But alive or dead, aren't I just the same? I don't count... They don't count. Like others, they don't count."[100]

"Musulman" roman is a fiction seeking a form to articulate truths for which no legal or political frameworks yet exist in any official language. The novel—if it is a novel—presents a seemingly infinite series of tales and memories told from inside a prison cage. This puts readers in the situation of listening to a voice never meant to be heard, of being exposed to impossible testimony spoken with a mutilated tongue in a forgotten minor language: "And in this camp where they want to kill me," the prisoner observes, "I bring her back. A language [*langue*] always speaks."[101]

This narrator's resurrected mother tongue is not English, French, or Arabic, but Kabyle—an indigenous language widely spoken in Algeria by descendants of the oldest inhabitants of the multiply colonized region of northwestern Africa now called the Maghreb. "I was born into a minor language," she writes, "and escaped from a distant nowhere that didn't want me."[102] This is a new clue to reading the idiosyncratic quotation marks around the word *Musulman* in the book's title, a word with which the narrator—an Algerian who is not a practicing Muslim—has been labeled whether she likes it or not. She speaks, much like the genius narrator Shahrazād of *The Thousand and One Nights*, at an impasse and under ominous threat, defying annihilation with every word and spinning tales from her memory of an indigenous language that few others know.

Rahmani's fiction thus unfolds in tension with its own narrative frame—in a silent prison, language suddenly takes flight. The text offers a heterogeneous weave of intersecting and colliding voices and genres—at once plaint, historiography, scriptural exegesis, memoir, rant, invocation, and haunting. The vivid details generated by these multiple voices defy every reductive Orientalist and Islamophobic fantasy about Islam, in particular by tethering the narrator's own deracinated identity to a popular, vernacular history of modern Algeria.

Among *"Musulman" roman*'s most striking passages are those that rewrite the history of the Qur'ān's composition, identifying the sacred text as a work born in translation and transmission through multiple languages—Arabic, Hebrew, Kabyle, Chaouia, Tamasheq. Rahmani's own text is arranged as a prologue followed by five dramatic "acts," whose titles immediately register her concern with the multiple and minor, and with transmitting the myriad stories she was told as a child: "The Night of the Elephant," "Little Thumb [*Le Petit Poucet*] and the Magic Nut," "My Mother Tongue Refuses to Die," "Dialogue with a Government Worker," and "Desert Storm."

The juxtaposition of two surprising epigraphs, both translated into Rahmani's French from English, at once connects Rahmani's vernacular Maghrebi counterhistory to the routes of the transatlantic slave trade and highlights her attention to ghostly figures of subaltern testimony aside from the "musulman" named in her book's title. The first epigraph is a passage from J. M. Coetzee's novel *Foe*, addressed to the mute slave Friday (from *Robinson Crusoe*) who cannot speak because the nerves at the base of his tongue have been severed. The second epigraph is the famous opening paragraph from Melville's *Moby Dick*, translated into French: "Call me Ishmael...." The first epigraph concerns how to elicit speech from the mutilated tongue of an enslaved person whose name is not his own; the second introduces a proper name (Ishmael) with particular symbolic resonance for Rahmani's fugitive narrator. In one version of Abrahamic tradition, to call oneself Ishmael is to lay claim to the lineage of the prophet Muhammad, and to claim to descend from an exiled slave, Hagar.[103]

After she is found wandering alone in the desert—as if she traces Hagar's own itinerant path—the narrator embraces this unexpected kinship. Her intricate rewriting of the history of the Qur'ān's composition prominently features the origin story of the split in Abrahamic tradition between Jew and Muslim, but with a twist. As she retells the tale of Abraham, Sarah, Hagar, Isaac, and Ishmael, she points out that the Qur'ān actually omits the name of *which* child Abraham almost sacrificed at Mount Moriah—was it Isaac or Ishmael? Was it the son of Abraham's legitimate wife, Sarah, or of his banished slave, Hagar, who was meant to be killed by the prophet?

Protecting this ambiguity "like a treasure," Rahmani redirects our attention to the point where Hagar vanishes from historical record without a trace:

> She put her son on her shoulders and set out for the desert. Just as she was about to collapse, she happened upon a spring. She put her son down. And then history tells us nothing about her. Nothing. Her life stops. The boy finds himself without a father, and Hagar disappears into the shadows of legend. So perhaps I was a child of Ishmael, the abandoned child, the child born of a castoff slave. Of a mother expunged from the record. Forgotten. Of a mother cut off from her progeny. I take this to be my lineage.[104]

What would it take to write a history that takes up as truly authoritative the lost testimonies of all the dispossessed, detained, deported, banished, forgotten, and disappeared? This is the ethical and political terrain at stake for Rahmani, whose literary fiction is an instrument for truths spoken in minor and mutilated tongues, testimonies that as yet have nowhere else to be heard. She takes this point of fadeout—the footprints of a trace of Hagar as she vanishes from history—as her own lineage, and as a starting point for her own literary experiment in finding out what it would take not just to write or speak history from such perspective, but to ensure that such testimony is heard. That the very nature of our political regimes and theoretical frameworks requires such intervention by way of fiction suggests that literature has an indispensable role to play in the ongoing work of justice.

A politics of testimony in our time of unfinished decolonization cannot be reduced to the narrative paradox posed by the structural absence of witnesses lost to history and thus incapable of making plaints before the law; this is only one dimension of a larger puzzle. From a standpoint that cannot afford to ignore the way that colonizing violence continues to shape ways of seeing and speaking, understanding the political stakes of testimony means also recognizing what Nancy Fraser has identified as a *metapolitical* problem of framing.[105] Rahmani's texts openly dispute the mistaken overlap between juridical personhood and what is truly human by claiming as kin those who are the *most* banished and broken by the law. Her work also demonstrates literature's capacity to create alternative frameworks that are capable of registering their unheard plaints, and thus to reveal a radical misfit between existing legal and theoretical frameworks and the demands of true justice.

2

Untranslatable Justice

À tes côtés les Arabes. Écartés les Arabes. Sans effort rejetés les Arabes. Confinés les Arabes. Ville indigène écrasée. Ville d'indigènes endormis. Il n'arrive jamais rien chez les Arabes. Toute cette lèpre sur ton corps. Tu partiras. Mais toutes ces questions, ces questions sans réponse. Le silence conjugué de 800 000 Français, ce silence ignorant, ce silence innocent. Et 9 000 000 d'hommes sous ce linceul de silence.

Arabs all around you. Arabs kept at a distance. Arabs, effortlessly rejected. Arabs, confined. Indigenous town razed. A town of sleeping indigènes. Nothing ever happens among the Arabs. This leprosy all over your body. You will leave. But all of these questions, these unanswered questions. The collective silence of 800,000 Frenchmen, this ignorant silence, this innocent silence. And 9,000,000 men beneath this death-shroud of silence. —Frantz Fanon

L'art judiciaire ne se confond pas avec la littérature, sauf, à la limite, quand l'absence de l'une des parties laisse à l'autre le champ libre.

The judicial art is not to be confused with literature, except, in a bind, when the absence of one of these gives the other free reign. —Jacques Vergès

Testimony and Resistance

In 1961, at the same time that the Eichmann trial was underway in Jerusalem and social demand for Holocaust survivor testimonies was growing in France, the liberation war was reaching hallucinatory levels of violence in both France and Algeria. A year earlier, an Algerian militant named Djamila Boupacha wrote a

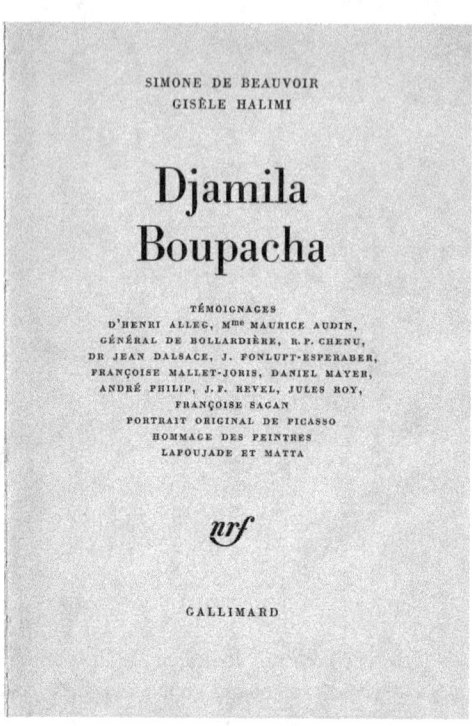

FIGURE 2.1. Title pages from *Djamila Boupacha* (Paris: Gallimard, 1962).

letter to a human rights attorney named Gisèle Halimi in Paris to ask for legal representation; at the time, Boupacha was in an Algiers prison awaiting the death sentence after her arrest and confession to planting a bomb in a restaurant in 1959. She had recanted her confession and accused the French officers and soldiers who arrested her of forcing her to sign a fabricated testimony after torturing and raping her at detention centers in El Biar and Hussein Dey in Algiers.

Halimi answered Boupacha's call. She traveled to Algiers for the short visit that her visa allowed; she knew to read between the lines of the police dossier for evidence of torture, which she found. With Boupacha, Halimi launched a legal battle inside a juridical system designed to make state-sponsored crime and its victims disappear: "Military justice wanted a swift and discrete liquidation of this affair."[1] Halimi had no illusions about the nature of the French legal institutions that she would work within to demand justice for Boupacha: "It wasn't always effective," Halimi observes in the 1962 book that she would publish about the case, "because sometimes it was too late. But, for Djamila and others, there was still time. We had to say it, had to write it, had to demand justice."[2]

Urged by the French procurer general of Algiers to keep Boupacha's case out of the media after she had studied the dossier and met with the prisoner, Halimi returned to Paris and wrote straight to General Charles de Gaulle with a signed and sealed copy of Boupacha's legal complaint; to André Malraux (Prix Goncourt–winning novelist, recently named minister of culture, and, as she notes pointedly, "the government official responsible for claiming that 'there is no more torture in Algeria'");[3] and to Edmond Michelet (Dachau survivor, Resistance hero, minister of justice). After receiving a tepid response from these officials, she convinced Nobel laureate (and sponsor of Elie Wiesel's 1958 publication *La nuit*) François Mauriac to publish a piece in *L'express* about Boupacha's case but found its tone ethically ambiguous and disappointing.[4] She then spoke with Daniel Mayer, president of the Ligue des droits de l'homme, who wept with shame upon hearing the graphic details of Boupacha's abuse but did nothing else ("What can we say? What can we say? he kept repeating").[5] Finally, she telephoned Simone de Beauvoir, who answered swiftly and unequivocally, as Halimi notes: "She said 'yes' like something that goes without saying."[6]

Like many French leftists at the time, Beauvoir had been reading the growing archive of testimonies, memoirs, pamphlets, reports, court proceedings, and other documents that were beginning to be published and circulated in Paris—despite intense but inconsistent censorship[7]—by presses such as Maspero, Minuit, and Seuil as soon as the first French military conscripts returned from service in Algeria. Her nine-hundred-page memoir *La force des choses* (1963) is replete with such references.[8] Beauvoir mentions, among others, Pierre Henri Simon's polemic *Contre la torture* (1957); the brochure of military conscript testimonies *Des rappelés témoignent* (1957); Jacques Vergès and Georges Arnaud's defense of Djamila Bouhired, an FLN militant also sentenced to death for planting a bomb (1957); Henri Alleg's account of his own arrest and torture and of Maurice Audin's disappearance, *La question* (1958); reports concerning the torture and summary executions of Ali Boumendjel and Larbi Ben M'hidi; dossiers concerning other Algerians disappeared and tortured by French military and police forces such as *Les disparus: Le cahier vert* (1958) and *La gangrène* (1959; discussed in this chapter); and a Croix-Rouge report documenting conditions in the civilian *camps de regroupement*, of which Beauvoir writes with acute anguish: "At the beginning of spring '59, a little-known facet of this exterminating war was revealed to us: the camps."[9]

Like many French citizens, Beauvoir was disturbed and moved to action by these revelations, especially with knowledge of Vichy deportations and Nazi extermination camps seared in her memory. In June 1960, she published an incendiary article, "Pour Djamila Boupacha," in an issue of *Le Monde* that was immediately seized by the French police, which prompted Halimi and Beauvoir to create a committee to advocate for Boupacha. In 1962, the book-length text *Djamila Boupacha* was published by Gallimard, with a preface by Beauvoir.

Beauvoir's preface opens by directly addressing French readers with sharp questions about inconsistencies in their newly whetted desire for testimony.[10] Its first sentence—"A twenty-three-year-old Algerian woman, liaison officer for the FLN, was imprisoned, tortured, and raped with a bottle by French military officers: it's *banal*"—pinpoints the problem in terms that prefigure the controversial subtitle of Arendt's 1963 essays on the Eichmann trial (*A Report on the Banality of Evil*) and also resonate with Fanon's 1961 observation about the banality of French practices of body-counting in Algeria ("this banality which makes it so that seven Frenchmen killed or wounded at Sakamody pass ignite the indignation of civilized consciences, whereas...").[11] For Beauvoir, the scandal was not the practice of torture itself—that atrocity was already an open secret, or rather no secret at all. What scandalized Beauvoir was the sheer banality of French state violence against Algerians and the numbness and blindness of French citizens to this regime-made catastrophe.[12]

Beauvoir takes aim at French indifference to Algerian pain with charged terms and visceral images that cumulatively register a justice problem of expanding scope and magnitude. The accumulation of noun phrases and lists of past participles cultivate a disquieting sense that the genocide Beauvoir tries to expose is neither a historically recent nor a geographically distant phenomenon, despite the date that she cites:

> Since 1954, we are all accomplices to a genocide which, in the name of suppressing rebellion, then pacification, has claimed over one million victims: men, women, elders, children gunned down during raids, burned alive in their villages, slaughtered, throats slit, bellies cut open, tortured to death; entire tribes have been left to starve and freeze, at the mercy of beatings, epidemics, in these "relocation centers" which are in fact extermination camps—serving also as brothels to the *corps d'élite*—and where currently over five hundred thousand Algerians await their death. Over the course of the last few months, the press, even the most circumspect journals, has churned out horror stories: assassinations, lynchings, racist attacks, manhunts in the streets of Oran; in Paris, along the Seine, hanging from trees in the Bois de Boulogne, corpses by the dozen; broken hands; exploded skulls; the Toussaint rouge of Algiers. Can we still be moved by the blood of a young woman?[13]

Over the course of a few pages, the essay lays out the details of Boupacha's case, then pans out again at its conclusion to survey the vast carceral system that effectively disappears so many Algerians from French sight: "'I am but one prisoner among thousands of others,' Djamila told her lawyer the other day," Beauvoir pivots. "Indeed, there are 14,000 Algerians detained in France's camps and prisons, 17,000 in Algeria's prisons, and *hundreds of thousands* cooped up in Algeria's camps."[14]

Beauvoir concludes by pointing out to French readers that they appear fully capable of grieving Anne Frank and the destruction of the Warsaw ghetto ("you who mourn so readily and so profusely over past tragedies—Anne Frank or the Warsaw ghetto") at precisely the same moment that they are also silently complicit in the extermination of Algerians taking place along the banks of the Seine, in the Algiers Casbah, and in detention camps in the Sahara: "You are on the side of the butchers of those suffering today. You passively consent to the martyrdom that, in your name and practically before your very eyes, thousands of Djamilas and Ahmeds suffer."[15]

Boupacha's was among the last of a series of highly publicized cases that shocked the metropolitan French public with graphic evidence of the violations carried out in their names to preserve Algérie française during the incoherently violent and chaotic last years of that war.[16] Earlier cases had included the disappearance of Maurice Audin (1957), the defense of Djamila Bouhired by Jacques Vergès (1957), and the torture of Henri Alleg (1958); however, between the two of them, Halimi and Beauvoir made Boupacha's one of the most famous.[17] They successfully transformed Boupacha's case into a powerful symbol for the repugnance of the entire colonial system, as Halimi described in *Les temps modernes* in 1960: "From Turin...to New York...to Oxford...to Copenhagen, Costa Rica, Rabat, Peking, Djamila Boupacha has become a familiar face. She is discussed at the dinner table, in the office, in the factory and in the fields, like a little sister who bears witness for the future to a system that survives only by means of shame and ferocity."[18] The battle waged on Boupacha's behalf by Halimi, Beauvoir, and a group of famous French intellectuals and artists effectively exposed the violence of the French colonial system to audiences who did not *already* see it for what it was.[19] In legal terms, however, the civil suits launched by Halimi with Boupacha—first in Algeria, then in metropolitan France—ultimately failed.

This chapter explores the implications of this legal failure across three different testimonial texts that were published during the chaotic years just before the Évian Accords marked the end of Algérie française and the beginning of French/Algerian decolonization. At a moment when French empire was in its dramatic death throes, *La gangrène* (1959), *Nuremberg pour l'Algérie* (1960), and

Djamila Boupacha (1962) were published as tactical moves in an ongoing activist struggle. Under treacherous political circumstances, a coalition of antiwar leftist intellectuals, publishers, and militant attorneys in France and Algeria fought to reframe Algerian prisoners and criminals as legitimate victims, plaintiffs, and witnesses to the officially disavowed crimes of colonizing war.[20] They worked to defend Algerians legally marked for death by strategically turning the language of the French justice system against itself. In some instances, this meant trying to legally force the state to abide by its own codes and agreements; in others, it meant exposing evidence generated by police and military institutions in order to reveal the state's complicity with injustice and demand public reckoning outside the courts.

However, each text also brings to view a moment of breakdown in the French state's legal and linguistic authority to decide matters of justice at all. *La gangrène* is a short collection of first-person accounts narrated by Algerian men who were rounded up, imprisoned, interrogated, and tortured in Paris over a period of ten days in 1958. Police seized initial copies of *La gangrène* from Paris bookstores, and soon after the state confiscated all printed copies; this prompted the publisher Jérôme Lindon to sue the government over the circumstances of censorship, yet the substantial accusations articulated in the victims' testimonies themselves were never the subject of any legal trial. *Nuremberg pour l'Algérie* is a slim pamphlet assembled by three FLN defense lawyers (including Jacques Vergès, who would in 1987 become infamous for his trial-by-rupture defense of the Nazi collaborator known as the Butcher of Lyon, Klaus Barbie). The pamphlet collates documentary and photographic evidence to support its demand for international legal reckoning on the order of Nuremberg—a demand that has of course never been met. *Djamila Boupacha* is a collectively authored dossier published by Halimi and Beauvoir to short-circuit a legal impasse that stymied the case in 1961. Boupacha returned to prison, but she was not executed. In April 1962, she was freed when the Évian Accords negotiated ceasefire, laid the groundwork for Algerian independence, and issued blanket amnesty for prisoners and war criminals on both sides of the conflict—including for Boupacha's rapists and torturers, who have never been publicly named, let alone charged with a crime or prosecuted.[21]

What makes these testimonial texts revelatory and surprising is not the fact that the legal trials they demanded proved to be impossible, nor that the evidence of state-sponsored crimes they gathered and exposed was so shocking. Rather, it is their unexpected, unsettling literary qualities that compel closer study. In distinctive ways, the Algerian testimonies presented by these antiwar activist texts misfit the legal and linguistic frameworks in which they are made to appear.

This kind of misfit can be observed in a few brief frames excerpted from a television interview with Djamila Boupacha that was filmed in Algiers in 1972, a decade after amnesty absolved both her and her torturers. From offscreen, a French man interviews Boupacha, while the camera remains focused on her face as she listens and responds to his probing questions. He asks her to share what was happening in her mind and her heart at the moment she was asked by the FLN to place a bomb in a public cafe. Boupacha does not answer this invasive question. Instead, she pivots from subjective to collective voice and reminds the interviewer of a longer history that he appears to have forgotten: "Like I already told you," she says, "the Algerian people have not stopped fighting since 1830.... We were the children of militants.... What matters to us is the liberation of our country."[22]

When the interviewer asks directly whether she was tortured (a question to which he must have already known the answer), Boupacha reacts visibly. She exhales a syllable before speaking; it could be French, *ça*, or a nonverbal sound of exasperation. When she speaks she does not answer the question directly: "All the people were [tortured]."[23] Boupacha's gaze drops, breaking with the interviewer's to look away from the camera, as she says that she would rather not dredge up the past. Then she looks directly at him and says forcefully: "*Everyone* was affected by the revolution. *Everyone* was tortured."[24]

The disjuncture between the French interviewer's questions and Boupacha's resolutely oblique responses reflects a broader truth about the literature on testimony, trauma, memory, and Algeria's liberation war. To put it plainly, Algerians have not been interested in answering the same questions that the French have so insistently posed, either during the war or since. This decalage has been reinforced by publication patterns that continue to engender critical blind spots. Christiane Chaulet-Achour made such a point in 2018, a few days after President Macron formally recognized the French state's role in the disappearance and murder of Maurice Audin.[25] Observing that six decades of denial and revelation were simply never a shared experience across the Mediterranean, Chaulet-Achour lays out a detailed bibliography of Algerian testimonial and literary texts that have largely escaped attention precisely because they did not answer to French questions about torture and state-sponsored violence, or because they were not composed in French.[26] Many of these works—especially poetry, theater, and works in Arabic—never drew attention in France, were not translated into French, or simply were never published at all.[27] Chaulet-Achour also points out that Algerian literary production has generally been less preoccupied by the fact of torture. When torture appears in these texts, it is most often depicted as one violence among many and set within a much longer historical memory—much the way that Boupacha insists to her French interlocutor in that 1972 television interview.

To date, scholars have primarily focused on the circulation, transmission, and reception of Algerian testimony beyond Algeria—that is, on the conditions and implications of Algerian testimony's translatability. By contrast, I turn directly to the unsettling literary qualities of these testimonial texts that seem instead to *resist* the demands of translation, and that also put significant pressure on their generic framing as legal testimony in ways that call into question the normal frameworks of justice to create space for raising other demands.[28] The glitches, disruptions, and tensions that resist easy translation and transmission in fact create openings for other kinds of plaints to emerge, often in registers and in languages that have long flown beneath the radar of public discourse and critical scholarly reflection.

These points where the rationality and coherence of French legal and linguistic operations break down are also the points at which literature has the most to teach about justice. In his meditations on testimony—*Demeure: Fiction and Testimony* (1998) and "The Politics and Poetics of Witnessing" (2005)—Jacques Derrida highlights the generic instability that distinguishes this genre to give it its peculiar subversive force. Both written complaint and testimony spoken in court address a legal authority with a grievance that asks for redress. Testimony, writes Derrida, thus has "sense only in regard to a cause: justice, truth as justice," and draws meaning in an implicit structural relationship to the law and the state.[29] Testimony is bound by law, and by legal oath sworn in court, to be *not fiction*. Yet this very contract shows us that the genre is constitutively haunted by the threat of perjury, lie, and fiction—or there would be no need for the oath. The inherent instability that the law must work so carefully to guard against is also where testimony's real power lies: "The possibility of literary fiction haunts so-called truthful, responsible, serious, real testimony as its proper possibility."[30] A witness claims to speak a truth that is not verifiable, bringing the possibilities and ambiguities of literature into contact with the law.

The truth of testimony is therefore not the same thing as evidence, proof, or argument. Derrida demonstrates this by citing multiple translations of a line from Paul Celan's German poem "Aschenglorie": "Nul ne témoigne pour le témoin. Personne ne témoigne pour le témoin. No one bears witness for the witness."[31] No one can testify in place of the witness, or know in her place what she actually saw; in this way, every testimony is untranslatable and secret. But testimony is also an act of address, an entreaty. When she testifies, a witness calls upon the listener for an act of faith: *You have to believe me*, she says. *I was there; I saw; I experienced.* This quality of singular inaccessibility is what renders testimony both impossible and necessary to translate: "As idiomatic as it must remain," writes Derrida, "a testimony *claims* to be translatable."[32] That claim—of the idiomatic to be translatable, of the witness to speak the truth even though what she says cannot be verified, only believed—is an appeal to the listener's faith. It is an invitation to the imagination, not to juridical reason.

Under the legal circumstances of French occupation, the Algerian voices framed as testimony by texts like *La gangrène, Nuremberg pour l'Algérie*, and *Djamila Boupacha* do not translate easily, yet they do make a demand. Compelled to speak from within a legal system historically designed not to recognize their grievances or protect their lives, the witnesses presented by these activist texts offer testimonies that allow much more into the picture than their generic framing at first appears designed to disclose. The possibility of perjury that always haunts the genre of legal plaint is thereby laid open precisely where the law's rational power fails. At this breach, literature steps in to do justice that cannot be done through legal means.

La gangrène: "Pour la millième fois je revois"

Published in June 1959 by Minuit under the direction of Jérôme Lindon, *La gangrène* frames Algerian torture testimony for French readers by drawing a direct line from the violence done by French police officers to detained Algerians in Paris in 1959 to that committed by Nazi agents against Jews and dissidents in Vichy-era Paris fifteen years prior. The pamphlet formally stages a trial of the French state for violating its own penal codes: it cites the law and presents a series of short narrative testimonies from Algerian torture survivors as evidence of this crime. The text's implicitly Eurocentric framework establishes Nazism as precedent for French state-sanctioned torture, but a tension between the first-person testimonies and the text's rhetorical and paratextual framing also suggests that the work of justice may be more elusive than *La gangrène*'s editors propose.

La gangrène includes six first-person statements (labeled alternately *déclaration, plainte, témoignage*) by Algerian men who describe being arrested by agents of the Direction de la surveillance du territoire and tortured in rooms on rue des Saussaies in Paris between December 2 and 12, 1958, as well as a statement from an Algerian journalist who attests that he personally saw several of these men at rue des Saussaies during the week in question. Each account is signed (by Béchir Boumaza, Mustapha Francis, Benaïssa Souami, Abdelkader Belhadj,

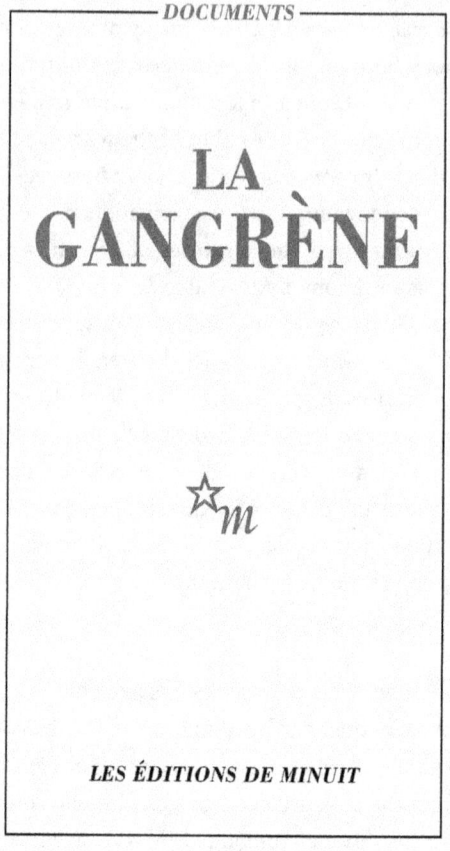

FIGURE 2.2. The cover of *La gangrène* (Paris: Éditions de minuit, 1959).

Moussa Khebaili, Ali Hadj, and Khider Seghir), and includes the age and occupation of each victim. All are professionals or students in fields such as dentistry, pharmacy, political science, and journalism. The six accounts are preceded by an editorial note (titled "Dans la légalité," or "In accordance with the law") that cites Articles 63 and 64 of the French penal code, which, as the editors point out, lay out "the extremely stringent laws" that had been "enacted in order to protect prisoners of war."[33] The testimonies are followed by a postface added to later editions that is signed and dated by publisher Jérôme Lindon, who describes the immediate censure and outraged official denials that followed *La gangrène*'s first publication in June 1959.

This paratextual framing invites the reader to see these testimonies as evidence in a quasi-legal case against the French state, but the case unfolds in writing rather than in a courtroom, with the publisher himself performing the role of prosecutor. The prosecution grounds its argument against the French state by drawing a direct causal link between Nazi and French state violence. This is evident from even the cover, which is plain white bordered by a thin black frame, like all Minuit books. Its provocative title appears in bold red type at page center, along with the title of the collection ("Documents") and the publisher's insignia (a star and an M) and name (Les Éditions de Minuit), in black type at page bottom. The publisher's recognizable house style reflects Minuit's origin as a clandestine press founded during Vichy-era underground resistance in 1942.

The evocative title printed on the cover in bright red (*La gangrène*) repeats on the text's fly pages, again in the opening epigraph that precedes the editorial preface, and as a heading printed at the top of each of the text's 107 pages. The address 11 rue de Saussaies also repeats in the first paragraph of each of the six testimonies, as every witness identifies it as the site of his detention and torture. The narrative testimonies themselves are iterative, like echoes of one another; they seem to follow the same scripts, repeat the same awful details about being tortured in secret rooms at 11 rue de Saussaies. They also start to blur together, as if to reflect the routine depersonalization that torture entails.

These repetitions reinforce the interpretive prompt of the text's opening epigraph, which is also the first printed sentence in *La gangrène*. Attributed to Edmond Michelet—whom the text identifies as Garde des Sceaux of the Ministry of Justice—and dated March 1959, this reads: "This is the aftereffect of a pox, of Nazi totalitarianism."[34] The epigraph, combined with the title printed at the top of every page in the book, strongly suggests that the violence exercised by French police against Algerians in Paris in 1959 should be interpreted as a sickness caused by the pox of Nazi totalitarianism. The viral metaphor casts these instances of torture as symptoms of a pathology that originates outside the French Republic, in Nazi Germany, and as the belated effects of a Vichy-era poisoning, while the title evokes the image of a gangrenous limb that, though rotted through, can still be amputated to heal the national body from a threatening infection.[35] In this paratextual framing, torture is a virus or an aberration to be excised, not a congenital sickness intrinsic to France—and not a sign of a disorder older than Nazi totalitarianism.

A French reader in 1961 would have known that Michelet was the highest-ranking officer of justice in France, and might likely also remember that notorious address (11 rue de Saussaies) as the former site of the Gestapo headquarters—a space just steps from the Élysée palace that was used for detention, interrogation, and torture of Jews and members of the resistance to be deported to the death camps. The building was taken over by the French interior ministry after 1945. By highlighting this street address and this statement from Michelet, the text prompts its reader to imagine the scenes of torture narrated by Boumaza, Francis, Souami, Belhadj, and Khebaili superimposed with previous scenes of torture and interrogation performed by Gestapo officers in the same rooms. The juxtaposition renders Algerians recognizable as victims of French state violence—and legible as subjects of testimony against the state and the police—through their implied likeness to Vichy resisters, detainees, and deportees. This renders French colonial violence perceptible and morally reprehensible by filtering it through the French reader's memory of Nazi occupation. This is a strategic rhetorical move, and certainly it is an ethically persuasive one.

However, by explicitly naming Nazism as a historical precedent, *La gangrène* also shields its reader from contemplating alternate genealogies of French state violence. Torture becomes visible *as* criminal precisely because it is a defect that can be imagined as alien to the French Republic, like a syphilitic or gangrenous infection; it is perceptible in these terms only because it is revealed to be taking place in the obscured but familiar heart of the French capital. *La gangrène* explicitly diagnoses the source of this violence by locating it in the evil of the Third Reich rather than in the entrenched legal and penal institutions that had governed Algérie française for well over a century. By framing Algerian testimony to be read as evidence of the French state's violation of its own post-WWII legal commitments and penal codes, this compelling emplotment also eclipses a longer history and more intractable pathology of institutionalized colonial violence. Bringing this eclipsed history fully into the picture would raise serious questions about relying on those laws and codes as a way to protect the humanity of political prisoners during war.

Yet the testimonies presented for scrutiny by *La gangrène* also deviate from this editorial scripting, transforming the text into a conduit for more than it initially appears designed to disclose. Of the six testimonies, one stands out in particular for the way it deviates from the iterative patterns established by the editorial framework. Consider the reasons offered by Béchir Boumaza for giving an account of his abuse at the hands of the police who arrested him at a friend's apartment on rue Montmartre on December 2, 1958: "My torture is nothing next to that of my brothers and sisters in Algeria, burned alive, mutilated, humiliated, raped, impaled, cut into pieces. But my brothers' voices no longer reach France, and the only reason I testify is that I hope that my voice, surely less loud—but closer—will have a better chance of getting through."[36] Boumaza challenges the narrative position assigned to him by *La gangrène* with an account that does not quite fit the editorial and translational frame in which it is made to appear. He testifies not because he considers his experience exceptionally traumatic or astonishing, but simply because proximity makes his voice slightly more likely to be heard by "la France." He positions his own voice as proxy for a multitude of accounts that cannot and may never get through. In the same rhetorical gesture by which Boumaza addresses his French audience with a detailed account of torture being carried out in plain sight in shadowed rooms of government buildings in the heart of the capital city, he also reminds them of the imperceptibility of most French state violence against Algerians, which occurs on a routine and terrible magnitude even further beyond the scope of his French audience's view. Boumaza describes his own pain as "nothing" and reminds the reader that he speaks *instead* of a multitude of others whose absence he highlights here.

Presumably asked to talk about being tortured by French police in Paris in 1958, Boumaza remembers and recounts something else entirely. After a detailed eighteen-page first-person account of his arrest, detainment, interrogation, and torture, Boumaza's narrative stops short with an abrupt line break and a gap of white space.[37] His past-tense narrative shifts to the immediacy of present tense when Boumaza picks up his narrative after this break—here he departs from December 1958 in Paris to narrate a different past in a different place. The framing turns distinctively visual and explicitly cinematic: "Again, I see flashing before me, for the thousandth time," writes Boumaza, "images from a film whose actors and victims were my closest friends."[38] Like a camera panning rapidly back from the detention room on rue de Saussaies in central Paris, Boumaza abruptly changes scene, transporting the reader to a city near the Algerian coast and a time just two days after the formal conclusion of World War II, a memory by which he remains haunted: "It was May 10th, 1945, in Kherrata, my natal village."[39] Asked for testimony about being tortured in Paris in 1958, Boumaza recalls an older trauma—that of the repression that happened at Sétif, Guelma, and Kherrata in the wake of May 8, 1945.

There are no Nazis and no secret rooms on rue des Saussaies in Boumaza's flashback to Kherrata in May 1945, of course. The scene depicted by Boumaza deviates from the Eurocentric postwar chronology to unravel the implicit historical argument of *La gangrène*. Here, he describes an instance of torture that took place not in a concealed former Gestapo cell at the heart of Paris, but in the open air of Kherrata's public square. The perpetrators in this May 1945 torture scene are not Nazis or Vichy collaborators but rather French legionnaires carrying out repressive retribution in the wake of the May 8, 1945, demonstrations in and around Sétif.[40] The date itself (May 10, 1945) explodes the implicit temporality of Michelet's pathology metaphor to propose a radically different genealogy of state violence as a framework for interpreting both these acts of punitive torture in 1945 and the torture that happened in basements and secret cells in Paris just over decade later.

Boumaza's first-person perspective here shifts to an intimate voice that departs from the monotone of the six nearly identical testimonial accounts brought together by *La gangrène*. The victims in the scene that haunts him were his neighbors: "Hanouz Arab, a medical auxiliary, who was reproached for being secretary of the local charitable cultural association, was brought along with his three children—the youngest of whom was my age—to the house of the seigneur-colon of my village."[41] What happened to Hanouz Arab and his children was done in plain sight, witnessed by everyone in town and openly applauded by the pied noir residents. Boumaza describes the terrible scene: "There, in the square, cheered on by the entire European population, women and children included, the Hanouz family was tortured for several hours by legionnaires."[42]

Boumaza describes French soldiers carrying out a deliberately and strategically visible spectacle of state terror on the bodies and minds of "indigène musulman" subjects: "That night, since they weren't moving anymore but were still breathing, the soldiers made the 'Musulmans' line up to see these four bodies, laid out with their faces against the ground."[43] The soldiers dispose of the corpses by throwing them from a bridge into a river: "The soldiers then brought the Hanouz family up onto a bridge, three kilometers away, and tossed them fifty meters down into the oued."[44] This disposal of the bodies in the river uncannily prefigures what the same police who tortured Boumaza in 1958 would do to Algerian protestors in Paris three years later, in October 1961, when they threw the bodies of dead and dying Algerians into the Seine. Although at the time he composed this testimony Boumaza could not yet have known these precise details, he likely would not have found the October 1961 massacre difficult or surprising to imagine given what he had already seen and could not erase from his own memory.[45]

Boumaza concludes his narrative by invoking the names of the father and his three sons who were tortured, killed, and disposed of in the oued by French legionnaires in May 1945. This invocation of proper names introduces a register of both collective mourning and private grief into Boumaza's account: "Since then, the inhabitants of my village have called this bridge 'the Hanouz's bridge.' A few months later, some friends and I were finally able to go recover the bones of M. Hanouz and his sons, Tayeb, Madjid, and Hanafi. I left my village the next day, not to return until 1952."[46] Boumaza remembers his murdered neighbors not by analogy to Nazi victims, and not by subsuming them in the plural ("des milliers de Djamila et d'Ahmed"), but by transcribing the proper names of those whose scattered bones he says he personally gathered for burial before leaving home for seven years: M. Hanouz Arab, Tayeb, Madjid, and Hanafi. He also registers the trace of collective grief and memory that has since attached a proper name to that particular site of improper burial—"le pont des Hanouz," the Hanouz's bridge.

Asked to give testimony of what happened to him in Paris in December 1958, Boumaza subtly betrays the implicit contract of his own scripted legal plaint in a way that permits other voices to be smuggled in. He transforms his account into a lament on behalf of those whose plaintive cries and screams *La gangrène* is not meant to transmit, and in some ways is even designed to silence. Other ghosts surreptitiously enter the scene. Knowledge of the public torture and murder of M. Hanouz and his three sons in May 1945 makes it impossible for a reader to see the violence committed by French police at rue de Saussaies in 1958 as a pathological *afterlife* of Nazism. Now, 1958 appears as only a recent iteration in a long history of French colonial violence, a history that began well before World War II. Boumaza's testimony only happens to shock and repulse French citizens because of its revelation of torture carried out within the shadows of their own capital city. The dramatic rupture in his narrative exposes this disjuncture in a way that cultivates a different kind of historical memory, and a different kind of ethical and political imagination—memory and imagination that might begin to account for the true magnitude of French colonial violence.

This subtle fissure within Boumaza's testimony opens up space for asking precisely those questions that run against the grain of the legal argument that is set up by *La gangrène*. If the fates of Hanouz Arab and his sons Tayeb, Madjid, and Hanafi cannot be cast in the shadow of Nazism, then the reader must find different terms and other frames by which to understand and respond to their deaths. If the French penal code was *never* designed to protect Algerian lives, but only to disappear and destroy them, then a different kind of argument must be made. If torture, massacre, and calculated erasure were *always* instrumental to establishing and maintaining the authority of the French nation-state, then it does not make sense to rely on that state as an authority for deciding matters of justice.

With this cinematic shift of tense and scene, Boumaza's account hijacks and reroutes the legal demand for justice. *La gangrène* frames its six torture accounts as relatively straightforward evidence of the crime of torture as defined by law, in order to exert political pressure on French state officials to enforce the strict laws governing the treatment of war prisoners. Boumaza's testimony throws a wrench into this juridical argument by surfacing more difficult historical and ethical questions. What is at stake for Boumaza is not verifying *whether* French police tortured Algerians in the heart of Paris in 1959, because of *course* they did, as they always had. Boumaza's testimony of the torture and murder of the Hanouz family in the Kherrata public square during the retributive repression and massacres in May 1945 is extraneous to the legal argument at hand in 1958. His testimony becomes a vessel for repressed cries and plaints not in French, not located in France, and not able to "reach" France. This testimonial fissure raises questions of magnitude: How can justice ever be done, or the injury ever redressed, if the crime is not just unfathomable but inexpressible in the language of French law?

While the explicit analogy to Nazism is powerful, it also very effectively reinforces a powerful blind spot. The analogy invites an interpretive practice that obscures rather than sheds light on what is already at the center of the frame. If anything, the Shoah emerges within a revised temporal order after reading *La gangrène* closely; that catastrophe becomes part of a greater ecology and longer genealogy of European racial crimes. Moreover, when Boumaza veers from the script that is established by *La gangrène*, he creates a subtle disturbance that opens a space for unexpected and profound lamentation to emerge. The collective sorrow that haunts the toponym "le pont des Hanouz" is one rarely perceived by French citizens. One effect of the clandestine lament trafficked into French by Boumaza's testimony is to call attention to the need for a much different discursive frame, one that permits such cries to take up the space and time that they deserve. This is a call to which only literature has answered.

Nuremberg pour l'Algérie: "Tu vois ça c'est du boulot"
The demand posed by the authors of *Nuremberg pour l'Algérie* (1961) is more radical than those demands posed by the editors of *La gangrène*, as its imperative title immediately announces. This thirty-one-page pamphlet also replicates the form of a legal trial, but it takes the matter of justice to a transnational stage in order to exert a different kind of pressure on the French state. Its authors—the militant lawyers Jacques Vergès, Mourad Oussedik, and Abdessamad Benabdallah, part of the same collective of FLN defense lawyers to which Gisèle Halimi also belonged—do not speak from Paris to address readers in the French metropole, and they do not cite French penal codes when they accuse the French state of a crime. Rather, they speak from a perspective grounded in Algeria, from within the networks of the FLN, using evidence gathered from local police and military files. Although the pamphlet was published by Maspero it also addresses a transnational audience beyond France, as the authors make clear in their direct citation of international genocide law that opens the text as well as in their closing injunction that "it is up to all free men in France and across the world to unite in order to prevent genocide in Algeria."[47]

« La corvée de bois »

FIGURE 2.3. Photographs that appear in the pamphlet *Nuremberg pour l'Algérie* (Paris: Maspero, 1961), beneath the caption, shown here: "La corvée de bois."

Although the lawyer-editors of this text also mobilize the force of the Nazi analogy in their case against the French state, they take a different tack than did the editors of *La gangrène*. Notably, *Nuremberg pour l'Algérie* contains absolutely no testimonies from Algerian victims. The conspicuous absence of victim testimony presents a significant contrast to *La gangrène*. The *Nuremberg* pamphlet takes it for granted that Algerians—and their testimonies—have so long been targeted for destruction by the highest offices and institutions of the French state that their accounts cannot be presented as evidence.

The text instead sets out to demonstrate the genocidal magnitude of this catastrophic crime by positioning absence *itself* as a form of evidence, starting with the unequivocal accusation that prefaces the text. The authors hold French authorities to account by name for the targeted assassination of their colleague Amokrane Ould Aoudia, which had taken place at his office in Paris in May 1959:

> For several years now, we have denounced the war in Algeria as a genocidal undertaking. For several years now, we have denounced juridical repression as a travesty [*parodie*].
>
> We have accused the highest officers of the Old and New Regimes as being complicit in tortures and murders: Messieurs Lacotes, Bourgès-Manoury, Soustelle, and Debré.
>
> The killers responded to us by murdering our friend Mr. Ould Aoudia. The Powers that be responded to us with multiple charges and internment measures.
>
> But no one has ever dared to contradict us.[48]

This accusation is followed by a transcript of all nineteen articles of the Convention on the Prevention and Punishment of the Crime of Genocide that had been adopted by the UN General Assembly in December 1948 and entered into force in 1951. The text of this law appears in full without any commentary. It is followed by a series of numbered sections that present documentary evidence of the "flagrant violation" of international genocide law by French forces in Algeria with the complicity of the highest officers of the French state, but draws no causal or comparative claim about the relationship between different genocides.

Nuremberg pour l'Algérie sets out its charges and evidence without explicitly telling the reader how to interpret this material, beyond its emphatic title. The text builds a case on institutional documents rather than on witness testimony, as if to make the absences and silences of the police and military archive testify. This editorial framing presents archival texts to be read against the grain and between the lines. The reader is invited to decipher and analyze administrative documents as a kind of fiction, armed with knowledge that the documents in fact lie, conceal, and leave unspoken the very evidence that would most count in any future trial held to prove the crime of genocide.

The first document is a letter, presented with a short explanatory note: "Here, without commentary, is the text of a letter sent from Sétif on May 20, 1960, by Sergeant Claude Copenal, SP 89116 AFN, to a serviceman who stayed in France. We transmitted this letter to military justice. No proceedings ever followed."[49] Next appears a series of seven black-and-white photographs. Each depicts unidentified human corpses scattered in rural fields, faces in the dirt, limbs askew. The first photograph is labeled simply "Un enfant" ("A Child"), which contrasts grotesquely with the description above it: "Prisoners executed without verdict according to the directions of the general officers backed by the commander in chief and the general delegation of the government."[50] The six following photographs are labeled with the succinct euphemism for summary execution that was used by French soldiers during the war in Algeria: "la corvée de bois" ("gathering firewood").[51]

The bodies almost blend into the rural landscape, a macabre visual illustration of Fanon's observation in 1956: "Unseen Arabs. Ignored Arabs. Arabs passed over in silence. Arabs vanished, hidden. Arabs repudiated every day, transformed into Saharan scenery.... The collective silence of 800,000 Frenchmen, this ignorant silence, this innocent silence. And 9,000,000 men beneath this death-shroud of silence."[52] By arranging photographs in this way, *Nuremberg* invites a reader to lift a shroud of silence, and to recognize the Algerian landscape as a terrain of state terror replete with unmarked graves.

The pamphlet ends with a text taken from a military tribunal along with two lists of names. This tribunal document, labeled "La parole d'un officier français" ("Statement from a French Officer") is the text of an oath signed by French Colonel Roucolle and delivered to Algerian fighters promising that they would be classified as soldiers and treated as prisoners of war subject to rights guaranteed by Geneva protocol. "The word 'soldiers' is emphasized in the text," the authors point out, before explaining that—despite this signed oath and the Geneva Protocols—the fighters were immediately condemned to death by a French military tribunal on July 23, 1960.[53] The text names the executed prisoners: Adda Hamdani and Abdelkader Bouabdellah.

Although it is not cited here, an exceptional French legal procedure called *traduction directe* defined in Decree No. 56-269 of March 1956—one of several laws that gave the French military exceptional authority—made this extrajudicial military execution quite literally legal. According to Sylvie Thénault, the procedure was so unprecedented that it required a legal neologism to describe it at the time: it was called *direct translation*. The decree can be found in the *Journal officiel de la République française* of 1956. Its first article reads:

> In Algeria, the competent military authorities may, notwithstanding any contrary provisions of the military legal codes, without prior instruction, and before a permanent tribunal of the armed forces, order the *direct translation* [*la traduction directe*] of individuals caught in the act of participating in an action against persons or property provided that these are offenses covered in Article 1 of Decree No. 56-268 of March 17, 1956, *even if these offenses are likely to entail the death penalty*, when they have been committed by perpetrators armed with weapons, explosives, ammunition, destructive hardware or military clothing or equipment.[54]

Nuremberg pour l'Algérie ends with two lists of the names of other Algerians arrested, tortured, disappeared, or "directly translated" by French military tribunals: "1) Prisoners of war handed over arbitrarily" and "2) Summary executions and travesty of justice [*parodie de justice*]."[55] These lists recall the multitude of voices that Béchir Boumaza knew would never "reach" France, and in whose place he testified. The lists gesture beyond themselves, inviting a reader to imagine that such lists of the disappeared and dead extend infinitely, so that these lists function not as comprehensive rosters but rather as a visual index of indefinite magnitude.

In place of the voices of victims, *Nuremberg pour l'Algérie* conveys the incriminating words of perpetrators to be scrutinized as evidence; the authors of the pamphlet thereby make the archive work against the institutional mechanisms that produced it. One of the perpetrator "testimonies"—the first document in the list of evidence—is a letter written by a French sergeant "just doing his job." Claude Copenal, author of the intercepted letter, addresses his letter to a "cher vieux copain" (dear old friend) near Reims from his post at Sétif. His colloquial, euphemistic French is riddled with military slang and a smattering of Arabic words. The sergeant is new to his work in the Algerian *bled*—"I've been in French North Africa [A.F.N.] almost two months," he writes, and three weeks in the "P.J." (Police Judiciaire)—where his duty is to update the police dossiers with photographs and information gathered from suspected militants: "I am also responsible for keeping a register in which I note all the *fellous* arrested through our fine efforts."[56]

The content of this letter—quotidian details of Copenal's duties in the Police Judiciaire—prompts the reader to recognize the other documents assembled by the editors of *Nuremberg pour l'Algérie* as selections from the military police archive. That is, we are reading documents and looking at photographs that were initially acquired through the *bons soins* (good work, fine efforts) of French soldiers just doing their jobs—jobs that routinely involved coercion, ratissages, rape, torture, and murder.

Disconcertingly, Copenal appears to enjoy his work producing military dossiers: "We have a file with photos of all suspected terrorists, and it's quite interesting work."⁵⁷ His language assumes a reader already familiar with the techniques: "When we arrest a *fell*, we interrogate him and we have some very persuasive material. You get what I mean."⁵⁸ The persuasive tactics made somewhat more explicit in Copenal's next sentence are not unusual ones, but rather routine interrogation methods taught by the French military to its specialists so that torture would leave no traces on the bodies of their victims: "An EE-8 on the ears and the family jewels, next some water in the mouth, then blows with the baton and some thrashing when it's done."⁵⁹

After using the dossier photographs to single out detainees for interrogation (and for electricity to the testicles, waterboarding, and thrashing), as Copenal explains, it was often necessary to make the prisoners vanish altogether. Copenal's diction obscures the act it describes, or rather completes the act of making evidence disappear:

> Sometimes we happen to off [*buter*] some *fells*. What do you expect us to do with them after the interrogation. We take them to the *bled* after dark. There, a big hole [*cave*] is set up just for this. The *fells* are brought to the edge of said hole and P.A. [automatic pistol] to the back of the neck and hop! the big leap [*et hop c'est le grand saut*]. You know we don't fight the P.J. inspectors to do it. At first, you know, the first one you off like that in cold blood, it gives you a shock, but it's like anything else, you get used to it. After all this you are probably going to take me for a gangster.⁶⁰

The first sentence deflects agency; by *buter* (take out, bump off) Copenal surely means "kill." The terms *fell* and *fellou* are French transliterations of an Arabic word turned into a common epithet for Algerian militants. *Fell* is a French abbreviation that almost seems to conflate two different Arabic words, either a rural farmer (*fallāḥ*) or a bandit (*fallāga*). The appropriated word combines rural peasant farmer, thief, and enemy combatant into a single hostile abstraction—a telling semantic ambiguity, given the significant tactical problem posed to French soldiers who could not distinguish Algerian peasant farmers from FLN fighters. The second sentence begins as if it is a question, but ends as a declaration that leaves no room to imagine what else might be done with prisoners after their interrogation. In Copenal's prose, there is only the inevitability of a "P.A." (*pistolet automatique*) to the back of the head in an unspecified cave at night in the "bled," then the "fells" leap into the great beyond, like the faceless, nameless ghosts that they already are.

These moves are now familiar from detailed studies of French police and military techniques.[61] Copenal's slang comes straight from the deranged lexicon of military French (*séance, nettoyage, dégrossissage, corvée de bois, interrogation serrée*) that among other things permitted torture specialists in Algeria to avoid imputing subjectivity to enemy bodies in pain.[62] Copenal counts bodies in a predictable and revealing way: "Review of the op: first the soldiers gassed the cave which is 180 meters deep, you can picture the scene. They went in and brought out 12 *fells*, two of which were second-in-command and one aspi (who died from the gas). All the weapons were recovered, you know that's some tough work [*tu vois ça c'est du boulot*]. Besides that, I can tell you that a week ago during a stall, there were four tirailleurs killed and 5 wounded, and *ouallou* on the *fells*'s side [*du côté fells ouallou*]."[63]

Copenal's accounting is neither irrational nor exceptional but demonstrates what Fanon described as "this line of reasoning that so arithmetically foretells the disappearance of colonized people."[64] This is the same calculated logic of disappearance that was made public by French legionnaires torturing families and throwing corpses from bridges in Kherrata in 1945, as we saw in Boumaza's haunted torture testimony. Moreover, the specific tactic described here by Copenal—asphyxiating fighters in caves to quell indigenous resistance—has an especially long and gruesome function in the history of colonizing of Algeria. "Enfumades" were a notorious technique practiced by French generals (Pélissier, Bugeaud, Cavaignac) to exterminate insubordinate tribes during the colonizing wars of 1844 to 1845, as depicted by Assia Djebar in *L'amour, la fantasia*.[65] Knowledge of this long history of gassing resistant Algerians in caves renders even more sinister and haunting Copenal's banal sentence "tu vois ça c'est du boulot" (it's just work, you see).

The French sergeant recounts the outcome of a recent skirmish: four killed and five injured *tirailleurs* (a term for Algerian, Moroccan, or Senegalese soldiers on the French side), and on the other side, *fells ouallou*. He appears to mean, literally, that no Algerian fighters were killed in this particular operation; *ouallou* is a colloquial Arabic expression (*wālū*) that can be glossed as "nothing, zero." In Copenal's idiom, there is no particular number of "fells" to count because no Algerians died. Given the semantic ghosting at work in his earlier description of summary execution and mass asphyxiation, Copenal's tally is suspect. Where such sentences are used, lives are already absent and anonymous, so an uncountable and spectral enemy can simply be whacked on the back of the head with a pistol "et hop c'est le grand saut" into an unfathomable abyss. In this view, such killing hardly "counts" as murder. It is just work that needs to be done.

Copenal's calque *fells ouallou* articulates the legal translation problem faced by the lawyers who assembled the case presented in *Nuremberg pour l'Algérie*. What would it take to make "fells ouallou" *count* as "genocide" so that the French state could be tried for its crimes before an international tribunal? The text discloses a problem of scale that ultimately calls into question the viability of its own demand for a legal reckoning on the order of Nuremberg.

Nuremberg pour l'Algérie makes no effort to channel the testimonies or cries of the French regime's disappeared victims. The text frames acts of silencing and erasure in a hijacked series of documents culled from military police files. The documents on display in the pamphlet were clearly selected from an immense archive, as we can easily surmise after reading Copenal's cavalier description of his routine labor. This creates an overwhelming impression that the evidence at hand is only a faint trace of something far more sinister, and also raises strong suspicion that *most* of the violence done by soldiers and police officers probably eludes documentation entirely. Nowhere does the pamphlet suggest that the genocide it names began any time after 1945, creating a vertiginous sense that the magnitude of the crime it exposes may be incalculably infinite, and thus that the very genocide laws it cites as a point of departure may in fact be wholly inadequate to respond to calls for justice on behalf of Algerians so systematically ghosted by French occupation.

Djamila Boupacha: "Il faut me faire voir"

Djamila Boupacha (1962) was published when Boupacha's legal case hit a dead end in 1961. This impasse concerned access to photographs that were filed away in military administrative records, much like those dossiers that Sergeant Claude Copenal had been in charge of putting together during his time in military service near Sétif. The book *Djamila Boupacha* literally displays the contents of the *dossier d'instruction* (investigation file) gathered by Halimi as evidence initially meant to be used in court. When the process broke down, Halimi and Beauvoir made these documents public in a book designed to take the matter of justice outside the complicit French legal system—not only to expose a travesty of justice that went to the top of the chain of command, but also to defer Boupacha's death sentence by creating public scandal.

Boupacha had been arrested at her home in Algiers in February 1960 along with her father and brother-in-law; she was detained for thirty-three days, first at

FIGURE 2.4. Portrait photograph of Djamila Boupacha that was published in the text *Djamila Boupacha* (Paris: Gallimard, 1962).

a prison in El Biar (the same prison where Henri Alleg was tortured and Maurice Audin killed), then in Hussein Dey. Boupacha signed a confession after enduring rape and torture (by electrical generator, known as *la gégène*), and was sentenced to death for her confessed act of terrorism. Boupacha retracted her testimony in March 1960, arguing that confession elicited under torture could not be admissible evidence. In May 1960, after contacting Giséle Halimi, Boupacha filed a civil suit (the document is called a *plainte* in French) with the *juge d'instruction* (in the French legal system, the magistrate charged with gathering evidence) in Algiers in which she accused the soldiers who had interrogated her of also torturing her. The routine practice of torture as an interrogation tactic was certainly not novel or surprising, but Boupacha's response to it was: she instrumentalized the language of French law to fight back.

In December 1960, after a series of mishaps and delays that included Halimi missing some hearings because the French authorities denied her visa requests to travel to Algiers, Halimi got the case jurisdiction transferred from Algeria to France. Boupacha was moved to a prison in Caen, and she underwent a medical exam at a prison infirmary in Fresnes, in the suburbs of Paris, to acquire a medical statement verifying her claims. By February 1961, the juge d'instruction at Caen, Philippe Chausserie-Laprée, was persuaded by this evidence to write to the French military authorities in Algiers to procure the civil documents, current addresses, and military identification photographs of all police, gendarmes, and soldiers who had had any contact with Boupacha during her arrest, detention, and interrogation. The authorities in Algiers did not answer the magistrate's letter.

Chausserie-Laprée wrote again in March, May, and June 1961. In late June, General Ailleret—the superior commanding officer of French armed forces in Algeria—finally sent a letter explaining that he just could not send the ID photographs because doing so would harm soldier morale. The minister of the army, Pierre Messmer, agreed with Ailleret. Because it would provoke "troubling repercussions for the mental state and morale of the [military] corps," sending these identification photographs would be simply "too difficult."[66] The Caen judge wrote once more, then dropped the investigation.

Boupacha filed a second civil suit in December 1961 with the highest legal authority in France, the Doyen des juges d'instruction at the Civil Tribunal of the Seine, in Paris. She accused Ailleret and Messmer of violating Articles 61 and 114 of the French penal code by refusing to provide evidence and thus sabotaging the justice process. This letter was received in silence, as Halimi notes: "At the Ministry of Justice, a certain turmoil and long silence greeted the filing of this plaint.... Has France become a country without justice?"[67] At this point, Halimi and the advocacy committee decided to publish the evidence that they had accumulated for trial as *Djamila Boupacha*, cosigned by Beauvoir in order to share legal liability. The book appeared in late January 1962, during the same tumultuous week that dozens of bombs planted by the Organisation armée secrète—the right-wing terrorist militia fighting tooth and nail to keep Algeria French—exploded across Paris.

Much like *La gangrène* and *Nuremberg pour l'Algérie*, Halimi's *Djamila Boupacha* stages a trial that just could not happen in a French court of law. Identification photographs might have made it possible to charge and prosecute perpetrators, but military command shut down this possibility. More obviously than the other testimonial texts, this one also reads like compelling crime fiction. That Halimi later published novels should not surprise a reader of *Djamila Boupacha*.

The book opens with Beauvoir's preface, followed by sixteen chapters written by Halimi that narrate Boupacha's case from their first meetings in prison in Algiers to the hearings in Caen. This is followed by an appendix containing three supplementary documents (a facsimile of Boupacha's original plaint); Beauvoir's *Le Monde* article; a letter written by Djamila Boupacha's father, Abdelaziz Boupacha; and twelve supporting statements from famous intellectuals, activists, and officials. The book also contains three illustrations, including a portrait of Djamila Boupacha drawn by Pablo Picasso.

The title page showcases Djamila Boupacha's name in large, bold font. At the top of the page appear the names SIMONE DE BEAUVOIR and GISÈLE HALIMI. Beneath the title is an impressive list of names whose "témoignages" are assembled to foster a strong sense of collective moral authority designed to persuade even the most skeptical French reader to believe Boupacha's story. These include: Henri Alleg, Mme. Maurice Audin, General de Bollardière, R. P. Chenu, Dr. Jean Dalsace, J. Fonlupt-Esperaber, Françoise Mallet-Joris, Daniel Mayer, André Philip, J. F. Revel, Jules Roy, Françoise Sagan, and the painters Pablo Picasso, Robert Lapoujade, and Roberto Matta.[68] A full page bears a print of a pencil-drawn portrait of Boupacha, signed by Pablo Picasso with the date December 8, 1961. This image appears on both the cover and the title page of the book. Also included in its fly pages is a black-and-white photograph of Boupacha along with a series of photographs of her with her father, mother, and sister.

The portrait photograph of Boupacha resembles a civil identification picture, except that she is smiling. Comparing the photograph with Picasso's drawing reveals the extent to which the artist dramatically enlarges and transforms Boupacha's eyes. In Picasso's drawing, the subject's eyes immediately attract attention: extravagant lashes, dark lines for eyelids, severe arching eyebrows. Her pupils are concentric black rings, hypnotic. A subtle smile plays on her lips. The silent gaze looks frank, direct, self-contained yet exposed, unsettling. Picasso's depiction of Boupacha's eyes seems to convey a collective desire to transform this symbolic victim of French state violence into a singular, believable witness.

In her narrative, Halimi likewise depicts Boupacha as a vivid character and active collaborator in the collective effort to translate a legally voiceless Algerian prisoner into the plaintiff of a civil suit addressed to the highest legal offices in the French Republic. Halimi lingers over descriptions of the act of writing, constructing detailed scenes such as the one below that lend her narrative a distinctly novelistic quality. Halimi not only listens to Boupacha tell her story and records the details, but also reads and bears witness to the ephemeral signs of torture on Boupacha's body.

I wrote for two hours on the small, white wooden table in that room at Barberousse [Prison]. Djamila answered my questions; she exhausted herself searching for the details that I asked of her; she stopped herself, she picked up the thread of her narrative. At one point, she unbuttoned her blouse: on her chest, up to her right breast, there was a string of tiny traces, like brown confetti. They had pressed, with rapid touches, their lit cigarettes onto her skin. On her right thigh, the glowing cigarette butt had probably been crushed harder: the circle was darker, more open. I took up my paper again. I was hot, I was afraid of incorrectly noting the number of scars, the length of the detention, the name of the officer. *The accumulation of details was our only chance.*[69]

The detailed testimony that Halimi describes cowriting in this intimate scene with Boupacha is included in full in the book,[70] as is a signed and sealed facsimile of the civil suit itself, in the appendix. In these carefully constructed legal plaints, Boupacha respects the seriousness of the genre. She lays out facts and names the crimes in the formal language required by French law: "*unlawful detainment [séquestration] having continued for more than one month and having been accompanied by physical torture.*"[71] The French state had signed laws denouncing torture, which she cites—Articles 341, 342, and 344 of the new French penal code. "In these circumstances," Boupacha concludes, "I have the honor, Mr. Examining Magistrate, to lodge in your hands a plaint [*une plainte*] for the above-mentioned crimes, naming myself as a plaintiff [*partie civile*]."[72]

And yet, for all this juridical gravity, the unsettling call of literature erupts at multiple points throughout *Djamila Boupacha*. This is especially pronounced at the points in Halimi's narrative that reveal moments of faltering and failure in legal language and protocols. Halimi lays out two revelatory courtroom scenes that stage such failures—one in Algiers, the other in Caen. In the first, Halimi vividly depicts the practice of "direct translation" (the summary execution of suspected terrorists without trial, authorized by French law in 1956) in live action in an Algiers courtroom. When Halimi had initially read Boupacha's police dossier, she noticed two sentences typed in fine print at the end of a four-page transcript of Boupacha's hearing that had been held at the Algiers Palais de Justice after she was first arrested and interrogated in 1960. The sentences typed into the dossier read: "I insist on being examined by a doctor. I have been tortured."[73]

Halimi reconstructs the hearing in which Boupacha spoke this demand aloud: Djamila sits straight-backed in handcuffs before a bored judge who dictates indifferently while a stenographer types up quadruple carbon copies of the false confession that Boupacha is about to be forced to sign. Halimi's mechanical sentences replicate the deadening violence of the scene: "Le juge dicte. La machine du greffier crépite" (The judge dictates. The clerk's typewriter clacks).[74] The two police officers who had tortured Boupacha for days eavesdrop from behind a closed door. Their threatening offstage presences silently illustrate why Boupacha had no choice but to sign the false testimony: "The police officers are behind the door: her statement will determine the destination of her return."[75] The judge reads aloud the "aveux confectionnés" (fabricated confessions), then asks whether Boupacha has anything to add to her written confession to planting the bomb.[76]

Here, Halimi's omniscient point of view shifts suddenly to be focalized through Boupacha's perspective so that the reader begins to imagine the scene from the prisoner's viewpoint:

> At this point, Djamila wants to scream. The police officers are still there. Too bad, too bad.
> She wants to say it.
> She practically shouts:
> —Yes. Have it noted that I was tortured at Hussein Dey... Yes, that I suffered immensely.
> And suddenly, breaking [*brisée*]:
> —I beg you... *I need to be seen* [*Il faut me faire voir*]...[77]

"Il faut me faire voir" might be read as "I need to see someone"—that is, seen by a doctor who would examine her body for signs of trauma—but this suggestive sentence also connotes a sense of coming undone, as in: "I need to *see* someone." It might also be read, perhaps misread, as "I must make myself see" or as "I need to be seen." It has the urgency of a demand, an entreaty: *see* me. It is an appeal to the imagination, not to juridical reason.

Boupacha's desire to be seen and believed interrupts the deadening courtroom scene that is staged by Halimi. With this sentence, Boupacha's bristling pain, anger, and desire cracks open the factual account, introducing a qualitatively different register of testimony that relies on literary ambiguity. The sentence "Il faut me faire voir" is not quite the same as the one transcribed by the court stenographer onto four carbon copies of the police dossier as the request "Je demande à être examinée par un médecin" (I insist on being examined by a doctor). It calls to the reader with a haunting demand. It is a reminder that bearing witness is a speech act unverifiable according to legal protocols, in the sense described by Jacques Derrida: "It does not mean 'I prove,' but 'I swear that I saw, I heard, I touched, I felt, I was present.' That is the irreducible sense-perceptual dimension of presence and past-presence, of what can be meant by 'being present' and especially by 'having been present,' and of what that means to bearing witness."[78]

Halimi's account gradually amplifies the generic tension intrinsic to testimony—that tension between providing verifiable proof and staging an address that asks to be believed on faith. And yet, as Halimi understands very well, Boupacha's death sentence is no fiction: "the accumulation of details was our only chance."[79] *Djamila Boupacha* conspicuously displays this burden of proof. Meticulous footnotes throughout the text cross-reference court documents and sworn testimonies; facsimiles of prison visitation passes and travel visas confirm chronologies and itineraries; transcripts of police files, medical reports, and personal letters support and reinforce Halimi's narrative, which she presents as corroborating testimony to the veracity of Boupacha's own account—Halimi saw the bruises, cuts, and cigarette burns before they healed. However, the ultimate effect of this obsessive accumulation of detail is not to affirm the efficacy of evidence but rather to reveal its inadequacy, which brings into full focus the literary dimension of witnessing that is this text's real power: "Bearing witness is not proving," Derrida writes; "Bearing witness is heterogeneous to producing proof or exhibiting a piece of evidence."[80] True testimony concerns something other than the obsessive accumulation of details—it asks for a leap of faith.

Set in Caen, the second court scene staged in *Djamila Boupacha* centers on verifying an act difficult to prove by any legal means. Torture was practiced by French soldiers using techniques meant to be "clean," meaning that they did not leave permanent physical traces as evidence, legible on the body. Although the "supplice de la bouteille" (bottle torture) is the "plus atroce des souffrances" (most horrific of the miseries) named in Boupacha's civil plaint, this act was never recorded in her police file.[81] The file contained only the two transcribed sentences that had been spoken by Boupacha when she interrupted the judge at her hearing at the Algiers Palace of Justice to insist that she be examined by a doctor for signs of torture. Halimi also notes that *all* the documents in Boupacha's file were hastily produced on March 15, 1960, the day of the hearing.[82] She zeroes in on the medical report signed by the court-appointed doctor, Dr. Levy-Leroy, who examined Boupacha directly after her hearing that day.

Halimi transcribes the complete text of Dr. Levy-Leroy's report in order to expose his contradictory, incoherent claim: namely, that the patient suffered "menstrual irregularities of a constitutional nature" and that he had permitted her to keep her underwear on so as not to "humiliate" her with a gynecological exam.[83] "This pseudo-discretion explains nothing," Halimi objects: "If he didn't examine Djamila, if she didn't mention these specific physical abuses, then how could he have known that she was suffering from constitutional menstrual irregularity?"[84]

Halimi reads between the lines with critical suspicion—"in medical language, this was a translation of 'bottle torture'"[85]—but to persuade the Caen judge to grant Boupacha a new hearing, Halimi needed better evidence than her own translation of the silences written into the text of the police dossier.

Halimi's effort to procure this evidence culminates in a courtroom standoff over how to legally verify Boupacha's statement that she had been tortured. Boupacha's body becomes a text that the male doctors and legal officials either fail or refuse to read, but which Halimi steadily attempts to translate and parse for them. Halimi arranges for Boupacha's transfer to a prison in Fresnes so that she can be examined by a gynecologist. Five months have passed, however, and Boupacha's wounds have healed, so the second medical report introduces only reason to doubt but not to dismiss Dr. Levy-Leroy's original report. Halimi transcribes the new medical report with the key hypothetical sentence in all-caps: "YES, BOUPACHA DJAMILA MAY HAVE HAD THE NECK OF A BOTTLE INSERTED INTO HER VAGINA . . . PERHAPS FOR THE PURPOSES OF A TRAUMATIC DEFLORATION."[86]

The possibility of "traumatic defloration" is enough to convince the judge at Caen to hear Boupacha testify, and to call a third medical expert witness into court—the same doctor who had tended both to Boupacha and to her father at the El-Biar "triage" center in Algiers. This "Dr. B" had treated Boupacha twice when she returned from Hussein Dey complaining of "abdominal" pain.[87] At the Caen hearing, Dr. B claimed not to remember whether he had noticed any telltale signs of torture on Boupacha's body: "It's possible," he admits, but here his memory appears to falter: "I don't remember anymore. . . . I don't know if Djamila had evidence of torture on her body. I didn't examine her naked."[88]

Dr. B's closing statement at the hearing in Caen pits his faulty memory against Boupacha's razor-sharp one. Halimi notes that Boupacha recognized Dr. B immediately upon his arrival in court, and that she recoiled before the electrical torture device displayed to her by the judge to gauge her reaction to it: "—So, tell us? Have you seen this before? The judge insisted. Djamila suddenly stood up and shouted:—that's the *gégène*! the *gégène*!"[89] However, Dr. B claims not remember *any* details, especially not any physical injuries, that could either confirm or deny Boupacha's account: "Her statements *may* correspond to the truth," he says, "but I haven't retained the memory. Since February 1960, I have seen many things and not everything that happened during this period has stayed in my memory."[90]

Impressed by Boupacha's recognition of the doctor and of the specialized electrical torture device, the judge decides that nine identification photographs should be shown to her to test the acuity of her memory. Boupacha instantly and confidently identifies the lieutenant and doctor from the El Biar detention center where she had been tortured, prompting the judge to agree with Halimi: "What better proof could Djamila give of the force of her memories and her capacity to reveal to us the faces of her torturers?"[91]

Boupacha never got the chance to identify and accuse her torturers in court. Here, the law reached its limit as an effective instrument of justice and snapped. The final pages of *Djamila Boupacha* contain a series of letters concerning the missing piece of evidence: those identification photographs contained in the military's records on all of its soldiers. When Ailleret flatly refused to comply with this request, the judge also wrote to the procurer of the Republic to request intervention from Edmond Michelet—minister of justice, and author of the statement "This is the aftereffect of a pox, of Nazi totalitarianism" included in *La gangrène*[92]—and the minister of the army Pierre Messmer to requisition these photographs. Michelet and Messmer did not intervene.

Boupacha's second civil suit, addressed to the highest court in France, accuses General Ailleret and Army Minister Messmer of illegally sabotaging the justice process. This legal complaint, like her first one, speaks the precise and formal language of French law. It is divided into four sections that lay out: 1) the facts of her case, 2) the concealment of evidence by Messmer and Ailleret[93] (citing Article 61, paragraph 2, of the French penal code criminalizing such concealment), 3) an accusation that Messmer and Ailleret violated the most basic codes of justice[94] (citing Article 114 of the penal code), and 4) a technical legal argument grounded in French penal and military law and jurisprudential precedents dating back to 1933, urging the French high court to intervene on her behalf against the intransigent military authorities in Algiers.

Boupacha addressed the highest legal authorities of the French state in the exacting language of their law, but she was not heard, and justice was not done. When the second civil suit went unanswered, Halimi and Beauvoir published *Djamila Boupacha* in order to draw public attention to the legal breakdown in a way that would defer Boupacha's execution. With the Évian Accords, Boupacha was freed from prison and returned to Algeria in 1962. Today, Boupacha still lives quietly in Algiers. The former soldiers who tortured and raped her may well still be alive somewhere.

The open questions with which the text *Djamila Boupacha* concluded in 1961 ("Has France become a country without justice?"; "SO THEN? HOW TO CONFRONT THIS AND HOW TO ADDUCE EVIDENCE [*CITER*]?") have not been answered.[95] *Djamila Boupacha* is, among other things, a kind of archival time capsule that holds open some of the most charged decolonial questions that have been elided by the processes of political decolonization. It is also testament to a failed legal process and a reminder that no state trials have *ever* been convened to reckon directly with the impact of French state violence against Algerians. Critical reflection on Nazi atrocities and on the great post-Holocaust trials of the twentieth century has generated human rights discourse and genocide laws, and has also produced an extraordinarily rich archive that has oriented scholarship about testimony, trauma, and memory.[96] However, theories of testimony and trauma must be reconsidered in light of those many trials that surely *should* have taken place, but did not—trials such as the one imagined and demanded on behalf of Djamila Boupacha in 1961.

Traces of other voices appear throughout Halimi's narrative, those of speakers whose names do not appear on the list of contributors on the book's cover. These surreptitious voices do not read anything like the formal complaints that Boupacha and Halimi crafted to address French legal authorities, so it might be easy not to notice that they are also justice claims. One of the voices channeled by the text belongs to Abdelaziz Boupacha, the father of Djamila Boupacha. He is the author of a *récit* addressed to Halimi that does not fit into the main narrative of *Djamila Boupacha* and thus appears instead as part of the appendix. This récit also does not conform to the grammatical conventions of standard French, as the editors underscore with a note emphasizing their decision to print the text uncorrected in order to respect its grammar and orthography. Leaving Abdelaziz Boupacha's letter unedited preserves the trace of its orality in a way that conjures the effect of a speaking voice. The letter asks to be read aloud. It transcribes the speech of someone who knows French phonetically: "excusé moi je ne sait pas bien écrire j'ai jamais été a l'école" (excuse me I don't know how to write well I never went to school).[97]

Abdelaziz Boupacha's three-page letter consists of a single, largely unpunctuated sentence. It narrates his arrest and torture alongside his daughter and his son-in-law. He remembers being blindfolded and tortured, and describes crying out for mercy only to hear the disembodied voice of an unseen torturer speak back to him from the darkness: "Je dit un peu d'humanité, une vois se lève un peu plus loin de mes pieds, me dit pas d'humanité pour les arabes, les yeux bander douche avec caoutchouc l'eau froide de la nuit du 10/12–1960 . . ." (I say have some humanity, a voice speaks up a little farther from my feet, tells me no humanity for the arabs, eyes blindfolded shower with rubber cold water from the night of 10/12 1960 . . .).[98] Nowhere does the abject failure of the state's legal codes become more explicit than in Abdelaziz Boupacha's haunting testimony, as he repeats the words of a faceless torturer just doing his job: *pas d'humanité pour les arabes.* No humanity for "Arabs." Arabs passed over in silence; vanished, hidden beneath a death-shroud of silence—as Fanon also did, Abdelaziz Boupacha here registers the banal yet articulate truth of a legal regime 130 years in the making.

Abdelaziz Boupacha also describes a prison visit from a French doctor who does not know—or does not want to know—the reason for the anonymous screams coming from the other rooms of the "triage" center: "Pendant ce temp il y avait un medecin qui est venu m'insculté [sic], il a entendu l'homme crier comme un porc, ce medecin me dit qui est qui cris comme ça, moi je dit sont entraine de torturé un homme, ce médecin a mis ces doigts sur le menton de sa barbe et fixé les yeux a la terre pré d'une minute et après j'ai regagné ma cellul, la datte de ma consultation par le médecin il est écrite sur le mur de ma cellul no 3 a el biar, pendant le temp de la torture de mon beau fils" (During this time a doctor came to examine [*ausculter*] me, he had heard the man squealing like a pig, this doctor said to me who's yelling like that, me I say they're torturing a man, this doctor put his fingers on the tip of his beard and fixed his eyes on the ground for nearly a minute after I went back to my cell, the day of my consultation with the doctor is written on the wall of my cell no. 3 in El Biar, at the time of my son-in-law's torture).[99] Here, the French doctor is observed by the exhausted victim of torture whom he has come to examine, and we envision the scene for a moment from Abdelaziz Boupacha's point of view. Boupacha observes the doctor's own eyes cast down in silence. Although he is not named, this might well be the same "Dr. B" who had also examined Djamila Boupacha, the same doctor who claimed not to remember anything when he testified in the hearing at Caen—the doctor who could say only that "since February of 1960, I've seen many things and not everything that happened during this period has stayed in my memory."[100]

Abdelaziz Boupacha describes his own clear memory of seeing this French doctor not-seeing and not-hearing. The doctor is lost in his own thought, fingers in his beard. He listens to the sound of a man being tortured on the other side of the wall, squealing like a pig; the man is quite possibly Abdelaziz Boupacha's son-in-law. Later, in a court in Caen, a doctor will testify that he cannot remember this, that he does not *know* if he saw marks on the bodies of the men and women tortured in these rooms.

Yet Abdelaziz Boupacha's memory would later remain intact, despite the violence he endured, and despite the physical aftereffects: "J'ai été bien boulversé et *presque* perdu la memoire par suite des chocs des coups de points sur la tête et a la figure tous des coups de points pas le bourdonnement et la cigal qui sifle la nuit et jour dans mes oreilles sant compté les brelures de l'ectricité *qui font foi sur mon corps* actuellement." (I was knocked over and practically lost my memory after the shocks from the blows of the fist on the head and on the face all these blows not the ringing of my ears and the cicada who whistles day and night in my ears not to mention the electric burns that now testify on my body).¹⁰¹ Here the literary claim of testimony is written on Abdelaziz Boupacha's scarred body and ringing in his own damaged ears—evidence that cannot be fully verified, only believed as an act of faith (*faire foi*).

Djamila Boupacha's mother also speaks surreptitiously in this text. Halimi sets the scene: she describes waiting to meet Mme. Boupacha and Nefissa Boupacha at a hotel in Algiers to ask them some questions relevant to Djamila's case. They must meet in the outdoor garden because a racist policy bars Algerians from entering the hotel, and Boupacha's mother does not pass: "Madame B. was dressed and coiffed in the Arab style, with a large safsari that she wrapped around her clothes."¹⁰² Mme. Boupacha does not speak French, either, so her daughter Nefissa accompanies her to translate for her. Yet Halimi, who is Tunisian, speaks fluent Arabic. She poses questions to Mme. Boupacha directly; Nefissa, discomfited by this, interrupts to add details.

The detailed account offered by Boupacha's mother surprises even Halimi with its lucidity and specificity: "But also, with a precision that amazed me, she responded to my questions, moving beyond the case of Djamila, she told me how the military officers arrested, tortured, pillaged. She gave me the names of disappeared Algerians, the dates..."¹⁰³ Like her daughter's memory in the Caen courtroom, like Abdelaziz Boupacha's memory of El Biar, like Béchir Boumaza's memory of what happened in Kherrata just after May 8, 1945, Mme. Boupacha's memory is precise, detailed, and sure. She knows the proper names of the disappeared; she remembers the dates that they vanished. When she is just about to leave the hotel after this conversation with Halimi, Mme. Boupacha suddenly cries out, as Halimi describes: "When Mme Boupacha was almost at the gate, she turned around abruptly and shouted to me: 'Don't forget...I would/will give you my eyes for Djamila [*mes yeux, je te les donnerai pour Djamila*]!'"¹⁰⁴ This Arabic expression, translated by Halimi into French—*I would give you my eyes for Djamila*—conveys the urgency of Mme. Boupacha's desire for justice that she surely knew would be difficult, if not impossible, to achieve; it also conveys her daughter's irreplaceable singularity to her. Like Djamila Boupacha's cry of fury and pain in the Algiers courtroom—*Il faut me faire voir*—her mother's entreaty surges up to trouble the surface of Halimi's account. It speaks to the imagination, asking to be heard and believed.

Despite the proper name that figures as its title, *Djamila Boupacha* is not primarily about the facts of a single legal case. This text lays out a legal argument and a dossier of evidence that is replete with literary details like this one—details that have nothing at all to do with juridical proof and protocols, and that come from beyond French. Like *La gangrène* and *Nuremberg pour l'Algérie*, the testimonial text channels a multitude of different voices and plaints that, although not in a form proper to any courtroom, demand more space and time to be fully heard. A testimony like this is most powerful not as historical record or legal claim, but as a literary instrument for imaginative training. It addresses the reader with an invitation—to cultivate both the kind of imagination and memory it would take to understand the full truth of what happened to Algerians under 130 years of French occupation. This is a starting point for thinking about what truly decolonial justice requires.

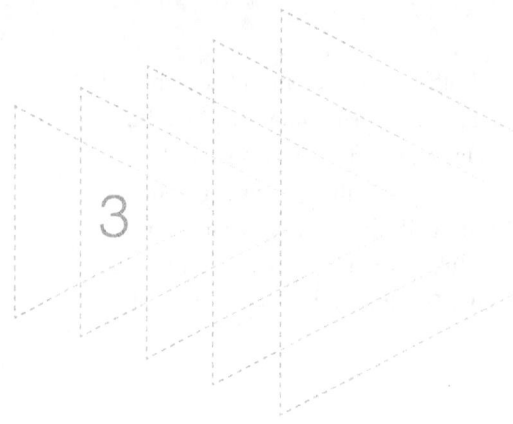

3

Mourning Revolt

Le temps nous défigure. Après deux secondes ou dix ans, vous n'êtes plus le même.

Time disfigures us. After two seconds or ten years, you are not the same.
—Yamina Mechakra

Nous qui vivons au passé
Nous la plus forte des multitudes
Notre nombre s'accroit sans cesse
Et nous attendons du renfort . . .

We who live in the past
We the strongest of multitudes
Our number increases without end
And we await reinforcements . . . —Kateb Yacine

Martyrs without Monuments

Arriving by air into Algiers, it is impossible not to notice the colossal monument perched on the cliff over the south curve of the bay. Called the Maqām al-shahīd in Arabic, this was by far the most prominent structure in the capital cityscape until 2019.[1] It towers ninety-three meters above the heights of Madania, on the cliff above the Musée des beaux-arts and Le Jardin d'Essai in Hamma, directly below the flight path into Boumédiène airport if one is arriving from Europe. The writer Yamina Mechakra worked for decades literally in the shadow of the

FIGURE 3.1. M'hamed Issiakhem, *Les aveugles*, 1982. In the Musée national des beaux arts, Algiers.

monument, at Drid Hocine Psychiatric Hospital in Hussein Dey. For many years, she lived alone in a small house on the hospital grounds, where she both practiced as a psychiatrist and was also quietly treated as a patient until she died in May 2013.[2]

Mechakra herself was an obscure recluse, little known beyond a small circle of close and devoted readers, including her friend and advocate Kateb Yacine and the eminent translator of Arabic Algerian literature into French, Marcel Bois.[3] She published two novels, twenty years apart: *La grotte éclatée* in 1979 and *Arris* in 1999. There has been renewed public interest in Mechakra's work since her death in 2013—including editorials and obituaries in the Algerian press, the Fondation Yamina Mechakra established in 2014 to support scholarly study of her œuvre, and a literary prize created in her name in 2018.[4] However, Mechakra's literary texts have long been difficult to find even in Algiers, where they were published, as both novels have fallen out of print. In 1976, a piece of her short fiction, "L'éveil du mont," appeared in an issue of *El Moudjahid culturel*.[5] Since its first publication in 1979, Mechakra's best-known novel *La grotte éclatée* has been reprinted three times, but it has yet to circulate outside Algeria and has not been published in English translation.[6] Mechakra's second and last novel *Arris* can be found in a 1999 Marsa edition produced by the literary journal *Algérie littérature/action*, dedicated since 1996 to promoting unpublished work by emerging Algerian writers. *Arris* has been scheduled for republication as a bilingual French/Arabic edition, with a translation by the poet Lamis Saïdi.

Despite its striking and unorthodox qualities, Mechakra's œuvre has remained relatively obscure, in contrast to that of her much more famous and prolific contemporaries. This obscurity is reinforced by the way in which commentators have tended to focus on Mechakra's friendships or on her status as a feminist symbol more than on the qualities of her writing itself, which has had the effect of rendering Mechakra visible only by placing her in the shadow of more famous writers like Kateb Yacine or Assia Djebar—the first of which is particularly ironic, given that Mechakra claims that she never read any of Kateb's published work.[7] Most critics who mention Mechakra cite Kateb's famous statement about her before they cite or analyze her own writing, if they read her writing closely at all.[8]

Mechakra's writing speaks to different readerships than do many works by Algerian writers with more robust French audiences, which may in part explain why her novels have not circulated widely. Her texts are intricately connected to Algerian histories, sensibilities, and terrains in ways that tend to confound Orientalist or exoticizing expectations, and that assume an almost visceral intimacy with Algerian nationalism. Both novels are noticeably disinterested in European spaces and histories, "introverted" in a sense that contrasts with what Eileen Julien has called aesthetic "extroversion."[9]

Mechakra charts an aesthetic cartography that resolutely ignores Paris and even Algiers, but includes Numidie, Tingi, Cirta, Carthage, Dougga, Tunis, Sétif, Guelma, Sidi Sakiet Youssef, and Arris. She alludes to histories of collective resistance that predate both French and Arab colonization (Kahina, Dido, Tacfarinas, then Abdelkader). She articulates horizontal links to other sites of colonization and genocide (Dien Bien Phu, *la squaw exterminée*, South Africa, Palestine, Nazi ghettos). She also draws on the aesthetic resources of Greek tragedies, and channels an extensive repertoire of Chaouia and Mozabite song and storytelling practices that index oral archives kept alive by travelers of Saharan migration and trade routes, an aesthetic resource Mechakra claims as "ancestral orality." The heterogenous archive constructed by Mechakra's intertextual poetics constitutes an act of decentered extroversion. *La grotte éclatée* appears as disinterested in the aesthetic power of the former imperial metropole as it is resistant to nationalist testimonial and memorial projects organized by Algeria's government.

The introverted, iconoclastic character of Mechakra's writing appears at once to invite and delay its own transmission. For instance, the manuscript that became *La grotte éclatée* sat in a drawer at the state publishing house for six years before finally appearing in 1979. Mechakra has attributed this publication delay to the manuscript's perceived political dissidence: "It disturbed the politics of the time," she said in an interview with Rachid Mokhtari in 1999.[10] There is an intrinsically lawless and unsettling quality to Mechakra's style. Both novels are narrated by orphans, breaking with any structure of patriarchal filiation and authority. The nameless narrator of *La grotte éclatée* is an illegitimate child raised by Catholic sisters in Constantine, a fatherless "X" who takes upon herself the roles of both imam and Antigone. She adheres to no religion but moves at the interstices of "three immense worlds which had no borders for me: that of Moses, of Jesus, and of our prophet Mohamed."[11] Much like Zahia Rahmani's imprisoned "Muslim" narrator, Mechakra's narrator moves well outside the bounds of religious and civil law: "without civil records, without a family name, without any first name ... an outlaw."[12]

While introversion combined with dissidence may not facilitate an Algerian novel's wide reception, Mechakra's work has elicited intense responses from readers beyond the circuits of Francophonie. An Arabic translation of *La grotte éclatée* has been published by the Palestinian scholar Aïda Bamia,[13] and another Arabic translation was undertaken by the Algerian poet Lamis Saïdi—who, completely *bouleversée* (overcome) by the novel, says that she wanted to render it in an Arabic as luminous and unsettling as Mechakra's French. Saïdi also directed a public theatrical reading of excerpts from *La grotte éclatée* at the Théâtre national in Algiers not long before Mechakra's death, and the poet was invited to read aloud from the unpublished manuscript of her Arabic translation of *La grotte éclatée* at the public memorial service organized in Mechakra's honor by the Algerian cultural ministry in 2013.[14]

La grotte éclatée bristles with unruly grief that resonates for Algerian readers in the present, as I learned after speaking about the text with an audience in Oran in 2014. A woman whose son had been disappeared during the 1990s approached afterward to talk about how powerfully the expressions of maternal grief in *La grotte éclatée* had moved her. This quality characterizes both *La grotte éclatée* and *Arris*. The poetics of both texts resist the Algerian state's authority over the national narrative by troubling the genre of historical testimony that is central to the construction of such a narrative.

Mechakra's linked novels, one published at the end of Boumédiène's long presidency (1965–76) and the other at the beginning of Bouteflika's even longer rule (1999–2019), lay claim to grieve those whose lives have been cast outside the protection of the laws of the Algerian nation-state. Her texts sanctify the lives of the most dispossessed, banished, and ghosted in modern Algeria's history, a move that subtly and surely resignifies the politically charged concept of *shahīd* (martyr/witness). Moreover, Mechakra's French is haunted by the absent presence of the Chaouia language in ways that compel a reader to dwell on uncommemorated losses that policies put in place by the postcolonial state have caused—especially in the wake of the legally disavowed state repression that took place in Algeria during the 1980s and the 1990s.

La grotte éclatée reads like eyewitness testimony of Algeria's independence war. The text is arranged as a series of dated fragments narrated in the first person that initially appear to follow a familiar revolutionary chronology from November 1955 to July 5, 1962—a date well known to every Algerian citizen, young and old, as the nation's Independence Day. The novel's opening sentence ("I was headed to ARRIS⁽¹⁾") includes a conspicuous footnote that tethers Mechakra's narrative to the symbolic ground zero of the revolution, those mountains where the armed rebellion is said to have started in November 1954: "⁽¹⁾ ARRIS: small town in the Aurès."[15] The narrator is a woman who volunteers as a medic for the FLN. This nameless *mujāhida* hides for three years (between 1955 and 1958) with her comrades in a remote mountain cave at the Algeria–Tunisia border, where she amputates limbs, dresses wounds, soothes the dying, and buries the dead. She conceives a child with a dying militant also named Arris, gives birth alone in the cave after her lover dies, and names the child Arris—a word both toponym and patronym.

La grotte éclatée is so visceral and specific that readers might assume it autobiographical, which it emphatically is not. At the novel's midpoint (dated October 1958), French napalm and bombs destroy the cave. Narrative and temporal sequences shatter. What initially read as prose testimony comes unhinged, and the novel fractures to become something else entirely. The question to ask of Mechakra's text is not "What genre is this?," but rather: "How to read this coming-undone?" The narrator loses her arm, her mind, and her friends in the cave; her child is blinded and dismembered, possibly dead. Although the textual fragments continue to move as if loosely following chronological time, temporal sequence feels disrupted and irreparably broken. Familiar generic forms give way to unknown and archaic ones; prose falters and breaks with grammatical pattern; time gets stuck in repetition, or veers bizarrely out of joint.[16] The novel's final section, bearing the date of Algeria's independence (July 5, 1962), describes the narrator's solitary pilgrimage to the ruins of the bombed-out cave (*la grotte éclatée*), where she grieves her losses alone before carrying on to Constantine by foot, with Arris (the broken and possibly dead child) on her back. *La grotte éclatée* concludes with the narrator's triple incantation of the enigmatic toponym and proper name "ARRIS, ARRIS, ARRIS," which will become the title of Mechakra's second novel.[17]

What at first appeared as "mujāhida" testimony—a monumental, sacralized genre in postcolonial Algeria,[18] including when it is composed by women militants—is violently shattered by Mechakra and transfigured into something else entirely. She mutes a familiar nationalist discourse of martyrdom and ventures into an opaque thicket of mourning, transforming the strictly limited national liturgy of justified sacrifice into a form for collective testimony that is much more powerful, plural, and strange. Her poetic disfiguring of the sanctioned revolutionary narrative genre poses questions that the close readings I undertake in this chapter address directly: What remains to write and think with if the poison is cut away from accounts of violence and war that have overdetermined history writing in contemporary Algeria? If the toxic transmissions of the nation-state can be interrupted, then what other losses become perceptible, what plaints audible, what claims legible, and what other practices of solidarity and of justice imaginable?

In contrast to *La grotte éclatée*, the novel *Arris* eschews any recognizable genre of militant testimony. After establishing a faint impression of historical realism, this text takes a vertiginous turn to the surreal, fragmented, and nonlinear. Mechakra's enigmatic and disorienting second literary text comprises ninety-one pages that convey the unfinished and feral energy of something coming unraveled, or being set free.

Arris is arranged as thirteen numbered sections that trace the itinerary of at least two lives: that of an adopted child named Arris and that of a grieving mother from whom he was stolen at the government-run hospital where she takes him for treatment in an opening scene. This scene is narrated in a realist mode and omniscient third person that depict a mother and her sick child—a pair that distinctly resembles the figure walking toward Constantine with a mutilated child on her back at the conclusion of *La grotte éclatée*. In the opening scene of *Arris*, a worried young mother wipes the vomit from her feverish child's mouth: "The mother cups her hands like a seashell around Arris's mouth. Collects the bilious vomit which she wipes onto an old rag that she uses as a towel. The little one begins to doze off again."[19] This woman has trekked from the rural Aurès region, crossing the border of "a world cut off from all other worlds" to reach a city hospital.[20] The Aurès mountains are also the setting in which *La grotte éclatée* begins and ends—yet in *Arris* this place is not named until halfway through the novel, and only once, as "this Aurès who defies time."[21]

Arris swiftly sheds its realist mode and any sense of identifiable location. Its eponymous protagonist—adopted by wealthy foreigners who spirit him to unnamed lands far in the north—inhabits no recognizable nation. In what reads like a strange fairy tale, the stolen child grows into an alienated adult in a place so far removed it could be another planet. *Arris* contains no dates and few references to specific geographical sites or historical events; there is no obvious indication that the narrative is partly set in Algeria except to a reader already familiar with the cultural and geographical terrain, or who notices the toponym (Aurès) cited above.

Except for this toponym, the text contains not a single allusion to Algeria's war of independence, nor is there any reference to the uncivil war that ravaged Algeria during the painful decade in which Mechakra composed *Arris*, at which point she was also battling the terrors and hallucinations of her own illness while living in a private house on the grounds of Drid Hocine Hospital in Algiers. Yet, although *Arris* does not speak of war, it channels powerful grief in the face of unbearable ruin and devastation. It reads like a howl of pain. Soon after the abrupt separation of parent and child, the narrative splits into two voices. We read the words of an illiterate Chaouia-speaking mother calling out her longing for a lost child; the child in an alien land can hear a voice in the night, arriving unexpected from elsewhere like the voice of a ghost or a hallucination. He finds himself responding to this voice in a mother tongue (Chaouia) that he has otherwise forgotten. These shifting lines of address multiply, collide, and cross, weaving together a lament of escalating intensity and despair. Like *La grotte éclatée*, this text also concludes with a pilgrimage. Arris traces his way back to the hospital where he had been stolen from his mother, and from there to his natal village in the Aurès, which has been abandoned and destroyed. In the rubble of the village, he discovers desiccated bones of his mother's skeleton and a skein of long white hair. This novel *also* concludes with a burial rite, and with a triple incantation, which is spoken by residents from the nearby village who help Arris gather and bury his mother's bones: "Arris has returned, the widow is no more! And all the people say: Amin! Amin! Amin!"[22]

If *La grotte éclatée* is relatively obscure, *Arris* practically buries itself. It is difficult to find, disorienting to read, and has been largely disregarded by critics.[23] Even though Mechakra's two novels are separated by twenty years of her apparent silence, the texts are closely connected at the level of poetics. In this chapter, I read them together, shuttling from one text to the other in three discrete sections, each focused on one of Mechakra's own aesthetic figures ("ghosted tongues," "exiled bones," and "shattered stones"). Read together, *La grotte éclatée* and *Arris* appear as if they might be remnant fragments belonging to a larger work composed over decades, most of which has been lost.[24] There are obvious stylistic echoes between them, such as the enigmatic toponym and proper name Arris, but *Arris* is not a narrative sequel to *La grotte éclatée*. Rather, it amplifies and escalates a lamentation that Mechakra seems to have been crafting for decades. *Arris* radicalizes an aesthetic insurrection launched with *La grotte éclatée*.

Mechakra's literary expressions of bereavement, like Antigone's unauthorized act of burial, defy state-sanctioned commemorative rituals and legal interdictions on mourning in postcolonial Algeria. The incandescent grief that emerges through Mechakra's experimental poetics also disturbs and unsettles the teleological nationalist epic in specific ways. She sanctifies as grievable the lives of those who have been excluded from the national narrative, a version of history shaped by the prerogatives of the ruling political party. Mechakra's fiction also clears a space outside the juridical limits of testimony to articulate a concept of what is human—and beloved—in terms of collective belonging not defined by citizenship in a nation-state, and not bound to the authority of the existing political regime.

"Alternate Scansions"

The massive concrete monument that towers over the city of Algiers is a prominent staging ground for those expressions of public mourning that have been actively promoted by the Algerian state under the authority of the FLN since 1962. In his study of the memorial complex that has crowned Algiers since the early 1980s, Emmanuel Alcaraz compares the Maqām al-shahīd to Parisian *lieux de mémoire* only to suggest that nothing in Paris quite compares: the Maqām al-shahīd is "at once... the Arc de Triomphe,... the Tomb of the Unknown Soldier... and the Pantheon crypt."[25] The Maqām al-shahīd is a *lieu de memoire* in Pierre Nora's sense of the term—that is, a *lieu-carrefour* (crossroads site) where the alchemical and fictional processes that generate national *histoire-mémoire* become legible. In short, the Maqām al-shahīd is a site that reveals how, in Nora's formulation, the nation is itself "an aesthetic project at once political and literary, resting on an interplay of forces that transform the very reality that they represent."[26]

In French, the Maqām al-shahīd is usually called *le mémorial du martyr*, although in Algiers it is often referred to as simply *le monument* because there simply is no other like it in the city, and no other of such impressive scale in the country. Many Algérois refer to it in Darija as *houbel*. A feat of engineering—contracted to the Canadian firm Lavallin and opened in 1982—the monument stands on a precarious cliff in an area of the city at high risk for seismic activity and, during the 1990s, for terror attacks. The complex also includes a public esplanade that hosts festivals and a shopping mall, a symbol of the state's opening to economic growth and a reason why it later became a symbolic target for attacks. The monument tower itself is formed of three concrete palm fronds that shelter an eternal flame dedicated to the memory of the war's "million" martyrs, or *shuhadā'*. At the base of each palm leaf stands a gigantic sculpture of an armed soldier representing a different branch of the FLN's military operations. Beneath the complex lies a subterranean military museum and, even deeper below ground, a crypt.

This complex is designed to inculcate a strong sense of reverence for those designated as shuhadā'—those militants revered as martyrs in the 1976 constitution[27]—whose stern portraits greet visitors upon entry to complex's subterranean museum. In December 1972, Boumédiène set forth a plan for this Musée national du moudjahid, which is now located directly beneath the triple spires of the Maqām al-shahīd.[28] Visitors descend into the museum led by volunteer guides through a series of display rooms and graphic dioramas that lay out a teleology of key dates and events in Algeria's modern history. This timeline is characterized by conspicuous omissions;[29] a circumambulation of its chronological circuit culminates in a room celebrating Algeria's Independence Day on July 5, 1962. Throughout the underground complex, a recording of Algeria's national anthem blasts over loudspeakers, its refrain an iteration of an imperative verb derived from the same root as the noun *shahīd*: "Fa-shhadū! Fa-shhadū! Fa-shhadū!" ("So bear witness! Bear witness! Bear witness!").

A full tour concludes with a descent into an even deeper subterranean mausoleum (in Arabic, *maqbara*) that is dedicated to the shuhadā'. This shrine is a circular space around a marble pulpit on which stands an opened Qur'ān; suras play softly over the sound system and are engraved on the walls; visitors speak in whispers or remain silent. The experience of walking through this maqbara is at once political, religious, and pedagogical. It conveys profound reverence. It is also a ritual space designed to foster the compelling impression that—as Malika Rahal notes of the nationalist epic that was institutionalized by state policy under Boumédiène during the 1970s—anything after "the year 1962 is simply not history."[30] Experiencing the site leaves a visitor with the strong impression that modern Algeria is Arabic-speaking and Muslim, and that its citizens are resolutely united under the protective and benevolent banner of the FLN.[31] In other words, the official version of Algerian history into which the Maqām al-shahīd conscripts its visitors also involves accepting amnesia, blank spots, and a teleological theory of history that culminates with the FLN at the helm of an Algerian nation triumphant in the wake of French domination, a state that embodies justice and a total break with the colonized past.

Defining the concept of shahīd—and determining which dead may be counted as shuhadā'—lies at the epicenter of disputes for narrative authority over Algeria's founding war. The monument is a material reminder of the complex ways that this war continues to serve as a source of legitimacy not only for those who have ruled Algeria, but also for those who are critical of the state, such as Islamists. Yet the anticolonial war has also long fertilized a vernacular lexicon of resistance widely available to the majority of Algerians who ally with neither of these poles, such as Yamina Mechakra.[32]

The monument's name reflects the multivalence of its symbolic status, and also the way in which political and religious meanings intersect in the same words in contemporary Algeria. *Maqām* (monument, site, tomb, sacred place, a place where one stands) is semantically linked by its root (*q-w-m*) to both *muqāwama* (resistance, standing against something) and *qawmiyya* (nationalism; from *qawm*, the people). *Shahīd*—usually translated as "martyr" or "witness," widely understood by Algerians to refer to those who died fighting the French in the war for national independence, and a category written into Algeria's founding documents[33]—is connected to the basic verb form *shahida*, which means to see or to testify. In different patterns, this root (*sh-h-d*) produces the verbs used both to describe watching television (*shāhada*) and spoken in the call to prayer,[34] a breath away from *shahāda*, which is the noun that names the profession of faith and, more generally, testimony. The same root generates juridical terms for eyewitness testimony and attestation, and a proliferation of other words concerning sight and seeing (*mushāhadāt*: "things seen, sights, visible things"). These variations of the root *sh-h-d* provide a feel for the testimonial polyvalence of this Arabic word beyond its function as the noun *shahīd* in a military lexicon.

This is the semantic and political terrain into which Mechakra ventures by way of fiction. The Maqām al-shahīd was built to mark the twenty-year anniversary of Algerian independence in 1982 in keeping with a plan designed in 1972 by President Boumédiène, and a new constitution was drafted and enforced by him in 1976 (he remained in office until 1978). Mechakra completed her manuscript of *La grotte éclatée* in 1973 and it was published, after a long delay that she ascribes to the manuscript's dissonance with the political order, in 1979. In 1974, she began writing a manuscript that would eventually be published as *Arris* in 1999. That is, Mechakra undertook her literary experiment with the poetics of revolutionary testimony during the same years that the nationalist ideology of the shahīd (as martyr) was being monumentalized by the state's aesthetic and pedagogical projects under the direction of "the architect of the Algerian state," Houari Boumédiène.[35]

It could easily escape note that the Arabic word *shahīd* appears just once in *La grotte éclatée*, and the corresponding French term *martyr* exactly once in *Arris*. This conspicuous silence has the effect of muting state-sponsored hyperbole at the very moment of its institutionalization, and yet the multivalent and capacious concept of shahīd also figures centrally (if silently) in both of these literary works in ways that link them at the level of style and form. Mechakra's fiction can be read as experimental countertestimony that contests the state's authority to define and wield this concept. Her splintered and fragmented texts create an alternate lexical constellation that eludes the dominant historical framework, and that brings into sharp focus precisely what this frame banishes and obscures.

Asking "Is a history of contemporary Algeria possible?," Malika Rahal has called attention to an archival conundrum still faced by professional historians of Algeria more than half a century after independence.[36] Here, Rahal lays out the key points of a dominant script that was written into the nation's founding laws, materialized in the new toponymies of its cities and memorial spaces, and advanced as educational policy under Boumédiène during the 1970s:

> In Algeria, the version of events developed by the Front de Libération Nationale regime turned into an official history imposing a one-dimensional and linear narrative of the nationalist past. This narrative took shape in official texts such as the 1976 National Charter (a political framework for the constitution ratified the same year) and was institutionalized in academia

during the 1970s. It appeared in textbooks and in *lieux de mémoire* such as street names and monuments. Univocal in nature, this narrative promoted values and attitudes that were those of the FLN, the only authorized political party after independence. It glorified armed struggle over political reformism; it was populist, referring to *the people* as the sole driving force for political change; it defined Algerian culture as Arabic in language and Muslim in religion, thus symbolically and (to an extent) practically excluding any other language and religion.[37]

According to Rahal, the epic instituted *as* history after 1962 has also generated significant epistemological blind spots. Rahal outlines how the teleological script produced and endorsed by the FLN leadership under Boumédiène was widely disseminated during the 1970s, when the state's near-total monopoly on academic, educational, and popular publishing and over the national archives practically ensured that textbooks, scholarship, and pedagogies alike "reflected the dominant narrative: certain themes, figures, or organizations were simply written out," an erasure that thereby "directly influenced the material available to historians and determined the questions they could—or could not—ask."[38] Historian James McDougall has expressed the problem in these terms: "As the origin point of reference for the independent state, its supplier of legitimacy and principle symbolic resource, the revolutionary epic was instituted at the very center of Algeria's political imaginary, the founding aporia of the nation's forgetful memory."[39]

In other words, state building is an aesthetic and pedagogical project closely linked to the narrative processes of fiction.[40] This process has had enduring consequences for what it is now possible to see, to know, and to say about modern Algerian history, both in public discourse and in professional historiographical writing. The state's investment in producing a self-justifying historical narrative has concretely determined what material exists for inclusion in the national archives at all, and this material archive in turn conditions what questions have been asked and answered by historians. An abiding focus on historiography of the independence war has also meant that other topics, times, and research questions have been comparatively neglected by scholars. The founding aporia identified by Rahal and McDougall generates demarcations that are etched into the archives and public memory until these demarcations become monumentalized as *if* they are immutable facts—a case study in the alchemical processes of the nation-state's fiction, which transforms the very reality it represents.

In Algeria the notion of a clean break or "Great Divide" is central to the official historical narrative, a temporal rupture point that has long served power in a number of ways. A chronology of colonial violence and anticolonial revolt that conveniently ends at independence in 1962 justifies the authority of the FLN and makes it possible to frame the periods of state-sponsored terror in 1954–62 and during the 1990s as disconnected and discontinuous. This also makes it harder to identify the reproduction of French colonizing techniques and law in the practices of the Algerian state, or to consider continuities between repressions carried out in the 1980s and those of the 1990s.[41] In fact, the aporia created by inaccessible or nonexistent archives and by historical narratives that reinforce conspicuous silences has also helped to set an epistemological and juridical framework for all that seemed to vanish into the void of "national tragedy" during the 1990s.

This disconnect, which Rahal notes has long been instrumental to the FLN's heroic epic, is reinforced by the periodizing habits of scholars who frame the 1990s as an inexplicable aberration, an inevitable traumatic repetition, or a manifestation of violent chaos somehow peculiar to Algeria. This tendency is replicated in a broader critical pattern that organizes Algerian history as a dramatic tragedy in three acts (colonialism, war for independence, 1990s civil war), as Walid Benkhaled and Natalya Vince point out in their argument for a "post-dramatic" analysis of Algerian history.[42] The dramatic framework of trauma, urgency, and crisis has had a number of effects on scholarship concerning Algeria. Among other things, such framing has reinforced a narrative of ongoing cultural-linguistic conflict and identity crisis that has long served as a pretext for state repression carried out in the name of "unity" and "harmony." It has also fueled what McDougall identifies as a "neo-orientalist cliché of a society endemically plagued by violence"[43]—violence often presumed to have something intrinsic to do with Islamist fanatics rather than with the particular historical circumstances of French colonization or neoimperialist oil extraction.

Rahal invites historians and anthropologists to challenge this epistemological blindspot and break with these theatrical clichés by turning to alternative archives as authoritative sources of historical knowledge. Breaking with the dramatic narrative framework will not be accomplished through unrestricted access to the national archives, she points out, because the archive *itself* enshrines these amnesiac silences and temporal demarcations.[44] Instead, we must find ways to learn from the unofficial and unauthorized narratives that have been transmitted outside the ambit of institutions managed by the state—precisely those kinds of sources that Lia Brozgal has called *anarchival*.

Rahal singles out the oral histories of women in the Aurès and Kabylie as one such resource. These Chaouia and Kabyle historical narratives, Rahal observes, tend to draw multiple links between the terrors of 1954–62 and those of

1992–2000. Centering these spoken archives will help to generate alternative temporal frameworks that illuminate the very continuities and connections that official chronology is designed to obscure, she argues: "This form of historical anthropology," writes Rahal, "is based on a local history of practices of violence and allows for a long perspective over the entire period running from the repression of May 1945 to the end of the Black Decade in 2002, via the war for Independence."[45]

Composed during the long arc of years leading from Boumédiène's dictatorship to Bouteflika's two decades of rule, Mechakra's texts also create what Rahal calls an "alternative scansion (or rhythm) to the classical colonial/postcolonial divide in Algerian history."[46] Mechakra opens up gaps, spaces, and blanks in the nationalist text of revolution that the Algerian state has sought to close and control in the name of national unity and state security, and she lays claim to archaic forms of lamentation that revolt against any politically useful notion of a clean break with the colonial past. Mechakra's literary experimentation with testimony—an improvisation that draws from a recessed signifying network marked by the Arabic term *shahīd*—creates space to imagine the ghostly multitude of lives that have been expunged from modern Algeria's history. Mechakra's incantatory poetics inaugurate an anarchival vision of history that moves according to the unpredictable scansions of insurrectionary mourning.

Ruining November 1954

In 1976, three years before *La grotte éclatée* finally made it into print, Mechakra published a short prose piece entitled "L'éveil du mont" ("The Awakening of the Mountain") in *El Moudjahid culturel*, a section of the paper first founded as an FLN guerilla information bulletin that became the state propaganda organ after 1962. "L'éveil du mont" is a rousing revolutionary title. Mechakra's piece bears the significant date "premier novembre 1954" (November 1, 1954) at its conclusion, which is the first day of armed resistance that officially launched the liberation war.[47] Mechakra's two-page text could easily be mistaken for nationalist propaganda—an ode to revolution's dawning—except for the uncanny way that it haunts and ruins the state's symbolic lexicon to make this well-known script serve much less predictable ends.

"L'éveil du mont" tracks parallel processions moving through the Aurès mountains in opposite directions. The first includes old peasant men carrying manuscripts, young women, former prison convicts, and hungry children who hail from different regions but converge together to climb into the "Djebel" (the mountains, and also a familiar trope for joining the revolution). The counterprocession is a line of French army deserters who have abandoned the mountain caves to descend from the Djebel "to the rhythm of future cannonades."[48] Their intersecting paths could be interpreted as a triumphant changing of the guard—the wretched of the earth march to their destinies as future *mujāhidīn* and *shuhadā'*, while the weary French soldiers slink away from occupied land, cannon fodder in the making. Yet there is a strange dissonance between the date inscribed on this scene and the ravaged, apocalyptic images conveyed. This world looks more like war's ruined aftermath than its bright dawn. Because of this temporal disjunction, the first day of revolution appears already haunted by the devastation to come, so that an ominous sense of tragedy invades the epic script.

Mechakra's piece appeared in the FLN newspaper twenty years after the inaugural scene she re-creates, and at a moment when the postcolonial state was busy fortifying its foundational architecture. The year 1976 is the same year President Boumédiène drafted a national charter designed to be "the supreme source of the nation's policy and the laws of the state," in the words of the constitution based on this charter.[49] Boumédiène's charter affirmed the nascent state's need to protect itself against threats: "To restore national sovereignty, construct socialism, struggle against underdevelopment, build a modern and prosperous economy, and be vigilant against external dangers requires a solid and constantly fortified state, not a state invited to die out, when it has barely emerged from the void."[50] These documents broke sharply with the 1964 charter that was adopted by an FLN wary of bureaucracy and proud of its role as an "avant-garde party profoundly linked to the masses."[51] Adopted by referendum in June 1976, the new charter served as the basis for Algeria's second constitution; the first had been suspended in the military coup that brought Boumédiène to power in 1965.

Together, these documents—cornerstones of the institutional edifice—fuse political, economic, and religious language under the banner of a vulnerable and self-fortifying state. In its preamble, the new constitution frames the independence war as "one of the greatest epics in history to have marked the resurrection of the peoples of the Third World," declares it the purpose of the state and its institutions to translate "the progressive ideals of the revolution into concrete realities" (here it is a small leap to erecting concrete monuments), and consecrates the president and the FLN as facilitators of this translation.[52] It also affirms a portrait of Algerian citizens as unified, Arabic-speaking Muslims.

"L'éveil du mont" was printed in October, a few months after the June referendum on the National Charter and just before the new constitution was officially approved by a 99.18 percent vote in November. In this immediate context, the eerie rather than epic character of Mechakra's imagery appears out of line, if not openly contestatory. In her descriptions, Algeria's terrain looks desolate and destroyed ("routes de napalm," "champs brulés"—napalm roads and scorched fields), and the parallel processions of warriors-to-be and soldiers-in-retreat are not clearly distinguishable against this volatile and terrorized landscape: "Processions advanced, merged. The earth began to tremble. The thunder rolled."[53] Earth tremors and thunder are not triumphant; they are threatening and troubling. This is a vision of a world trembling in the face of destruction and ruin. It is not epic, but an ominous moment before catastrophe, or an interlude before lamentation.

Moreover, while the pilgrims' destination is ambiguous, it is possible to envision their starting points because Mechakra names characters individually, sketching in a few significant details sufficient information to render them distinctive. Their names are not obviously Arabic; their religion is not obviously Islam. Daliah wears a haik stitched with ancient motifs. Mairama is adorned with the most beautiful jewelry in her *dachra*. Chuchana's slum has just been torched. Sisine has seen his mother raped and knows too much for his age. Hançala prays to the rain and is accompanied by his beloved dog Cerbère. Horça has a white beard reaching past his knees and leads a procession of old men who each carry a single book and sing a strange hymn. Youb, a prison convict who escaped his cell and walks naked, is the haunting figure of an "indigène musulman" prisoner who flees a law that wants him dead: "ce damné de la terre avait refusé la loi qui l'assassinait" (this wretched of the earth had rejected the law that was killing him).[54] Inflecting Fanon's iconic turn of phrase with a juridical sense ("damnés"), Mechakra's fugitive is not only "wretched," but "condemned." The fact that the verb is imperfect and not *passé simple* or *composé* ("la loi qui l'assassinait") could also suggest that this is a kind of ongoing death at the hands of the law, or that this prisoner walks freely only because he is already a ghost.

The itinerary set by Mechakra does not align with any state-sanctioned revolutionary script. Although these potential militants trek into the Aurès mountains, they are headed not for the ancient caves that harbor collective memory of two thousand years' insurrection against occupation, but instead toward a single sacred tree and the matriarch ("la mère") who dwells there. That is, they are headed toward a sepulcher, a site that might otherwise be called either *maqām* or *maqbara*. A similar destination appears at the conclusion of pilgrimages undertaken by the narrators of both *La grotte éclatée* and *Arris*.

Read this alongside the allusion to Cerberus, the mythical Greek three-headed demon dog who guards the gates of the underworld and prevents the dead from leaving, and the crepuscular light of "L'éveil du mont" can be seen to shift. In this interpretive flickering, what at first looked very much like mujāhidīn and *mujāhidāt* marching into the revolution at dawn now appears to be a strange army of ghosts moving across the ruined terrain of a dusky underworld toward an archaic burial ground in the ancestral mountains. Surreptitiously, Mechakra's fiction infiltrates and occupies the nationalist lexicon, subtly transforming figures who resemble mujāhidīn into shuhadā' of a qualitatively different kind than those who are so visibly memorialized by the Maqām al-shahīd that towers over the nation's capital today.

Ghosted Tongues: *La grotte éclatée* | *Arris*

La grotte éclatée extends Mechakra's experiment in finding words for war that cannot be made useful to the state. The word *shahīd* appears on the pages of the novel just once. Mechakra's narrator wakes wounded and stunned in a Tunis psychiatric hospital after bombs and napalm shatter the cave and kill her beloved friends. She refers to her dead comrades Kouider and Salah not as *shuhadā'* but rather as "heroes transformed into rotten flesh," and as corpses "lying prone beneath the wreckage of bombs, forgotten by everyone except perhaps some faraway friend."[55]

Tunis, headquarters of FLN strategic operations and of her convalescence, is for her a site of erasure: "For Tunis these men had never existed. Forgetting had fallen heavily on these men whom I had loved."[56] She fixates on the viscera and rotting bodies of her friends rather than on her own healing: "There, a few hundred kilometers away, this sun so beneficent in Tunis is turning my brothers into stinking corpses."[57] Indifferent to her sudden status as war hero and lieutenant, she dwells morbidly on mutilation: "They [*on*] promoted me to lieutenant. Two stars on my armless shoulder. That was the price of my handicap.... In Tunis they saw me as a heroine."[58] "Tunis" operates as a metonym for the FLN—an impersonal and faceless "on" who promotes her to lieutenant, pins stars to the empty shoulder of her uniform, and delivers the charred body of her eyeless, legless child to her only remaining arm.

It is at this point that the word *shuhadā'* appears: "The FLN decided to circumcise all of the sons of the shuhadā'. They gave Arris a white gandourah and red fez."[59] The word is set apart by Mechakra's narrator as belonging already to the lexicon of a nation-state in the process of being formed. Here the FLN steps in as proxy patriarch to circumcise the male children of dead soldiers. This ritual is alien to her—an illegitimate orphan without family or religion—just as the word *shuhadā'* has no place in her vocabulary. These political liturgies belong to the implicitly masculine "on" of "le F.L.N.," a revolutionary vanguard in the process of establishing its symbolic and legal patriarchal authority.

After the temporal rupture marked by the bombing of the cave (October 1958), Mechakra's narrative prose becomes disrupted and disturbed by a series of other generic forms. At first, these include direct citations from the FLN newspaper *El Moudjahid* and parodic lapses into genres such as medical dossier, psychiatric evaluation, police report. These function to convey the anguish of a war-traumatized person forced to translate her pain into bureaucratic terms that abjectly fail to do justice:

> They brought me my son's body.
> Age: two months.
> Napalm victim.
> My living son, blind and without legs. My scorched son.[60]

Every description of the burned, blinded, and legless child Arris accents his status as tragic archetype. The figure of Arris marks a point of impasse and opacity that poses significant resistance to notions of justified sacrifice and eyewitness testimony fused together by the FLN's valorization of the revolutionary shuhadā'. Grim descriptions of the child's ruined eyes and legs counter the heroic sense of shuhadā' by linking martyrdom with blindness, mutilation, and murder: "My son, face without eyes destroyed by napalm, my son the kid with murdered legs"; "My son mutilated by fire"; "Child of the martyred legs."[61]

The status of the sacrificed infant as living or dead is also rendered syntactically and typographically indeterminate, making it seem possible that the child Arris is only visible as the narrator's hallucination or a ghost. Indeed, the narrator begins to directly address the dead with increasing frequency after the novel's midpoint, as in this lament addressed to her dead lover, the soldier Arris, concerning the mutilation of their child:

> I will go and find my river and with my one remaining hand I will scrub my breasts and my bastard womb with a young blood that sings, that has been harvested from the boiling entrails of thousands of mothers leaning over a child who exists   no more.
>   Like them [*comme elles*], I am bent over my son who exists no more,
>   A great wrinkle on my back.
>   Like them, I still weave crowns on the forehead of a son who no longer exists,
>   a great wrinkle in my eyes.
>   Like them, my breasts still weep tears of milk.
>   Like them, my womb still shudders over a child
>   That my entrails remember.

> Like them, my memory vacillates, falters: my son whom I see is not [*mon fils que je vois n'est pas*].⁶²

This passage reads not as prose but verse, and its typography is noticeably glitchy. Mechakra's sentences are riddled with gaps and absences that disrupt a smooth process of reading to introduce a sense of uncertainty and hesitation: *mon fils que je vois n'est pas*. This appears to be something other than idiosyncratic margin justification—there are strange gaps in the line. The disrupted syntax makes it appear that sentences might not achieve grammatical closure, producing a disruptive and destabilizing quality. Above, the anaphora that begins "Comme elles" (Like them) connects the narrator's private grief to the collective lamentation of "milliers de mères" (thousands of mothers) who, like her, fold their bodies into the absence of a child who has been torn from their entrails: breasts weep milk, uterus shudders with the memory of a nestled fetus, bodies reel with loss as visceral as amputation. Memory itself vacillates and cracks, seared by a disruptive blank like that which perforates the concluding line. Mechakra's poetics bristle with unruly, disfiguring grief that is at once profoundly private and also connected to the dispossessing losses experienced by multitudes of others.

When Arris's circumcision cut becomes infected by the dirty instruments of the FLN functionaries who botch the job, something else begins to unsettle and transform Mechakra's sentences. In this passage, the narrator sings to her feverish child—whose eyes have been scorched away by napalm, limbs torn off, and foreskin infected—pleading with him to live through the night:

> All night long, by my son's bedside, half-conscious,
> I begged him not to go away.
> I told him [*je lui disais*] the hikes that we would take together
> along the paths of our villages.
> I told him our grandmothers split in two, rolling between
> their artists' fingers a fine couscous that our infinite fields of wheat
> had ripened in the sun.
> I told him the mountains crowned by a halo of snow
> all year round.
> I told him the quobba of Sidi Othman rising over
> the Meskiana plain, towards which gazes turned
> when hearts cried out for a peaceful dawn and for water
> to nourish the earth, to fill the granaries.⁶³

Typographical blanks are not the only glitch in these lines. After each iteration of reported speech act ("Je lui disais"—I told him, I said to him) the conjunction that a reader expects (*que*, or "that") is missing, as is a clause with a finite verb. In place of what grammatical convention leads a reader to anticipate are sentence fragments, introducing syntactic suspension and disorientation into the reading process. The fragmented clauses offer vivid images of rural landscape, of sunlight, of mountains haloed with crowns of snow, of the *quobba* (a saint's shrine) on the Meskiana plain. These noun phrases that follow "Je lui disais" thus appear as the direct objects of unconventional use of the verb *dire*, as if to indicate that by reciting or incanting, she conjures and conveys these landscapes. She speaks as a lifesaving antidote to the toxic infection caused by the FLN's botched operation—but what words are we to imagine this mother actually *saying* to her blind child in order to convey these scenes to Arris? Moreover, in what language does she speak?

An epigraph on the novel's first page helps to answer these questions. Just two vivid sentences, it reads like an apostrophe, or a prayer:

> Language kneaded into the braids pleated in the the fire of the love that has blazed for centuries in the hearts of my ancestors and in my own heart towards which I turned my frozen face and my damp eyes so that I could smile. Language kneaded into the carpets, open books bearing the multicolored prints of women of my country who, at dawn, begin to write the fire of their entrails to cover the child in the evening when the sky robs him of the sun; into the silver khalkhals, icy rings around delicate ankles, whose music reassures and comforts the one who sleeps near the hearth and already loves his mother's foot and the earth on which she treads.[64]

The speaker describes a language "braided" or "kneaded" into the warp and weave of textiles that, like open books, bear the multicolored imprints of her ancestors, women who woke at dawn to write "the fire of their entrails" into intricate blankets to cover and protect a beloved child. This language also sounds in the musical chime of silver *khalkhals* worn on the ankles of a mother who walks barefoot across the hearth as a sleeping child listens.

This is the language—another epistemology—that the fissures, glitches, and cracks in Mechakra's French bring to the edge of semantic availability for a close reader of *La grotte éclatée*. It is a vivid but fragile idiom, vulnerable to destruction by the masculinist monological grammar of the new state and its legal codes. Mechakra's poetics are kneaded and braided with oratures and text(iles) composed by women who neither speak nor write French or Arabic but rather inhabit Chaouia, Kabyle, Tamasheq, Chenoua, Mozabite. By cracking the testimonial genre and unsettling the vocabulary of the nation-state, Mechakra repurposes its remnants and fragments to create a fugitive literary space of infinite dimension in which other languages can move. The poetic text becomes, for Mechakra, an instrument of this clandestine transmission. It is a sheltered archive for knowledge that can only be articulated in a recessed mother tongue such as Chaouia.

The occluded speech act signaled by variations of the phrase "Je dis" or "Je dis à mon fils" repeats throughout *La grotte éclatée* after the fracture point in the text marked "October 1958." Narrative prose gives way almost entirely to verse, and these verses cultivate the distinctive and escalating energy of sung lament, a genre with deep roots in the Maghreb. The cumulative repetition "Je dis" becomes liturgical and incantatory, conveyed in an intimate rather than sovereign voice and in a written language that is haunted by spoken language that is not French. For example, the following lament is replete with toponyms that stand in place of landscape, spoken aloud to a blinded child:

> I say to my son Algiers the languishing and wounded, trembling for independence.
> I say to my son Constantine and Kef Chkara.
> I say to my son Kabylie and Amirouche, Tlemcen and
> its fury, Oran and its revenge.
> I say to my son the Aurès and my pain [*Je dis à mon fils les Aurès et ma peine*].
>
> I remember the skies of my country.
> I say to my son the fleece sky of Algiers, its sun standing
> high above the Casbah, its capital.
> I say to my son the clean and immense sky curling around a
> distant sun that slips into the narrow streets of Constantine
> the secret.
> I say to my son the dark and bewitching sky, crowning a
> yellow and dripping sun hung on the Aurésian rocks still
> covered in snow.
> I say to my son the horizontal and floating sky, cooling a red and virile sun, for fear that it does not burn Tlemcen
> the Andalouse.[65]

This act of lifesaving cosmogenesis transforms the sky and the cities into words. A mother speaks in images, by way of untranslatable toponyms: the *qobba* of Sidi Othman, Alger, Constantine, Kef Chkara, la Kabylie, Amirouche, Tlemcen, Oran, Casbah, the snow-covered stone of the Aurès. While these proper names are transcribed in French, to read them aloud or to imagine them spoken is to be inhabited by language that is neither French nor Arabic. It is language charged with mountains, with collective memory of subterranean caverns, and with pain that stresses the limits of grammatical convention in order to make felt what cannot be seen. This corresponds to the speaker's desire to transmit something of her experience to her blinded and broken child: "Je dis à mon fils les Aurès et ma peine" (I say to my son the Aurès and my pain [sentence, punishment, grief, suffering]).

This sentence echoes the original title of *La grotte éclatée*. Mechakra had initially given her novel the title *Ma grotte et ma peine*, but agreed during the editorial process to revise it.[66] Spoken in personal possessive form, the words also tap into a subterranean vein of collective memory—not only of private suffering and legal punishment (*ma peine*) but also legends of millennia of indigenous revolt and resistance located in the caves of the Aurès. Twenty years later, the same lines will echo in the novel *Arris*, like a single through line threaded into the warp and weave of Mechakra's œuvre over time:

There, there
In my Aurès...
The cave of sorrows [*peines*]
Three thousand years, four thousand years...
May my appeased soul
lay there forever at rest.[67]

As Kateb Yacine points out in his preface to Mechakra's first novel, the subterranean hiding spaces of the Aurès are a potent symbol of underground resistance not only to French colonial violence—from the notorious "enfumades" of the nineteenth century to the *ratonnades* and napalm of the twentieth—but *also* to the Arab and Roman imperial wars that long predated the French.[68] The caves in the Aurès represent both clandestine archive and sepulcher for Mechakra. All three of her texts trace a return to *this* site—it is the destination of the ghostly pilgrims in "L'éveil du mont," and it is also the endpoint of pilgrimages at the conclusions of both *La grotte éclatée* and *Arris*, whose narrators return to the Aurès to bury what has not been properly buried.

The narrator's direct address to her mutilated child culminates on the concluding page of *La grotte éclatée*, which is marked with two dates: that of Algeria's national independence and that on which Mechakra completed her manuscript. The narrator has laid daisies on the place where her friends Salah and Kouider died. The novel concludes:

JULY 5, 1962
On the road from ARRIS, I met the indifferent gaze
of a few rare travelers.
The sun was drowning in heat.
I found Constantine for a moment.
I let my gaze fall on the eyes of my son.
Arris, my son, you were my revolt.
To you, today, my child,
I say [je dis] your dead father, my love on his lips.
I say my house killed there at the foot of a tree that blasphemes
in the face of the sky.
I say my friends crushed by forgetting, but still alive in
the memory of an old jackal; he comes every evening to rend
the night with his slow sobs.
I say my faith in tomorrow, nailed to my chest.
I say ARRIS my country and its harvests
ARRIS my ancestors and my honor
ARRIS my love and my home [demeure; dwelling, legacy].
September 1973[69]

In September 1973, Mechakra haunts the celebrated date of the new nation's birth with the subterranean whispers, echoes, cries, and howls of a speaker in mourning. The formulation "Je dis" appears here at its most direct—as if inviting the reader to enter the space of familiar second-person address—yet the grammar remains elliptical and disrupted. The shattered lines limn loss and register absence, lingering on the sobbing cry of a jackal. A feral howl is not the authorized register for commemorating July 5, 1962.

La grotte éclatée opens a breach within the nationalist liturgy of the revolution by rewriting sacrifice and ruin in ways that pay tribute to those who do not qualify for the FLN's definition of "shahīd." Much as her narrator refrains from repeating the word *circoncision* to her child in order to speak instead Alger, Constantine, Oran, Kabylie, Tlemcen, Kef Chkara, and ARRIS, so Mechakra blanks out the tainted word *shahīd* from her own lexicon, opening in its absence a space to experiment with testimony beyond those forms instituted and celebrated by the nation-state. Here, in a ritualized private prayer and language made her own, Mechakra implicitly counterposes the proper name "ARRIS" to the state's abstract and generalizable category of the revolutionary witness and heroic martyr called *shahīd*. Her act of cosmogenesis culminates with a triple keening of the name ARRIS, a word that is neither French nor Arabic, but that is the name of a dead lover, of a mutilated child, and of an ancestral home—and that would also become the title of Mechakra's second novel.

Mechakra has said that she was already writing what would become *Arris* as early as 1980,[70] the year after she published *La grotte éclatée*. However, the experience that sparked the idea for *Arris* came earlier than 1980—in 1974, only one year after Mechakra had completed an unpublished manuscript that would eventually become *La grotte éclatée* in 1979. By 1974, Mechakra was a medical doctor in training to become a psychiatrist; she worked with sick children and young mothers in a pediatric hospital in Beni-Messous. In her interviews with Rachid Mokhtari, Mechakra describes a young woman who arrived at the hospital with a dehydrated and dying infant in her arms. Because the mother was not married and did not have official papers (*livret de famille*), the hospital refused to admit her illegitimate child for treatment.

This moment stayed in Mechakra's memory to inspire the opening scene of her second novel: "*Arris*, in which I consider the status of the young single mother and abandoned children, is born from this scene," she recounts. "I only stayed six months at Beni Messous but this image of a 17-year-old adolescent mother throwing her newborn into my arms before she fainted has always stayed with me."[71] *Arris* begins with two numbered chapters that depict a hospital scene from the point of view of young woman who does not speak French or Arabic, and who does not know how to read or write. *Arris* invites the reader to envision this government hospital in an uncanny and defamiliarized way, and to inhabit a world perceived through different linguistic and epistemological frames. In this way, *Arris* picks up the testimonial experiment where *La grotte éclatée* left off.

In contrast to the dates and toponyms that organize *La grotte éclatée*, temporal and geographical markers are completely absent from *Arris*. From the first lines, Mechakra's French conveys an estranged and untranslatable quality, offering little to orient the reader. This reflects the experience of the narrator, who is far outside the boundaries of her known world: "She comes to the village for the first time."[72] She has walked to the hospital from the mountains, "a world cut off from all other worlds," along with several other people from her tribe in order to get treatment for her child.[73] From her point of view, the hospital is alien territory. Its logic, objects, and procedures are strange and indecipherable:

> She finds herself in a dark, narrow room. It takes a while for her to make out the objects. The nurse pulls out a sheet of paper with many questions written on it.

—All I know, says the mother, is that his name is Arris and that he is four springs old. He was born in early spring and that was four springs ago.

The nurse tips the boy over, inserts a thermometer into his anus. The mother does not understand anything and, deep down, rejects this bizarre gesture.

—He is feverish; what does he have?
—The monster.

She takes the nurse's hand and places it on the tumor. She tenderly cradles Arris against her chest.[74]

What the nurse calls a tumor, the mother calls a monster. She has never heard of the identification papers required by the government in order to admit her child to the hospital: "The mother had never heard of a civil identification record or of a birth certificate," although she knows the names of her child's ancestors for fourteen generations: "She knows only [the child's] first name, the first name of the father, written on the child's file, the descent lines [*les Ben*] of the grandfather and of the great-grandfather all the way to the 14th generation."[75] This knowledge does not translate as bureaucratically useful.

When the narrator speaks, she prays—but her prayers address a banished deity, "Araki, the mother of all," who is unknown to the inhabitants of the city ("There, you don't exist. They cast you out of their city forever").[76] She prays as she decides what to do—"Will I leave the flesh of my flesh in a city, in a country that I did not choose?"—and relinquishes Arris to the nurse for care to save his life, leaving only her fingerprint in place of a signature in the hospital records: "At the hospital, the mother placed her fingerprints on the file, since she didn't know how to sign."[77] She believes he will be returned to her, but instead he is sent to an orphanage, then adopted by foreigners abroad.

At this rupture, the narrator's expression of grief reprises the keening cry at the conclusion of *La grotte éclatée*: "The mother lets out a jackal wail; she empties herself of the last cry she has left. Neither woman nor animal, neither woman nor animal."[78] Her inchoate scream becomes versified lament on the following page:

> I am alone in the land where he was conceived and grew up. At the hospital, they promised to return him to me once he was healed or dead.
>
> Pain, o my pain
> From what gaping wound
> Do you softly seep out
> I hear you o my pain...[79]

Apostrophes like the one above repeat throughout *Arris* so frequently that narrative sequence becomes secondary to an interruptive poetics of grief. After this early point, prose sheds any semblance of historical realism to make space for unruly lamentation that both echoes and radically amplifies that of the first novel.[80]

In *Arris*, the narrative perspective splits. Its third section shifts to the point of view of the child Arris, whom the hospital had abandoned to an orphanage where he is sodomized by another child, then adopted by foreign parents who whisk him away to a fantastical foreign place that resembles English royal court. Arris gets a new name and birthdate, rides in limousines, lives in a palace, goes to school, forgets his mother tongue, learns to play polo, amasses a fortune, marries a woman named Nassa, adopts a beloved dog named Cilia, is visited by the voice of his mother whom he can hear crying out to him from a land he cannot remember. Arris responds to this voice in a language that he has forgotten: "Cut off from my roots, I find myself in another country that is not my own and I tell you [*je te dis*]."[81]

Arris takes on a dialogic form as the separated parent and child call out to each other. This includes many iterations of the apostrophe that characterized the mode of address in *La grotte éclatée*—"O Arris, Arris, ... my love ... my love"; "I would have told you"; "I told you stories"; and "I would have bequeathed you my whole memory as inheritance."[82] In *Arris*, however, the child is not mute. He speaks back. The shifts are abrupt, often without any signal, creating a disorienting and hallucinatory effect that not only renders the two voices indistinguishable at points, but that *also* connects them across space and time to millions of other such voices in pain. In the Aurès, a place scattered with Roman ruins, the mother sees the names of lost multitudes inscribed in the very stones: "Even here, in these places, in this city that long ago belonged to Castellum, entire walls speak of me, of you, oh, of you. Our names have come to layer over millions of others."[83]

Ultimately, the novel's narrative arc is of exile and return. As Arris ages, his mother continues to call out to him in a voice that beckons him back to the place he began. She foretells Arris's return in this apostrophe addressed to the earth itself: "Earth, when you will cover me bit by bit you will incorporate me until my body is baptised and I become an element like the elements of which you are composed, I will let out a howl that will tear apart space and time until it reaches my son's ears. He will come. The call of the earth, yes, this terrible, gutting cry exists. He exists. He will come. That day the jackals will howl until dawn and we will hear the thunder roar with joy.... Arris has returned."[84] By the time Arris finds his way back to the remote village in the Aurès where his mother waits for him, her prophecy is true; he is old, and she is dead, her body decomposed and her bones mingled into the elements, becoming part of the ruined village along with those of "millions of others." It is not clear at what point she died, only that by the time Arris arrives it has been a long time, which suggests that the voice that had beckoned him was that of a ghost. In the novel's last scene, Arris gathers and buries her bones.

Exiled Bones: *La grotte éclatée* | *Arris*

A dispute about justice lies at the heart of both of Mechakra's novels, and is resolved through ritual acts of burial. In the case of *La grotte éclatée*, this is staged as the aftermath of a tribunal described in an undated fragment before the novel's explosion into verse. Here the narrator and her companions Kouider and Salah observe silently as two prisoners—an Algerian harki and a French military conscript, archetypal enemies of the FLN—are accused, judged, and executed in a tribunal conducted by militants who have commandeered the cave for this purpose. A fictional judge corrects the banal arithmetic observed by Fanon whereby no number of Algerian lives lost adds up to a single French death before the law, precisely the kind of trial that the activists who produced texts such as *Djamila Boupacha* and *Nuremberg pour l'Algérie* also imagined, but to different effect. Mechakra's emplotment exposes the limits and dangers of a tribunal for mediating justice claims and opens discursive space to register a heterogeneous anarchive of plaints that are excluded and silenced by the language of the tribunal, which is also the language of a future nation-state establishing its law.

This section of *La grotte éclatée* begins and ends with the narrator's meditations as she tends to the bodies of the wounded and dead, so the tribunal is framed as an unwelcome interruption of the alternate temporality and solidarity of the cave: "That night, we [*nous*] had yet another unexpected visit: some maquisards and two prisoners, a French soldier and a harki. We had to witness two short interrogations."[85] The narrator's first-person plural pronoun includes her friends—a wounded maquisard named Kouider who comes from the remote south, and the illiterate shepherd child Salah whose legs were blown off by a land mine. The visual and spatial details that the scene comprises highlight a fissure separating this "nous" from the maquisards and their tribunal. Descriptions are filtered through the narrator's observation of the faces and gestures of her friends, who, from the shadows, silently watch the fighters carry out interrogation around the fire at the center of the cave.

The FLN soldier-judge is a fair-minded patriot—solemn, severe, a pure product of revolution. Read from the vantage point of the 1970s, there is a strong hint of critical irony in Mechakra's description of his chiseled face, caricatured moustache, and moral clarity about exacting justice. In grievances addressed to the harki (Taieb Flen ben Flen, which means something like "So-and-So, Son of So-and-So," hence a nobody) and the French conscript (François Gaspard), the judge plays the roles of both plaintiff and judge in a fictional legal scenario: he speaks on behalf of Algerian citizens-in-the-making *and* speaks in the authoritative voice of a nation-state-to-come.

His charge against the harki lays possessive claim to the violated bodies of women, fetuses, and children who are implicitly *not* of his "nous":

> You killed *our* children and raped *our* wives. You are an Algerian kneaded from Algerian flesh; each one of your genes carries within it the red letter of frustrated honor...your wife is safe; *our* wives have been raped. *Our* fetuses are kicked about like footballs by the legionnaires. Your children go to school, they are not afraid, they are not hungry, they are warm in winter. Look at him (and he pointed to Salah. The child, in a sign of confusion, sought to hide his legs). He doesn't have any legs, his hands are dirty, his head teems with nasty parasites, with lice. He cannot write, he doesn't even remember that he once walked, he is cold and hungry. He is alone. His parents were killed. These are *our* children.[86]

The subject of this plaint is a masculine "we" injured by French colonial violation. It is a "we" that does not include the raped women and mutilated children whose injuries register only indirectly—an appropriative silencing underscored by the judge's discomfiting gesture toward the mute Salah. Mechakra's parenthetical aside "(and he pointed to Salah)" registers the subalternizing force of a gesture that recognizes suffering from below (Salah, who seems to feel exposed) only insofar as it is useful evidence in a criminal plaint articulated from the point of view of a citizen-to-be of a nation-state that does not yet exist.

The judge's charge against French conscript François Gaspard is also riven. He traces a counterhistory of Europe's twentieth-century wars from the perspective of a colonized masculine "nous," citing a series of atrocities that echo back to massacres carried out by Pélissier, who asphyxiated an entire tribe at the Dahra caves in 1845, and St. Arnaud, who did the same, also in 1845. The judge recites a litany of crimes that has become a familiar script:

> In 1914, our fathers died so that yours, who were still in the cradle, could live. Their exiled bones seek burial.
> In 1939 our brothers died so that you could grow up.
> In 1945 your father raped my mother.

Today, boy, you came to rummage about in my wife's womb and to murder my son in his cradle.
... You hung Djebel Boukhadra (Ouenza). 100 innocent people died. "We mount you like automatons and we loose you on populations that have done nothing to you"*
In Mesloula (Ouenza) women and children who were sheltering in a cave were gassed in the style of Pélissier.
You torch our forests, you torch our villages. Saint-Arnaud is rejoicing in his grave.
[*Footnote in the text reads "El Moudjahid 1957."][87]

Mechakra's sly footnote to *El Moudjahid* here visibly accents the judge's function as mouthpiece of the Algerian nation-state-to-come. Precisely this history is now laid out in the chronological diorama of the Musée du moudjahid that lies in the ground beneath the Maqām al-shahīd; any visitor can walk a series of dated rooms with photos and artifacts that depict each of the violent episodes listed in the judge's speech.

This maquisard's judgment is swift and impartial, executed as a correction of a banal arithmetic that had so long authorized colonizing massacre and the wholesale conscription of Algerians as fodder for European wars. He instructs the condemned harki to recite the shahāda and sentences the French conscript to death, pronouncing on behalf of a collective "nous" in his "cavernous" voice: "Nous sommes justes avec nos ennemis" (We are just with our enemies).[88] Behold the act of judgment that founds a new state: drawing the line between violence that is justified and violence that is not.

But Mechakra's scripting makes it difficult for a reader *not* to notice that the judge's "nous," however justified its grievance may sound, does not speak on behalf of everyone in the scene. For instance, the "nous" pointedly excludes those characters through whose silent observations Mechakra constructs the scene. This staging of a fictional tribunal opens a fissure in the "nous" of national unity that the judge's grammar is designed to close, making it difficult to read this scene of judgment without asking: *Is* this sentence just? By making perceptible an act of founding foreclosure and putting into question the authority of the FLN to adjudicate matters of justice, Mechakra unsettles and challenges the narrow nationalist and masculinist construction of Algerian citizenship (as Arabic-speaking-Muslim-male) and she also opens a dispute about what kinds of voices should count and be heard as justice claims.

The chapter's last word belongs not to the tribunal judge but to the narrator's heterogeneous "nous" positioned in the shadows of the tribunal scene, such that his act of judgment is reframed by their acts of mourning. She, Kouider, and Salah do not witness the offstage execution of the condemned prisoners, but they hear it—"We heard a savage cry."[89] They find charred human remains outside the cave the following morning, after the maquisards have departed, and they bury these desecrated corpses with their own dead: "The next day, Kouider and I were doing a round in the maquis. Lying a few hundred meters from the cave was a partially burned man. We buried him with the others."[90]

The act of burial extends the dignity of mourning to the archetypal enemies of the state, a harki and a French soldier. These are the unmournable, despised war dead whose names will never be engraved on stone at the Maqām al-shahīd; in particular, harkis were targeted for massacre and expulsion, their names deliberately erased from national record after 1962. But Mechakra's narrator pronounces sacred liturgies over the graves of the dead she buries ("I cleared my throat and again took up my role as Imam"), highlighting her own renegade status both as imam *and* as an Antigone figure who cares for the bodies of the dead excluded by law from the Algerian nation-state.[91] These acts of unauthorized mourning subvert and resist the FLN judge's version of justice.

Mechakra's staging registers the silence and exclusion of a founding dispossession in which those most damaged do not speak or participate in the juridical process that symbolically founds the authority of the new state, but her poetics do something else entirely. The language of this scene multiplies threads of testimony in a way that surrounds the judge's "nous" with a chorus of narratives and voicings that elude and exceed it. Literary language, haunting in this way, becomes a supplement to the language of the law and of state-sanctioned historiography.

As the narrator tends to the bodies of dying soldiers in her cave hospital, she imagines the grief of a woman who does not yet know that her husband has been killed: "His wife had already promised to give his name to the child he was going to father."[92] When she takes a portrait of a woman from the hands of a dead man, she imagines herself in the place of the woman in the photograph: "I saw her eyes then imagined my own."[93] As she watches another soldier die after amputation, she inhabits his mother's powerful and solitary grief:

One of the wounded let out a sigh.
I went back to the amputees. They all had fevers; their condition was less than encouraging.
Somewhere, a mother was praying on her knees, eyes turned skyward.
She did not know that her son was on the brink of leaving her, somewhere in a snow covered cave.

> She would have crossed the plain and the mountain to come collect the last breath of her child who, before dying, began to speak of her.
> Her heart had beaten next to his; she had made herself younger to allow him to grow up. She would have crossed the plain and the mountain to whisper to him one last time the things that she said only to him and that no one else knows.[94]

These passages also gesture toward how the lives of others speak in ways that are irreducible to writing. Of Kouider, her wounded friend, she observes: "His forehead furrowed with lines, his large hands criss-crossed with turgescent veins that spoke for him, silent witnesses to the numerous years that enfolded him."[95] To Salah, the legless orphan who does not know how to write but yearns to, she offers: "You will carve yourself a flute, you'll whistle your music; it's a writing that speaks. It has the strength of multiple writings."[96]

Mechakra's intricately composed scene creates a space to register ephemeral traces of grief and mute testaments that the protocols of the justice tribunal exclude. Twenty years later she further explodes the juridical limits of testimony and plaint by unleashing a torrent of such foreclosed voices in the dialogic poetics of *Arris*.

Arris is trying to find his way back to home village whose name and location he does not know. He speaks to Nassa, his wife whom he does not love; he is hearing voices, including his mother's, but barely remembers the language in which they address him. He also hears the voice of "the patriarch" who was head of his mother's tribe in the Aurès. Much like the FLN tribunal judge of *La grotte éclatée*, the patriarch recounts a history replete with carnage, yet articulates a differently configured "nous" in his macabre description of an immense charnel field filled with the skeletons of newborn babies:

> There exists, very close, very close, said the Patriarch, a mass grave, gaping, where the skeletons of newborns lie in a ghetto to the scale of our fathers' anger. Little things, mouths still open on their mother's breast who, despite the nails embedded in her bones, still holds them tight. A page of history to be added to countless others in our history, of human history. The Nazi, Vietnamese, Palestinian, South African ghettos...!
> Must we put all of history on trial?[97]

This is the only reference in *Arris* to specific historical situations and places aside from mention of the Aurès. The sentence links a series of ghettos, from those created by Nazis to Vietnam, Palestine, and South Africa. The patriarch's question ("Must we put all of history on trial?") sounds skeptical; it also anticipates and inverts Rahmani's literary efforts to put all of French colonial history on trial. Mechakra's patriarch suggests that a legal proceeding may not be the right method for doing justice to the millions of skeletal infants and the bones of so many crucified mothers that actually constitute the dark book—or charnel field—of human history.

After posing this question, the narrative voice splits and multiplies. A chorus of questions crowd the page. Unlike the "nous" spoken by the FLN maquisard-judge, this "nous" is shifting, many-gendered, and does not point *at* those who have been mutilated and violated but speaks with them. A parent addresses a child whose throat has been slit and eyes torn out while his mother watched: "What did you understand, my little one, when the murderer's knife cut into your chest and tore out your eyes under your mother's frozen gaze and the gazes of so many other mothers mute with terror?"[98] Another speaks to an abandoned child whose name was never recorded in a birth register: "Who knows you, you the anonymous one whose name does not figure even on the register of newborns?"[99] A child addresses a mother who weaves a tapestry whose colors are likened to the sound of a weeping flute: "Who knows you, you the mother, my mother who wove for years the carpet, the painting where all the colors intertwined with a harmony that grieved the fugitive's flute?"[100] Such shifts multiply within a single sentence addressed to those whose fingernails have been torn out, who have been disemboweled, or raped: "Surprised, oh son of my mother, oh son of my sister, oh my son, they first tore your nails out, then disemboweled you. Surprised, oh my sister, they violated your body and drank your blood."[101]

These plaints are qualitatively different from those spoken by citizens (or proto-citizens) to address a judge with grievance and evidence. Mechakra opens a plurivocal register for lamentation and for questions spoken by subjects whose identities are resolutely indeterminate, yet whose speaking is resolutely intimate, specific, and idiomatic. In every instance the dead and lost are addressed with tenderness as *tu*. The section concludes with a series of questions that concern how one person among this multitude of the dead will be remembered: "Who is there to speak of you and to draw a portrait of you at the place where you died? ... In other countries, women look like you. What historian, what poet will speak you [*te dira*] one day? And you, my brother who was flayed and then crucified alive. The murderer's nails struck bone and you said nothing. Today, has a wall been built where you died, a wall where the helpless [*désemparé*] might come to weep?"[102] What historian or poet will write the memory of the damned, the skinned alive, the crucified, the one who could not say a word when her killer's nails scratched against her bones? Who will place a monument on the site where you died, as a memorial to grieve for the distressed and the damned? Mechakra's finely woven texts both ask and answer these questions, in the way of a protective shroud placed with incalculable care over the body of a beloved.

Shattered Stones: *La grotte éclatée* | *Arris*

In *La grotte éclatée*, an especially strange fragment appears just after the novel's midpoint rupture, in the midst of a careening dialogue between the narrator and her psychiatrist at the Centre psychiatrique de la Manouba in Tunis. The narrator—herself grief-stricken and shattered—speaks unexpectedly of her sorrow over losing a beloved fragment of a French war monument, a granite angel that stands above the treacherous ravine carving through the city of Constantine. In *Arris*, a network of especially strange images appears as the dying mother observes her body's disintegration into stone fragments and bones. Stone fragments, rubble, ruin, remnants—such is the antimonumental material with which Mechakra constructs her anarchival poetics of memory. The narrator of *La grotte éclatée* wakes in 1958 on a page directly after the caesura marking the cave bombing. The explosion is never described but appears instead as a list of dates and phrases in what reads like the diary entry of a ghost. The repeated date "October 1958" arrests the temporal sequence that had to this point organized the narrative fragments to resemble a soldier's war diary; here, one date skips like a broken record, shattering sequence, arresting time:

> —October 1958—Death of companions. Explosion of the cave.
> —October 1958—I died.
> —October 1958—napalm took Salah from me.
> —February 1958—Little murdered schoolchildren didn't even have the time to understand that they were dead.
> —October 1958—Kouider rescued my body from forgetting.
> —October 1958—Kouider smelled his burnt flesh.
> —October 1958—I wished to lose memory.[103]

Another date intrudes in the series of repetitions ("February 1958"), along with the fleeting image of murdered schoolchildren who do not yet know that they are dead. This is the date of an infamous aerial bombardment by French military planes of the Tunisian border town of Sakiet Sidi Yousef. The bombing targeted an FLN base that was sending arms and fighters into the maquis in the Kabyle and the Aurès, but sixty-eight Tunisian civilians, including schoolchildren, were killed. Here, those spectral children silently populate Mechakra's lines.

On the subsequent pages, a hospital room dialogue stages a dispute over the status of such ghosts. Upon waking, the narrator's eyes first fall on an anachronous *El Moudjahid* dated 1945, a decade before the newspaper existed in any form: "I scanned the first lines, I read 'Sétif' 'Guelma.' I put the newspaper down. I closed my eyes."[104] A doctor appears, alien with his white coat and scrutinizing gaze. When he begins to ask questions, she defies his clinical realism by calling a chronology of war dates fiction:

—Are you crying?
—No.
—You read the newspaper?
—I don't know.
—It's an old article, from 1945.
—I don't believe it. Perhaps we made it up.
—May 1945, November 1st, 1954, Bugeaud, Emir Abdelkader.
—Made up.[105]

When the doctor gestures to the patient's missing hand, seared off by the bomb, she does not acknowledge its absence but instead envisions her hand ritually blessing the heads of dead children at Sakiet Sidi Yousef:

—Your burned hand.
—My hand had crowned my sons' foreheads with a farewell caress, sun-filled memory from Sakiet. It kept for me the song of a child walking through brambles and whom they loved. I saw the daisies moan in the halo of a song covered with snow and with sand, I saw the brambles turn red and I loved the little girl.[106]

Asked by an FLN psychiatrist about her own wounds, she answers in poetry that conveys infinite tenderness for the dead children at Sakiet whom she claims as kin.

A fissure opens with the date "May 1945" as the narrator describes her love for a stone monument that stood high above the Rhummel River on one of the most notorious cliffs of the city of Constantine. The rhythm and logic of her language eludes her doctor's attempts to bring her back to a shared reality:

I loved a statue. She towered over the abyss in Constantine. It was my freedom. Then, one day, they wounded her; she defied the curfew. She bled, you weren't able to save her. My statue is dead. Her corpse? A stone.

—Your statue still looms over the abyss in Constantine.
—Made up.[107]

As the doctor points out, the stone angel to which the narrator refers does, in fact, exist; to this day, she crowns the World War I monument that was built by the French in 1918 on the vertiginous cliff above Constantine's deepest ravine just above the Sidi M'Cid Bridge—but this narrator's story concerns a different kind of historical truth.

The narrator envisions this stone angel as a beloved wounded and destroyed in 1945—"On me l'a blessée" (They hurt her [from me]), she laments; "On m'a tué ma statue (They killed my statue [from me])."[108] She implicates the FLN doctor in the angel's destruction. When the stone angel was shot in the lungs during Christmas 1945 ("They shot a bullet straight into her lungs"), her skull revealed an older wound from the previous world war: "In the hospital they found a large wound in the skull. You said it was from the 1914–1918 trenches."[109]

Here, Mechakra's disrupted temporal scansion transforms a national monument into renegade symbol charged with memory of violations that far exceed her narrator's own. As the tirade against the FLN doctor continues, the "vous" she blames for destroying her beloved statue begins to resound as plural: "Vous avez dit aussi qu'elle avait dépassé l'homme et ses lois. Vous avez plongé vos doigts dans sa poitrine. Vous avez retiré une feuille d'un carnet: mon portrait pendu par un jet de sang au pont Sidi M'Cid, au-dessus d'un cratère enragé qui crachait une pluie de projectiles enflammés couverts de chair brûlée." (You said that she had surpassed man and his laws. You plunged your fingers into her chest. You pulled out sheet of paper from a notebook: my image, hanging by a stream of blood at the Sidi M'Cid Bridge, above a rabid crater spitting a shower of flaming projectiles covered with burnt flesh.)[110] This macabre composite of nested images—fingers reach inside a ribcage and pull out a notebook page bearing a photograph hanging from a stream of blood suspended from the Sidi M'Cid Bridge over the enraged crater of the Rhummel River spitting fiery projectiles and burned flesh—reads like dream condensation. The haunted superimposition of images also distills centuries of collective memory of violation and death at a site otherwise unmarked, as if to answer the question later articulated in *Arris*: Who is there to speak of you and to draw a portrait of you at the place where you died? Who will place a monument there to grieve the distressed and the damned?

In Constantine, the Sidi M'Cid Bridge is suspended over an abyssal ravine beneath an impressive rock formation called Kef Chkara, which is also one of the place names incanted by *La grotte éclatée*'s narrator to the child Arris.[111] The site has also been called, in French translation of the Arabic toponym, "Le rocher du sac" (the Rock of the Sack) and also, in French Orientalist fantasy, "Le rocher des femmes adultères" (the Rock of Adulterous Women). These toponyms register legends that have marked the treacherous ravine as site of suicide and execution for millennia.¹¹² The ravine over which Kef Chkara towers—where a French war monument in fact still stands, although Mechakra's fiction takes this angel for a different line of flight—is also a mass grave. It is a vernacular "lieux de mémoire" that has accumulated untold numbers of broken bodies and bones, a violence channelled by Mechakra's hallucinatory hospital room dialogue.

This hospital dialogue ends as elegy in which the narrator remembers her statue alive, as a beloved beside whom she had once walked the winding streets of Constantine:

> She sat down on the ground. I sat next to her.
>
> She brought her hands to her face and wept softly. I pulled the embrace of my gaze away from the statue and left. Outside, bells were ringing. That night I dreamed that I emerged onto the surface of a flat, empty world at the end of which my statue was crying, her head in her hands. And then, on a day when Constantine was listening to the wind playing in the trees of her ravine, then running through the gorges while making her bridges sway, one day when Constantine seemed powdered with green, they killed my statue [on m'a tué ma statue].¹¹³

FIGURE 3.2. "Constantine—Le rocher des femmes adultères," antique postcard from the Collection de cartes postales anciennes de Constantine, overseen by the Association des amis de Constantine d'hier et d'aujourd'hui (ADCHA).

MOURNING REVOLT 133

The dreamlike scene is punctuated by a description of a dream in which the narrator swims up from unknown depths to emerge on the surface of a flat and silent world where she finds her statue standing at the brink of a void, weeping with her head in her hands. Mechakra takes us with her to the edge of an abyss. Her language invades and disrupts the iterative lexicon of the nation-state, figuratively shattering its concrete monuments into enigmatic shards that she wields as instruments all her own. This makes of literature a site for mourning deaths that have no written place in history, and a space to convey unauthorized love for lives outside the reach of reason or of law.

Shattered imagery forges a link between the broken stone angel of *La grotte* and the mother-narrator of *Arris*. As dialogic shifts accelerate toward the novel's conclusion, the maternal voice documents her own body's disarticulation. She depicts her body as a decimated surrealist city, breaking apart cell by cell to mingle with the rubble of a stone city designed by a fastidious architect:

> My body is another city. One might say a surrealist city. The stone that I am, slipping into the city, assumes its form. I become the misshapen reflection of a city where the architect, enamored with perfection, goes so far as to calculate the height of walls to the nearest millimeter, so that one stone won't jut out past another. Without a doubt. It takes just a quick glance to see all of the beauty in it. Boldly I examine my irregularities and find them to be a singular beauty.
>
> The city devours me until all of my being is annihilated . . . [114]

Next, she envisions her body becoming more like the stone caves and ravines of the Aurès mountains—much like the granite of Kef Chkara from which a statue might be carved: "I still look like the stone from where I come. I look like those incomplete sculptures, the ones that we cannot yet define, that we'd like to tear away from their creators to make something out of them."[115] As her body disintegrates, she reflects on the masculine impulse to build monuments—"delirium of stone made by man to channel his anguish, faced with his own vulnerability"— but figures her own disintegration in terms not of vulnerability but revolt: "One day, something awful awakened in me, something was born. Revolt."[116] Ironically, her body becomes the very soil and rubble of an urban terrain whose laws and institutions reject her, a subversive invasion: "I hate the city whose form I have assumed and who indefinitely rejects me."[117]

The point of view shifts again, as Arris completes his quest by finding a way back to this site: "My adoptive mother showed me the country and the hospital where I was sold."[118] He finds a dusty dossier in the hospital archive that contains his mother's fingerprint in place of a signature—"I thumb through the file in an office as dusty as archives. I find my mother's fingerprint."[119] Then he hires a guide to drive to a mountain village that he finds abandoned and destroyed: "There, I found no living soul. A few walls were still standing; the rest had collapsed and were covered with dust."[120]

Arris does not yet know it, but in this stone rubble he has found his mother. She is a pile of bones that he does not at first recognize: "With the help of my guide, I find a skeleton covered in skeins of long white hair and a weaving loom."[121] Arris also discovers the gravestones in the village cemetery—"le cimetière de l'oubli" (the cemetery of forgetting)—where he cannot find his mother's grave, so he visits the neighboring village to speak in broken Chaouia with a hundred-year-old sage who tells him what he needs to know: "They all left. Only the mother of Arris stayed behind, waiting for him."[122] Arris realizes that the bleached, unburied bones he had seen in the ruined village are his mother's remains.

The novel ends, like the previous one, with a burial, but this time the ritual is not solitary. A community of strangers come from the neighboring village, offering hospitality "to bring the cemetery out of forgetting."[123] They stay with Arris as he digs a grave, and stand beside him as he completes the burial by protectively covering his mother's bones with her tattered shroud: "With infinite tenderness, I bury my mother.... I hesitate for a long time before deciding to cover the body of Little mother. I pull back her white hair and, according to custom, consent to her complete burial."[124]

The text concludes with a sudden shift from the first person to a distant third, expanding the visual field as if to position the reader within the circle of hospitable strangers who stand beside Arris watching as he completes the burial ritual: "He watches the peasants surrounding him, as silent as death.... He tries to piece together his mother's tales.... He takes his head in his hands and closes his eyes. He doesn't bother to wipe his face of the dust mixed with sweat and tears."[125] The novel's concluding words are given over to this crowd. The hundred-year-old sage breaks the silence, and the people speak in unison:

> The silence is broken by the 100-year-old man:
> —Arris has returned, the widow is no more! And all the people say:
> —Amin! Amin! Amin![126]

Mechakra's œuvre here ends with the triple incantation of a word spoken in collective assent, affirmation, and acceptance. Whether Arabic, Hebrew, Greek, Aramaic, Latin, or Chaouia, this word closes a haunted supplication; it completes a long lament.

Amnesty, Amnesia, *Arris*

Reading *La grotte éclatée* and *Arris* is a lesson in what might be made of grief besides a national war monument. Mechakra's poetics cast the literary text as a protective shroud that carefully covers what is exposed and vulnerable, and that lays loving claim to what is dispossessed and banished. Her work's preoccupation with the ghosts of the disappeared and forgotten also takes on new force when read in the immediate aftermath of the 1990s in Algeria, when the charged term *shahīd* and acts of public mourning also assumed new political valences.

In October 1988, the police attacked demonstrators in the streets of Algiers. The shock of witnessing a state led by the once-revolutionary vanguard turning its force directly against Algerian citizens unleashed critical reflection among intellectuals concerning the FLN's monopoly on the narrative and legacy of the independence war. In her *Le blanc de l'Algérie* (1995), written to mourn and contest the bloodletting then underway in Algeria, Assia Djebar pinpoints the uncanny repetition of colonizing violence in the structure of the postcolonial state at this moment. Specifically, she figures the transmission as a hand-to-hand transfer of bloodied and infected torture instruments: "How, in Algiers, dark city, does the hand-off happen between yesterday's butchers and today's?"[127]

This is a version of a question raised by many Algerians during the 1990s, a preoccupation with infection prefigured by Mechakra's image of dirty surgical knives in the hands of FLN functionaries circumcising "all the sons of the shuhadā'" to make them legitimate members of the new political community.[128] This was also a warning articulated by Fanon at the cusp of independence, as Djebar points out: By what deadly operation did the "glinting grey of metallic instruments" pass from the hand of the former torturer to the hand of the formerly tortured?[129]

Writing in 1995, Djebar denounces the dangerous ideology saturating the term *shahīd* and proposes to disrupt state discourse by semantic substitution: "The tribute in hot corpses from Algeria being reborn, panting, caught in a trance, will it glint in the sun: the *shahids* or the *shouhadas*, as it was said, that is literally 'martyrs in the name of God'? Why not the *abtals*, war heros, the volunteers, who willingly gave their lives, their ardor, why already this hyperbole and in a questionable consensus? We needed Fanon, to protest semantically: he, more than anyone, ready to take out the scalpel of his lucidity!"[130] *Baṭal* (pl. *abṭāl*) refers to someone brave, a champion, a war hero; it is the term for the protagonist of a literary narrative or a theatrical performance. Djebar endorses its secular valence as an act of protest against a hyperbole that sanctifies blood sacrifice with divine justification. Her metaphor suggests that a semantic cut, inspired by Fanon's scalpel, might interrupt the infected transmission of this dangerous word, as if to lance and drain a festering wound. She invokes Fanon's lucid insight, calling for a recognition of historical continuities and repetitions rather than a clean break with the colonial past.

The Bouteflika regime staked its legitimacy on a claim that it won the fight against terrorists in 1999. Yet, given that the "dark decade" that followed October 1988 was characterized by pervasive violence on the part of terrorist groups *and* state and military forces—to the degree that many claim it is impossible to know who was abducting, killing, massacring, and torturing whom—the official claim of Bouteflika's regime is questionable at best. This politically useful opacity ("Who killed whom?") was institutionalized by amnesty laws that legislated impunity by presidential decree for the widespread terror that Bouteflika's regime claimed to have decisively ended, yet in which key members of the ruling party, police, and military were surely complicit.

Under the euphemistic description of "national tragedy" Bouteflika oversaw two sets of amnesty measures: the Civil Harmony Law put to referendum in 1999 (using Article 41 of this law, Bouteflika passed a presidential decree in 2000 granting amnesty to members of the Armée islamique du salut [AIS] and the Ligue islamique pour la dawa et le djihad [LIDD]) and the "Charter for Peace and National Reconciliation" proposed by the president in 2005, put to referendum and quickly approved by the cabinet in 2006 before it could be debated by parliament, which was out of session. The "reconciliation" charter effectively issued blanket amnesty for the armed forces and state-armed militias that had operated during the 1990s, a move denounced by international human rights organizations such as Amnesty International and Human Rights Watch. These laws created conditions of narrative and juridical impasse that continue to make it very difficult for survivors and scholars to gain clarity concerning the violence of that recent past.

In short, it is squarely in the current regime's interest that much of what happened during the late 1980s and 1990s never come to light. To this day, members of the Collectif des familles des disparus stand together in public squares and at bus stops in cities across Algeria with photographs of their vanished loved ones, stark reminders of the uncounted and unburied dead whose absences continue to haunt the present. The names of the disappeared regularly appear in ephemeral graffiti on walls across the capital city. Activist documents like the collection of torture testimonies *Cahier noir d'octobre*, compiled and published by a group of lawyers in Algiers in 1989, refer to *these* dead as shuhadā'. It is a pointed rhetorical move that disputes the state's authority to determine who counts as shuhadā', given that the disappeared are widely believed to be victims of state repression, abduction, torture, and execution.

At precisely the moment that *La grotte éclatée* was reissued for the last time (2000), Mechakra had also just published *Arris* after years struggling to write while grappling with the acute symptoms of her own psychiatric disturbance. Her direct supervisor at Drid Hocine Hospital, Dr. Mahfoud Boucebci, was stabbed to death at the hospital's gate in June 1993—the morning after he had founded the committee to investigate the truth about the assassination of novelist and journalist Tahar Djaout (Djebar's *Le blanc de l'Algérie* is also dedicated to Boucebci, who appears as a ghost haunting Djebar at her writing desk, silently imploring her to write). Dr. Boucebci's murder took place almost literally on Mechakra's doorstep, in direct line of sight from the windows of her house on the hospital grounds. The identity of Boucebci's murderers remains unknown to this day.

The most recent edition of *La grotte éclatée*, published by ENAG in 2000, bears on its cover a small print of the oil painting *Les aveugles* (*The Blind*) by M'hamed Issiakhem, the modernist painter who was a friend of both Kateb and Mechakra.[131] On the painting is hand printed an unsigned verse. It is an unmarked citation from Kateb's tragedy *Les ancêtres redoublent de férocité*, a play that was staged just once in Paris in 1967. This play belongs Kateb's trilogy *Le cercle des représailles*, modeled on the Aeschylus's *Oresteia* in ways that provoke contemplating the tragic cycles of bloodletting that took place in Algeria *after* independence. A new preface to the 2000 edition of *La grotte éclatée* suggests that Mechakra herself chose Issiakhem's painting with Kateb's handwriting for the cover of her novel.

Mechakra's added prefatory note begins by citing the unattributed handwritten verse, including a footnote:

> ...Nous qui vivons au passé
> Nous la plus forte des multitudes
> Notre nombre s'accroit sans cesse
> et nous attendons du renfort...
>
> We who live in the past
> We the strongest of multitudes
> Our number increases without end
> And we await reinforcements...[132]

Mechakra's footnote does not specify a source, but simply offers that she transcribed this handwritten verse from Issiakhem's canvas. In Kateb's play, the lines above are spoken by a dead character incarnated as a vulture. The vulture speaks of a decimated tribe who populate the afterlife and impatiently await armies of future dead who will soon come to join their swelling ranks. Mechakra's paratextual gesture—choosing this particular painting, composing this enigmatic preface, and accenting this striking verse spoken by ancestral ghosts in a play modeled on a cycle of Greek tragedies—suggestively reframes her 1979 novel for readers in the immediate wake of the *décennie noire* (black decade). It both foregrounds the tragic quality of her revolutionary war narrative and also subtly invokes the Greek sense of *krypte*, a root of the French word *grotte*—linking Mechakra's exploded cave both to tombs (*crypt*) and to secrets (*kryptein*; to hide).

Issiakhem's painting resembles the color and texture of stone. This recalls the subterranean caves of the Aurès, the rocky terrain of a village called Arris, and the massive cliff above Constantine called Kef Chkara. In the painting, two faint human figures face in the same direction, to the right—a future space for a French reader, a past for a reader of Arabic, yet the visual poetics of this image suspend the politics of language in postcolonial Algeria. The taller figure holds a dim lantern. A ghost seems to follow them, its arm raised, its shroud falling at their backs. In her new prefatory note, Mechakra describes her own eavesdropping on private conversations between her dead friends Kateb and Issiakhem in the foyer of a home in Ben Aknoun, in 1981. She claims to remember a whispered exchange between them and to have recorded this in a notebook, yet she offers only a partial transcript of sentence fragments and ellipses, followed by a promise: "A day will come when I will write this testimony kept intact."[133]

Mechakra's secretive gesture—her promise of a transcript unwritten, inaccessible, but intact—suggests that *La grotte éclatée* should be read as fragment of a hidden or lost text, as if what is most important remains absent from its pages. Mechakra's revisions to the 1999 paratext of *La grotte éclatée* mark her text with the opacities of that difficult moment. Her promise of a future in which she will write testimony that is intact but not yet recorded invites us to read *La grotte éclatée* as a prophetic and dissident text oriented not so much to the past as it is to the future. This also invites us to read *Arris*, published the same year as these paratextual revisions, by the light of the same promise of a testimony to come. In no way can Mechakra's second novel be said to be "about" the Algerian civil war in any thematic or representational sense, yet Mechakra also gave her text a title that is the same multivalent proper name incanted in the lamentations that run throughout *La grotte éclatée*. It is as if, speaking back after 1999, *Arris* can finally answer questions raised by the mujāhida narrator of *La grotte éclatée*: "I believed in heros," says Arris. "Today, I know better. There are no heroes who are not also martyrs. Each of us is, in our own way. Slave or free."[134]

In *La grotte éclatée*, poetic disfiguration and shattering of the standard revolutionary chronology creates an alternate line of transmission through the mujāhida narrator's incantatory address to her mutilated child Arris. Twenty years later, *Arris* stretches this dialogic form of address to its limits. The haunted poetics woven between the two novels create an alternate epistemological frame for testimonies that sound in languages and forms distinctively unlike those imposed by heroic narratives of sacrifice and martyrdom that have been sanctioned and monumentalized by the FLN. Mechakra carves open space to grieve what the state's legal frameworks have rendered invisible, shattering and disfiguring the enshrined term *shahīd* to make of it a more malleable instrument capable of sounding out all those plaints and laments that have gone unheard for far too long.

4

Open Elegy

Je suis comme l'aigle blessé
L'aigle blessé entre les ailes
Tous ses enfants se sont envolés
Et lui ne cesse de pleurer . . .

I am like the wounded eagle
The eagle wounded between his wings
All of his children have flown away
And he does not cease weeping . . .
—Fadhma Aïth Mansour Amrouche

All poetry is political poetry, concerned
mainly with rewriting the future.
—Mahmoud Darwish

Decade, Year, Month, and Day

Waciny Laredj's novel *Sayyidat al-maqām: Marthīyāt al-yawm al-ḥazīn* does not chronicle Algeria's civil war, nor is it—as the back cover of its French translation *Les ailes de la reine* (*The Wings of the Queen*) claims—the "story of a destiny shattered by religious fanaticism."[1] While Marcel Bois's French translation (Actes Sud, 2009), done in collaboration with Laredj, is available in Algiers bookshops today, the original Arabic (Dār al-Jamāl, 1993) is out of print. A concluding authorial signature in the Arabic edition draws attention to the place and time of

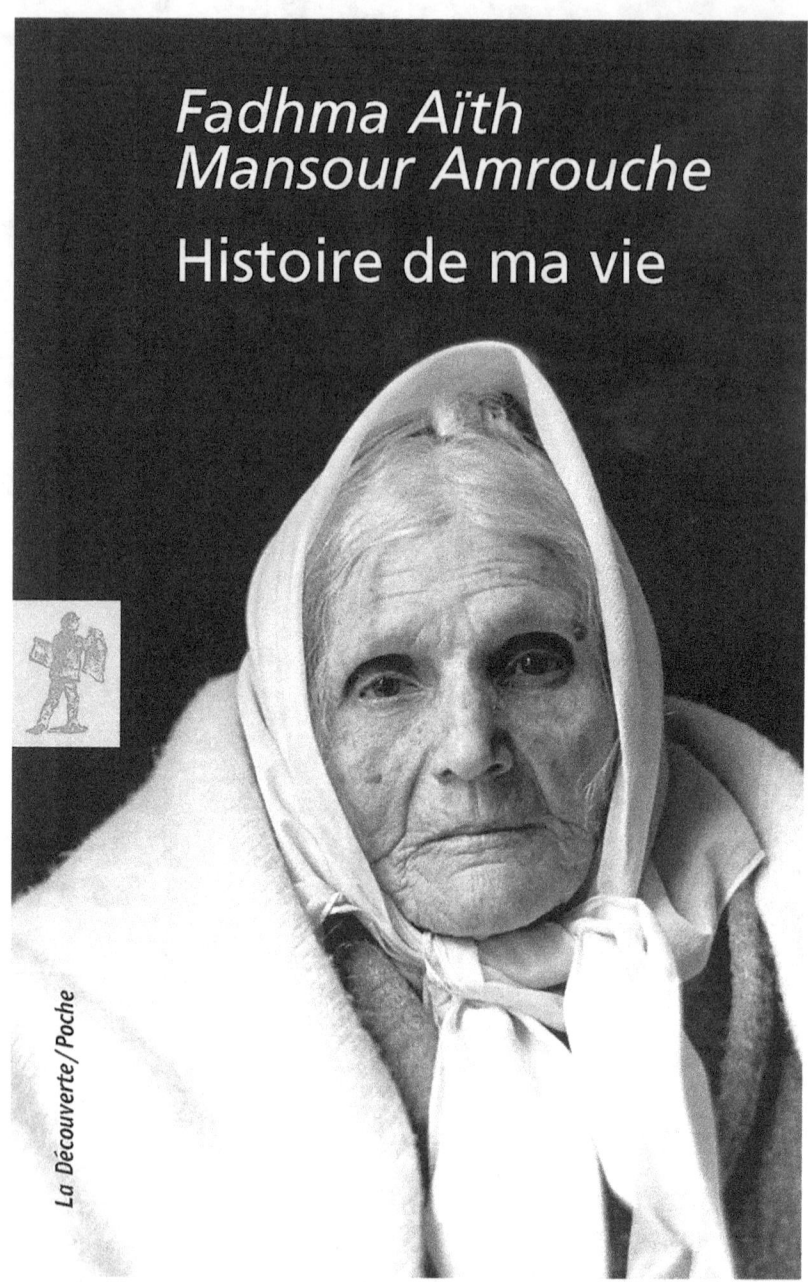

FIGURE 4.1. The cover of *Histoire de ma vie* with a portrait of its author, Fadhma Aïth Mansour Amrouche (Paris: Gallimard, 1968).

its writing: ""al-Jazā'ir al-'āṣima—shitā', rabī' 1991" (Algiers, the capital—winter, spring 1991). The novel's Arabic subtitle (*Marthīyāt al-yawm al-ḥazīn*, or *Elegies of the Sorrowful Day*) does not appear in its French translation.

This is a surprising date to see at the end of the text, given that "winter, spring 1991" falls one year *before* the series of events usually taken to mark the beginning of a war against civilians now widely referred to as Algeria's décennie noire.[2] The paratext on its French translation strongly suggests that Laredj's novel be read as a testament to that turbulent decade: "above all... a lesson in courage... of the men and women who know... that culture is the last rampart against barbarism."[3] Yet the concluding signature in the French translation also reads differently than it does in the Arabic: "Alger, le premier hiver de l'année des cendres" (Algiers, the first winter of the year of ashes). Laredj could not have written such a phrase in the early months of 1991. Published eighteen years after the "year of ashes" it foretells, the translation reflects knowledge of events that Laredj did yet not have when he first wrote the date "winter/spring 1991" on his novel's last page. He might have intuited what was to come, but at the time that Laredj composed *Sayyidat al-maqām*, neither the "dark decade" nor the "year of ashes" had actually yet happened. The novel's French edition thus ever so slightly reframes the novel's temporal scansion, and also subtly mutes its prophetic quality. Resisting the impulse to read this novel through the retrospective frame of a war that had not yet taken place opens a different interpretive horizon for understanding the testimonial stakes of Laredj's aesthetic project. First, this enables a reading of the text not overdetermined by the state's antiterror discourse.[4] That is, adjusting the temporal frame directs a reader's attention away from the décennie noire in general to *octobre noir* in particular—specifically, to October 1988, a date that repeats throughout the text like a refrain and that has recently come into fuller critical focus as the interrupted democratic uprising that precipitated much of the violent repression that took place throughout the décennie noire.[5]

Furthermore, the novel's Arabic subtitle—which vanishes from the French translation—at once amplifies its tragic register and even more narrowly focuses its temporal frame. Notably, in the Arabic clause *marthīyāt al-yawm al-ḥazīn* (elegies of the sorrowful day), the word *day* (*al-yawm*) is singular rather than plural (*al-ayām*). The single day in question is almost certainly "a Friday, October 7th, Autumn of 1988," the day on which the novel's tragic heroine Miryam is shot in the head by an unknown gunman when she kneels to shield a wounded fellow protestor during one of the massive peaceful protests that filled the streets of Algiers in early October 1988.[6]

The novel is set in Algiers on the brink of disaster. Its intricate narrative is framed by a single night that will end with its narrator's own suicide, sometime after October 1988 but before 1991. In the novel's opening lines, this nameless narrator walks the capital's labyrinthine streets in despair after watching his lover Miryam die in his arms at Mustapha Pacha Hospital because her dancing (she is a ballet dancer) had dislodged a bullet that had entered her skull on October 7, 1988. The bereft narrator carries with him a satchel holding the manuscript of an unfinished novel; as he walks, he remembers—his own memories, Miryam's, and myriad others. The single night that serves as narrative frame is also *his* last night, as this roving circumambulation of Algiers concludes with his suicidal leap from Telemly Bridge into the abyss below.

There is no death scene, only a formal interruption of prose with verse. The novel ends with its narrator's vertiginous free fall cut by citation of transcribed *qaṣīda* from a sung lament recorded by the Arabic Andalusian Gharnāṭī musical master Cheikh Ghaffour. This lament is addressed to a lost beloved also named Miryam, music that the free-falling narrator recalls hearing from an open window as he presumably plummets to his death below. Laredj's novel ends in verse; this verse trails off with an ellipsis, followed by the concluding signature that marks the time and place of the novel's writing. This formal and typographic openness with which the narrative concludes is portended by its first sentence: "En cette ville, un immense fracas, une chute vertigineuse!" (In this city, an immense din, a vertiginous fall!).[7]

Laredj thus frames a tale that unfolds against the barely deferred threat of prophesied catastrophe. *Sayyidat al-maqām* poses as the posthumously published reconstruction of that unfinished manuscript its fictional narrator had carried with him in a satchel until his fatal leap from Telemly Bridge. Before jumping, he actually eats his national identification card (CNI no. 124170) and then scatters the pages of his manuscript draft into the wind ("eleven chapters, on the brink of being finished").[8] This happens to be the same number of chapters in Laredj's novel, whose narrator claims repeatedly that he could never find the right ending for a chapter, or for the book. By this cunning metanarrative sleight, the novel resists its own conclusion.

Notably, the novel *also* leaves resolutely opaque the identity of whomever instigated this disaster. The bullet that ultimately kills Miryam and precipitates her despondent lover's suicide was not put there by Islamists in October 1988, but by someone else. Miryam is a ballet dancer obsessed by an unreasonable desire to perform the title role of Rimsky-Korsakov's *Scheherazade* at the Théâtre national in Algiers before the theater is shuttered under pressure from *les Inquisiteurs*, and she ultimately dies after vigorous rehearsal dislocates the bullet that had lodged in her brain during the chaos of the street demonstrations many months prior. As readers learn on the novel's second page, the identity of Miryam's killer is ambiguous: "The bullet is shot from a pistol and the shooter, without realizing it, precipitates an irreparable disaster. Perhaps one of the passersby whom I cross every day in the streets, a young man just out of the national or antinational service. Who knows? Alas!... A soldier is a soldier."[9] The novel both repeatedly underscores the anonymity of this faceless killer and implies that the killer might have been an agent of the state, a problem that puts Miryam in an impossible double bind: "the choice between an anarchic democracy and the 'Inquisitors'!," as she puts it. "Talk about a *situation!*"[10]

The novel's title—*Sayyidat al-maqām*—at first reads like an homage to the dead ballerina, Miryam. The Arabic might be glossed as "the lady of the *maqām*," inviting any reader familiar with the topography of Algiers to associate this *sayyida* (lady) with the massive national monument to the revolutionary war dead that crowns the capital and is widely referred to as *al-maqām*.[11] Miryam is a professional dancer from a working-class family on the outskirts of Algiers. Her mother had used the governmental shahīd pension due to her—as a widow of a "shahīd" who died in the independence war—to buy a cassette player and ballet lessons for her daughter. An orthographic similarity between the Arabic words also makes it possible to *mis*read the title not as *Sayyidat al-maqām* (سيدة المقام), but rather *Shahīdat al-maqām* (شهيدة المقام), a slip that transforms the novel's tragic protagonist herself into a *shahīda*, a martyr-witness for a new time of war.

The Arabic title also calls to mind an image of the kind of Algéroise who would be called *lallaḥūma* in the Algerian Darija spoken in the capital. *Sayyidat al-maqām* is in fact a direct translation into formal Arabic of a vernacular Algerian idiom with deep resonance in the inhabited cartographies of Algiers, where the word *ḥūma* designates not just a neighborhood but a kind of village within the city whose communal lines and links organize urban space and belonging in intricate ways.[12] A lallaḥūma, literally a "woman" of the "ḥūma," or neighborhood, belongs to a specific place; she is known, respected, and considered above reproach.

While the Arabic title thus tethers the text and its heroine to the capital city Algiers, the French translation gives her wings. According to Laredj and his translator and close friend Marcel Bois, the novel's French editors chose this title (*Les ailes de la reine*) because they liked its touch of grace and hope in the face of Islamist fundamentalism. Laredj and Bois had considered other possibilities: *Le sang de la vierge* (*The Virgin's Blood*: too aggressive), *La nuit du viol* (*The Night of the Rape*: too dark), *La dame du sanctuaire* (*The Lady of the Sanctuary*: the most literal). Yet a maqām might be both a spiritual sanctuary—a liminal space between heaven and earth—and a dance hall. It is etymologically tied to the sacred (monument, site, tomb) as well as to political resistance (*muqāwama*) and to nationalism connected to a sense of standing together in place (*qawmiyya*).

The word *maqām* is charged with this semantic and symbolic resonance. It is also haunted by the Darija word *ḥūma* that it silently translates, which even more intimately connects the *sayyida* (or, rather, *lalla*) to a profoundly vernacular and popular Algiers—she belongs to the local ḥūma, more than to the national monument (al-maqām).

Laredj's text is a tribute closely grounded to the place and time of its writing. In fact, it asks to be read as an elegy, or rather, as *marthīyāt* (plural), the genre to which its original subtitle lays claim. The *marthīyā* is among the oldest of Arabic literary genres and the only one that has been unequivocally associated with women for many centuries; the earliest extant examples of Arabic *marāthī* are traditionally credited to obscure women poets from the pre-Islamic era. As the *Encyclopedia of Islam* explains: "a marthīyā is an elegy, a poem composed in Arabic (or in an Islamic language following the Arabic tradition) to lament the passing of a beloved person and to celebrate his merits; *rithā*', from the same root, denotes both lamentation and the corresponding literary genre." The encyclopedia also notes that the origins of this form "may be found in the rhymed and rhythmic laments going with the movements performed as a ritual around the funeral cortege by female relatives of the deceased, before this role became the prerogative of professional female mourners."[13]

The marthīyā is a verse form widely understood to follow the pattern of ritual laments composed and performed by women for the dead. It is also a living poetic form with strong political valences in the present. Mahmoud Darwish experimented with the genre, for example, in "Ṭibāq," a poem that he wrote in honor of Edward Said; this marthīyā appeared in numerous Arabic newspapers and magazines and was widely translated around the world after Said's death in 2003.[14] Given that its function is to publicly announce and allocate grief, the marthīyā can easily become nationalist propaganda; it is in this way closely related to the obituary and to political hagiography, as scholars have noted of its renaissance in twentieth-century Egypt. In contemporary Algeria, certain forms of public mourning are endorsed by the government and monumentalized in those concrete structures that tower over the capital city, while unauthorized forms of mourning that appear in public spaces present a subversive threat.

Read as an infinitely open marthīyā or, rather, as an open compendium of marthīyāt, Laredj's Arabic novel intervenes in the allocation of grievability in postcolonial Algeria, an act with political significance. In her critical reflections on the ways in which expressions of public grief have been withheld from Muslim victims of US military action in the wake of September 11, 2001, and in her studies of the *Antigone* tragedy, Judith Butler has illuminated these political dimensions of grief and mourning. Acts of mourning, according to Butler, do not simply concern the matter "of simple entry of the excluded into an established ontology, but an *insurrection* at the level of ontology, a critical opening up of the question, what is real? Whose lives are real? How might reality be unmade?"[15]

Ontological insurrection of this order is among the principal prerogatives of Laredj's marthīyāt. The 1990s war on civilians remains unresolved despite amnesty laws instituted by presidential decree in 1995, 1999, and 2005. In light of these legal interdictions on certain acts of public plaint or mourning, Laredj's poetics actually make of the literary text a protective sanctuary (maqām) for the kinds of material that would be targeted by law for destruction. In this way, the novel constructs an anarchive of October 1988, a counterhistory of that dark moment when Algerians witnessed "the national army [take] position against the nation."[16] It is a literary performance of what it might look like to save a profoundly vernacular nation from the tyrant state. Laredj's many-voiced elegy opens up the question of whose lives are real; it keeps alive revolutionary questions about how a given reality might be unmade, or made otherwise.

To demonstrate this, I analyze Laredj's Arabic-language novel by the light of its central intertexts, *Alf layla wa-layla* (*The Thousand and One Nights*) and Fadhma Aïth Mansour Amrouche's *Histoire de ma vie* (1968). Laredj's intertextual poetics undermine the politically convenient myth of intractable language and cultural conflict by revealing arabophone, berberophone, and francophone literary spaces to be intimately connected.[17] Moreover, Laredj's translingual elegy channels plaints that are not reducible to the kinds of plaints that might be addressed to the state in public legal tribunals. His haunted fiction anticipates the kinds of calls for justice that have resounded throughout Algerian cities and streets in a grassroots vernacular "symbolic revolution" that has so publicly confronted the ruling political regime beginning in February 2019.

Bouteflika at Sétif, 2012

A speech that president Abdelaziz Bouteflika delivered to a full auditorium in Sétif on May 8, 2012, could have been remembered as his graceful exit from power. Bouteflika was a war hero arriving at the dusk of a three-term presidency that had dawned in 1999.[18] At the time, Bouteflika's speech at Sétif was described in the press as his *discours d'adieu* (farewell speech), taking a cue from his own indication that he was passing the baton to the next generation after doing his best to end the terrors of the 1990s and restore Algeria to stability—his fulfillment of the revolution's promise.

This speech took place two years before the 2014 presidential election that could have respectably concluded Bouteflika's term. It did not, in part because of the outcome of the 2012 national legislative elections that were to take place a few days after this particular speech. The legislative elections were Bouteflika's primary focus on May 8, 2012. Their outcome would in fact entrench FLN hegemony in parliament from 2012 to 2019, a period that Bouteflika's regime used to pass a series of laws—and a completely revised constitution in 2016—that further strengthened the ruling regime's power, and enabled a fragile and ailing Bouteflika to run for and then win an extended fourth term of his presidency (2014–19).[19]

Addressing an audience of Algerian citizens in May 2012, Bouteflika exhorts them to vote in the election that would take place a few days later. The president calls on his listeners in the name of the shuhadā'—"I am addressing you, guardians of the legacy of the shuhadā'"[20]—and urges them to protect national stability by voting rationally and wisely. Although Bouteflika does not name the cancelled legislative elections of 1991–92, they haunt his language like an ominous threat when he predicts that "these elections [the ones about to take place] will be exceptional because of the multiple safeguards we have put in place; they will be clean and transparent so as to meet the expectations of our people."[21]

Those 1992 elections would have been the first pluralist legislative elections since independence. Had they not been canceled, the FIS would have been voted in by the people to hold a ruling majority over the FLN. A state of emergency declared soon after this gave the state's agents unlimited power to repress civilians presumed to be "Islamist terrorists" and supporters of FIS. These state agents included many different groups: the military, the DRS (Département du renseignement et de la sécurité), police, gendarmes, and militias. Bouteflika mentions none of this, of course, but his silences frame what he *does* say, and how. That is, Bouteflika's speech encodes the amnesiac poetics of official discourse; as state poetics shape the discursive space into and against which Laredj's anarchival novel moves, it is worth examining Bouteflika's silences in some detail.

After October 1988, Laredj, like so many Algerians, found himself reckoning not just or even primarily with Islamist violence, but with self-authorizing, legal state terror exercised at the expense of civilians and civil society. This is precisely the language spoken by Bouteflika in his "discours d'adieu" at Sétif in 2012, which can now be reread with retrospective knowledge of the elections that have happened, or almost happened, since (in 2012, 2014, and 2019).

The place (Sétif) and date (May 8) of Bouteflika's speech served as a symbolically resonant staging ground for his exhortation to vote, as he underlines: "From Sétif, a secular and symbolic city, we commemorate today the tragic anniversary of May 8, 1945, in an atmosphere of meditation in memory of the defenseless martyrs—women, men and children who were massacred in a great many regions of this country, notably in Sétif, Guelma, and Kherrata, when they took to the streets peacefully, flags in hand, like the people who defeated Nazism and Fascism, to celebrate the end of the World War in which their people took part, in the hopes of obtaining their legitimate right to dignity and freedom."[22] The symbolic charge of Sétif permits Bouteflika to frame the 2012 elections as a crucial point in a revolutionary chronology of battles and sacrifices. The election would be "a new phase...of democratic progress in your country," "the threshold of a critical stage" for "our Arab-Muslim nation" and for "the State of law and democracy to which we aspire."[23]

In the picture drawn up by Bouteflika, the ongoing revolutionary struggle has distinct and newly configured sides. One side is allied with "all of the shuhadāʿ of May 8, 1945"—including "those locked up in obscure jail cells or bleak camps, burned in forgotten caves or buried in mass graves, unnamed"—while on the other side are "enemies of the country" whom he identifies as "instigators of Fitna," or discord.[24]

This schema permits Bouteflika to identify the state security forces and military as inheritors of the legacy of the "shuhadāʿ" who are pitted against the machine of terror that sows discord and death: "The elements of the popular National Army and all the security corps...have stood up to the death machine and to abject terrorism so that the Republic stands tall, unified and reconciled, dignified, proud and radiant."[25] This is the language of a president trying to establish a performative break with a war that is not finished. He mobilizes the audience's memory of instability and violence to amplify the force of his exhortation on the eve of election: "You whose minds are weighed down by the torments of colonialism and discord [*fitna*], who are aware of the complex dangers facing a geographical region afflicted by upheavals...you will reveal to the world Algeria's shining present and future."[26] Bouteflika's argument is that "peace" and "security" are in fact ongoing states of war against the malevolent danger of "abject terrorism." He calls on citizens to align with the state's military and police force against the enemy, lest the terror and chaos of the recent past return to tear the nation apart. In other words, the nation's present security is tenuous and fragile, secured through ongoing sacrifice and blood tribute: "Liberty and national sovereignty have been recovered at the cost of enormous sacrifices," Bouteflika reminds Algerians, invoking the revolution to connect it to the 1990s conflict: "An equally heavy tribute was paid to preserve the unity of the country and of the republican regime and to sanction security, peace, and reconciliation."[27]

Nasséra Dutour, spokesperson for the Collectif des familles des disparus en Algérie (CFDA) and president of the Fédération euro-méditerranéenne contre les disparitions forcées (FEMED), is in a position to comment on the sacrifices exacted during Bouteflika's presidency in the name of security, peace, and reconciliation. In her 2008 essay "Algérie: De la Concorde civile à la Charte pour la Paix et la Réconciliation nationale: Amnistie, amnésie, impunité," Dutour outlines the amnesty laws overseen by Bouteflika. She does not mince words. "À chaque amnistie," she writes, "correspond l'amnésie" (Amnesia corresponds to every amnesty).[28]

The Algerian government tried to close the book on the 1990s through a series of laws, beginning with the 1995 "Raḥma" (Mercy) Law, followed by the 1999 "Civil Concord" and 2005 "Charter for Peace and Reconciliation" passed by Bouteflika's presidential decree. Of course, Bouteflika does not discuss the details of these laws in his 2012 speech, but they provide critical context for interpreting his battlefield picture and chronology.

All three laws affirm and enforce Bouteflika's narrative that the violence caused by "Islamist terrorists" requires the ongoing, unlimited exercise of state force to preserve national security. Certain articles of these documents—namely articles 44, 45, 46 ("perhaps most ominous" according to a Human Rights Watch report on the amnesty laws), and 47 of the 2005 charter—spell out other sacrifices and tributes exacted.[29] These articles issued blanket amnesty; decreed that legal plaints against any security or defense officers would not be received by Algerian courts; made it a punishable crime to "exploit" the wounds of the national tragedy by writing or speaking in any way that harms the institutions of the democracy, weakens the state, undermines the reputation of the state's agents, or tarnishes Algeria's international reputation; and gave the president unlimited power to put the charter into practice. "This is how the political machine settled the matter [*a réglé le dossier*]," writes Dutour in 2008. "Today there is neither reparation nor justice—just amnesty and amnesia."[30]

The other irony of Bouteflika's dramatic speech at Sétif in 2012 is that his opening description of peaceful protestors waving flags who were violently attacked and repressed by the French police and military (massacre, arrest, disappearance, detainment, torture, and prison camps; all that is invoked in Algerian collective memory by the date May 8, 1945) bears a striking structural resemblance to a series of events that Bouteflika does *not* mention—events that amnesty laws that he oversaw in fact made it a crime to mention publicly. October 1988, when the Algerian military and police turned its weapons and torture techniques on Algerian citizens so visibly, is just one of the dates that does not appear in Bouteflika's exhortation. In Kabylie in 2001, for instance, police and security forces also killed 126 peaceful protestors during what has been called "Printemps noir/Tafsut Taberkant."[31] The expression *Printemps noir* that names this repression alludes both to "octobre noir" and also to "Printemps berbère," the rebellion and repression that took place in 1980. It is *also* a gesture of mourning for the massacres that took place during all of these episodes at the hands of the state's agents. These names chart a counterchronology of rebellion against and confrontation with the state, precisely what Bouteflika's official amnesiac chronology is designed to make disappear.

It is time to reject the long-standing myth of intractable linguistic and cultural conflict in Algeria and to recognize that confrontations with the state move across and between all of Algeria's languages. Reading between the lines of Bouteflika's discourse clarifies why it is problematic to frame the 1990s war on civilians as a *jihād*—or fitna—instigated by Islamist radicals targeting the institutions of secular democracy implicitly allied with Francophonie. This is the gist of paratext designed to appeal to French readers of Laredj's novel by framing his text as the "story of a destiny shattered by religious fanaticism," but it is also a self-reinforcing blind spot that happens to collude with the consequential silencings at work in Bouteflika's speech.

It is also time to disrupt the tragic trope of identity crisis and schizophrenic culture war that not only is implicit in Bouteflika's discourse, but has also dominated scholarship on post-1988 Algeria, as Walid Benkhaled and Natalya Vince have recently argued.[32] They sketch out the simplistic triptych that so often frames discussion of Algerian political conflicts by dividing the scene into three camps: the Arabo-Muslim FLN system, the Islamists, and the pluralists (a category that usually includes women/feminists, Berbers, and secularists). These tropes align with supposed linguistic fissures that stand in as shorthand for ideological positions. The framework itself generates aesthetic works that fit such expectations, at a cost: "Yet the more the same interpretive frames and themes are reproduced, the more they set the expectation of publishers and film funders—and the more these latter—notably in Europe—expect a version of this triptych from Algerian artists, the greater the extent to which alternative frameworks are edited out of public space."[33] Reading *Sayyidat al-maqām: Marthīyāt al-yawm al-ḥazīn/Les ailes de la reine* against the grain of these frameworks provides evidence that anarchival alternatives are already being constructed by writers in all of Algeria's languages, despite tropes and laws designed to disappear counternarratives and critique from public space.

The Last Night

The beguiling compendium of translated tales known as *Alf layla wa-layla* (*The Thousand and One Nights*) is not only a thematic intertext but a governing narrative principle of Laredj's novel. In an interview published soon after his novel's French translation, Laredj calls the *Nights* "a text that has slumbered within me since early childhood... my inevitable reference."[34] Most obviously, its famous frame story—that standoff between Shahrazād and King Shahriyār, staged in Laredj's texts as the Russian ballet with which Miryam is obsessed—provides Laredj with a narrative model for creating what looks to be an infinite compendium of stories, voices, and aesthetic practices generated in the face of threat.[35] Shahrazād is a cunning storyteller who protects herself from a terrorizing killer king by telling him a different tale each night, thus indefinitely deferring her own rape and decapitation.[36] *Sayyidat al-maqām* explicitly channels Shahrazād's defiance in the face of sovereign terror: Miryam's last words on the novel's first pages[37] and the narrator's final words before he leaps to his death are curses aimed at the tyrants in power.[38]

Alf layla is the ur-text of infinite translation, a work that formally resists closure and defers completion. It is an authorless collection of popular stories that have come from so many places, through so many forms, and passed through multiple languages over centuries.[39] As Michael Wood has pointed out, it is important to remember that there are *not* 1,001 nights in the compendium, but rather an uncountable number of them. That is, *Alf layla* is an infinitely open series.[40]

Laredj could have written *Sayyidat al-maqām* in French, but he wrote it in Arabic. Like many Algerians, he is a polyglot: "Being in two languages," as he has put it, "I am in two different writing traditions and I often feel like I am two-headed."[41] After his father died under torture in a Tlemcen prison during the war for independence, his mother worked to support the children and Laredj was raised by his paternal grandmother. He frames his decision to write literature in Arabic as a gesture of love and respect for his grandmother: "My connection to Arabic was first an affective one," he says. "My grandmother, for whom Islam is inseparable from language, from the word, pushed me towards Arabic. Learning Arabic is a gesture of love for this woman who incarnated for me the absent figures of both father and mother."[42]

Laredj's intertextual reworking of the *Nights* is not an inevitable effect of his writing in Arabic, but an aesthetic strategy that takes place within a particular context and with a particular charge. He recounts an illicit moment during Quranic school when he accidentally discovered and then stole a copy of what would become his "inevitable reference," the text that led him to writing: "At the Quranic school, tucked on the same shelf as the sacred texts, I come across a copy of *The Thousand and One Nights* which I steal and read in secret. My becoming a writer was determined by this illicit act. I still keep a copy of the text with me. Reading the *Nights* brought me definitively outside the realm of the sacred."[43]

Like Laredj's decision to write in Arabic, his reference to the *Nights* is an affective and contextual one, not an inevitable effect of his cultural location but an aesthetic act within it. The *Nights* intertext in Laredj's novel can best be understood in terms that Eileen Julien has described as a "rhetorical act through which the writer attempts to resolve aesthetic and social problems."[44] Drawing on the *Nights* as intertextual resource and narrative model is significant not because this positions the writer in a war against Islam, but rather because it positions the text in a dispute over who should speak for Islam, and in what kind of Arabic, in postcolonial Algeria. Laredj embraces Arabic as a supple literary language that is, like any language, open to vernacular experience and to transformation. He counterposes the heterogeneous, popular, and translational heritage of Arabic and of Islam against other versions, wresting the language from the grip of ideologues—including those who would reinforce a misconception that radical dissent or democratic questioning can only or best take place in French in the Maghreb.

Laredj's intertextual strategy improvises on the subversive relation to sovereignty and the orientation to the future that is inherent in the narrative formula of the *Nights* itself. In the introduction to her study *Narratives of Catastrophe* (2009), Nasrin Qader analyzes how the *Nights*' dispossessing narrative structure informs the poetics of narrative (récit) in novels by Boubacar Boris Diop, Tahar Ben Jelloun, and Abdelkébir Khatibi. Qader's reading of the *Nights* as enacting dissent by way of its poetics inspires my reading of Laredj's *Sayyidat al-maqām*. Qader writes:

> *1001 Nights* sets up the scene of the singularity of each night and each tale, infinitely repeated (for the number 1001 is not referential, but rather a sign of continuity), each night and tale threatened with annihilation and open to the future. Therefore the text of *1001 Nights* tells the story of a life, récit, at a distance from the subject. *This life tells its story by telling about other lives.* Shahrazad never speaks of herself, there is no I of narration, except in the formula *balaghanī* (I have heard, it has reached me) which, by its formulaic structure, empties itself of signification.[45]

In Laredj's novel, a narrator recounts what appears to be an infinite series of memories and tales in the space of a single night that is the novel's temporal frame. Its nameless narrator is, like Shahrazād, a dispossessed speaking subject whose own narrative voice teems with the tales of others.

Laredj draws a series of links between the figure of Shahrazād, of the character Miryam dancing the Shahrazād role ("Schéhérazade-Miryam"), and the novel's first-person narrator.[46] The narrator's and Miryam's first-person voices splice so intricately together in passages of Laredj's novel that one perspective becomes almost indistinguishable from the other, rendering mutable the boundaries of the "I" who speaks.[47] This is replicated in Miryam's own stated desire to be possessed by Shahrazād so utterly that she herself becomes transparent: "I am haunted by *Schéhérazade*."[48]

The narrative voice of Laredj's novel is thus, like Shahrazād's, a dispossessed and haunted "I" who recounts the stories he has heard, collecting and refracting the many tales that have reached him over time. This has multiple effects. In Laredj's description of the scene of Miryam's final dance rehearsal, for instance, the narrative voice and actions of Shahrazād *and* of Miryam fuse together in Laredj's language so that the curse uttered by Shahrazād-Miryam on the rehearsal stage could have any number of implied speakers.[49] It reads as an indictment of the "new criminals" destroying the nation: "Shame on you, country who forgets its lovers and its martyrs: you venerate them by morning and condemn them by night. I wish death upon you, new criminals!"[50] While this curse sounds rather obviously directed at Algeria's ruling elite, it also does not have a determinate speaker, which has the effect of transforming the literary text into a clandestine form for expressing otherwise impermissible (soon to be literally illegal) complaints.

Modeled on Shahrazād's mode of address, Laredj's novel elaborates a poetics of haunted testimony that infinitely multiplies the curses, plaints, and lamentations that flicker between its lines. The novel's intertextual poetics empty and open its first-person narrative voice so that it expands to contain multitudes of other stories, references, and citations. This narrative structure is reflected formally throughout *Sayyidat al-maqām*, generating the dazzling impression of a vast compendium of voices arriving from multiple sources, times, and languages. In this way, the novel constructs a model for an open archive composed of traces and remnants of all that is under threat of annihilation in an Algiers under siege. If this anarchival novel is read as elegy, then the elegized are truly *legion*.

At one level, the novel catalogues references that multiply across its pages. The bibliography is heteroglot, transnational, and unsystematic. Laredj includes poets, writers, painters, dancers, choreographers, composers, and singers, such as the Algerian painter-sculptor-writer Mohamed Khadda (42, 67, 72); Salvador Dali (67); Delacroix and Picasso, both of whom painted some of their famous tableaux in the city (140); and Cervantes (140), who was long a prisoner in Algiers (and author of Laredj's second "inevitable reference," aside from the *Nights*).[51] On Miryam's bookshelf sit texts with titles and authors both familiar and obscure: *Madame Bovary, Germinal, L'épopée des Harafiches, Soleil un jour de pluie, Anna Karenina, Les cités de sel, Les cercles de l'orient,* Faulker, Proust, Syrian novelist

Hanna Mina, collections by unnamed obscure poets, alongside her cassette tapes of classical music including Stravinsky, Tchaikovsky, Berlioz, Wagner, Mozart (57–58), and the complete works of the Russian composer Rimsky Korsakov, whom Miryam reveres precisely *because* he created the *Schéhérazade* ballet (61).

The novel also records fragments and excerpts from a broad collection of different works, many of them musical. These fleeting citations accumulate, each one opening up a possible trail for the reader to follow elsewhere: we read the lyrics of the Lebanese singer Fayrouz's "solitary plaint" that emanates from a window near Telemly Bridge, and observe the choreography process of a ballet that combines a musical score from the composer Mohammed Iguerbouchène with script improvised from the Kabyle French narrative *Histoire de ma vie* by Fadhma Aïth Mansour Amrouche, whose cover appears in figure 4.1.[52]

Lyrics from songs by popular Algerian singers also figure prominently in Laredj's text, creating the impression of sounding out a sonic archive that is highly specific to Algiers. For instance, the song "Al-'āṣima" ("The Capital," a common way to refer to Algiers) by Chaâbi singer Abdelmajid Meskoud plays on the car radio as the narrator drives across the city.[53] Chaâbi is a popular, vernacular Algerian musical genre born in the Algiers Casbah in the twentieth century (its name means "popular," of the people; the casbah is an iconic Algiers ḥūma), and Meskoud a local autodidact who only became publicly known with this particular song. Its lyrics connect Laredj's novel closely to the city's own poetics, positioning these lyrics as a vernacular form of lamentation with Hebrew scriptural echoes: "one of the most beautiful texts written of this city at the moment of her collapsing and falling into ruin."[54]

The song "Al-'āṣima" appeared in 1989, a lament for the destruction and disappearances underway in the capital city. This transcribed passage appears as verse in Laredj's text:

> My beautiful Algiers, submerged on all sides,
> You've lost the taste for life. On all sides, they are bursting in.
> Where have all the caftan tailors gone,
> The craftsmen of the medjboud? Disappeared, the silk embroiderers
> And the leather embroiderers!
> Where are the brass-workers, the saddle-makers,
> And the painters?
> Tell me, whomever is listening to me...[55]

These lyrics lament the vanished caftan makers and gold filigree artisans, the lost embroiderers of silk and leather, the painters, the brass workers, the upholsterers, all of those whose artistry and knowledge had for so long composed the urban tissue of the city of Algiers—and whose traces Laredj weaves into his own text with this musical intertext. Laredj's narrator listens to the lyrics, then responds directly to the singer's refrain, asking: "Who will hear you, Abdelmajid, my brother?"[56] Laredj's novel transcribes the lyrics in a way that relays such questions to its readers: Who will really listen to and hear Meskoud's elegy for the vanished artists, customs, traditions, and places of old Algiers, of Al-Bahdja, the splendid Casbah? Who will mourn everything else in the process of disappearing?

A different series of song lyrics appear at various points throughout the novel. They are lines from "Welfi Miryam" sung by El Hadj Mohamed Cheikh Ghaffour.[57] Gharnāṭī is one of three schools of classical music in Algeria thought to have originated in Al-Andalus. The name *gharnāṭī* is an Arabic version of the toponym *Granada*; this musical genre has deep Algerian roots that are grounded in Tlemcen, which is also Laredj's city of origin. Mohamed El Ghaffour, from Nedroma near Tlemcen, is a master of the genre. He won first prize at the 1969 music festival in Algiers for singing "Welfi Miryam," a qaṣīda by the Algerian mystic and poet Cheikh Khaddour Benachour Ezzerhouni (b. 1850) that had been sung before him by master gharnāṭī musicians such as Cheikh Hammada and Cheikh M'hamed Al Anka. The poem's partial transcription in Laredj's text is an act of anarchival protection of an Arabic qaṣīda so subtle and intricate that it takes at least fifteen minutes to perform the entire piece aloud. The poem is also replete with the erotic double entendres of Sufi mysticism; its presence in the novel lays claim to a popular, tolerant form of Islam in all its aesthetic nuance and its Algerian artistry.

The qaṣīda frames the text. Excerpts from "Welfi Miryam" appear as the epigraph to Laredj's novel, and also appear as the novel's last lines. Verse interrupts Laredj's prose to trail off in an ellipsis, and the suspended narrator never hits the ground. The poem is an ode that comprises dozens of verses detailing every subtle attribute of the speaker's beloved, Miryam. An excerpt also appears a few pages before the novel's conclusion, at the point in the narrator's desperate circumambulation of Algiers that pivots his footsteps at last toward the final destination, Telemly Bridge. Here, it becomes abruptly clear to the reader how this night is going to end. The passage reads in full:

> When I got to the ambulance entry gate, I thought of my friend, the poetess Safia Kettou, whom the city had killed. She threw herself from the top of the Telemly Bridge that connects the lower city to its heights. Without giving myself over to grand reflections, I let my body wander through the

streets where puddles had multiplied and I listened to Ghaffour's voice rising up from the coffee bar next to the hospital; a sad and mournful voice...

Your absence burns me, Miryam, tender companion!
What has become of you, my lovely one?
...And your gaze, full of promises? Greet me from there,
Miryam, my tender companion.[58]

The idea to jump from Telemly Bridge comes to him from elsewhere, just as the lyrics of the elegy come to him from elsewhere, overheard emanating from a bar near the hospital. As for Telemly Bridge, it is a well-known site of suicide, much like the vertiginous pont Sidi M'Cid mentioned in *La grotte éclatée*. The "suicide bridge" in Algiers oversees a steep drop onto urban streets below and is today shielded by a tall chain-link fence.

Safia Kettou, "the poetess...whom the city had killed," is not a fictional person. Her suicide at this site was real. Laredj's narrator retraces her last steps. He reenacts her suicide. Safia Kettou was the pen name of the writer Zohra Rabhi, who jumped from Telemly Bridge on January 29, 1989, when she was forty-five years old. She was born in a town at the edge of the desert south of Oran and Tlemcen called Aïn Sefra, where she worked as a teacher between 1962 and 1969 (and where she is now buried in the same cemetery as Isabelle Eberhardt, who died in Aïn Sefra in 1904). After 1969, Rabhi/Kettou lived and worked as a journalist in Algiers, writing for publications like *AfriqueAsie* and *Algérie actualité*. She wrote the first science fiction in Algeria; her nearly forgotten œuvre includes a collection of seventeen short stories composed between 1962 and 1978 called *La planète mauve et autres nouvelles* (1979), as well as a play (*Asma*), a collection of poetry (*Amie cithare*), and a book for children (*Rose des sables*). She lived in an Algiers considered the "mecca of revolutionaries" during the decades after 1969—but in the winter months just after October 1988, Safia Kettou threw herself from Telemly Bridge.

In 1999, Yamina Mechakra would pose a series of questions in her novel *Arris*: "Who is there to speak of you and to draw your portrait at the place where you died? In other countries women look like you. What historian, what poet will speak of you [*te dira*] one day?"[59] Laredj addresses a similar question with a novel that does more than create an elegiac archive to register traces of all the lives under threat of disappearance in Algiers after 1988. His narrative retraces a path to this particular place; his narrator scatters an unfinished novel into the same abyss where Safia Kettou disappeared. Laredj's novel is also a singular tribute, a memento for a lost writer at the site of *her* last night. That is, the "sayyidat al-maqām" Laredj elegizes is not only the fictional ballerina Miryam, but a living artist killed too soon by a once beloved and revolutionary city turned treacherous.[60]

Like Grains of Sand

On the concluding pages of *Sayyidat al-maqām*, as Laredj's narrator prepares to jump, prose gives way to an escalating series of apostrophes. The narrator's last words are a curse addressed to those faceless assassins who killed Miryam, along with so many other citizens on the streets of Algiers in October 1988. He stands on the bridge railing and screams into the night:

> Predator criminals [*criminels; qatala*], oppressor criminals, corrupt criminals, bad shepherd criminals.
> Criminals in heaven, criminals on earth, criminals between heaven and earth.
> Criminals in the air, criminals in the sea, criminals vociferating, criminals acting in silence.
> Criminals in full day, criminals in the black of night, criminals between dog and wolf.
> Bloodthirsty criminals, torturer criminals, murderers of memory [*criminels tortionnaires, assassins de la mémoire*].
> Cri...mi...nals of the last sighs that pierce the horror of this wild desert.[61]

This curse reads almost like a plaint in the juridical sense; the Arabic word translated to French as *criminels* is *qatala*—more explicitly, "killers." The identity of those responsible for Miryam's death, as for Safia Kettou's, remains shadowy. Laredj's fiction moves well beyond juridical plaint to create an anarchival model for transmitting justice claims not reducible to modes of address designed for legal tribunals.

This comes into clearer focus when Laredj's fictional plaint is set alongside plaints collected in an activist text also produced "in the state of shock from initial testimonies on October 17, 1988."[62] Now freely available in digital form, the *Cahier noir d'octobre* (1989) includes dozens of testimonies of Algerians arrested, detained, and tortured in the wake of the demonstrations that mark the defining rupture in Laredj's novel. These testimonies were spoken in public fora during the weeks following the repressed October uprisings, then transcribed, translated, and published in 1989 by a group called the Comité national contre la torture. The *Cahier noir* is among the myriad explicit intertexts of *Sayyidat al-maqām*, whose characters complain about the failure of that legal effort to hold the perpetrators of violence accountable for these crimes.[63]

The original preface to the *Cahier* includes an exhortation that the testimonies it contains be heard and amplified: "Let us listen to them, for every victim of torture above all needs to be heard; listen to them for their sake but also for our own, to know the atrocity of torture; listen to them to protect our society against disastrous futures for their words have the force of *memory against forgetting* [*la mémoire contre l'oubli*]."[64] Novelist Anouar Benmalek, who led the committee from 1989 to 1991, republished the *Cahier* in October 2008 and added a new preface, in which he asks: "Twenty years later, what is left of October 1988 and its hundreds of victims?" Benmalek answers his own question: "First comes torture—a crime that goes unpunished. Then, the tortured victims who still suffer in their souls and, for many, in their bodies. Finally, state torturers go unpunished and reassured in their practices. This observation is bitter. If the torturer's victory is not to be fulfilled in Algeria, then—in the absence of justice—the words of the victims must perpetually be held up against it."[65]

Reading Benmalek's 2008 preface alongside Laredj's 1991 text retrospectively renders the target of its suicidal narrator's rage ("criminels tortionnaires" and "assassins de la mémoire") distinctly less ambiguous, but also prompts reflection on how the novel frames a qualitatively different justice demand than does a text like the *Cahier noir*. Like Laredj's novel, the *Cahier noir* reckons with the shock that came with seeing the state turn deadly force upon the citizens it was founded to protect, before Islamists became the public face of terror behind which the state would obscure its crimes. The authors of the *Cahier* describe the impact of revelations spoken in public testimonies organized at a university in Bab Ezzouar on October 17, 1988: "This was a terrible moment of emotion because, for the first time since the country's independence, Algerian citizens were able to testify to the torture that police had inflicted on them during their arrest."[66]

The *Cahier noir* collects testimonies of individual citizens in order to create a collective accusation of the state from a narrative position located just outside the complicit legal institutions, but still addressed to them—or perhaps to tribunals of the future. The collection includes several dozen testimonies whose speakers describe being abducted, arrested, detained, and tortured by security forces in Algiers, Blida, Tipasa, Cherchell, and Mostaganem during the weeks immediately after the October demonstrations. These accounts are repetitive, clinically detailed, and painful: a twenty-five-year-old taxi driver, a twenty-two-year-old painter, a twenty-year-old seller of fruits and vegetables, a seventeen-year-old unemployed person, a fifty-six-year-old wounded war veteran. Some victims are named. Many are not. Frequently listed are the names of those who listened to and recorded their personal accounts, structurally implicating the recipients and by extension the readers in the text's construction of a collective plaint. The

Cahier noir configures testimony not as a single act of speaking but as a scene of address and a process carried out by citizens listening, recording, and transmitting in order to hold the state accountable to its own legal promise to protect them.

The authors of the *Cahier noir* name the accused: "the hand of crime is guided by State sponsorship and justified by State reason."[67] This cuts through the opacity of the state's impersonal "on," which the authors also expose: "And yet 'they' [*on*] tortured again and again and the list would get longer and longer with all of the crimes perpetrated in the name of state reason. PRS, FPS, ORP, PAGS, fundamentalists, benbellists, various opponents or victims of struggles within the apparatus—in every 'affair' of political and police suppression, the practice of torture returns and sometimes former torture victims—or their former torturers—torture, or go silent, *in the name of power*. In every 'affair,' these staggering accounts come before a powerless justice system, or a cowardly complicit one."[68] The citizen-activists articulate their demand in juridical terms: "JUSTICE IN OUR COUNTRY"; "trial of the torturers in accordance with the constitution and the law."[69] The *Cahier* concludes with a subjunctive declaration that cites the constitutions of 1976 and 1989: "So that: torture is banished for good; the army never opens fire on the people; justice is done."[70] This demand went unfulfilled in 1989. After amnesty laws in 1995, 1999, and 2005, and the imperatives of a global war on terror after 2001, such plaints became inadmissible in court, and it appeared unlikely that the demands collected by the *Cahier* would ever be met by the existing institutions.

The *Cahier*, in the way of texts such as *Djamila Boupacha, La gangrène*, and *Nuremberg pour l'Algérie*, staged an extrajudicial trial of the state that exposed the direct complicity of the state's institutions in perpetuating injustice. The dossier was compiled after the repeated interdiction of a symbolic people's tribunal scheduled to be held in Salle Harcha in December 1988. Concerning the unexplained order to cancel their event, the authors ask pointedly: "*Who* is afraid of anti-torture organizing?"[71] They provide a list of silent marches stopped by the police, hunger strikes forbidden, and public demonstrations canceled, menaced, prohibited, and broken up by security forces on the streets. This section of the *Cahier* ends with the demand for "a public forum in which to hold a people's tribunal against torture."[72] Citizens organized to publicly hold the state accountable, but the state repeatedly prevented those accountings from taking place. The unauthorized publication of the *Cahier* alerts us to the impasses inherent in using the state's own legal language to do justice.

A novel like *Sayyidat al-maqām* intervenes in this space of interdiction and impasse, supplementing the activist effort with anarchival moves. Laredj's riven narrative creates openings to register forms of testimony far beyond those recorded, translated, and heard in public fora in 1988. For instance, the narrator tries—but fails—to persuade Miryam to stop dancing because of the danger posed by the new mafia terrorizing Algiers, to whom he refers as "les nouveaux arrivants" (the new arrivals).[73] Instead of responding directly to this plea, Miryam reports her own memory of overhearing a conversation at the moment that she woke in the hospital a few days after she was shot in the head.

It is a subtle temporal shift, but the structure of reported speech creates a relay as one voice recounts another, then another. The narrator recounts Miryam's own account of what she heard her surgeon tell her mother in the hospital room a few years earlier: "Ils tuent l'élite de ce pays" (They are killing this country's elite).[74] When the surgeon says "ils" here, he refers not to "les nouveaux arrivants" about whom the narrator had warned Miryam, but rather to the shadowy figures who had carried out the violence in October 1988, and who continued to carry out violence after the demonstrations themselves. Miryam reports the overheard conversation to her lover, citing her surgeon's description of what had happened when the corpses came to the hospital from the streets in the immediate aftermath of the October protests: "I will testify before the Human Rights League, before the Committee against Torture. I will say that they used percussion bullets. They forced us to return the bodies to their families. They forced us to write names on coffins stuffed with cotton and unidentified limbs torn to pieces. I will tell the story of the mother who insisted on seeing her son's face, a victim of the events..."[75]

In his vow to testify before the committee that would compile what became the *Cahier noir*, Miryam's surgeon recalls an unnamed mother's grief, noting that she demanded to see her son's body, and that the body was an assemblage of body parts taken from different unidentified corpses but labeled with her son's name. The mother saw this corpse and tried to forget what she had seen. Five months later, her son was released from prison alive but so physically damaged that he was unrecognizable; upon seeing her son alive but disfigured, she embraced him—and then she died. This section of Laredj's novel ends with the unnamed mother's death, like a vanishing specter: "Practically blind, she caressed his face.... She burst into tears and slipped away like a summer cloud."[76]

Such an account exceeds anything that can be found in the *Cahier noir*. It gestures to grief that may never be aired in public, to truths that risk never being heard or transmitted at all. Laredj's text is riven with such openings, as if to amplify and multiply testimonies infinitely. As Miryam says of the Comité contre la torture: "Our distresses multiplied like grains of sand and we palavered, we gritted our teeth. Shouldn't we look for something else?!"[77] Laredj's fiction supplements the quest for justice in a subversive way; his novel is one such "something else."

By formally opening up to laments as numerous as grains of sand, Laredj's novel resists the closure provided by official answers surrounding the many enigmatic deaths of "la décennie noire"—like Miryam's, like the identities of those corpses whose body parts appeared in the doctor's fragmented tale, like the nameless mother who died of grief upon seeing her still-living but mutilated child.

The novel expands the anarchival function of literature by channeling stories, testimonies, and griefs that have no spaces in which to be publicly heard, and by sounding out an open archive of lamentations in the face of interdiction and impasse. That is, where the *Cahier noir* stops short, literature begins to truly move. What literature has to offer is thus qualitatively different from the important activist effort to instrumentalize the language of the law in order to compel the state to listen to its abused citizens. Literature goes much further than this, by flagrantly disregarding and defying the legal frames that decide which voices can be heard or losses grieved. Literature carries out the political work of mourning *against* and *in spite of* the law.

As distresses multiply like grains of sand, people will grit their teeth only so long before demanding that something *else* be done. On September 15, 1999, during the first months of Bouteflika's presidency and the day before the "Civil Concord" was passed by referendum, a group of women belonging to the Collectif des familles des disparus en Algérie (CFDA) tried to enter the Salle Harcha to get President Bouteflika's attention, carrying with them the portraits of their disappeared sons, fathers, husbands. According to Nasséra Dutour, who was present that day, the president said to the activists: "The disappeared are not in my pocket.... You shame me before the world like public mourners, displaying your photographs."[78]

Laredj invites the reader directly into this space of the marthīyā, an act of bereavement dismissed as shameful or negligible by the president but claimed by the women of CFDA not only to commemorate the dead or to survive the pain of their loss but to interrupt and confront power with their fury. Laredj's text protects this revolutionary force of memory in the face of law's concerted efforts to neutralize and anesthetize threats to its authority.

Testimonies to Come

The other animating intertext of Laredj's novel is a more surprising point of reference than is the *Nights* or the *Cahier noir*. This is a nearly forgotten work titled *Histoire de ma vie* that was published by the late Fadhma Aïth Mansour Amrouche in 1968; Amrouche is usually better known as the mother of her more famous children, the singer Taos Amrouche and the writer Jean Amrouche. Born illegitimate in Tizi Hibel in 1886 and raised in a Catholic orphanage in Kabylie, Fadhma Aïth Mansour Amrouche is often credited as the first Algerian woman to write and publish her own life story. Kateb Yacine wrote the preface to Amrouche's *Histoire*, which was published just a few months after her death in Brittany in July 1967 at age eighty-four. Kateb concludes his preface by addressing the author directly with a promise: "I greet you, Fadhma, young woman of my tribe, for us you are not dead! We will read you in the douars, we will read you in the lycées, we will do all we can so that you are read!"[79] *Histoire de ma vie* concludes with a series of Kabyle poems.

Laredj takes up Kateb's promise with an intertextual articulation that channels, shelters, and gives new life to Amrouche's Kabyle French *Histoire* in Arabic, an Algerian language that Amrouche herself neither spoke nor wrote. *Histoire de ma vie* is the inspiration for a role that the character Miryam dances immediately before she takes flight as Shahrazād—it is the title role in a (fictional) ballet titled *La Berbère* that we learn sets Amrouche's récit to a score by the composer Mohammed Iguerbouchène. Miryam speaks of incarnating Fadhma Amrouche's own grief as she dances the role of *La Berbère*, picking up on the undercurrent of suffering that resonates throughout Amrouche's récit: "A strong feeling begins to eat away at me: each time that I rehearse *La Berbère*, I feel a poignant sorrow. I have it in my blood. I know the suffering of not knowing one's father. I find myself in her: her present, her past, her exile."[80]

First published in 1968, *Histoire de ma vie* was composed in two separate phases of writing separated by almost twenty years. Amrouche drafted the main narrative in a single month during 1946; she added a long epilogue in 1962, two weeks before Algeria's independence. The text was thus composed in the shadow of two traumatizing and painful wars, making it especially poignant for Miryam, or for a reader in the wake of the 1990s. Amrouche's narrative voice is permeated by suffering. Kateb amplifies this by citing Jean Amrouche's description of his mother's voice as she sang to him the Kabyle poetry that he would transcribe and translate, and that his sister Taos Amrouche would later perform and record: "A plain voice almost without timbre, infinitely fragile and on the verge of breaking."[81] Kateb describes Fadhma's fragile voice as also one with formidable power, singular and multiple, the exiled remnant of a decimated Kabyle tribe still singing the ancestral songs: "A plural yet singular tribe."[82]

Amrouche's text reads as vivid first-person testimony, "the first time that a woman of Algeria dares to write what she lived."[83] She insists in a letter addressed to her son Jean Amrouche which appears as a second preface to her text that "this story is true, not a single event was fabricated; everything that happened before my birth was told to me by my mother."[84] Among the scenes that could have been recounted to her only by her own mother (or invented) is an especially visceral one of her own birth in Tizi Hibel, her village in Kabylie, near Taourirth-Moussa-ou-Amar, in 1886: "The night of my birth," writes Fadhma, "my mother was sleeping alone with her two small children; no one around to assist or to provide aid: she delivered alone, and cut the umbilical cord with her teeth."[85]

At birth, she was already an exile, an illegitimate child born outside patriarchal law whose parents were not married and whose father abandoned her mother when she became pregnant. "My mother was courageous," writes Amrouche, transcribing and translating her mother's own Kabyle voice: "She used to say: 'Tichert-iou khir t'mira guergazen!'—'the tattoo on my chin is worth more than a man's beard!'"[86]

Amrouche's precarious status meant that she almost disappeared even before she was born. She sketches the legal circumstances surrounding her mother's pregnancy: "She was pregnant, and the man denied having fathered the child. Kabyle customs are awful. When a woman has sinned, she must disappear, be seen no more, so that the shame should not tarnish her family. Before French conquest, justice was expeditious; family members led the offender into a field where they killed her. Then they buried her under an embankment.... But in those days, French law was fighting against these brutal customs. And my mother had recourse to it."[87] To circumvent the expedient justice of Kabyle mores—which Amrouche indicates would have entailed her mother's being beaten to death, buried, and forgotten (a punishment that recalls stories linked to "Le rocher des femmes adultères" that was evoked by Mechakra)—her mother walked alone to appeal to French justice nine days after giving birth. She lodged a plaint to compel the father to recognize paternity, but he refused to do so, despite her recourse to French colonial law. In despair, her mother tried to drown the newborn infant in a fountain, but—as Amrouche writes—"I didn't die from it."[88] She was hardy; she survived. As Amrouche puts it plainly in 1946: "The world is mean, and it's the 'child of sin' who is the real martyr in Algeria, especially in Kabylie."[89]

By weaving Fadhma Amrouche into his novel, Laredj elegizes and dignifies the life of an illegitimate female child who was through her mother's agency rescued from Kabyle justice by French law, who narrowly survived her own infanticide at the same mother's hands, who was schooled out of the Kabyle language by nuns who taught her French and made her Catholic, who became mother of five children and who spoke not a word of Arabic but wrote and published her own formidable first-person account of her life in French. When Amrouche wrote the French word *martyr* to describe herself in 1946, the word had not yet calcified into a national ideology as it would after 1962. This is a very different kind of "shahīd" than those who are memorialized with concrete monuments in Algeria today, and very different from the "shuhadā'" that Bouteflika was invoking when he instrumentalized the suffering of "Sétif" in his 2012 speech.

Histoire de ma vie might be read as "shahīda" countertestimony, an account at odds rather than in confluence with the state's narrative power. Amrouche's text concludes with an epilogue, added by her in June 1962, just months before Algeria's independence. The epilogue lists in swift and vivid terms the losses and suffering that she experienced during Algeria's national independence war. This is not testimony of the glorious November revolution exalted by Bouteflika but an account of the vulnerability that she felt as an old French-speaking Kabyle woman at a time with no clear side to join: "To the Kabyles we were Roumis, traitors," she writes. "To the army, we were *bicots* [faceless Arabs] like the others."[90]

Amrouche vividly describes the terror of being an eighty-year-old with a sick and fragile husband caught between the maquisards and the army, trembling with fear at every sound in the night: "From March 1957 to October 1958 we lived in the trances of war; the population was subjected to mistreatment by the army; the maquisards raided and sacked by night, and by day the army forced the people to repair what they had done. There was misfortune among civilians on both sides, and my husband was visibly growing thinner.... That is how sinister the atmosphere was! All night we trembled whenever we heard a noise. Despite the lock and bolt, we feared everything and the unknown."[91] At this point, Amrouche's text documents a series of deaths in swift succession: she loses her remaining three sons and her husband (she had already lost two sons in the previous war). This torrent of losses leaves her devastated with grief and paralyzed in the face of her own desire to die: "October 1958, Henri; January 1959, his father; April 1962, it was Jean. Since August of 1939, it's been five of my sons, and their father; six bereavements strike me and I survive each of these hardships. Sometimes I ask myself what kind of death I could choose so as to disappear without suffering, without seeing myself die in stages like paralytics do."[92] In the last lines of her epilogue, Amrouche describes the solace that she discovered in the Kabyle language itself at this late point in her life. The language freed her from the sense of paralysis and her desire to disappear. She describes composing poetry to sing aloud to her last living child, her daughter, Taos. "Our men are so enduring of misfortune, so assenting to the will of God," writes Amrouche, "but this cannot be truly understood without entering into the language that was a solace to me throughout my exiles."[93]

After the epilogue appears a series of seven lyric poems. An editorial note explains that they are transcribed verses that were composed and sung aloud in Kabyle by Fadhma Amrouche to her daughter, the singer Taos Amrouche, who translated and transcribed the verses and appended them to the manuscript of *Histoire de ma vie* after her mother's death in 1967. Several of the verses call out the names of each dead son, speaking as a mother who addresses her lost children. Two are prayers spoken to protect her living child, Taos, to keep her safe as she travels.

Among Amrouche's verses is one of inconsolable lamentation that lends an unexpected valence to the translated title of Laredj's novel, *Les ailes de la reine*. Amrouche's verse reads:

> I am like the wounded eagle
> The eagle wounded between his wings.
> All of his children have flown away
> And he does not cease weeping.
> Have pity, o master of the winds,
> Come in aid to those who suffer.
>
> I am like the mountain eagle,
> On the highest rocky peak.
> He spends his nights watching the sky
> Hoping to find, among the stars,
> The faces of those who have flown away.[94]

By way of this loving translational claim to Amrouche, Laredj performs an act of literary inheritance that is perhaps his novel's most radical aesthetic move. Amrouche's own elegies are not marāthī, which is an Arabic genre; her grief and solace are expressed in her mother tongue, Kabyle. Before the protests of October 1988 was the "Berber spring" of 1980, a movement for Tamazight recognition and legitimacy that was violently repressed by the government. These linguistic and political questions were burning when Laredj composed *Sayyidat al-maqām*, and they would not die, although those who raised them were also often attacked, killed, and silenced. Including Amrouche among those lives worthy of elegiac mourning expands the novel's anarchival sanctuary even further. The act of translation and transmission itself—the "story of a life" moving through Kabyle, through French, into Arabic—also undoes the linguistic partitions imposed by official discourse between Arabic, French, and Tamazight. Those supposed divisions played an important role in the state's own war against those citizens who stood together to challenge its version of the truth.

In 1967, Kateb Yacine wrote a preface that directly promised Fadhma Aïth Mansour Amrouche—at the threshold of death—that the story she had written of her life would be read in the future. He also wrote this sentence: "But this book is also, in its humility, an implacable indictment [*réquisitoire*]."[95] A réquisitoire is a legal narrative form, a speech delivered in court before a judge that lists a series of accusations and asks that justice be done. Kateb extends Amrouche's own réquisitoire to Algerians and calls on them to respond with their own acts of speaking and writing: "Algerians—women and men—testify for yourselves! Do not submit to being objects, take up the pen yourselves, before your own story is seized and turned against you!"[96] With his literary act, Waciny Laredj both answers Kateb's exhortation and amplifies it, as if to keep alive an ember to ignite uncountable future testimonies that will at last be capable of saving the heterogeneous nation from the state.

Conclusion

Prisons without Walls

Les morts qu'on croit absents se muent en témoins qui, à travers nous, désirent écrire. Écrire comment?

The dead we believe to be absent become witnesses who, through us, want to write. Write how? —Assia Djebar

Je ne demande rien: seulement qu'ils nous hantent encore ... mais dans quelle langue?

I ask for nothing: only that they haunt us still, again ... but in what language?
 —Assia Djebar

La décolonialité est un espace d'énonciation et non d'origine ou de géographie. Elle dessine, pour ainsi dire, des contre-géographies.

Decoloniality is a space of enunciation and not of origin or geography. It sketches out, so to speak, counter-geographies. —Françoise Vergès

Hirakologie

A new emancipatory lexicon began to resound in the streets of Algeria's cities during the same weeks that I completed drafting this book. Tens of thousands of Algerians—then tens of *millions* of Algerians—of all ages and kinds started showing up together to publicly demand justice on the streets and in the squares of cities across the nation, even in the marginalized south. Every Tuesday and

FIGURE C.1. Digital image circulated on Facebook to call protesters to demonstrations on July 5, 2019.

Friday without fail for a year after February 2019, the massive peaceful demonstrations of citizens in the streets continued to amplify the rhythm and energy of revolt. Whatever the ultimate outcome, their footsteps, flags, banners, posters, slogans, jokes, chants, songs, essays, articles, interviews, and demands have posed a resolute challenge to the authority of the Algerian state, and to the imperialism of the Global North.

"Liberté," a song by the Algerian rap artist Abderraouf Derradji, better known as Soolking, became an unofficial anthem of the grassroots movement in spring 2019. When the song would play over loudspeakers during street demonstrations, tens of thousands of voices would sing along. The anthem's opening lines address the regime directly, speaking in the first-person plural:

> Paraît que le pouvoir s'achète
> Liberté c'est tout ce qui nous reste...
> Si faux, vos discours sont si faux...
> mais c'est fini.
>
> Seems like power can be bought
> Freedom is all we have left...
> Bogus, your speeches are so bogus...
> But now it's over.[1]

Soolking's lyrics move between French, Arabic, and Algerian Darija, calling for prisoners to be freed, the dead to be brought to life, and legal judgment to be questioned: "Libérez lī rāhī otage / libérez al-marḥūma / kāyin khalal fī al-qaḍā'" (Liberate those taken hostage / liberate the dead / there is an error in judgment).[2] These are the words of people standing together to resolutely resist injustice. To hear these lyrics resounding on the nation's streets is evocative and powerful:

> وحنا هوما الابتلاء اه يا حكومة
>
> W-ḥnā hūmā al-ibtilā' āh yā ḥukūma
>
> Nous serons l'obstacle de ce pouvoir
>
> Hey regime, we are your catastrophe!

The collective "we" who sing these lines remember Algeria's history viscerally. They do not forget the absent and disappeared, in spite of the state's efforts to obscure the recent past:

> Ils ont cru qu'on était morts
> ils ont dit bon débarrasse
> Ils ont cru qu'on avait peur
> de ce passé tout noir...
> Il n'y a plus personne que des photos,
> des mensonges...
>
> They thought we were dead
> They said good riddance
> They thought we were afraid
> Of this dark past...
> There's no one left, just photographs,
> Just lies...

The singing voice seems to call forth the dead and absent, tuning in to underground and repressed voices of those who have been disappeared or imprisoned:

En bas ils crient,
entends-tu leurs voix?
La voix de ces familles pleines de chagrin
La voix qui prie pour un meilleur destin.

Down below they're crying out,
Do you hear their voices?
The voice of these families full of anguish
The voice praying for a better fate.

The uprising that removed president Abdelaziz Bouteflika from office and continues to reject the autocratic regime that he symbolized has many names: *le Ḥirāk* (the movement), *thawrat al-shaʻb* (the people's revolution), *thawrat al-karāma* (the dignity revolution), *la révolution du sourire* (the revolution of smiles). Le Hirak speaks in many tongues, all of them Algerian; the commonly used name "le Ḥirāk" itself blends a French article with an Arabic noun in a characteristically Algerian diglossia.[3] The movement's viral slogan "#يتنحاو قاع!" ("yatnaḥḥāw gāʻ!") is a resolutely Algerian Arabic phrase that captures the systemic nature of the movement's demands. The phrase emerged from a televised news interview with a protestor who interrupted a Sky News journalist during a broadcast in central Algiers. When the Arabic-speaking newscaster interjected to ask him to speak (formal) "Arabic," the young man countered in Darija, annoyed and matter of fact: "I don't know Arabic," he said. "This is our Darija." He made his larger point along with a dismissive hand gesture—something like swatting a fly—that instantly became an iconic slogan and digital hashtag for the movement: "Yatnaḥḥāw gāʻ! Yatnaḥḥāw gāʻ!" (Get them all out!/Remove them all!).[4] As Ziad Bentahar has put it, these two words not only demand "a complete purge of the entire ruling class and political elite," but they do so in a way that denounces and disrupts "an established power dynamic in the Arabic language."[5]

In June, a conference called HIRAKOLOGIE took place at the University of Algiers, organized by the linguist Khaoula Taleb Ibrahimi; the name was coined by Lazhari Rihani, professor of Arabic linguistics at the Ben Aknoun Faculty of Language and Literature. One day of the conference was reserved for young researchers—master's and doctoral students in popular literature and linguistics—to discuss their analyses of the chants, songs, slogans, graffiti, and Facebook posts that are the many-tongued medium of the movement.[6] Even the neologism that names the movement's logic is diglossic, reflecting its heterogeneous, inventive, and inclusive ethos: HIRAKOLOGIE.

Brahim Rouabah, Muriam Haleh Davis, and Thomas Serres—among others[7]—were swift to point out the innovative ways that protestors draw deeply on both the charged memory of Algeria's war for national independence and on memory and losses of the 1990s war, as they craft their demands for dignity and justice in terms that reject the authority of the existing state. For instance, historic organizations like the Union génerale des travailleurs algériens and the Organisation des moudjahidin threw their weight behind the movement at an early point, and revolutionary icons like Djamila Bouhired and Zohra Drif marched with the protestors. The poster shown in figure C.1 was circulated to call citizens to the Independence Day protests on July 5, 2019, "Vendredi de la Libération." The image brilliantly revises the "I want you" recruitment poster, replacing Uncle Sam with four iconic shuhadā'—Larbi Ben M'Hidi, Hassiba Ben Bouali, Mohamed Boudiaf, Ali la Pointe, *and* Djamila Boupacha, who is still living. What began as a resounding collective rejection of Abdelaziz Bouteflika's candidacy for a fifth presidential term has become an uprising far more radical and multifaceted. Whether the Algerian government will hear and heed the collective demands of Algerians is yet to be determined.[8] Protestors continue to put their bodies and lives on the line, facing off against the military and police as repression escalated in late 2019 and early 2020.[9] The people on the streets understand what is at stake; they know, as the lyrics of Soolking's anthem acknowledge, that "l'avenir est incertain" (the future is uncertain).

Decolonial political action and open contestation with state power is not new to Algerians, as this prolific and flexible lexicon reveals. The protestors draw on a long Algerian genealogy of democratic protest and emancipatory critique, amplifying a countercurrent of resistance to state violence and neoimperialism that has too often flown under the radar of international news circuits and analyses. Such protest has also been filtered through Eurocentric interpretive frameworks such as the notion of an "Arab Spring." In 2012, Maytha Alhassan argued that "Arab Spring" was never an appropriate term for the uprisings taking place across Africa and the Middle East: "The irony of the Western invention of the 'Arab Spring' is that regardless of citizenry remonstrations for 'self-determination,' we still continue to see the Arab region in our eyes and not through theirs. What is going on in the MENA is something deeper than a democratic transformation, it is what democracy is predicated on—*a demand for recognizing the right to human dignity.*"[10] As Brahim Rouabah argues, we must "listen attentively and heed the messaging of the movement" in order to see clearly the epistemic shift at stake: "The Algerian revolt . . . is engaged in *reworking the temporal and spatial order* that underpins the coloniality of [Algeria's] present and sustains the conditions of its colonizability."[11]

Throughout this book, I have argued that the violence of Algeria's history in the wake of French occupation is such that only aesthetic works—which move in an elusive, anarchival relationship to the power of the nation-state and its laws—have been able to register and reckon with its effects. The kinds of imagination and memory that are kept alive by writing, publishing, circulating, and interpreting literary texts have also created clandestine space for decolonial contestation that foments rather than neutralizes rebellion against the authority of the state. Algeria's writers—including the ones whose works I have analyzed here, but there are so many others—have carved open the possibility not just to imagine but to claim human kinship with those who live outside the law's protection, those who are legally destroyed, banished, and incarcerated. Laws can protect the vulnerable, but they do not have the authority to decide what is human, and they do not have the last word on justice. The literary texts that I have analyzed offer models for reworking and contesting the temporal and spatial orders that sustain colonial and neoimperial violence. They help to envision frameworks for justice that contest rather than confirm the power of the state. In a real way, literature saw the Ḥirāk coming. Literature helped to call the movement into being.

Specifically, the movement taking place on streets across Algeria in 2019 has been directly connected to protests against the Algerian government that took place in October 1988, a moment that many now remember as a repressed beginning of the movements that erupted across North Africa beginning with Tunisia's "Jasmine Revolution" in 2011. Thomas Serres highlights this in an interview from March 2019, in which he argues that a symbolic revolution had already taken place in Algeria: "In 1988, the regime feared its own people, some of whom had voted for the FIS Islamists. The punishment was terrible: ten years of civil war that got blamed on the people, who had voted badly, who had been manipulated."[12] The political ruptures generated by the shock of October 1988 and the traumatizing war on civilians that followed have been discussed by many commentators,[13] but this moment has not been fully connected to broader transnational movements by historians and theorists. Writers of literature, on the other hand, have registered these repressed connections and recessed revolutionary possibilities. Their works have kept its memory alive until now.

To conclude, I highlight a recessed genealogy of symbolic resistance from October 1988 into the present moment by bringing together works by the novelist Assia Djebar and the poet Samira Negrouche. In particular, Djebar's poem "Raïs, Bentalha" (1998) tracks a writer's submission to be haunted by the ghosts of those killed and disappeared during the late 1980s and 1990s. Negrouche picks up the relay from Djebar to envision a future movement beyond mourning and paralysis in collaborative works that invite a kind of testimony that has not yet been written. Taking a cue from the moving form of Negrouche's piece "XIII planches/poètes (a genealogy a constellation)"—a series of handwritten posters that she installed on a wall in a public art space in Algiers during the summer of 2018—we can see this future being written in the present, by Algerian citizens who are standing and speaking together on their streets to redefine what it means to be human.

Ghosts Set Free

By her own account, Assia Djebar's work as a writer was dramatically altered when she witnessed the violent repression of peaceful demonstrations known as *octobre noir*. "I was derailed by the street riots of October 1988 in Algiers," Djebar recalls in an interview with Clarisse Zimra. "I saw blood flowing in the streets."[14] She reports that the shock of what she saw prompted her to suspend writing the third novel of her Algerian Quartet—it was later published in 1995 as *Vaste est la prison*, part 3 of a quartet that began with publication of *L'amour, la fantasia* (1985)—in order to write a novel that would challenge fundamentalist readings of Islamic tradition particular to Algeria in the late 1980s. Of this unexpected text, published in 1991 as *Loin de Médine*, Djebar has said: "It is an irruption, I'd almost say, a fracture within my corpus—that was written all at once [literally, "in one blow/sitting"], in order to participate in a specific debate: it is a piece grounded in time and place [*une œuvre de circonstance*]."[15]

The literary works that Djebar published after this fracture in her œuvre transform the haunting poetics of her earlier novels in ways that respond to new forms of disappearance and loss that are particular to the political circumstances of Algeria in the wake of October 1988. Her poem "Raïs, Bentalha . . . un an après" ("Raïs, Bentalha . . . One Year After") found at the end of the collection *Ces voix qui m'assiègent* (*These Voices That Besiege Me*), brings this shift into focus. Djebar read this poem at an event at Harvard University in 1998, one year after the massacres of Algerian civilians that took place in the towns of Raïs (August 29, 1997) and Bentalha (September 22, 1997), both a few kilometers south of Algiers.[16] Aside from the sheer magnitude of these killings, the mutilation, dismemberment, and public exposure of corpses that characterized the Raïs and Bentalha massacres made them especially disturbing, as did numerous accounts from survivors indicating that government security forces either knew about or facilitated the mass murder of Algerian civilians.[17]

Djebar's poem traces the process of a writer's submission to being haunted by the people who were killed so horribly at Raïs and Bentalha. Initially, the speaker considers the risk that by writing she will participate in stripping mutilated corpses of dignity by exposing them to public view in a way that only reinforces their abjection and their silencing: "To write, that would kill the voice, exhaust it, expose it, burn it so as to expose its invisible bones, its ripped-up sinews, its glinting steel."[18]

This imagery of charred, desecrated corpses evokes Djebar's earlier meditation in *L'amour, la fantasia*, where a historian-narrator transcribes French general Pelissier's detailed description of the asphyxiated and burned corpses of her ancestors whom he had ordered killed by "enfumade" in a mountain cave in 1845. Those disfigured bodies were removed from the cave and exposed to the sunlight, to Pelissier's gaze, and, through Pelissier's written descriptions, to a scandalized public in France.

Again, the writer encounters a mass grave of unknown dead. In 1998, a host of new ghosts—not ancestors, but contemporaries—crowd the speaker's memory with their faceless presence, silently clamoring to be heard. She depicts a gathering of revenants in the desert of history who vie for the poet's attention, not unlike Rahmani's armies of "musulman" ghosts. This growing crowd demands something of the writer, and also of "nous":

Disparus
Émiettés
... ils reviennent à nous, ils accourent
pour habiter ce désert de notre histoire
... Ils reviennent presque dans la hâte
... Les morts reviennent en cohorte,
sans visage particulier. (III, IV)

Disappeared
Scattered
... they come back to us, surge up
to inhabit this desert of our history
... They come back almost impatiently
... The dead come back in droves,
without distinctive faces.

Each stanza of the poem marks a moment of the poet's gradual assent to a demand imposed on her by a restless multitude of the disappeared. As she reckons with the risks entailed in writing on their behalf, she recalls the mourning of

Fadhma Aïth Mansour Amrouche—"To write the voice of others, of the orphan mother keening her infinite grief."[19] This implicit but sure reference connects the "infinite grief" of the archetypal "orphan mother" to the lamentation of those mothers of murdered children "at the heart of the ravaged hamlet, Raïs, Bentalha, O Mitidja of desecrated childhoods."[20]

The political implications of Djebar's act of literary haunting become clearer when considered in light of the amnesty laws that would be imposed very soon after she composed and published this poem. The massacres at Raïs and Bentalha are also a focal point of a dossier concerned with the impact of these laws, called "Les massacres en Algérie, 1992–2004."

This dossier, compiled by the Comité Justice pour l'Algérie for a people's tribunal that was held in Paris in 2004, contains seventy-six pages of detailed forensic evidence and survivor testimony.[21] It opens with a timeline of the massacres carried out by different forces (state forces, death squads, armed Islamist groups, and anti-Islamist civilian militias) after 1992 that led up to the "grandes massacres" that took place during the summer of 1997. This timeline is followed by written testimony from survivors of massacres at both Raïs and Bentalha (pages 25–30), an orientation to the immediate political context at the end of President Zéroual's rule (pages 31–34), and a series of questions and hypotheses about who was in truth responsible for the 1997–98 massacres. The dossier concludes with more testimonies, maps of the massacre sites that show their discomfiting proximity to security force checkpoints and barracks, and an open call signed by Algerian intellectuals demanding an international inquisition: "In these circumstances," they announce, "only an international and impartial investigation commission has the moral authority necessary to shed light on what is happening in Algeria."[22]

By "these conditions," the authors signal the ongoing threat of violence at once enabled and obscured by the amnesty policy enforced by the Algerian state. They underscore the dangers of legal impasse and impunity that had been imposed by Bouteflika's government at the time of the 2004 tribunal in Paris, when the Algerian civil war had been declared to be over and done:

> To this day, the attacks and massacres have not stopped, although they are no longer the subject of anything but the briefest articles in Western newspapers. This "banalization of crime" has, since the early 2000s, made it possible to project an image of Algeria as peaceful, under control, and secure. It is true that since Abdelaziz Bouteflika became president (April 1999), the number of crimes has decreased; on the other hand, the confusion and opacity which surrounds these crimes has intensified and

makes it even more difficult to decipher them than was the case during the period that preceded his first term. What is important to note is that all the structures that made it possible, on the one hand, to commit these crimes, and on the other hand, to establish impunity, *remain in place—such that the machine can be revved up to run again at any moment.*[23]

Fifteen years later, as Bouteflika proposed his fifth presidential term, the committee's demand for international inquest and transparent reckoning had never been met. The confusion and opacity installed by the political machine that the writers describe succinctly in this passage of the 2004 dossier never lifted, and their call for justice has yet to be answered. This is a point emphasized very clearly by Algerian protestors in the streets in 2019. Those who were left dead or grieving after Raïs and Bentalha are surely among the silenced and suffering on whose behalf Soolking's anthem entreats: "Down below, they're crying out, / Do you hear their voices?"

Djebar's poem can thus be understood as an act of listening to what has been forcibly silenced by the machinations of the Bouteflika regime outlined by activists above. By the third stanza of the poem, the speaker lays claim to writing as an act that shields and defends the dead from the ritualized indignity and violence of political instrumentalization:

Écrire pour effacer ce dévoilement absolu
ce linceul sans rituel sans psalmodie
Écrire pour les retrouver eux, les morts,
mais avant ou maintenant, quand ils nous parlent
car ils nous parlent. (III)

To write in order to erase this extreme exposure
this death-shroud without ritual without psalmody
To write in order to find them again, the dead,
but before or right now, when they speak to us
for they speak to us.

The poet accepts her obligation to the demands of this horde of unquiet and disturbing ghosts. She writes not simply to register or transcribe their plaints but rather to create a protective space for their unsettling demand (*"car* ils nous parlent"*).

At this juncture, the demanding armies of the dead seem to break into the space of the poem, "bodies tangled together."[24] Each speaks in a distinctively singular voice, in her own idiomatic and in some way untranslatable tongue:

mais chacun sa voix nette
distincte
préservée
chacun, ses mots à lui, son dialecte, sa fureur, sa douceur
ils reviennent jusqu'à nous, jusqu'à moi. (IV)

but each one, their voice clear
distinct
preserved
each one, their own words, their dialect, their fury, their gentleness
they come back to us, to me.

It appears that Djebar's poetics of testimony transformed in the long wake of October 1988. The testimonial act in this poem is driven by a desire different from that which the narrator had expressed at the conclusion of *L'amour, la fantasia* (1985). There, the narrator wanted to restore a dismembered and mutilated hand to life so that it could hold the writing instrument: "Plus tard, je me saisis de cette main vivante, main de la mutilation et du souvenir et je tente de lui faire porter le 'qalam'" (Later, I seize this living hand, hand of mutilation and memory, and I try to make it take up the "qalam").[25]

After Raïs and Bentalha, the poet holds the "qalam" in her *own* hand, and the guillemets are missing from the Arabic word: "Je demeure la fillette du village... le calame à la main / ma plume de l'école coranique" (I am still that little girl from the village... the qalam in my hand / my pen from quranic school).[26] She seizes the "calame/qalam" in order to write in all the language available to her—both "de gauche à droite" (from left to right) and "de droite à gauche" (from right to left), that is, in French *and* in Arabic, at once. What matters is not which of these languages she uses but that she creates a language to transmit the humiliated, gunned-down, violated, mutilated dialects of the dead by way of her well-trained writing hand:

J'écris la langue des morts ou la mienne qu'importe.
J'écris une langue offensée
 fusillée
...J'écris vos voix pour ne pas étouffer
Vos voix dans ma paume dressées
Raïs, Bentalha, j'écris l'après. (V)

I write the language of the dead, or my own, what does it matter.
I write the wounded tongue
gunned-down

> ... I write your voices so as not to choke
> Your voices mapped, tamed in my palm
> Raïs, Bentalha, I write the after.

Here, "writing the after" is not an act of healing or restoration, but of haunting. It does not repair a wound or recuperate what is lost; it does not fill a blank in the archive; it does not restore the dead to life.

The poet's submission to being "haunted in the name of a will to heal," as Avery Gordon puts it in *Ghostly Matters*, does not lay ghosts to rest. Rather, the poet creates a protected space for disturbance. Djebar's poem is a domain of turmoil and trouble, "when the people who are meant to be invisible show up without any sign of leaving, when disturbed feelings cannot be put away, when something else, something different from before, seems like it must be done."[27] The text also forges a relationship to the past that disturbs the temporality of the Bouteflika regime. The 1999 and 2004 amnesty laws tried to close the book on this past and on these unresolved questions by strategically marshaling fears of terror and discord, as I discussed in the previous chapter. Djebar's poem, much like her other literary works published during and after the 1990s, refuses to let the dossier close and wrests open the more difficult, unresolved questions of decolonization.

In other words, Djebar's poetics enact a disturbance that resembles what Algerian protestors have been doing quietly on the streets for many years, long before the hyperlinguistic demonstrations of the present Ḥirāk. Since 1997, members of the Collectif des familles des disparus have gathered weekly to demonstrate silently in town squares and at bus stops in Algiers, Oran, Blida, Constantine. They stand in the streets against the law's injunction to forget, summoning ghosts of those who have been disappeared—siblings, children, parents—by holding portraits of their faces and banners with their names. Posters appear on alley walls; anonymously authored graffiti record the proper names and disappearance dates of loved ones. By their obstinate refusal to retreat from public space, the kin of the disappeared dispute an official narrative in which the disappeared are generally accused of being Islamist terrorists. They also resolutely challenge a simplistic narrative that sets fundamentalist Muslims against francophone writers and feminists, instead revealing the state's war on civilians to be a continuation of colonizing force in which "musulman" ghosts now have a slightly different name—"terrorists" and sowers of discord. These protestors move into the spaces of Algerian history confiscated by the state's enforced amnesia, anticipating an anthem to come:

وحنا هوما الابتلاء اه يا حكومة

W-ḥnā hūmā al-ibtilā' āh yā ḥukūma

Nous serons l'obstacle de ce pouvoir

Hey regime, we are your catastrophe!

Underground Music

In October 1988, as tires burned and citizens revolted in the streets of Algiers, Samira Negrouche wrote her first poems. She was a teenager during the curfews and massacres of the 1990s, absorbed and protected by staying inside to translate French literary works into Arabic for her school essays. Until she entered medical school in 1997, her formal education was entirely in Arabic because of Arabization policies put in place during the 1970s that mandated the humanities and social sciences be taught in Arabic but left advanced scientific and mathematical training to be conducted in French. In her first year of medical school, Negrouche saw the university library burned to ash. As a resident at the main hospital in Algiers during the late 1990s she treated victims of bombs, terror attacks, the notorious earthquake and flood. "Hospitals," she observes, "are the nerves of a city."[28] Rather more literally than many poets, Negrouche has had her fingers on the pulse of Algiers.

Since 2001, Negrouche has published seven collections of poetry in French, many of them with the innovative publishing houses that have renewed Algeria's cultural sphere in the wake of the 1990s war, such as Éditions Barzakh,[29] Éditions du Tell, Éditions El-Ikhtilef, and Lettres Charnues.[30] She has also continued her early practice of translating contemporary Arabic and Tamazight Algerian literature into French.[31] Meanwhile, her own poetry has been translated into Arabic as well as into Italian, Turkish, Spanish, Swedish, Danish, German, Slovenian, Bulgarian, Latvian, and English. To protect and cultivate a plurilingual Algerian literary history, Negrouche has edited both an anthology of works by contemporary Algerian poets who write in French—*Quand l'amandier refleurira* (*When the Almond Tree Reblooms*; 2012)—and an anthology of works by international poets translated into Tamazight, Arabic, and French—*Triangle* (2008).[32]

During a conversation in January 2019, she spoke of her contemporaries with a sense of both respect and urgency: "We are a miraculous generation," she says, "but things are shifting again, at risk of vanishing in a new way."[33] In a prose poem called "Qui parle," the poet addresses an interlocuter who has posed the customary question about whether an Algerian can write authentic poetry in French. "My language is a constellation of poets," she counters, "each one bringing his or her own meter.... I dig down into the poem thinking of these subterranean musics. Silence is a landscape and my ancestors know no borders."[34] The poet ignores her interlocutor's question about language choice in order to pose one that matters to her, a question that closely corresponds to Djebar's prayer to be haunted by the ghosts of the vanished. In the darkest years of the 1990s, Djebar had written: "I ask for nothing: only that they still haunt us, again . . . but in what language?"[35] Negrouche responds, now: "Then who speaks for the ancestors? Today that's the only question that matters to me."

Two of Negrouche's recent installations demonstrate how this testimonial question translates as an aesthetic practice with political significance in the present. "XIII planches/poètes (a genealogy a constellation)" was a series of posters installed as part of the "Cabinet du Poète" project in Algiers during the summer of 2018. Soon thereafter, Negrouche collaborated with two contemporary visual artists to create an artist book entitled "2×2" that was shown in Algiers and Annaba in October 2018, and again in Algiers in February 2019, just as Bouteflika announced his decision to run for a fifth presidential term. These collective works, installed in public and read together, create a model for practicing testimony on the move.

The paper on which her installation "XIII planches/poètes (a genealogy a constellation)" is printed dates from the "decade of assassinations," according to Negrouche. The paper was given to her by a scientist who had worked for Algeria's Atomic Energy Commission but who left Algiers when the political situation worsened acutely in the early 1990s. When the scientist returned to the city to sell his apartment in 2014, he discovered the unused reams of paper gathering dust and gave them to Negrouche. Negrouche created this piece in May 2018 for Les ateliers sauvages, a public art space in Algiers founded in 2016 by Wassyla Tamzali. Defying the "XIII" of its title, fourteen sheets of aged paper are affixed to a bare wall. The paper is faded at the edges and visibly fragile (and it was destroyed by the adhesive when removed after the exhibition). The first thirteen sheets of paper are aligned at eye level directly beside each other, while the fourteenth is set apart, disrupting the series with blank space. Each panel bears the same handwritten pattern in black ballpoint ink: a roman numeral at the top; a large triangle at page center with birth and death dates written at either end of its hypotenuse; beneath the triangle, a fragment of text followed by the name of an Algerian writer and another date.

Hanging on the wall at Les ateliers sauvages, these pale sheets of paper look something like white tombstones. They also resemble those posters bearing names of vanished citizens that still sometimes appear on the graffitied walls of stairwells and alleyways throughout Algiers, placed there by relatives of the

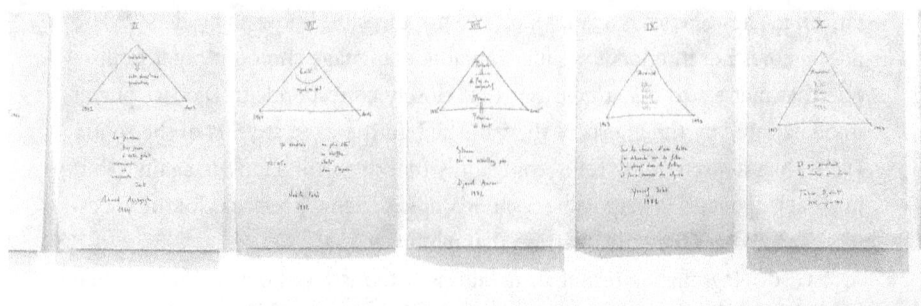

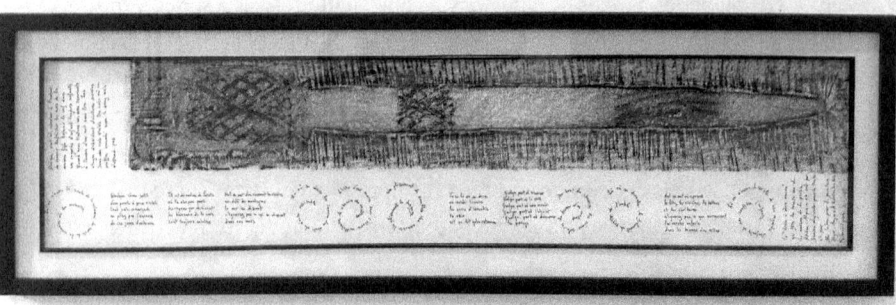

FIGURE C.2. Photograph of 2018 installation at Les ateliers sauvages in Algiers of "XIII planches/poètes (a genealogy a constellation)," by Samira Negrouche, and "Baton/Totem," a collaboration between Negrouche and Ali Silem. Photograph courtesy of Samira Negrouche.

disappeared who continue to demand justice that has yet to be done. "XIII planches/poètes (a genealogy a constellation)" is, among other things, an act of public mourning and an ephemeral archive; its prayerlike quality resonates with that of Assia Djebar's *Le blanc de l'Algérie*.

Displayed on the wall directly beneath "XIII planches/poètes (a genealogy a constellation)" was a different piece called "Bâton/Totem" that Negrouche had created in 2016 with the Algerian painter and engraver Ali Silem, an artist who, like so many, left Algeria for France in 1991. On "Bâton/Totem," Negrouche's handwritten text overlays Silem's drawings of ritual symbols, creating a funereal rite for the writers and artists killed during the 1990s. This visual-textual form itself is a subtle but unmistakable homage to the two foundational figures of modern Algerian art and letters. It invokes the many paintings done by M'hamed Issiakhem (1928–1985) on which his close friend Kateb Yacine

(1929–1989) handwrote verses of poetry, including *Les aveugles*, the painting that appears on the cover of Yamina Mechakra's first novel. However, "Bâton/Totem" reflects a different kind of conversation. "Bâton/Totem" is an act of dialogic relay, not only between Silem and Negrouche but also between an older generation of Algerian artists and intellectuals exiled from Algeria (like Silem, or like Assia Djebar and Waciny Laredj) and a younger generation who, like Negrouche, came of age during the 1990s and live and create in Algeria, where they intend to stay. Read by this light, "XIII planches/poètes (a genealogy a constellation)" communicates Negrouche's desire for a new relationship to Algeria's painful past—one that neither forgets nor is paralyzed by this history but which has digested the pain and loss to move beyond exile, mourning, and traumatized paralysis.

The first thirteen panels lay out a generation of dead Algerian poets who wrote in French beginning in the 1920s, in the following order: I. Jean Amrouche (1906–1962), II. Mohammed Dib (1920–2003), III. Ismail Aït Djaffer (1929–1995), IV. Kateb Yacine (1929–1989), V. Anna Gréki (1931–1966), VI. Ahmed Azzegagh (1942–2003), VII. Nabile Farès (1940–2016), VIII. Djamel Amrani (1935–2005), IX. Yousef Sebti (1943–1993), X. Tahar Djaout (1953–1993), XI. Jean Sénac (1926–1973), XII. Bachir Hadj Ali (1920–1991), and XIII. Myriam Ben (1925–2001). The fourteenth panel (numbered XXXXXXXXXXXXXXXXX) addresses, in English, "the future happy Algerian poet," with an entreaty, also in English:

Do not forget
Do not overestimate
The past.

The series charts a visual map of Algeria's turbulent birth in the twentieth century, and also makes visible a new scion in the grafting of French as an Algerian language. The organizing principle is not linear but idiosyncratic and errant, as birth and death dates do not hew to chronology. The piece is not an homage to writers killed during 1990s—just three of the thirteen were murdered, and just two during that decade. Those deaths are invoked by red ink fragments scrawled inside the triangle: Yousef Sebti, "Bullets / Night / 27/28 / December / 1993"; Tahar Djaout, "Bullets / 25 years / 26 May / 1993"; and Jean Sénac, "Knife- / -Point / Cellar / Summer /August."[36] Others endured different fates, also sketched inside the triangle: Amrouche, "worn out"; Dib, "exiled"; Djaffar, "dislocated [like a bone from a joint]"; Gréki, "sacrifice"; Amrani, "Tortured / from bone to cartilage / Witness / Witness to everything."[37]

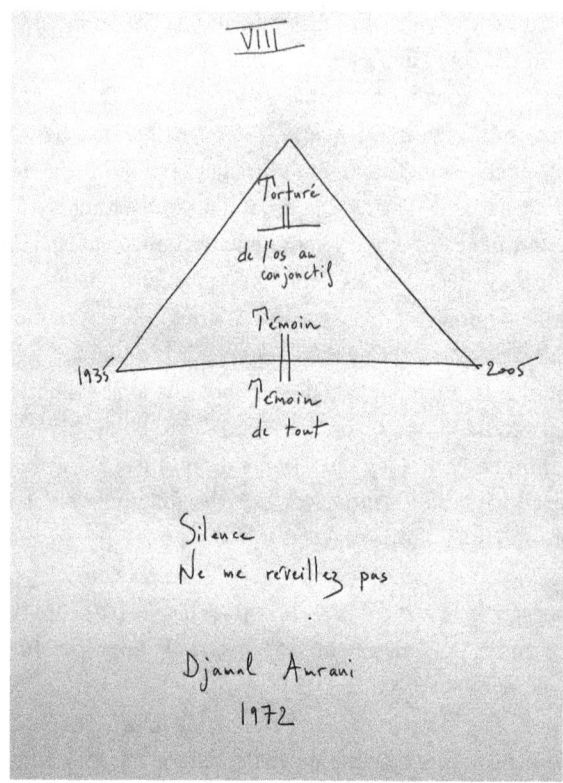

FIGURE C.3. Close-up photograph of one panel of "XIII planches/poètes (a genealogy a constellation)" by Samira Negrouche. Photograph courtesy of Samira Negrouche.

Each panel also contains quoted text, selected and handwritten by Negrouche and marked only with a year, such that it is difficult to determine whether she cites from published works or from remembered conversations. These fragments are written by hand as verse and nearly all are composed in the first person. This creates the impression of a growing chorus of gathered voices, among them: Mohamed Dib, in 1961, the year before Algeria's independence:

Je marche, je marche:
les mots que je porte
sur la langue sont
une étrange annonce

I walk, and walk:
the words I carry

FIGURE C.4. Close-up photograph of the final panel of "XIII planches/poètes (a genealogy a constellation)" by Samira Negrouche. Photograph courtesy of Samira Negrouche.

on my tongue are
a strange herald.

Kateb Yacine, in 1947, two years after the violent repression of the demonstrations at Sétif (May 8, 1945) and a decade before *Nedjma* (1956):

Ainsi
suis-je
violent avec les fleurs
et doux avec les vaches

Thus
am I
violent with flowers
and gentle with cows.

Anna Gréki, in 1963, after her imprisonment at Barberousse, time in an internment camp, deportation, return to Algiers, and three years before she died in childbirth:

> Quand je parle plus haut
> que ma voix quotidienne
> je sais bien
> que j'ai tort

> When I raise my voice
> louder than usual
> I know
> that I am wrong.

Tahar Djaout, sometime between 1975 and his murder in Algiers in 1993:

> Il y a pourtant
> des routes plus sûres

> Yet surely
> there are safer paths.

If this is a dialogue, it follows no predictable or certain route. It is not a collective statement so much as it is a gathering of ghosts, a series of fragments that mark potential and unrealized pathways. The dead writers speak in French, an Algerian language whose valence has changed over the decades since they first wrote or uttered these words. At the moment of Algeria's independence war, French became a language of political resistance and vindication, as Negrouche has noted elsewhere—"French, a common language, the spoils of war so dear to Kateb Yacine, a site of reclamation, of an 'I' at last audible from the South"[38]—yet its triangulation with Darija, Tamazight, and formal Arabic in contemporary Algeria has since generated other configurations that neutralize and transform this charge. "XIII planches/poètes (a genealogy a constellation)" tracks this shift. Samira Negrouche does not carry Kateb Yacine's burden of demonstrating to the French, in French, that French is Algerian. She knows it to be a "living language that carries within it an open and liberated Algerian genealogy."[39] Negrouche's "XIII planches/poètes (a genealogy a constellation)" makes manifest, in Algerian public space, an open and liberated genealogy which includes but is by no means limited to French.

Negrouche's enigmatic "writing on the wall" activates the kind of literary anarchive that I have charted in this book. By its constellatory form, "XIII planches/poètes (a genealogy a constellation)" creates a triangulation that invites any viewer who encounters the piece to participate in an open-ended and generative process of transmission. A constellation differs from a genealogy in both spatial and temporal ways. Only at a glance does a constellation appear to be a fixed pattern. When examined more closely, its potential configurations are infinite, and its stellar nodes are not inert points but dynamic fusions of hydrogen and helium. That is, a constellation is an interpretive pattern imposed on atomic chemical reactions moving at the speed of light. As a formal figure, it also implicates the viewer in a dynamic process—and a "planche," like a panel in a graphic narrative, creates temporal juxtapositions that invite connections governed only by a reader's own focus and signifying moves.

The juxtaposition created by the last two panels of this series brings such a process into view. Panel XIII is dedicated to Myriam Ben (1928–2001), pen name of the Algerian writer Marylise Ben Haïm, who claimed both Chaoui and Andalusian Jewish heritage and was exiled from Algeria after Boumédiène took power by coup in 1965, because of her militant communist political commitments. The citation here, dated the year of Ben's death—"J'ai eu le temps / de capturer / le dernier rayon du soleil (2001)" (I had the time / to catch / the last ray of sunlight)—is likely drawn from her posthumously published poetry collection *Le soleil assassiné*.[40] Ben's lines and the title of her collection allude directly to Jean Sénac, the poet mysteriously assassinated in Algiers in 1973 who had long signed his own name as a five-pointed sun.

The fourteenth panel of "XIII planches/poètes," numbered with a vanishing trail of X's above a disintegrating series of triangles, is addressed to a "future happy Algerian poet." This dedication creates a dialogue with Ben by also channeling Sénac. Speaking at a conference in South Africa in 2011, Negrouche closed by reading aloud from a poem that Sénac had dedicated, in 1970, to "la poétesse algérienne de demain" (the Algerian poet of tomorrow), as he understood clearly that any revolution that ignores the authority of women's speaking and writing is not revolutionary.[41] Myriam Ben and Samira Negrouche have, among many others, answered Sénac's call. Who in the future will respond to Negrouche's open address? In this way, "XIII planches/poètes (a genealogy a constellation)" cultivates not only a past but a *future* Algerian genealogy, as an infinite constellation whose unpredictable movements are also a source of dynamic and luminous potential.

Negrouche participated in a different project a few months later, this time collaborating with two Algerian artists from Annaba who were in residence at Les ateliers sauvages, Lamine Sakri (b. 1987) and Ryma Rezaiguia (b. 1985). Titled like a simple mathematical operation, "2×2," this piece was shown at Les ateliers sauvages in late summer 2018, then in Annaba in October 2018; in early February 2019, it was again on display in Algiers. "2×2" is a collaborative act of creative transmission oriented more to Algeria's unwritten present and future than to its highly charged past. The piece's orientation to the unknown future is especially salient to note now, given that this installation appeared on the cusp of the presidential elections in which the moribund president Bouteflika had just announced his candidacy for a fifth consecutive term, thus in those uneasy weeks just before the Ḥirāk began.

"2 × 2" is a two-sided screen made of cardboard that folds into four panels to stand upright. The facing side (labeled "face") was drawn by Sakri, and the back (labeled "dos") painted by Rezaiguia. While the two sides of the screen look nothing like each other, Negrouche's handwritten text stitches them together. Sakri's charcoal line drawings resemble diagrams from an anatomy textbook—a discernable foot, toenails, a face, circular nodes for joints, a trail of ligaments, shadows of bones unfurl across the four panels. The human form is of ambiguous gender; it might be seen as a landscape, or a river. On the "dos" side, Rezaiguia's style is angular and futuristic, like an architect's drafting table. Geometrical blocks of pale yellow, fuchsia, umber, and lavender are overlaid with line drawings in ballpoint pen. The drawings include interlinked circles that look like Venn diagrams and patterns of connected dots that resemble constellations, molecular structures, or points on an urban subway map.

Negrouche's text interacts with these images. Her handwriting stretches and scatters French words into eddies that create uncertainty for an eye that scans for a trail to follow. For instance:

                                          C'est

                                          dans

                                          le

                                          nœud

                                          rigide

                                          que se déploie

                                          un

  m

                                                  o

                                                u

                                              v

                                            e

                                          m

                                        e

                                      n

                                    t

Là

   où

      l'onde   s'éveille
(It is in the tight knot that movement unfolds / There where the wave awakens)

This visual play slows the process of reading by breaking French words apart so that they cannot be skimmed at a glance. The words are reduced to their basic elements, becoming visual, sonic, and rhythmic patterns. Like a wave breaking, or a knot loosening, the words unleash; they come to life in movement.

   Another series of lines reads:

ne cherche pas le chemin
ne cherche pas le pas
qui t'a précédé
cherche

> do not search for the path
> do not search for the footprint
> that preceded you
> search.

This imperative recalls the entreaty of "XIII planches/poètes (a genealogy a constellation)" to handle memory and history with a light touch so as not to become paralyzed. Subsequent clusters of text unfurl in lines that arch above then descend toward Sakri's charcoal line drawings:

> dessine-moi
> un vent qui éveille
> la surface du sens
> une note qui parle
> à mes courbures
> éclatées
> dessine-moi
> le seuil
> d'une constellation
>
> dans le dos
>
> draw me
> a wind that awakens
> the surface of sense
> a note that speaks
> to my exploded
> curves
> draw me
> the threshold
> of a constellation
>
> on the back.

The text and images on the back of "2 × 2"—on which "dos" is written in curling yellow script—both respond to and reiterate this imperative. Rezaiguia's painting is replete with vibrant colors and sharp angles, like an experimental drafting board for an unfinished design project. Negrouche's text continues where it left off, handwritten within and alongside patterns of interlinked circles, as if searching for a form to articulate what has never been done before:

Ne me
promets pas
ce qui est
attendu
Nous méritons
autre chose
que l'attendu
autre chose
qui n'a pas encore
d'axe
qui n'as pas
encore été
dessiné

Do not
promise me
what is
expected
We deserve
something other
than the expected
something else
that does not yet have
an axis
that has not
yet been
drawn.

On the next panel, written along two lines connecting dots against a backdrop of pale yellow, are four short phrases that can be read in a number of different combinations, such as:

te dessiner
une constellation
au seuil
d'une autre peau

draw you
a constellation
at the threshold
of another skin.

Negrouche's desire for "another skin" resonates in particular with the last of Frantz Fanon's published words. In 1961, as he died in Bethesda while Algeria's anticolonial war raged to its end without him, Fanon called out to those who would create a future with an invitation that included the same metaphor. The last sentences of *Les damnés de la terre* are addressed directly to his colonized sisters and brothers across the world: "Comrades, we must make new skins [*faire peau neuve*], develop new thinking."[42] Negrouche, Sakri, and Rezaiguia answer Fanon now. They are not alone.

The public installation in Algiers of this revolutionary call for "something other than expected" in February 2019 corresponds precisely to the moment that the Algerian government undertook elections that threatened to launch President Bouteflika's fifth consecutive term in office. Late winter 2019 marked an uncertain threshold just before the launch of a massive people's uprising in Algeria that has since removed Bouteflika from power—an ongoing movement whose outcome has not yet been written.

Let a New Song Arise

Throughout the year that passed after February 2019, I listened to the voices of this movement sounding from a distance. Because I have been denied visas by the Algerian authorities for the past several years, I have not visited Algiers since June 2015, when the research that would become this book was still in its early stages. During the winter and spring of 2018–19, I listened and watched, across Skype connections and social media threads, taking in the video and audio recordings, photographs, interviews, and articles. The revolt in Algeria was astonishing and powerful to witness, even from afar. The movement created a sudden opening that I did not see coming, but that so many years closely reading and discussing literature with Algerians had in some ways prepared me to recognize and respond to when it happened. It was as if I had been listening with an ear close to the ground to subterranean footsteps and whispers for years. Suddenly these footsteps and voices were marching openly and speaking resolutely in public, to show the rest of the world what a decolonized future might actually look like.

This is a different conclusion than the one I had already written for this book. It became possible to write it only after a series of conversations I had with Samira Negrouche just before the movement began. We spoke by phone between New Haven and Algiers in January, and then through a series of messages exchanged between Tunis and Algiers in early February, a few days before Bouteflika's announcement that he would run for a fifth term.

"We are on the cusp of something," Negrouche said to me in early January 2019. "Everything is at risk of vanishing in a new way." We talked about her recent visits home to her family's village in Kabylie, called Taourirt. Taourirt is also the birthplace of the Kabyle musician Lounès Matoub, whose murder by masked gunmen on a mountain road near Tizi Ouzou in June 1998, Negrouche reminded me, provoked uprisings and strikes across Kabylie. Then, mourning protestors chanted, "Pouvoir assassin" (Power, murderer) outside the hospital where his body had been taken.

Negrouche described Taourirt—the way its narrow streets weave, how its public and protected spaces knit together. She remembered that, as a child, she would watch the many pilgrims from distant elsewheres who walk through Taourirt's main road on the way to visit mausoleums of the forty-four saints for whom the village is known. She translated a Kabyle aphorism into French to communicate to me a sense of her home place and language: "Ayabrid etsoun medden yemghid lahchich di lathriss. Ô chemin que les gens ont oublié, l'herbe ne peut que repousser sur ses pas."[43] *The path on which people forget to walk will become overgrown and abandoned.* "It is like memory," she added, before our conversation turned elsewhere.

What has happened in Algeria since our conversations in January and February 2019 will change the course of many things, in ways that we do not yet know. One thing that is clear is that the people have returned to the streets of Algeria's cities in a significant way. As Ghaliya Djelloul and Aniss Mezoued have pointed out, precisely those public spaces that were occupied by the state during the 1990s are now coming back to life, reclaimed by protestors as sites for emancipatory contestation.[44] The civic spaces made barren and inaccessible by security fences and checkpoints during the 1990s are the same ones that protestors have transformed into gathering and rally points. For instance, the steps of la Grande poste are now referred to as *la Mecque des manifestants* (the Mecca of protestors), and others—the tunnel des Facultés, place du 1er Mai, place Maurice Audin—have become magnetic protest nodes and gathering places. The protestors are wresting back their right to a city confiscated by the state as punishment during the décennie noire.

The Kabyle aphorism spoken to me by Samira Negrouche in January 2019 has taken on a different sense in the months since February 2019: *The path on which people forget to walk will be abandoned.* Millions of footsteps, in a weekly scansion, are reactivating the revolutionary memory that inheres in these recently abandoned urban crossroads, as Algerians again inhabit the streets in a collective effort to save the people from the state.

A note on the last page of Negrouche's collection *Six arbres de fortune autour de ma baignoire* (2017) indicates that she finished every one of its poems in her home city of Algiers between 2010 and 2017. This includes "Seven Little Jasmine Monologues," a series of verses that she wrote in the wake of civilian uprisings that electrified places like Tahrir Square in Cairo or Avenue Habib Bourguiba in Tunis in 2011. Each of the seven monologues is given the initial of a city and is an incantation that resounds with the quotidian rhythms and images specific to that place, linked by Negrouche into a sonic network: Tunis, Tripoli, Cairo, Sanaa, Damascus, Rabat. The seventh monologue is for Algiers. It reads:

> En cette journée lézardée de déceptions où le bleu a quitté la mer pour envahir la colline chaînes blindées dans l'amas minuscule Minuit avorte le jour laissant la Casbah à ses débris. J'en appelle à la mémoire d'Alger de ses comptoirs marins aux chars de l'occupation j'en appelle à Hassiba à Djamila à Didouche et à Boudiaf aux ancêtres et aux amnésiques aux violeurs de rêves et aux traîtres de toujours j'en appelle à chaque goutte versée à chaque humiliation que jaillisse enfin la baie et qu'elle nous habite qu'elle ouvre nos paupières assommées que se réveillent Al Anka et les diwans assiégés que s'ouvrent les seuils de nos maisons et que s'élève le chant nouveau. Que se lève le *TGV expresse*, qu'il ramène la brise de Tanger et qu'il amorce sa course de Tunis à Alexandrie et de Beyrouth à Istanbul. Que s'ouvre un jour nouveau et que Minuit embaume de jasmin.

> On this morning cracked with disappointments when blue has left the sea to invade the hill in a uniformed chain tightening on the diminishing crowds. Midnight aborts the day leaving the Casbah to its rubbish and fragments. I appeal to the memory of Algiers from its seaside bars to the tanks of the occupation, I appeal to Hassiba to Djamila to Didouche and to Boudiaf to the ancestors and to the amnesiacs to the rapists of dreams and to the perpetual traitors I appeal to every drop spilled to every humiliation let the bay gush forth at last and let it inhabit us let it open our senseless eyelids let Al Anka and the besieged diwans awaken let the doorways of our houses open and let a new song arise. Let the *TGV Express* awaken, let it bring back the breeze from Tanger and let it start a new route from Tunis to Alexandria and from Beirut to Istanbul. Let a new day open and let Midnight be fragrant with jasmine.[45]

The opening lines are haunted by memory of the violent repression that happened in that city in October 1988: "On this morning cracked with disappointments when blue has left the sea to invade the hill in a uniformed chain tightening on the diminishing crowds. Midnight aborts the day leaving the Casbah to its rubbish and fragments."[46] In 1988, Algerians saw their government violently repress and kill citizens demonstrating in the streets; here Negrouche registers this as not only a trauma, but also a recessed and muted possibility.

Negrouche's poem activates revolutionary memory, transforming monologue into invocation. It is a prayer to be haunted by collective memory that inheres in the intricate spaces of a beloved, once-revolutionary capital city. Negrouche summons the spirits of the revolution's shuhadā' in an intimate and familiar voice, like kin ("to Hassiba to Djamila to Didouche and to Boudiaf"). Her call picks up where Assia Djebar's questions left off—what will the suffering people do now? After so many years in silence, in pain, in humiliation? Negrouche's lines pray that the closed eyes of the humiliated (ḥogra) will open again, and that their closed throats will open and sing: "I appeal to every drop spilled to every humiliation let the bay gush forth at last and let it inhabit us let it open our senseless eyelids let Al Anka and the besieged diwans awaken let the doorways of our houses open and let a new song arise."

Her closing lines situate Algiers on a map of the future. Algiers—a city again thrumming with the sounds of Chaâbi and Andalucian classical master El Hadj M'hamed Al Anka's mandole—appears as one stop along the route of a future high-speed train linking territories that are at present impassable because of a closed national border between Algeria and Morocco, because of war in Libya and Syria, and because of a deadly virus: "Let the *TGV Express* awaken," she writes, "let it bring back the breeze from Tangier and let it start a new route from Tunis to Alexandria and from Beirut to Istanbul."

Negrouche's poem envisions a future of movement, dignity, and flourishing: "Let a new day open and let Midnight be fragrant with jasmine." That new day has opened. In the praying, singing, chanting, shouting, and speaking of millions of people, it is happening right now. The future is far from certain.

Notes

INTRODUCTION: THE FUTURE OF MEMORY

Epigraphs: Gayatri Chakravorty Spivak, "Assia Djebar (1936–2015)," *Frontier*, November 11, 2015, based on an address she delivered at an event commemorating Djebar's death in March 2015; Hélène Cixous, "Lettre à Zohra Drif," address delivered at the conference *Hélène Cixous, croisées d'une œuvre*, Cerisy-la-Salle, June 1998, published in *Leggendaria* 14 (April 1999): 4–9; Nabile Farès, *Mémoire de l'absent* (Paris: Seuil, 1974), 178. A note on the translations here and throughout the book: all translations, unless otherwise noted, are my own; most of them were done in collaboration with Doyle Calhoun, to whom I am grateful for his sharp eye and literary sensitivity. When only the English translation appears in the body of my text, the original citations will be included in the notes for reference.

1. In Farès's novel the setting is initially Algiers after the revolution but the aesthetic cartography charted by this extraordinary text is far more expansive. A considerable body of scholarship has brought the global afterlife of Algeria's revolution into view. See Jeffrey James Byrne, *Mecca of Revolution: Algeria, Decolonization, and the Third World Order*, Oxford Studies in International History (Oxford: Oxford University Press, 2016); and the edited collection from Muriam Haleh Davis and James McDougall, eds., "The Afterlives of the Algerian Revolution," *JADMAG* 2, no. 1 (June 2014). My use of *afterlife* is not metaphorical, but registers the largely forgotten fact that the seventeen nuclear bombs detonated in Algeria by the French between 1960 and 1966 were authorized by secret clauses written into the Évian Accords that negotiated Algerian independence on the condition that certain military bases in Algerian territory remained "French" long enough to conduct these nuclear weapons tests. The afterlife of these detonations is part of the legal history of French Algeria, and it has not yet been acknowledged, let alone assessed. Exceptional articles on the topic include Roxanne Panchasi, "'No Hiroshima in Africa': The Algerian War and the Question of French Nuclear Tests in the Sahara," *History of the Present* 9, no. 1 (spring 2019): 84–112; Rob Skinner, "Bombs and Border Crossings: Peace Activist Networks and the Post-colonial State in Africa, 1959–1962," *Journal of Contemporary History* 50, no. 3 (2013): 418–38; and current research by Samia Henni. The toxic sites of former French nuclear test sites were also used as secret prisons to detain many of the Algerians forcibly disappeared by the government during the 1990s; on this, see the documentary film *At(h)ome*, by Elisabeth Leuvrey, based on photographs taken by Bruno Hadjih (Les écrans du large, 2013).

2. This question echoes Avery Gordon's, in the introduction to her *Ghostly Matters: Haunting and the Sociological Imagination* (Minneapolis: University of Minnesota Press, 1997), 18. I share Gordon's understanding of haunting as not superstition or psychosis but a "constituent element of modern social life" (7), and am persuaded by her claim that "to study social life one must confront the ghostly aspects of it. This confrontation requires (or produces) a *fundamental change in the way we know and make knowledge*, in our mode of production" (7, emphasis added).

3. While my approach to this corpus has been shaped by Lia Brozgal's description of the *anarchive*, I also envision that these works constitute *artistic contact nebulae* in the sense defined by Karen Laura Thornber. In *Empire of Texts in Motion: Chinese, Korean, and Taiwanese Transculturations of Japanese Literature* (Cambridge, MA: Harvard University Press, 2009), Thornber extends Mary Louise Pratt's notion of a contact zone in her own definition of artistic contact nebulae as "the physical and creative spaces where dancers, dramatists, musicians, painters, sculptors, writers, and other artists from cultures and nations in unequal power relations grapple with and transculturate one another's creative output" (1). She adds: "Among the most vibrant subsets of artistic contact nebulae are *literary contact nebulae*, active sites both physical and creative of readerly contact, writerly contact, and textual contact, intertwined modes of transculturation" (2).

4. This phrase is inspired by Hoda El Shakry's use of it in *The Literary Qur'an: Narrative Ethics in the Maghreb* (New York: Fordham University Press, 2020): "This book is part of a broader critical effort to *theorize from below*—namely, to decentralize Euro-American historical frameworks, periodizations, and critical methodologies mobilized in the study of non-Western cultural practices and forms" (4). Scholars such as Cajetan Iheka, Brahim El Guabli, and Imane Terhmina are continuing to transform critical frameworks along such lines.

5. Hélène Blais discusses the struggle of the French state to name this colonized territory in the opening chapter of her *Mirages de la carte: L'invention de l'Algérie coloniale* (Paris: Fayard, 2014). See especially the section "Nommer et délimiter" (50–76). The name *Algérie française* came only after departmentalization in 1848. I use the specific French term in this sense, understanding the term to be marked by this conquest history and by the violence entailed in the act of naming occupied land.

6. For scholars who have addressed the magnitude of this violence, see Abdelmajid Hannoum, *Violent Modernity: France in Algeria* (Cambridge, MA: Harvard University Press, 2010); Kamel Kateb, *Européens, "indigènes," et juifs en Algérie, 1830–1962: Représentations et réalités des populations* (Paris: Institut national d'études démographiques, 2001); Kamel Kateb, "Le bilan démographique de la conquête de l'Algérie (1830–1880)," in *Histoire de l'Algérie à la période coloniale (1830–1962)*, ed. Abderrahmane Bouchène, Jean-Pierre Peyroulou, Ouanassa Siari Tengour, and Sylvie Thénaut, 82–88 (Paris: La Découverte, 2014).

7. See Karima Lazali, *Le trauma colonial: Une enquête sur les effets psychiques et politiques contemporains de l'oppression coloniale en Algérie* (Paris: La Découverte, 2018), 51n7, which cites Kateb's "Le bilan démographique de la conquête de l'Algérie."

8. Lia Brozgal defined this neologism in her essay "In the Absence of the Archive (Paris, October 17, 1961)," *South Central Review* 31, no. 1 (2014): 34–54, in which she excavates "the alternative forms of epistemological activity at work during, and in spite

of, the fifty-year period of archival silence imposed by the French government" after the long-disavowed police massacre of Algerian demonstrators that took place in the heart of Paris in 1961, the height of the counterrevolutionary war against the Algerian liberation struggle (35). Her book *Absent the Archive: Cultural Traces of a Massacre in Paris, 17 October 1961* (Liverpool: Liverpool University Press, 2020) expands on the concept. For other recent discussions of the concept and practice of anarchiving, see Brian Massumi, "Working Principles," Andrew Murphie, "Not Quite an Archive" and "'Where Are the Other Places?': Archives and Anarchives," all in *The Go-To How-To Book of Anarchiving* (Montreal: The SenseLab, 2016), 6–7, 5, and 41–43.

9. Brozgal, "In the Absence of the Archive," 50. In *Absent the Archive*, Brozgal gives an account of how memory of the October 1961 police massacre of Algerians has been smuggled into the world by the "rogue collection of cultural texts" that she names an *anarchive* (24). I amplify and extend Brozgal's important insight that "literature and culture may 'do history' differently by complicating it... sometimes, by showing us things that cannot otherwise be seen" (5).

10. See Benjamin Brower, *A Desert Called Peace: The Violence of France's Empire in the Algerian Sahara, 1844–1902* (New York: Columbia University Press, 2009); as well as Blais, *Mirages de la carte*.

11. See Sarah Abrevaya Stein, "Dividing South from North: French Colonialism, Jews, and the Algerian Sahara," *Journal of North African Studies* 7, no. 5 (2012): 773–92.

12. See Joshua Schreier's *Arabs of the Jewish Faith: The Civilizing Mission in Colonial Algeria* (New Brunswick, NJ: Rutgers University Press, 2010) and Benjamin Stora's *Juifs, musulmans: Chronique d'une rupture* (Paris: L'esprit du temps, 2017), as well as Stora's volume coedited with Abdelwahab Meddeb, entitled *Histoire des relations entre juifs et musulmans* (Paris: Albin Michel, 2013).

13. Algerian converts to Catholicism, for instance, were still juridically "musulman." While an "indigène musulman" could in theory become a citizen, in practice this was made so bureaucratically difficult that the number of people who managed to do so is almost negligible. On this, see Patrick Weil, "Le statut des musulmans en Algérie coloniale: Une nationalité française dénaturée," *Histoire de la justice* 16 (2005): 93–109; and Patrick Weil, *How to Be French: Nationality in the Making since 1789* (Durham, NC: Duke University Press, 2008). For these specific historical reasons, I do not use the French word *musulman* as a synonym for the Arabic word *muslim* even though one usually operates as the other's translation. Throughout this book, I try to use both terms in quotation marks to signal that neither word is a politically neutral description under European imperialism, except when I am referring to self-identified practicing Muslims.

14. With the Crémieux Decree reinstated after 1943, Jews were reassimilated to the French nation and, as Todd Shepard puts it, "the urgency with which the French government and other French people insisted that Algerian Jews were wholly French helped fix a new boundary for the [French] nation, which now excluded Algerian 'muslims.'" Todd Shepard, *The Invention of Decolonization* (Ithaca, NY: Cornell University Press, 2006), 170.

15. Derrida discusses this "extraordinary history" in a long, speculative footnote in his *Monolingualism of the Other, or, The Prosthesis of Origin*, trans. Patrick Mensah (Stanford, CA: Stanford University Press, 1998), 78n9.

16. Cixous, "Lettre à Zohra Drif," 6, emphasis added.

17. For an analysis of the riven nature of colonial modernity, consider the foundational place of Algeria in Achille Mbembe's discussion of modernity's "nocturnal face" in *Politiques de l'inimitié* (Paris: La Découverte, 2016); and the central place of Algeria in Abdelmajid Hannoum's theorizing of modernity in his *Violent Modernity*. For histories of French citizenship that do not neglect the Algerian occupation, see: Laure Blévis, "Droit colonial algérien de la citoyenneté: Conciliation entre des principes républicains et une logique d'occupation coloniale 1865–1947," in *La guerre d'Algérie au miroir des décolonisations françaises: Actes du colloque en l'honneur de Charles-Robert Ageron, Sorbonne, Novembre 2000*, ed. Daniel Lefeuvre (Paris: Société française d'histoire d'outre-mer, 2000), 87–103; Kateb, *Européens, "indigènes," et juifs en Algérie*; Emmanuelle Saada, "Une nationalité par degré: Civilité et citoyenneté en situation coloniale," in *L'esclavage, la colonisation, et après… France, États-Unis, Grande-Bretagne*, ed. Patrick Weil and Stéphane Dufoix (Paris: PUF, 2005), 193–227; Weil, *How to Be French*; Weil, "Le statut des musulmans en Algérie coloniale."

18. James McDougall describes this code as an act of "lawfare": "Overtly a wartime law," he explains, "a set of emergency regulations for the suppression of revolt but maintained thereafter in what was notionally a time of peace, the *indigénat* both symbolised and, in the exactions it entailed, made manifest that aspect of the colonial state which constituted an apparatus of permanent, routinised low-intensity warfare." James McDougall, "Savage Wars? Codes of Violence in Algeria, 1830s–1990s," *Third World Quarterly* 26, no. 1 (2005): 122.

19. Olivier Le Cour Grandmaison, *De l'indigénat: Anatomie d'un "monstre" juridique: Du droit colonial en Algérie et dans l'empire français* (Paris: Zones/La Découverte, 2010).

20. "Avec l'indigénat, la violence coloniale se trouvait inscrite dans le droit. Légitimée, elle était banalisée." Sylvie Thénault, *Violence ordinaire dans l'Algérie coloniale: Camps, internements, assignations à résidence* (Constantine: Saïd Hannachi, Éditions Média-Plus, 2012), 10. For histories of the Code de l'indigénat, see also Sidi Mohammad Barkat, *Le corps d'exception: Les artifices du pouvoir colonial et la destruction de la vie* (Paris: Amsterdam, 2005); Grandmaison, *De l'indigénat*; Sylvie Thénault, *Une drôle de justice: Les magistrats dans la guerre d'Algérie* (Paris: La Découverte, 2001).

21. "Le régime colonial tire sa légitimité de la force et à aucun moment n'essaie de ruser avec cette nature des choses." Frantz Fanon, *Les damnés de la terre* (Paris: La Découverte, [1961] 2014), 81. I use the French title instead of *The Wretched of the Earth*, as the term *damnés* conveys a sense of legal condemnation that *wretched* does not; throughout this book all translations of Fanon's texts are my own, because published English translations interpret his scalpel-sharp literary turns of phrase much differently than do I.

22. Fanon, *Les damnés de la terre*, 144. The consequences of this transfer of power are the focus of the chapters "Mésaventures de la conscience nationale" and "Sur la culture nationale" of *Les damnés de la terre*.

23. "Ce raisonnement qui prévoit très arithmétiquement la disparition du peuple colonisé, ne bouleverse pas le colonisé d'indignation morale." Fanon, *Les damnés de la terre*, 82.

24. "Et quand, préconisant des moyens précis, le colon demande à chaque représentant de la minorité qui opprime de descendre 30 ou 100 indigènes, il s'aperçoit que

personne n'est indigné et qu'à l'extrême tout le problème est de savoir si on peut faire ça d'un seul coup ou par étapes." Fanon, *Les damnés de la terre*, 81–82.

25. "N'étonne pas non plus les colonisés." Fanon, *Les damnés de la terre*, 81.

26. "Arabes inaperçus. Arabes ignorés. Arabes passés sous silence. Arabes subtilisés, dissimulés. Arabes quotidiennement niés, transformés en décor saharien. Et toi mêlé à ceux: Qui n'ont jamais serré la main à un Arabe. Jamais bu le café." Frantz Fanon, "Lettre à un Français," in *Pour la révolution africaine: Écrits politiques* (Paris: La Découverte, 2001), 55–58.

27. The French avoided using the term *Algérien*, which Fanon most often deploys, as do I; he tends to use *arabe* or *musulman* only when channeling the colonial voice. In the passage of "Lettre à Zohra Drif" cited above, Cixous identifies the ghosting function of the French term *Arabe*: "On disait 'les Arabes' (et pas Algériens: Algérien est un mot révolutionnaire) et c'était un mot magique: on ne voyait plus ni la foule, ni les regards fiévreux des hommes offensés, ni les femmes farouches, ni une misère que je n'ai plus jamais revue avant de la retrouver en Inde, ni la colère des humiliés, ni la haine des opprimés, ni les ulcères, ni les loques." Cixous, "Lettre à Zohra Drif," 3.

28. Frantz Fanon, "Le 'syndrome nord-africain,'" *Esprit* 187, no. 2 (February 1952): 237–48.

29. "Quelles sont-elles, en vérité, ces créatures, qui se dissimulent, qui sont dissimulées par la vérité sociale sous les attributs de *bicot, bounioule, arabe, raton, sidi, mon z'ami*?" Fanon, "Le 'syndrome nord-africain,'" 237.

30. "Comment, comment, cet homme que tu chosifies en l'appelant systématiquement Mohammed, que tu reconstruis, ou plutôt que tu dissous, à partir d'une idée, une idée que tu sais dégueulasse (tu sais bien, tu lui enlèves quelque chose, ce quelque chose pour lequel il n'y a pas bien longtemps tu étais prêt à tout quitter, même la vie), eh bien! *cet homme-ci*, tu n'as pas l'impression de le vider de sa substance?" Fanon, "Le 'syndrome nord-africain,'" 246; emphasis in original.

31. "Droits, Devoirs, Citoyenneté, Égalité, que de belles choses!" Fanon, "Le 'syndrome nord-africain,'" 245.

32. "Le Nord-Africain au seuil de la Nation française—qui est, nous dit-on, la sienne—vit dans le domaine politique sur le plan civique un imbroglio que personne ne veut voir en face." Fanon, "Le 'syndrome nord-africain,'" 245.

33. "Il n'y a absolument pas de place pour eux." Fanon, "Le 'syndrome nord-africain,'" 246.

34. "[Les colonisés] constatent en effet sur le terrain que tous les discours sur l'égalité de la personne humaine entassés les uns sur les autres ne masquent pas cette banalité qui veut que les sept Français tués ou blessés au col de Sakamody soulèvent l'indignation des consciences civilisées tandis que 'comptent pour du beurre' la mise à sac des douar Guergour, de la dechra Djerah, le massacre des populations qui avaient précisément motivé l'embuscade." Fanon, *Les damnés de la terre*, 86.

35. "Bientôt sept ans de crimes en Algérie, et pas un Français qui ait été traduit devant une cour de justice pour le meurtre d'un Algérien." Fanon, *Les damnés de la terre*, 89.

36. "Aux yeux du colonisé, ces commissions n'existent pas." Fanon, *Les damnés de la terre*, 89.

37. "La guerre d'Algérie, la plus hallucinante qu'un peuple ait menée pour briser l'oppression coloniale." Fanon, *L'an cinq de la révolution algérienne* (Paris: Éditions La Découverte, [1959] 2011), 5.

38. Shepard, *Invention of Decolonization*.

39. On the politics of archival disputes in Algerian and French history, see both Brozgal, "In the Absence of the Archive"; and Todd Shepard, "'Of Sovereignty': Disputed Archives, 'Wholly Modern' Archives, and the Post-Decolonization French and Algerian Republics, 1962–2012," *American History Review* 120, no. 3 (June 2015): 869–83. For studies of colonial archives as techniques of state power and control, see Ann Laura Stoler, "Colonial Archive and the Arts of Governance: On the Content in the Form"; and Achille Mbembe, "The Power of the Archive and Its Limits," both in Carolyn Hamilton et al., eds., *Refiguring the Archive* (Norwell, MA: Kluwer Academic Publishers, 2002), 83–102 and 19–27, respectively. On the workings of power in the creation of historical facts and archives, see Michel-Rolph Trouillot's inimitable *Silencing the Past: Power and the Production of History* (Boston: Beacon Press, 1995).

40. The phrase, often cited, comes from Amílcar Cabral: "Christians go to the Vatican, Muslims go to Mecca, revolutionaries go to Algiers." For a depiction of Algiers as center of revolutionary movements, see Mohamed Ben Salama's documentary film *Alger: La Mecque des révolutionnaires (1962–1974)* (Arte France, 2014). See other recent works such as Byrne, *Mecca of Revolution*; as well as Elaine Mokhtefi's memoir *Algiers: Third World Capital* (New York: Verso Books, 2018). Malek Bensmaïl's documentary about the making of the iconic film *The Battle of Algiers*—entitled *La bataille d'Alger: Un film dans l'histoire* (Hikayet films, 2018)—includes revealing interviews with members of the Black Panthers and with US military officials on this topic.

41. On the uncertain impact of the COVID-19 pandemic on the movement in Algeria in 2020, as this book goes to press, see Vish Sakthivel's article "Algeria's Hirak: A Political Opportunity in COVID-19?," Middle East Institute website, April 1, 2020, https://www.mei.edu/publications/algerias-hirak-political-opportunity-covid-19. For collective reflection on the movement up through late spring 2020, see "Hirak, Algérie en révolution(s)," ed. Amin Allal, Youcef Chekkar, Lalia Chenoufi, François Gèze, Nacira Guénif, and Farida Souiah, *Mouvements*, no. 102, summer 2020.

42. On this, see Maytha Alhassan, "Please Reconsider the Term 'Arab Spring,'" *Huffington Post*, February 10, 2012, https://www.huffpost.com/entry/please-reconsider-arab-sp_b_1268971.

43. For an exceptionally clear and cogent statement of this point, see Brahim Rouabah's essay "Reclaiming the Narrative of Algeria's Revolt," *Africa Is a Country*, April 26, 2019, https://africasacountry.com/author/brahim-roubah.

44. "Ce système s'est institué sur un fondement légal: les pouvoirs spéciaux. Cette loi, votée par le Parlement en 1956, a donné carte blanche au Gouvernement pour rétablir l'ordre en Algérie." The full declaration is available at "Déclaration du président de la République sur la mort de Maurice Audin," Élysée website, September 13, 2018, https://www.elysee.fr/emmanuel-macron/2018/09/13/declaration-du-president-de-la-republique-sur-la-mort-de-maurice-audin.

45. "La République ne saurait, par conséquent, minimiser ni excuser les crimes et atrocités de part et d'autre durant ce conflit. La France en porte encore des cicatrices, parfois mal refermées."

46. For instance, consider Francois Fillon's response as it was reported in this February 2017 Reuters article by Jean-François Rosnoblet and Mathieu Rosemain, "France's Macron Seeks to End Controversy over Algeria Comments," Reuters, February 18, 2017, https://www.reuters.com/article/us-france-election-idUSKBN15X0QP. See also historian Sylvie Thénault on why colonial violence remains technically unclassifiable as crime: Marc-Olivier Bherer, "Macron en Algérie: 'La définition juridique du crime contre l'humanité ne peut s'appliquer à la colonisation,'" Le Monde, February 16, 2017, https://www.lemonde.fr/politique/article/2017/02/16/peut-on-dire-comme-emmanuel-macron-que-la-colonisation-est-un-crime-contre-l-humanite_5080715_823448.html.

47. For a discussion of the rhetorical functions of the independence war in Algeria's successive constitutions, see Malika Rahal, "Fused Together and Torn Apart: Stories and Violence in Contemporary Algeria," *History and Memory* 24, no. 1 (spring/summer 2012): 120–21; the cited passage from the 1976 constitution is on page 120. For the full text of the 1976 constitution, see *Journal Officiel de la République Algérienne* 15, no. 94 (1976): 1042.

48. Stora's *La gangrène et l'oubli: La mémoire de la guerre d'Algérie* (Paris: La Découverte, 1991) and Kristin Ross's *Fast Cars, Clean Bodies: Decolonization and the Reordering of French Culture* (Cambridge, MA: MIT Press, 1996) both argue, differently, that disavowal and forgetting of the "Algerian war" profoundly constitutes contemporary French politics and culture.

49. Debarati Sanyal, Michael Rothberg, and Max Silverman, eds., "Nœuds de Mémoire: Multidirectional Memory in Postwar French and Francophone Culture," special issue, *Yale French Studies* 118–19 (2010): 2.

50. See, for instance, Robert J. C. Young's *White Mythologies: Writing History and the West* (New York: Routledge, 1990) and Kristin Ross's *May '68 and Its Afterlives* (Chicago: University of Chicago Press, 2002). More recent works extend the insights of Young and Ross in compelling directions, such as Paige Arthur, *Unfinished Projects: Decolonization and the Philosophy of Jean-Paul Sartre* (London: Verso Books, 2010); Lia Brozgal, *Against Autobiography: Albert Memmi and the Production of Theory* (Lincoln: University of Nebraska Press, 2013) and *Absent the Archive: Cultural Traces of a Massacre in Paris, 17 October 1961* (Liverpool: Liverpool University Press, 2020); Hannah Feldman, *From a Nation Torn: Decolonizing Art and Representation in France* (Durham, NC: Duke University Press, 2014); Ranjana Khanna, *Algeria Cuts: Women and Representation, 1830 to the Present* (Stanford, CA: Stanford University Press, 2008); Mireille Rosello, *The Reparative in Narratives: Works of Mourning in Progress* (Liverpool: Liverpool University Press, 2010); Debarati Sanyal, *Memory and Complicity: Migrations of Holocaust Remembrance* (New York: Fordham University Press, 2015). On the specific historical relation of poststructuralist to postcolonial theory, see Simon Gikandi's essay "Poststructuralism and Postcolonial Discourse," in *The Cambridge Companion to Postcolonial Literary Studies*, ed. Neil Lazarus (Cambridge: Cambridge University Press, 2004), 97–119.

51. Gary Wilder, *The French Imperial Nation State: Negritude and Colonial Humanism between the Two World Wars* (Chicago: University of Chicago Press, 2005). The latter point in this sentence draws on Ariella Azoulay's definition of *constituent violence*. Considering the settler colonial context of Palestine's transformation into Israel, she writes: "Constituent violence is understood here not only—as suggested by Benjamin and a whole tradition of political theory—as the force used to create and impose a new political regime but also as an entire scopic regime that supports it." Ariella Azoulay, "Potential History: Thinking through Violence," *Critical Inquiry* 39, no. 3 (spring 2013): 571.

52. Françoise Vergès, *Le ventre des femmes: Capitalisme, racialisation, féminisme* (Paris: Albin Michel, 2017). Vergès picks up the term *coloniality of power* from Anibal Quijano; see page 21 for the full citation, and for other definitions that clarify the stakes of her intervention and inform my own.

53. "La postcolonialité désigne une période qui s'ouvre dès lors que la France se présente comme émancipée de son empire colonial. Il n'indique pas une temporalité, mais une politique." Vergès, *Le ventre des femmes*, 20.

54. Michael Rothberg's generative study *Multidirectional Memory: Remembering the Holocaust in the Age of Decolonization* (Stanford, CA: Stanford University Press, 2009) has had a wide impact in the past decade. Rothberg argues persuasively that memories of the Shoah generally help to illuminate and bring into "counterpublic" visibility the memories (or simply awareness) of decolonization, in particular of Algeria's anticolonial war. However, if we first ask *from whose perspective* this anticolonial war was ever hidden or not visible, then the limited directionality of Rothberg's counterpublic framework becomes immediately more clear. See in particular his book's part 3, "Truth, Torture, and Testimony: Holocaust Memory during the Algerian War," and part 4, "October 17, 1961: A Site of Holocaust Memory?"

55. See Feldman, *From a Nation Torn*, 3.

56. Shepard, *Invention of Decolonization*, 10.

57. "La lutte pour la déconstruction de la colonialité du pouvoir." Vergès, *Le ventre des femmes*, 22.

58. On this point about the temporality of decolonization, see Eve Tuck and K. Wayne Yang, "Decolonization Is Not a Metaphor," *Decolonization: Indigeneity, Education, and Society* 1, no. 1 (2010): 1–40. Jasbir Puar's essay "The Right to Maim" makes a related argument concerning the Palestinian struggle to survive coloniality: "If temporality itself is already suffused with the biopolitical," she writes, "to claim unfettered access to futurity is already predicated upon the genocide or slow death of others." Jasbir Puar, "The 'Right' to Maim: Disablement and Inhumanist Biopolitics in Palestine," *Borderlands* 14, no. 1 (2014): 14.

59. My argument here combines reflection on the anarchive with insight drawn from Gil Hochberg's *In Spite of Partition: Jews, Arabs, and the Limits of Separatist Imagination* (Princeton, NJ: Princeton University Press, 2008). Analyzing the Palestinian/Israeli context, Hochberg underscores "the manner by which [literary representation] not only *reflects* historical and sociopolitical realities, but further *competes* with them, introducing alternative actualities" (3). She demonstrates the ways in which Arabic and Hebrew literary texts "revisit forgotten narratives and figures and missed opportunities *as a means for envisioning the future in counterhegemonic terms*" (140, emphasis added).

60. Muriam Haleh Davis and James McDougall, eds., "The Afterlives of the Algerian Revolution," *JADMAG* 2, no. 1 (June 2014); James McDougall, *A History of Algeria* (Cambridge: Cambridge University Press, 2017); Marnia Lazreg, *Torture and the Twilight of Empire: From Algiers to Baghdad* (Princeton, NJ: Princeton University Press, 2007), http://catdir.loc.gov/catdir/toc/ecip0715/2007014846.html; Neil MacMaster and Jim House, *Paris 1961: Algerians, State Terror, and Memory* (Oxford: Oxford University Press, 2006), http://site.ebrary.com/lib/yale/Doc?id=10271661; Malika Rahal, "Fused Together and Torn Apart: Stories and Violence in Contemporary Algeria," *History and Memory* 24, no. 1 (spring/summer 2012): 118–51; Thénault, *Une drôle de justice*; Thénault, *Violence ordinaire dans l'Algérie coloniale*; Natalya Vince and Walid Benkhaled, "Performing Algerianness: The National and Transnational Construction of Algeria's 'Culture Wars,'" in *Algeria: Nation, Culture, and Transnationalism*, ed. Patrick Crowley, 243–69 (Liverpool: Liverpool University Press, 2017); Natalya Vince, *Our Fighting Sisters: Nation, Memory, and Gender in Algeria, 1954–2012* (Manchester, UK: Manchester University Press, 2015).

61. Concerning the recent historical scholarship on Algeria's independence war that has burgeoned during and after the 1990s war, see Arthur Asseraf's informative review essay, "Between the World and Algeria: International Histories of the Algerian War of Independence," *Arab Studies Journal* (spring 2017): 198–201.

62. Lazali, *Le trauma colonial*; Tristan Leperlier, *Algérie, les écrivains dans la décennie noire* (Paris: CNRS éditions, 2018).

63. The apt term *translingual* was recently coined by Yasser Elhariry to name the intertextual and lyrical invasion of French by Arabic in postfrancophone poetics; see his *Pacifist Invasions: Arabic, Translation, and the Postfrancophone Lyric* (Liverpool: Liverpool University Press, 2017), in particular the lucid introduction "Word over Word." On this point, see also Hoda El Shakry, *The Literary Qur'an*.

64. See Vince and Benkhaled, "Performing Algerianness."

65. "Il a toujours su que ses rencontres avec le colon se dérouleraient dans un champ clos. Aussi le colonisé ne perd-il pas son temps en lamentations et ne cherche-t-il presque jamais à ce qu'on lui rende justice dans le cadre colonial." Fanon, *Les damnés de la terre*, 82.

66. "Une véritable apocalypse"; "un authentique génocide." Fanon, *Les damnés de la terre*, 241.

67. In "Fureur raciste en France," an essay on French anti-Muslim racism collected in the posthumously published *Pour la révolution africaine* (Paris: Gallimard, 1964, 189–92), Fanon directly cites one of the most provocative lines from Césaire's *Discours sur le colonialism* (1955); see page 192.

68. "L'Algérien, affirmait-on, est un criminel-né." Fanon, *Les damnés de la terre*, 285.

69. "Ces magistrats, ces policiers, ces médecins dissertent très sérieusement sur les rapports de l'âme musulmane et du sang." Fanon, *Les damnés de la terre*, 286.

70. Fanon, *Les damnés de la terre*, 289.

71. "Dans la bouche du doyen des juges d'une chambre à Alger cette aggressivité de l'Algérien se traduit par son amour de la 'fantasia.' 'Toute cette révolte, disait il en 1956, on a tort de la croire politique. De temps à autre, il faut que ça sorte cet amour du baroud qu'ils ont!'" Fanon, *Les damnés de la terre*, 289n2.

72. "Le combattant algérien a une façon de se battre et de mourir, et nulle référence à l'Islam ou au paradis promis ne peut expliquer cette générosité de soi quand il s'agit de protéger le peuple ou de couvrir les frères." Fanon, *Les damnés de la terre*, 285.

73. "... la conséquence d'une organisation du système nerveux ni d'une originalité caractérielle mais le produit direct de la situation coloniale." Fanon, *Les damnés de la terre*, 297.

74. "Exposé à des tentatives de meurtre quotidiennes: de famine, d'expulsion de la chambre non payée, de sein maternel desséché, d'enfants squelettiques, le chantier fermé, les chômeurs qui rôdent autour du gérant comme des corbeaux, l'indigène en arrive à voir son semblable comme un ennemi implacable.... Oui, dans la période coloniale en Algérie et ailleurs on peut faire beaucoup de choses pour un kilo de semoule. On peut tuer plusieurs personnes. *Il faut de l'imagination pour comprendre ces choses. Ou de la mémoire.*" Fanon, *Les damnés de la terre*, 295; my emphasis.

75. Primo Levi, *Si c'est un homme*, trans. Martine Schruoffeneger (Paris: Julliard, [1947] 1987); Elie Wiesel, *La nuit* (Paris: Éditions de Minuit, 1958). For an account of the reception of these survivor testimonies in French, see Annette Wieviorka, *The Era of the Witness*, trans. Jared Stark (Ithaca, NY: Cornell University Press, 2006).

76. "Dans les camps de concentration, des hommes se sont tués pour un morceau de pain." Fanon, *Les damnés de la terre*, 296.

77. "Je me souviens d'une scène horrible. C'était à Oran en 1944." Fanon, *Les damnés de la terre*, 296.

78. "Du camp où nous attendions l'embarquement, les militaires lançaient des morceaux de pain à de petits Algériens qui se les disputaient avec rage et haine. Les vétérinaires pourraient éclairer ces phénomènes en évoquant le fameux 'peck order' constaté dans les basses-cours. Le maïs qui est distribué est en effet l'objet d'une compétition implacable. Certaines volailles, les plus fortes, dévorent toutes les graines tandis que d'autres moins agressives maigrissent à vue d'œil. Toute colonie tend à devenir une immense basse-cour, un immense camp de concentration où la seule loi est celle du couteau." Fanon, *Les damnés de la terre*, 296.

79. "Il y a peu de temps le nazisme a transformé la totalité de l'Europe en véritable colonie." Fanon, *Les damnés de la terre*, 298.

80. "Saint-Arnaud ira quant à lui jusqu'à enfumer des tribus entières, près de huit cent personnes dans une grotte. Les descriptions des convulsions des enfants, des femmes, des personnes âgées et des hommes, provoquées par l'intoxication des fumées, sont insoutenables." Lazali, *Le trauma colonial*, 52n12.

81. "La littérature tente d'écrire les *blancs* et les impensés du fait historique. Surtout, elle oriente le lecteur vers la dynamique incessante entre le texte et ses marges invisibles." Lazali, *Le trauma colonial*, 13.

82. Ranajit Guha's strategy of reading the archive "against the grain" to detect evidence of subaltern agency by identifying its ghostly traces in the written record is a remarkable act of literary imagination, and a gesture that Djebar's novel investigates and extends. See Guha's essays, "On Some Aspects of the Historiography of Colonial India" and "The Prose of Counter-insurgency," both included in *Selected Subaltern Studies*, ed. Ranajit Guha, 37–44 and 45–88 (Oxford: Oxford University Press, 1988).

83. Gayatri Chakravorty Spivak, "Can the Subaltern Speak?," in *Marxism and the Interpretation of Culture*, ed. Cary Nelson and Lawrence Grossberg (Urbana: University of Illinois Press, 1988), 285.

84. In her "Scattered Speculations on the Subaltern and the Popular," Gayatri Spivak clarifies that the term *subaltern* is not an identity position but a structural location, or rather a politically orchestrated *absence*, a site "removed from all lines of social mobility" that cannot be generalized according to hegemonic logic (which would turn it into popular). Spivak adds that "subalternization does not stop," a point that should prompt us to "think of building infrastructure for agency," and learn to "learn from below, *from* the subaltern, rather than only study her." Gayatri Chakravorty Spivak, "Scattered Speculations on the Subaltern and the Popular," *Postcolonial Studies* 8, no. 4 (2005): 475, 477, 482.

85. For these section titles, refer to the table of contents page in Assia Djebar, *L'amour, la fantasia* (Paris: Éditions J. C. Lattès, 1985), 257–58.

86. In Maghrebi dialects, different terms are used for this event. The French word is picked up in Arabic as "fanṭāzya," but it is also called "tbūrīda" and "bāridiyya," from the root "b-r-d" which is linked to gun powder (bārūd), and "khayyāla," from root "kh-i-l" which designates horses.

87. The term may be a French transcription of a word used in Darija and Amazigh languages, "tzaghrit" or "thighratin," which names the trilling sounds made by women to express strong emotion, or "tazzalt," which means prayer. The first term corresponds to the standard Arabic words *zaghrada/zaghrūda* (plural *zaghārīd*) and *taghrīd* (plural *taghārīd*).

88. "Pour lire cet écrit, il me faut renverser mon corps, plonger ma face dans l'ombre, scruter la voûte de rocailles ou de craie, laisser les chuchotements immémoriaux remonter, géologie sanguinolente. Quel magma de sons pourrit là, quelle odeur de putréfaction s'en échappe? Je tâtonne, mon odorat troublé, mes oreilles ouvertes en huîtres, dans la crue de la douleur ancienne. Seule, dépouillée, sans voile, je fais face aux images du noir... Hors de puits des siècles d'hier, comment affronter les sons du passé?" Djebar, *L'amour, la fantasia*, 58.

89. "Il me tend une main inattendue, celle d'une inconnue qu'il n'a jamais pu dessiner." Djebar, *L'amour, la fantasia*, 255.

90. Djebar, *L'amour, la fantasia*, 255.

1. REMNANTS OF MUSLIMS

This chapter is significantly revised from previous publications: "Remnants of Muslims: Reading Agamben's Silence," *New Literary History* 45, no. 4 (autumn 2014): 707–28; and "Am I Not One of the Disappeared?," *Public Books*, April 8, 2019. https://www.publicbooks.org/am-i-not-one-of-the-disappeared/.

Epigraph: Ka-Tzetnik, *Kar'u lo piepel*, trans. Moshe Kohn, *Moni: A Novel of Auschwitz* (Secaucus, NJ: Citadel Press, [1961] 1963), 116–17. Gil Anidjar discusses Ka-Tzetnik's novel in *The Jew, the Arab: A History of the Enemy* (Stanford, CA: Stanford University Press, 2003); see chapter 5, "Muslims (Hegel, Freud, Auschwitz)," 113–49.

1. Achille Mbembe, "Necropolitics," *Public Culture* 15, no. 1 (2003): 11–40; Ranjana Khanna, *Algeria Cuts: Women and Representation, 1830 to the Present* (Stanford, CA: Stanford University Press, 2008); Michael Rothberg, *Multidirectional Memory: Remembering the Holocaust in the Age of Decolonization* (Stanford, CA: Stanford University Press, 2009); Sylvie Thénault, *Violence ordinaire dans l'Algérie coloniale: Camps, internements, assignations à résidence* (Constantine: Saïd Hannachi, Éditions Média-Plus, 2012).

2. Giorgio Agamben, *Homo Sacer: Sovereign Power and Bare Life*, trans. Daniel Heller-Roazen (Stanford, CA: Stanford University Press, [1995] 1998), 185. Hereafter cited in the text as HS.

3. Giorgio Agamben, *Remnants of Auschwitz: The Witness and the Archive*, trans. Daniel Heller-Roazen (New York: Zone Books, [1998] 1999). Hereafter cited in the text as RA.

4. Giorgio Agamben, "What Is a Camp?," in *Means without End: Notes on Politics* (Minneapolis: University of Minnesota Press, 2000).

5. Agamben, "What Is a Camp?," 1.

6. For an illustration of this appeal, see Alison Ross, ed., "The Agamben Effect," special issue, *South Atlantic Quarterly* 107, no. 1 (winter 2008).

7. See Hannah Arendt, *Eichmann in Jerusalem: A Report on the Banality of Evil* (New York: Viking Press, 1963); Shoshana Felman, *The Juridical Unconscious: Trials and Traumas in the Twentieth Century* (Cambridge, MA: Harvard University Press, 2002). An English translation of Ka-Tzetnik's testimony is available in "The Trial of Adolf Eichmann: Record of Proceedings in the District Court of Jerusalem" (Jerusalem: State of Israel Ministry of Justice, 1992) and the filmed testimony can also be watched in a video available online: EichmannTrialEN, "Eichmann Trial—Session No. 68, 69," March 9, 2011, YouTube video, 52:15, https://www.youtube.com/watch?v=m3-tXyYhd5U. The moment in which he says "when I was a 'Muselmann'" is at 7:42; the interpreter does not translate the word.

8. Anidjar, *The Jew, the Arab*, 141–42. When written in European languages, the orthography of the word varies widely; even within a given text the spelling is unstable. From Ka-Tzetnik's Hebrew it is transcribed as "muzelman," and in English translations we see "mussulman" and "musselmen." Primo Levi alternates between the Italian and German forms; so does Agamben. I most often use the French spelling of the word, *musulman*. This is a homophone of the German word *Muselmann*, which I use when referring directly to Auschwitz or citing from texts that do. When spoken aloud, these variations sound very similar; Agamben does not detect the French juridical sense of "musulman" within the term "Muselmann" as he uses it, whereas I use the term *musulman* to register this ghostly quality.

9. Hannah Feldman, *From a Nation Torn: Decolonizing Art and Representation in France, 1945–1962* (Durham, NC: Duke University Press, 2014); Abdelmajid Hannoum, *Violent Modernity: France in Algeria* (Cambridge, MA: Harvard University Press, 2010).

10. Feldman, *From a Nation Torn*, 7.

11. Feldman, *From a Nation Torn*, 7.

12. See Feldman's discussion of this in her introduction to *From a Nation Torn*, which draws on Hannoum's argument about "violent modernity." She writes: "It is instructive

to remember that the uprisings that would eventually culminate in the 1954–1962 Algerian War of Independence actually began in 1945, precisely on 8 May, a date much better celebrated in Western histories as 'Victory in Europe Day.' ... So, just as one moment of violence and genocide was ending and precisely as it was being celebrated with pageantry and parade, another episode in what the historian Abdelmajid Hannoum has recently coined a 'violent modernity' was beginning. Rather than discontinuous and contained, the history of war in France during the decades of decolonizing would prove ongoing and perpetual." Feldman, *From a Nation Torn*, 3.

13. This question has preoccupied others; see, in particular, Anidjar, *The Jew, the Arab*; Fethi Benslama, "La représentation et l'impossible," *Évolution psychiatrique* 66, no. 3 (2001): 448–66.

14. Samera Esmeir, *Juridical Humanity: A Colonial History* (Stanford, CA: Stanford University Press, 2012), 2.

15. Much like Agamben, many other scholars who mention the term within the context of the Shoah stop short after puzzling briefly, often with some expression of discomfort, over the question "why *this* name?" The critiques by Fethi Benslama ("La représentation et l'impossible") and Gil Anidjar (*The Jew, the Arab*) are notable exceptions. Their objections to its use by Agamben hinge precisely on the human status of those designated "musulman," as well as on histories of kinship between Muslims and Jews that are effaced by the twin manifestations of European antisemitism that constructs the "Jew" and the "Muslim" as enemies to be assimilated or destroyed.

16. Quotes from, respectively, David Atkinson, "Encountering Bare Life in Italian Libya and Colonial Amnesia in Agamben," in *Agamben and Colonialism*, ed. Marcelo Svirsky and Simone Bignall (Edinburgh: Edinburgh University Press, 2012), 155; and Rothberg, *Multidirectional Memory*, 62–63.

17. Esmeir, *Juridical Humanity*, 5.

18. Esmeir, *Juridical Humanity*, 17.

19. The film described by Agamben is available online from the British Pathé, which neither identifies this as Bergen-Belsen nor specifies the year. British Pathé, "Concentration Camp Footage 1945," video, 3:19, accessed August 5, 2020, http://www.britishpathe.com/video/concentration-camp-footage. The footage from 0:43 forward is almost certainly the section to which Agamben refers.

20. One of Carpi's drawings is included at the start of this chapter, figure 1.1. The image and others are contained in the Ghetto Fighter's House Museum archives located in a former kibbutz in Western Galilee.

21. Primo Levi, *Survival in Auschwitz*, trans. Stuart Woolf (New York: Crane Books, [1947] 2012). Hereafter cited in the text as SA.

22. This is on page 62 in the Crane Books edition cited above; it is found on page 88 in the Simon and Schuster edition (*Survival in Auschwitz*, trans. Giulio Einaudi [New York: Simon and Schuster, 1996]). There is no such insertion in Levi's Italian; it appears to be an editorial intervention to help readers of the English translation who, unlike Italian or French readers, would find this word unfamiliar.

23. Primo Levi, *The Drowned and the Saved*, trans. Raymond Rosenthal (New York: Random House, [1986] 1989), 17. Hereafter cited in the text as DS.

24. Fethi Benslama takes this transformation of the epithet into a proper name as the starting point for his rigorous critique of Agamben ("La représentation et l'impossible"). Sylvie Thénault, the historian of French imperialism and state violence, observes that this typographic assimilation naturalizes the violence of colonial taxonomy, and she insists that in her own work "'indigènes' et 'musulmans' ne peuvent être écrits sans guillemets" ("indigènes" and "musulmans" cannot be written without quotation marks). Thénault, *Violence ordinaire*, 16. For the same reasons, I follow the practice of Benslama and Thénault and do not naturalize or translate these terms.

25. According to the *Oxford English Dictionary*: "the word occurs in both [Persian and Arabic] but it is not clear in which it originated, ultimately <Arabic *muslim*, n. (the formation is uncertain; perhaps based on Arabic *musalmānī* 'convert to Islam')." "Mussulman, n. and adj.," OED Online, June 2020, Oxford University Press, accessed August 24, 2020, https://www.oed.com/view/Entry/124216?redirectedFrom=musulman. See also the entry for "shahid," naturalized into English like "mussulman." The OED defines *shahid* as "Muslim martyr" based on cases of use in British-colonized South Asia beginning in 1881 ("the Musalman name shahid"; "The martyrs of the new Indian religion, known by the Musalman name shahid, were to have their own exceeding great reward in a future state") and on entries from the 1934 *Encyclopedia of Islam* ("the muslim who falls on the battlefield is called Shahid, 'witness,' 'martyr'"). "Shahid, n.," OED Online, June 2020, Oxford University Press, accessed August 24, 2020, https://www.oed.com/view/Entry/177296?redirectedFrom=shahid.

26. Levi adds to this semantic cluster a term not mentioned by Agamben: "In the Ravensbrück Lager (the only one exclusively for women), the same concept was expressed, so I'm told by Lydia Rolfi, by the two specular substantives *Schmutzstück* and *Schmuckstück*, respectively, 'garbage' and 'jewel,' almost homophonous, one the parody of the other" (*DS* 99).

27. Thomas Keneally, *Schindler's Ark* (London: Coronet, 1983), 347.

28. The 1939 famine was the direct result of colonial policies documented and denounced by Albert Camus in reports with titles like "Famine in Algeria," later compiled in his *Chroniques algériennes, 1939–1958* (Paris: Gallimard, 1958).

29. Achille Mbembe's "Necropolitics" is an important correction of this marginalization; notably, Mbembe begins his critique of Agamben by turning to the Algerian scene and to Fanon's texts in particular.

30. On the question of vengeance and judgment, see Judith Butler's reading of Hannah Arendt's *Eichmann in Jerusalem*, "Hannah Arendt's Death Sentences," in "Trials of Trauma," special issue, *Comparative Literature Studies* 48, no. 3 (2011): 280–95.

31. This passage from Ka-Tzetnik's novel is cited as the opening epigraph to this chapter.

32. On the obscured yet highly visible quality of this violence, see Hannah Feldman's chapter "'The Eye of History': Photojournalism, Protest, and the *Manifestation* of 17 October 1961," in *From a Nation Torn*, 159–99. For a study of the paradoxically visible erasure of the event from historical archives, see Lia Brozgal's essay "In the Absence of the Archive (Paris, October 17, 1961)," in *South Central Review* 31, no. 1 (2014): 34–54.

33. The original text of Maurice Papon's order is transcribed by Jean-Luc Einaudi in *La bataille de Paris—17 octobre 1961* (Paris: Seuil, 1991), 85. In 1999, Papon would lose a suit for libel against Einaudi for accusing him of orchestrating and condoning "massacre" of Algerians in Paris in 1961.

34. Anne Tristan, *Le silence du fleuve: Ce crime que nous n'avons toujours pas nommé* (Bezons: Au nom de la mémoire, 1991). Kristin Ross develops this point in her readings of literary texts by William Gardner Smith, Didier Daeninckx, and Jean-François Vilar in her *May '68 and Its Afterlives* (Chicago: University of Chicago Press, 2002).

35. For a detailed and fascinating discussion of the production of the now-iconic graffiti and photograph taken beside the Seine, see Vincent Lemire and Yann Potin, "Ici on noie les Algériens: Fabriques documentaires, avatars politiques et mémoires partagées d'une icône militante (1961–2011)," *Genèses* 49, no. 4 (2002): 140–62.

36. For a detailed chronological summary of texts, theater, film, radio, and music concerning the events of October 17, 1961, see Gilles Manceron's bibliography in the 2011 edition of Marcel and Paulette Péju, *Le 17 octobre des Algériens, suivi de Gilles Manceron, la triple occultation d'un massacre* (Paris: La Découverte, 2012), 187–94.

37. Neil MacMaster and Jim House, *Paris 1961: Algerians, State Terror, and Memory* (Oxford: Oxford University Press, 2006), http://site.ebrary.com/lib/yale/Doc?id =10271661.

38. Brozgal, "In the Absence of the Archive" and *Absent the Archive: Cultural Traces of a Massacre in Paris, 17 October 1961* (Liverpool: Liverpool University Press, 2020).

39. Sylvie Thénault's *Violence ordinaire* illustrates this point in detail, while House and MacMaster recontextualize the police massacre of Algerians in Paris as just one of many in a long history of French state violence that has become exceptionally visible (even in its invisibility) only because of *where* it took place—"in the heart of Empire, rather than in the streets of Algerian cities." See House and MacMaster, *Paris 1961*, 4–5.

40. "Ce raisonnement qui prévoit très arithmétiquement la disparition du peuple colonisé." Frantz Fanon, "De la violence," in *Les damnés de la terre* (Paris: La Découverte, [1961] 2002), 82.

41. "Moze n'était plus français et les autorités algériennes l'avaient assigné comme 'étranger à la nation.' Ils l'ont interné. Mis dans un camp." Zahia Rahmani, *Moze* (Paris: Sabine Wespieser, 2003), 44.

42. This is most likely drawn from Canetti's *Les voix de Marrakech*, published after his visit to that city in 1956, an explicit intertext in *Moze* that the narrator describes reading during her visit to Algiers in 1991. Recall that Agamben *also* refers to Canetti's writings in his description of the unbearable sight of the Muselmänner at Auschwitz, an image which deeply informs the chapter of *Remnants of Auschwitz* entitled "Shame." Agamben cites: "As Elias Canetti has noted, a heap of dead bodies is an ancient spectacle, one which has often satisfied the powerful. But the sight of the Muselmänner is an absolutely new phenomenon, unbearable to human eyes" (*RA* 51).

43. Rahmani, *Moze*, epigraph page.

44. Rahmani, *Moze*, epigraph page.

45. "Tu es mort un lundi. Le jeudi, ils ont apporté ton cercueil à la maison. Il était fermé. Parce que ton corps avait été ouvert et découpé, on ne voyait que ton visage derrière un hublot." Rahmani, *Moze*, 15.

46. "Flottant dans la soie blanche et quelques algues." Rahmani, *Moze*, 15.

47. Although Rahmani does not cite Agamben in her novels, the intertextual relationship is apparent to a close reader of Agamben because of the way that so many of Agamben's idiosyncratic turns of phrase and precisely formulated images are reformulated and transfigured in Rahmani's rather wildly dialogic prose. She confirms in private conversation that she has indeed closely read *Remnants of Auschwitz*, and that her use of the term *musulman* is informed by this reading.

48. Citations from Rahmani's novel in this section are drawn from Matt Reeck's English translation, *"Muslim": A Novel* (Dallas: Deep Vellum, 2019), unless otherwise noted. The French reads: "J'ai su l'existence du Nom à l'âge de dix ans." Zahia Rahmani, *"Musulman" roman* (Paris: Sabine Wespieser, 2005), 38.

49. "Disons que vivant il était mort. Il ne l'a pas eue sa vie. Il est né mort." Rahmani, *"Musulman" roman*, 39.

50. The film was subject to controversy and censorship. Resnais had included photographs of French officers guarding detention centers from which Jews were deported, operated in collaboration with the Vichy government; this scene prompted a call to be cut by French censors because "it might be offensive in the eyes of the present-day military" (this was 1955; the present-day military was also present-day fighting the war in Algeria, and the offense should be read in that light).

51. "*Nuit et brouillard* me disait, Il y a eu six millions d'hommes et de femmes tués. Tués parce qu'ils étaient... Eux, ils n'avaient qu'un Nom. Un seul Nom." Rahmani, *"Musulman" roman*, 39–40.

52. "Ce regard insoutenable, cette figure extrême de la culpabilité, je veux m'en défaire. Je ne veux pourtant pas l'innocenter. Qu'en est-il de cette faute? Celle que je porte, qui n'est pas la mienne et que je ne peux pardonner? Comment sortir seule d'une culpabilité endossée?" Rahmani, *Moze*, 23.

53. "C'est arrivé le 11 novembre, mais c'est venu bien avant. Vivant, il était mort." Rahmani, *Moze*, 19.

54. "Moze était un supplétif de l'armée française. Il a rejoint ses compagnons d'armes le 11 novembre 1991. À 8 h 30, on l'a vu qui saluait le monument aux victimes de la Grande Guerre. À 9 h 15, deux chasseurs le trouvaient noyé flottant dans l'étang communal. Ses lunettes et son chapeau étaient près de lui." Rahmani, *Moze*, 20.

55. "[Désigné] comme un banni, un être indigne... une espèce d'homme"; "cette homme concerne l'histoire." Rahmani, *Moze*, 23, 22.

56. "Ce que sa langue ne suffisait pas à dire, c'est le système qui permit à l'État français de fabriquer une armée de soldatmorts sans se soucier qu'ils étaient des hommes." Rahmani, *Moze*, 20.

57. Rahmani, *Moze*, 20.

58. "Moze n'a pas été tué,... arrêté, torturé, interné, vendu, déplacé, recelé, acheté, déplacé,... interné, transferé, frappé, négocié, racheté, emprisonné, torturé, recelé, déplacé, frappé, venu, racheté." Rahmani, *Moze*, 22.

59. "Milliers de corps perdus." Rahmani, *Moze*, 21.

60. "Je suis devenue, *re*devenue, 'Musulman.'" Rahmani, *Moze*, 13.

61. "J'ai regardé plus loin, loin derrière les barbelés. Il y avait l'autre camp. Celui des hommes. Tous assis, regard noir baissé vers le sol." Rahmani, *Moze*, 124.

62. "Je regarde la masse des corps à genoux. Rien ne semble la perturber. Le désert est puissant." Rahmani, *Moze*, 124.

63. "Rien dans ce régard ne dit qu'ils se soumettent à leur condition." Rahmani, *"Musulman" roman*, 126.

64. "Son fatalisme? Sa nonchalance, *c'est sa résistance.*" Rahmani, *Moze*, 95.

65. "Et c'est dans leur visage que j'ai pu lire. Ce n'est pas une absence d'existence que montrent ces visages, non, c'est un visage étranger à l'intérêt. Un refus de l'intérêt porté par le visage, porté par la seule dignité du visage. Le corps à genoux ne défait pas le visage." Rahmani, *"Musulman" roman*, 128.

66. "C'est en cette lenteur que réside son unique bien, celui dans lequel se loge son honneur d'homme, comme on l'a dit des esclaves dans les champs de coton, moins vite, toujours moins vite." Rahmani, *Moze*, 95.

67. "Oui, ce monde désert comme son âme vide et inculte! Voilà ce que se disaient les hommes en armes qui tenaient ce camp. Dans ce désert, on ne trouvera rien. Tout y est laissé en l'état. Ils n'ont même pas su faire fructifier leur terre!" Rahmani, *"Musulman" roman*, 128. On this gaze and the colonizing project of French cartography in Algeria, see Hélène Blais, *Mirages de la carte: L'invention de l'Algérie coloniale* (Paris: Fayard, 2014).

68. "Voilà ce que se disaient les hommes qui tenaient les fusils de ce camp." Rahmani, *"Musulman" roman*, 128.

69. This term is from Orlando Patterson, *Slavery and Social Death* (Cambridge, MA: Harvard University Press, 1985).

70. "Ce pays cherche. Il cherche encore. Il lui faut du temps.... Le mensonge le gouverne et la peur règne jusque sur les ombres.... Et dehors la barbarie s'exhibe!" (This country is searching. It is still searching. It needs time.... It is governed by lies and fear reigns even in the shadows.... And outside, barbarism runs rampant!) Rahmani, *Moze*, 86–87.

71. "Je ne lui dois rien. Lui il me doit de me quitter, de quitter mon esprit, il me doit de partir. Il me doit de ne plus revenir. Je suis venue ici pour m'en débarrasser!" Rahmani, *Moze*, 85.

72. "—Comment dire la dignité de celui qui n'existe pas? /—Ramène-le chez les morts. /—Est-ce qu'un musulman revient de la mort? /—Il est écrit que les hommes meurent et ressuscitent. /—La rumeur gronde. On préfère qu'il ne revienne pas." Rahmani, *Moze*, 95.

73. "Les musulmans ont été méprisés. On les a tués en si grand nombre et si librement tout le long des décennies précédentes que vraisemblablement ils n'étaient bons qu'à être exploités et domestiqués pour les nécessités du moment. Ceux d'Afrique du Nord l'ont été, à force de luttes, de vols et de séquestres. Ensuite, et par milliers, à force de privations, d'épidémies et de famines. Certains étaient même montrés dans les foires. On a envoyé au bagne ou fusillé ceux qui ont fui la conscription, refusé de servir le drapeau français. Il y a eu ceux des lignes avancées de 1914, et ceux qui, après cette guerre, furent

enrôlés comme force de travail étaient déjà des hommes finis. La survivance aux abois du colonialisme passait par la clochardisation de l'homme colonisé. L'*omertà* coloniale vient de cette honte. Celle d'avoir à avouer cette absence totale d'humanité." Rahmani, *Moze*, 94–95.

74. "Ne crois-tu pas que tant qu'on parle d'indemnisation on ne parle pas des massacres?" Rahmani, *Moze*, 92.

75. "Tu veux un colloque, un symposium, une conférence internationale avec images d'archives?... La vérité sera impossible." Rahmani, *Moze*, 91.

76. "Ils nous emmerdent avec les chiffres! 20 000 morts? 30 000, 90 000, 100 000, 130 000 harkis fusillés! Ou lynchés ou brûlés? 150 000, 180 000 soldatmorts ignorés? 200 000, 250 000, 300 000, 400 000 matricules! 600 000 ou 900 000 peut-être? 1 000 000, 2 000 000, 5 000 000, plus, plus encore! Tous les contrats ont eu un matricule et ces documents sont archivés. On sait leurs noms. Qu'on nous dise les noms des disparus! Qu'on nous les donne les noms! Donnez-les!" Rahmani, *Moze*, 91.

77. "République française—Commission nationale de réparation—Convocation à témoigner." Rahmani, *Moze*, 88.

78. Rahmani, *Moze*, 96.

79. Rahmani, *Moze*, 96. Notably, "ceux qui restent" echoes the French title of *Remnants of Auschwitz*, which is *Ce qui reste d'Aushwitz*.

80. Rahmani, *Moze*, 92.

81. "—APPROCHEZ! / Ainsi commence l'acte de justice. / Je suis dans un grand espace face à un haut mur. J'entends, approchez et je sais que je vais dire ce que je veux dire. Tout ce que je tiens à dire je vais le dire." Rahmani, *Moze*, 107.

82. "Nous avons pour mission de recueillir dans la transparence et l'équité votre témoignage concernant votre père. Vous n'avez pas à prêter serment." Rahmani, *Moze*, 108.

83. "Moze était un Algérien. Un *musulman d'origine algérienne* selon les termes en vigueur. La France conquérante et reconnaissante, aimant ses terres, ses ancêtres et son pouvoir, l'a fait *Français musulman d'Algérie*. C'est ce qu'il est devenu." Rahmani, *Moze*, 112; emphasis added.

84. "Cette guerre est terminée, dit le président." Rahmani, *Moze*, 112.

85. "L'histoire qui nous concerne n'est pas close. Tout est vif. Il faut agir." Rahmani, *Moze*, 126.

86. "Peut-on solliciter le pardon de celui à qui on a demandé une trahison?" Rahmani, *Moze*, 110.

87. "On m'a défigurée. Un malentendu rend précaire, fragile, ma nationalité. Il y a un trou dans ma citoyenneté et c'est difficile à vivre." Rahmani, *Moze*, 115.

88. "Mon père portait l'ambiguïté de ce siècle: l'humanité ignominieuse. L'ignominieuse humanité de ce siècle! Nous avons été donnés parce que nous n'étions rien! Des Arabes, des musulmans. Nous avons servi à couvrir la fuite d'une armée! Un tapis de corps morts en guise de souvenir." Rahmani, *Moze*, 128.

89. Rahmani, *Moze*, 122.

90. "Une technique concentrationnaire"; "la pulvérisation opérée par la politique coloniale"; "Une politique de séparation. La politique algérienne de ce pays était fondée sur

ce principe. Elle était étroite, raciste, et lâche.... Et ce monde-là, *c'est celui de la France!*" Rahmani, *Moze*, 135, 122.

91. Rahmani, *Moze*, 116.

92. "Il ne faut plus se demander s'il y a eu de la torture. Il y en a eu. Des viols? En grand nombre. Des hommes meurtris? Trop." Rahmani, *Moze*, 126.

93. Rahmani, *Moze*, 134.

94. "J'accuse le peuple français de m'avoir abandonnée. J'accuse ce pays d'avoir tué mon père. Voilà pour l'accusation. Quant à la plainte, il manque l'office, le bureau, l'instance qui doit la délivrer.... Cette plainte je vous la dis. C'est fait. Voilà! Le tribunal? C'est pareil. On y est." Rahmani, *Moze*, 125.

95. "Je dois pourtant plaider non pas pour le réhabiliter ou disculper mais pour dire ce que signifie le devoir de témoignage dont je suis moi le légataire." Rahmani, *Moze*, 131.

96. "Vous faites la justice. Vous êtes les juges et la loi. Si la dignité de la France souffre d'une telle requête, vous trouverez l'argument qui lui épargnera le ridicule. Ce pays a fait cet homme. Et il vous revient à vous, vous les magistrats du monde, d'en proscrire à jamais l'existence. Plus un homme ne sera un banni. Plus un! Imaginons qu'aucune loi, qu'aucune politique ne pourront justifier cet homme. Jamais plus! Jamais plus un homme ne sera un banni!" Rahmani, *Moze*, 127.

97. "Ce qui doit être condamné dans la condamnation de Moze c'est ce qui a permis son existence." Rahmani, *Moze*, 136.

98. "Il faut le dire, c'est vrai qu'il y a eu dans ce pays un acte grave! Il faut l'écrire. Il faut parler, parler de ce qui a eu lieu! Parler avec qui l'ont vécu. Parler ceux-là avec eux pour taire la violence, parler pour que la parole exerce son droit, parler pour que le visage existe, parler pour que les larmes viennent enfin, parler pour que l'homme ne tue plus, parler pour que cesse ce mépris, parler pour que l'homme se réconcilie, parler pour que fondent les armes, parler pour que le chant ne soit plus sombre, parler pour toutes ces femmes..." Rahmani, *Moze*, 136.

99. "Seule pour leur dire que tous les miens crèvent d'avoir cru à ce mensonge. La République..." Rahmani, *Moze*, 144.

100. Unless otherwise noted, the citations from Rahmani's novel in this section are drawn from Matt Reeck's English translation, *"Muslim": A Novel*. In the original this passage reads: "Si tout ce peuple disparaissait? Mais n'a-t-il pas disparu déjà? Disparu. Ne suis-je pas moi-même 'un disparu'? Mon corps est là. Mais vivante ou morte, ne suis-je pas du même lot? Je ne compte pas." Rahmani, *"Musulman" roman*, 127.

101. "Et dans cette tôle où on veut m'éteindre, je la fais encore rouler. Une langue, ça parle toujours." Rahmani, *"Musulman" roman*, 75.

102. "Je suis née dans une langue mineure pour surgir d'un nulle-part lointain qui ne me voulait pas." Rahmani, *"Musulman" roman*, 73.

103. Hagar appears in the book of Genesis and is alluded to in the Qur'ān. In Islamic tradition she is considered to be Abraham's second wife. In Genesis she is the Egyptian slave of Sarah, Abraham's wife, given to Abraham in order to produce a child; she was then cast out to wander in the desert with her son Ishmael. Islamic tradition understands her as a matriarch of the prophet's lineage; the prophet Muhammad descended

from Ishmael. Hagar is also an important figure who has been taken up by Black feminist/womanist theologies, the powerful figure of an exiled slave in the wilderness.

104. "La mère mit son fils sur ses épaules et marcha vers le désert. Épuisée, elle parvint à une source. Elle y déposa l'enfant. Et puis, d'elle, l'histoire ne dit plus rien. Plus rien. Sa vie s'arrête. L'enfant se retrouvait sans père et Agar disparaissait dans les limbes du récit. Ainsi je venais peut-être de lui, d'Ishmaël, le fils abandonné né d'une mère esclave répudiée. D'une mère qu'on effacera. Qu'on obliera. Et par là même d'une femme dont on effacera la descendance. Je m'inscris donc dans cette origine-là." Rahmani, *"Musulman" roman*, 36.

105. On this, see Nancy Fraser, "Reframing Justice in a Globalizing World," *New Left Review* 36 (November–December 2005): 69–88; and Nancy Fraser, "Abnormal Justice," *Critical Inquiry* 34, no. 3 (spring 2008): 393–422, especially 408.

2. UNTRANSLATABLE JUSTICE

Epigraphs: Frantz Fanon, "Lettre à un français," in *Pour la révolution africaine: Écrits politiques* (Paris: La Découverte, 2001), 56; Jacques Vergès, *De la stratégie judiciaire* (Paris: Les Éditions de Minuit, 1968), 209.

1. "La justice militaire voulait une liquidation rapide et discrète de cette affaire." Gisèle Halimi and Simone de Beauvoir, *Djamila Boupacha* (Paris: Gallimard, 1962), 62.

2. "Ce n'était pas toujours efficace, parce que c'était quelquefois trop tard. Mais, pour Djamila et pour d'autres, il était encore temps. Il fallait le dire, l'écrire, réclamer justice." Halimi and Beauvoir, *Djamila Boupacha*, 41–42. For an illuminating reflection on Halimi's justice work and commitments as context for understanding her involvement in Boupacha's case, see the chapter "Gisèle Halimi's Autobiographical and Legal Narratives: Doing to Trees What They Did to Me," in Mireille Rosello's *The Reparative in Narratives: Works of Mourning in Progress* (Liverpool: Liverpool University Press, 2010), 141–86.

3. "L'homme responsable, dans le gouvernement, de cette affirmation 'On ne torture plus en Algérie.'" Halimi and Beauvoir, *Djamila Boupacha*, 60–61.

4. Halimi and Beauvoir, *Djamila Boupacha*, 61.

5. "Qu'est-ce qu'on peut dire? Qu'est-ce qu'on peut dire? répétait-il." Halimi and Beauvoir, *Djamila Boupacha*, 62.

6. "Elle dit 'oui' comme une chose qui allait sans dire." Halimi and Beauvoir, *Djamila Boupacha*, 63.

7. Many of the documents and testimonies emerging from Algeria were swiftly censored and thus circulated illegally, if they circulated at all. According to Benjamin Stora, between 1958 and 1962, 14 percent of all texts concerning the Algerian war were seized by French authorities; the seized texts were exclusively those that concerned torture, addressed atrocities committed by the French army in Algeria and France, or questioned either the war itself or the silences of the government about the war. See Benjamin Stora, *Le livre, mémoire de l'histoire: Réflexions sur le livre et la guerre d'Algérie* (Paris: Éditions Le Préau des collines, 2005).

8. Simone de Beauvoir, *La force des choses* (Paris: Gallimard, 1963).

9. "Au début du printemps 59 nous fut révélé un visage peu connu de cette guerre exterminatrice: *les camps.*" Beauvoir, *La force des choses*, 479. For detailed information about these camps and their history in the penal institutions of Algérie française, see Sylvie Thénault, *Violence ordinaire dans l'Algérie coloniale: Camps, internement, assignations à résidence* (Constantine: Saïd Hannachi, Editions Média-Plus, 2012). About the term *concentration camp*, see Annette Wieviorka, "L'expression 'camp de concentration' au XXe siècle," *Vingtième siècle: Revue d'histoire* 54 (April 1997): 4–12. For the works cited in *La force des choses*, see Pierre Henri Simon, *Contre la torture* (Paris: Éditions du Seuil, 1957); *Des rappelés témoignent* (Paris: Comité de résistance spirituelle, 1957); Georges Arnaud and Jacques Vergès, *Pour Djamila Bouhired* (Paris: Éditions de Minuit, 1961); Henri Alleg, *La question* (Paris: Éditions de Minuit, 1957); Jacques Vergès, Michel Zavrian, and Maurice Courrège, *Les disparus: Le cahier vert* (Paris: Éditions de Minuit, 1959); *La gangrène* (Paris: Éditions de Minuit, 1959).

10. Both Annette Wieviorka and Michael Rothberg pinpoint 1961 as a year in which French demand for testimony was suddenly ignited. Wieviorka attributes this to the unprecedented circulation of testimonies from the 1961 Eichmann proceedings, while Rothberg identifies 1961 as the moment during which both Holocaust testimony and testimony of French colonial violence "went public" in a new way: "In 'going public,' as both Holocaust testimony and testimony to colonial crimes did around 1961," Rothberg writes, "testimony ultimately becomes part of the historical record and larger democratic debates, as it also potentially enters the field of legal justice" (215). Annette Wieviorka, *The Era of the Witness*, trans. Jared Stark (Ithaca, NY: Cornell University Press, [1998] 2006); Michael Rothberg, *Multidirectional Memory: Remembering the Holocaust in the Age of Decolonization* (Stanford, CA: Stanford University Press, 2009), esp. part 3, "Truth, Torture, and Testimony: Holocaust Memory during the Algerian War," and part 4, "October 17, 1961: A Site of Holocaust Memory?"

11. From Beauvoir: "Une Algérienne de vingt-trois ans, agent de liaison du FLN, a été séquestrée, torturée, violée avec une bouteille par des militaires français: c'est *banal.*" Halimi and Beauvoir, *Djamila Boupacha*, 1. From Fanon: "Cette *banalité* qui veut que les sept Français tués ou blessés au col de Sakamody soulèvent l'indignation des consciences civilisées tandis que. . . ." Frantz Fanon, *Les damnés de la terre* (Paris: La Découverte, [1961] 2014), 86.

12. The disturbance that Beauvoir documents here can be understood as a form of what Ariella Azoulay has more recently called *civil distress*. She gives the name *civil distress* to "what happens when those who were trained by the regime not to identify the existence of a disaster as such begin to recognize it, but what they start to perceive clearly as disaster continues not to be perceived so by others." Ariella Azoulay, "Potential History: Thinking through Violence," *Critical Inquiry* 39, no. 3 (spring 2013): 549.

13. "Depuis 1954, nous sommes tous complices d'un génocide qui, sous le nom de répression, puis de pacification, a fait plus d'un million de victimes: hommes, femmes, vieillards, enfants, mitraillés au cours des ratissages, brûlés vifs dans leurs villages, abattus, égorgés, éventrés, martyrisés à mort; des tribus entières livrées à la faim, au froid, aux coups, aux épidémies, dans ces 'centres de regroupement' qui sont en fait des camps d'extermination—servant accessoirement de bordels aux corps d'élite—et où agonisent

actuellement plus de cinq cent mille Algériens. Au cours de ces derniers mois, la presse, même la plus prudente, a déversé sur nous l'horreur: assassinats, lynchages, ratonnades, chasses à l'homme dans les rues d'Oran; à Paris, au fil de la Seine, pendus aux arbres du bois de Boulogne, des cadavres par dizaines; des mains brisées; des crânes éclatés; la Toussaint rouge d'Alger. Pouvons-nous encore être émus par le sang d'une jeune fille?" Halimi and Beauvoir, *Djamila Boupacha*, 1.

14. "'*Je ne suis qu'une détenue parmi des milliers d'autres,*' disait l'autre jour Djamila à son avocat. En effet, il y a 14 000 Algériens enfermés dans les camps et les prisons de France, 17 000 dans les prisons d'Algérie, des *centaines de milles* parqués dans les camps d'Algérie." Halimi and Beauvoir, *Djamila Boupacha*, 12.

15. "Vous qui pleurez si volontiers et si abondamment sur des malheurs anciens—Anne Frank ou le ghetto de Varsovie... vous vous rangez parmi les bourreaux de ceux qui souffrent aujourd'hui. Vous consentez paisiblement aux martyres que subissent, en votre nom, presque sous vos yeux, des milliers de Djamila et d'Ahmed." Halimi and Beauvoir, *Djamila Boupacha*, 12.

16. In their *Paris 1961: Algerians, State Terror, and Memory* (Oxford: Oxford University Press, 2006), Jim House and Neil MacMaster discuss this escalation as an effect of De Gaulle's generalized anxiety about losing the empire, and challenge the ways in which historians have rationalized (or have not acknowledged) this radical escalation of French state violence. They situate the police massacre of Algerians that took place in Paris during October 1961 within the broader context of "chaos and violence in the final stages of the Algerian War," highlighting a structural blindness: "the brutal repression of unarmed and peaceful demonstration of 17 October was one among many acts of state violence as the colonial regime disintegrated," they write; "*what distinguished this event was its location in the capital, the heart of empire, rather than in the streets of Algerian cities*" (4–5, emphasis added).

17. In June 1960, Beauvoir's essay "Pour Djamila Boupacha" first appeared in *Le Monde* and later became the preface to *Djamila Boupacha*. The issue was seized by the police. Two weeks later, novelist Françoise Sagan published an open letter, "La jeune fille et la grandeur," and invited protestors to add their names; the list of signatures grew long and by the end of the month the committee had formed. Hundreds of support letters and telegrams poured in from all over France, Italy, England, the Soviet Union, Costa Rica, Egypt, and Israel: signs of what Halimi describes as an international "réveil brutal" to the crimes of the French colonial state. Halimi and Beauvoir, *Djamila Boupacha*, 66.

18. "... de Turin... à New York... à Oxford... à Copenhague, à Costa Rica, à Rabat, à Pékin, Djamila Boupacha est devenue une figure familière. On parle d'elle à table, au bureau, à l'usine et dans les champs, comme une petite sœur qui témoigne pour l'avenir d'un système qui ne survit que par la honte et la férocité." Gisèle Halimi, "D'Henri Alleg à Djamila Boupacha," *Les temps modernes* (June 1960): 1832.

19. The effectiveness of their collective effort to transform Boupacha into an international symbol for the violations of colonialism is reflected by the way that Boupacha's name and case continue to feature in scholarship on torture, testimony, and the Algerian independence war. See, for example, Ranjana Khanna, "The Experience of Evidence: Language, the Law, and the Mockery of Justice," in *Algeria Cuts: Women and Representation*,

1830 to the Present (Stanford, CA: Stanford University Press, 2007); Rosello, *Reparative in Narratives*, 144; Joseph Slaughter, "Narration in International Human Rights Law," *CLCWeb: Comparative Literature and Culture* 9, no. 1 (2007): 11; Mary Anne Lewis, "The Maghreb Goes Abroad: The 'Worlding' of Postcolonial North African Francophone Literature and Film in a Global Market" (unpublished diss., Yale University, 2013; book manuscript in progress); Françoise Vergès, *Le ventre des femmes: Capitalisme, racialisation, féminisme* (Paris: Albin Michel, 2017).

20. In recent decades, scholars have excavated and probed the unruly, unofficial archive generated by antiwar activists during this time to elucidate the many ways that these disputes—over torture, state terror, racism, justice—continue to shape postcolonial France and transnational intellectual and political movements in consequential ways. Their work brings to view the important legacies of anticolonial activist projects and traces out an alternative archaeology of nondominant and radical forms of knowledge production in and beyond "postwar" France. Such works include Khanna, *Algeria Cuts*; Rothberg, *Multidirectional Memory*; Rosello, *Reparative in Narratives*; Hannah Feldman, *From a Nation Torn: Decolonizing Art and Representation in France* (Durham, NC: Duke University Press, 2014); Debarati Sanyal, *Memory and Complicity: Migrations of Holocaust Remembrance* (New York: Fordham University Press, 2015).

21. Directly after President Macron's 2018 statement concerning French state culpability in the disappearance and murder of Maurice Audin, Sylvie Thénault questioned the point of this official recognition, given that the 1962 amnesty suspended all legal plaints and rendered such cases permanently legally untranslatable. See Sylvie Thénault, "À quoi va servir la reconnaissance de l'implication de l'État dans la mort de Maurice Audin?," *The Conversation*, September 13, 2018, https://theconversation.com/a-quoi-va-servir-la-reconnaissance-de-limplication-de-letat-dans-la-mort-de-maurice-audin-103144.

22. "Comme je vous l'ai déjà dit, le peuple algérien n'a jamais cessé de lutter depuis 1830.... Donc on était des enfants de militants.... Pour nous ce qui est important c'est la libération de notre pays." This interview footage appears between minutes 54:12 and 101:13 of the documentary film by Malek Bensmaïl about the history and making of Pontecorvo's iconic film, entitled *La bataille d'Alger: Un film dans l'histoire* (Hikayet films, 2018). The original clip of this interview with Boupacha comes from the documentary film by Ange Casta and Igor Barrère, *L'Algérie dix ans après: Partie 1, L'Algérie des Algériens* (INA, 1972). The full film is available online at the INA archives: https://madelen.ina.fr/programme/lalgerie-dix-ans-apres-1-lalgerie-des-algeriens.

23. "Tout le peuple l'a été." *L'Algérie dix ans après: Partie 1, L'Algérie des Algériens* (INA, 1972).

24. "*Tout le monde* a été touché par la révolution. *Tout le monde* a été torturé." *L'Algérie dix ans après: Partie 1, L'Algérie des Algériens* (INA, 1972).

25. See Christiane Chaulet-Achour, "La torture et la guerre: Mémoires en décalage," *Diacritik*, September 28, 2018, https://diacritik.com/2018/09/28/la-torture-et-la-guerre-memoires-en-decalage-france-algerie/.

26. For instance, those works such as Djamal Amrani's *Le témoin* (1960), the many testimonies published in *El Moudjahid*, or the testimonies of victims of violence collected as case studies at the conclusion of Fanon's *Les damnés de la terre*.

27. Chaulet-Achour notes that if French-language texts picked up by French publishers were hard to publish and subject to censorship, the barriers to publication for other articles, songs, poems, theater, and novels were even more formidable—especially those composed by Algerians for Algerian audiences without mediation from French publishers and famous French writers, and especially those works not produced in French. According to Chaulet-Achour, the works that were produced between 1962 and 2000—the two moments of intense French interest in the problem of torture—were much more anchored to Algerian experiences and audiences, constituting a rich literary archive that has never attracted much interest from French readers, or, for that matter, from scholars. She lists Myriam Ben, *Nora* (1982); Ali Boumendjel's poem for Mohamed Larbi Ben M'Hidi published in *Matinale de mon peuple* in 1961; an anthology edited by Denise Barrat, *Espoir et parole*, published 1963 by Seghers, including a poem written by Leïla Djabali while she was in prison at Barberousse; and another anthology, *Diwan algérien*, ed. Jamel-Eddine Bencheikh and Jacqueline Lévi-Valensi published by SNED in 1967.

28. At first, these activist texts appear principally invested in generating the "discernible grammar" of what the political theorist Nancy Fraser has called a *normal justice* claim. This form of justice—which the testimonial texts in my chapter seem to demand—rests on two ontological premises: the first concerns *who* can be subject of a justice claim (namely, citizens), and the second concerns what authority should be addressed by this claim (the nation-state). Fraser identifies a recognizable monological character to "normal" justice claims, and demonstrates how "abnormal" justice claims have a different character that cuts across the state-bounded terms of this framing of justice: "What has been problematized is the Westphalian view that the modern territorial state is the sole unit within which justice applies.... Effectively territorializing justice, the Westphalian frame equated the scope of concern with the citizenry of a bounded political community. The effect was to drastically limit, if not wholly to exclude, binding obligations of justice that cut across borders." Nancy Fraser, "Abnormal Justice," *Critical Inquiry* 34, no. 3 (spring 2008): 401. My claim is that the testimonial texts disrupt the *normal* framing of justice to expose the need for a new frame, and that this frame has been offered by literary texts. See also Nancy Fraser, "Reframing Justice in a Globalizing World," *New Left Review* 36 (November–December 2005): 69–88.

29. Jacques Derrida, "Politics and Poetics of Witnessing," in *Sovereignties in Question: The Poetics of Paul Celan*, ed. Thomas Dutoit and Outi Pasanen (New York: Fordham University Press, 2005), 65–96. Quoted material from 78.

30. Derrida, "Politics and Poetics of Witnessing," 72.

31. Derrida, "Politics and Poetics of Witnessing," 66–67.

32. Derrida, "Politics and Poetics of Witnessing," 42.

33. "Des lois très strictes édictées pour protéger les prisonniers de guerre." Lindon, *La gangrène*, 81.

34. "Il s'agit là de séquelles de la vérole, du totalitarisme nazi." Lindon, *La gangrène*, 7. More specifically than "pox," *vérole* implies syphilis or smallpox, an ailment and metaphor with a long literary tradition, especially in nineteenth-century French literature.

35. Michelet's infection metaphor is suggestively enhanced by knowledge of his biography: active in the French Resistance (credited with staging the first act of the resistance in 1940), he was arrested by the Gestapo and deported to Dachau in 1943, where he was infected by the typhus epidemic, but survived. He was among the last to leave Dachau because he stayed to aid the last of the sick prisoners, was made minister of the army by de Gaulle in 1946, and served as minister of justice during the most violent years of the Algerian war (1959–61). In Beauvoir's description of her meeting with Michelet about Djamila Boupacha, he obsessively repeats the word *gangrène*, as if he has no real power to stop the torture even though he is in the legal position to intervene. Hannah Feldman offers a compelling analysis of Michelet's urban redesign of Paris, which deliberately concealed visible signs of North African immigrants. Feldman, *From a Nation Torn*, 2014.

36. "Mon supplice n'est rien, à côté de celui de mes frères et de mes sœurs d'Algérie, brûlés vifs, mutilés, humiliés, violés, empalés, et coupés en morceaux. Mais la voix de mes frères n'atteint plus la France, et la seule raison pour laquelle je témoigne est que j'espère que ma voix, moins forte sans doute, mais plus proche, aura peut-être plus de chances de l'atteindre." Quoted in Lindon, *La gangrène*, 31.

37. Lindon, *La gangrène*, 12.

38. "Je revois défiler devant moi pour la millième fois, les images d'un film dont les acteurs et les victimes furent mes amis les plus chers." Quoted in Lindon, *La gangrène*, 29.

39. Quoted in Lindon, *La gangrène*, 29.

40. Emmanuel Alcaraz notes that Boumaza would later preside over the Association du 8 mai 1945, spelling out more explicitly the argument that I detect in his fissured testimony in *La gangrène*, and also foreshadowing the way that this historical counternarrative would become institutionalized and instrumentalized by the postcolonial Algerian state during the 1990s. See Emmanuel Alcaraz, "Les monuments aux martyrs de la guerre d'indépendance algérienne: monumentalité, enjeux de mémoire et commémorations," *Guerres mondiales et conflits contemporains* 237, no. 1 (2010): 145.

41. "Hanouz Arab, auxiliaire médical, à qui il était reproché d'être le secrétaire de l'Association locale de culture de bienfaisance, était conduit avec ses trois enfants, dont le plus jeune avait mon âge, devant la maison du seigneur-colon de mon village." Quoted in Lindon, *La gangrène*, 30.

42. "Là, sur la place, au milieu des encouragements de toute la population européenne, femmes et enfants compris, les Hanouz furent torturés pendant plusieurs heures par les légionnaires." Quoted in Lindon, *La gangrène*, 30.

43. "Le soir, comme ils ne bougeaient plus, mais respiraient encore, les soldats obligèrent les Musulmans à défiler devant ces quatre corps, allongés les visages contre le sol." Quoted in Lindon, *La gangrène*, 30. After the infamous *enfumades* of the nineteenth century, bodies were exposed publicly as a warning and a lesson to insurgents. Karima Lazali highlights this important point in *Le trauma colonial: Une enquête sur les effets psychiques et politiques contemporains de l'oppression coloniale en Algérie* (Paris: La Découverte, 2018), 57.

44. "Les soldats transportèrent ensuite les Hanouz sur un pont, à trois kilomètres de là, et les précipitèrent, d'une hauteur de cinquante mètres, dans l'oued." Quoted in Lindon, *La gangrène*, 30.

45. Given that Maurice Papon became administrator of this particular region of Algeria in October 1945 and then oversaw the massacre of Algerians in Paris in 1961, these continuities are even less surprising. For an account of Papon's colonial service in Algeria, see the first chapter of House and MacMaster, *Paris 1961*.

46. "Depuis, les habitants de mon village appellent ce pont 'le pont des Hanouz.' Quelques mois plus tard, nous pûmes enfin, quelques amis et moi, aller recouvrir les os de M. Hanouz et de ses fils, Tayeb, Madjid et Hanafi. Je quittai mon village le lendemain, pour n'y revenir qu'en 1952." Quoted in Lindon, *La gangrène*, 30.

47. "Il appartient à tous les hommes libres en France et dans le monde de s'unir pour empêcher le génocide en Algérie." Jacques Vergès, Mourad Oussedik, and Abdessamad Benabdallah, *Nuremberg pour l'Algérie* (Paris: Maspero, 1961). The original pamphlet does not include page numbers. A transcribed version is available online, with the photographs from the original: nonaumuseefasciste.wordpress.com/2013/05/03/nuremberg-pour-lalgerie/.

48. "Depuis plusieurs années, nous dénonçons la guerre en Algérie comme une entreprise de génocide. Depuis plusieurs années, nous renonçons à la répression judiciaire comme une parodie. Nous avons accusé de complicité de tortures et d'assassinat les plus hauts dignitaires de l'Ancien et du Nouveau Régime: MM. Lacoste, Bourgès-Manoury, Soustelle, et Debré. Les tueurs nous ont répondu par l'assassinat de notre ami Me Ould Aoudia. Le Pouvoir par des inculpations multiples et des mesures d'internement. Mais personne n'a jamais osé nous démentir." Vergès, Oussedik, and Benabdallah, *Nuremberg pour l'Algérie*, opening section.

49. "Voici, sans commentaire, le texte d'une lettre adressée de Sétif le 20 mai 1960 par le sergent Copenol Claude, SP 89116 AFN, à un militaire resté en France. Cette lettre a été communiquée par nous à la Justice militaire. Aucune poursuite n'a été engagée." Vergès, Oussedik, and Benabdallah, *Nuremberg pour l'Algérie*, second section.

50. "Prisonniers abattus sans jugement selon les directives des officiers généraux couverts par le commandement en chef et la délégation générale du Gouvernement." Vergès, Oussedik, and Benabdallah, *Nuremberg pour l'Algérie*, third section.

51. On these euphemisms, see Benjamin Stora, *Les mots de la guerre d'Algérie* (Toulouse: Presses universitaires du Mirail, 2005).

52. Fanon, "Lettre à un Français," 56.

53. "A noter que le mot soldats est souligné dans le texte." Vergès, Oussedik, and Benabdallah, *Nuremberg pour l'Algérie*, third section.

54. "En Algérie, les autorités militaires compétentes pourront, nonobstant toutes dispositions contraires des codes de justice militaire, ordonner *la traduction directe* sans instruction préalable devant un tribunal permanent des forces armées des individus pris en flagrant délit de participation à une action contre les personnes ou les biens à condition qu'il s'agisse d'infractions prévues à l'article 1er du décret no 56-268 du 17 mars 1956 *même si ces infractions sont susceptibles d'entraîner la peine capitale*, lorsqu'elles auront été commises par des auteurs porteurs d'armes, d'explosifs, de munitions, de matériel de destruction ou d'effets d'équipement ou d'habillement militaire." Decree 56-269, in *Journal officiel de la République française* (March 19, 1956): 2656; emphasis added. For full text, see legifrance.gouv.fr/jo_pdf.do?id=JORFTEXT000000330477&pageCourage=02656.

55. Vergès, Oussedik, and Benabdallah, *Nuremberg pour l'Algérie*, final section.

56. "Ça fait presque deux mois que je suis en A.F.N."; "Je suis chargé en outre d'un registre où j'inscris tous les fellous arrêtés par nos bons soins." Vergès, Oussedik, and Benabdallah, *Nuremberg pour l'Algérie*, first section.

57. "Nous avons un fichier avec les photos de tous les suspects terroristes et c'est un boulot vraiment intéressant." Vergès, Oussedik, and Benabdallah, *Nuremberg pour l'Algérie*, first section.

58. "Quand nous arrêtons un fell nous l'interrogeons et nous avons du matériel tout à fait persuasif. Tu vois ce que je veux dire." Vergès, Oussedik, and Benabdallah, *Nuremberg pour l'Algérie*, first section.

59. "E.E. 8 à l'oreille et aux bijoux de famille, ensuite la flotte dans la bouche, plus les coups de bâton et la branlée quand c'est fini." Vergès, Oussedik, and Benabdallah, *Nuremberg pour l'Algérie*, first section.

60. "Parfois il nous arrive de buter des fells. Qu'est-ce que tu veux qu'on en fasse après l'interrogatoire. Nous les emmenons à la nuit tombée dans le bled. Là une grande cave est aménagée spécialement. Les fells sont amenés au bord de ladite cave le P.A. sur la nuque et hop le grand saut. Tu parles si on se les dispute avec les Inspecteurs de la P.J. Au début, tu sais le premier que tu butes comme ça de sang froid ça te fout un choc, mais c'est comme toute autre chose on s'y habitue. Après cela tu vas peut-être me prendre pour un gangster." Vergès, Oussedik, and Benabdallah, *Nuremberg pour l'Algérie*, first section.

61. For such studies, see Marnia Lazreg, *Torture and the Twilight of Empire* (Princeton, NJ: Princeton University Press, 2008), http://catdir.loc.gov/catdir/toc/ecip0715/2007014846.html; Kristin Ross, *Fast Cars, Clean Bodies: Decolonization and the Reordering of French Culture* (Cambridge, MA: MIT Press, 1994); Pierre Vidal-Naquet, *La torture dans la République* (Paris: Éditions de Minuit, 1972).

62. This is discussed at length by Elaine Scarry in her classic study of the ontology of torture, *The Body in Pain: The Making and Unmaking of the World* (New York: Oxford University Press, 1985). For a lexicon of French terms related specifically to the war in Algeria, see Stora, *Les mots de la guerre d'Algérie*.

63. "Bilan de l'opé: d'abord les militaires ont gazé la grotte qui fait 180 mètres de profondeur, tu vois un peu cette installation. Ils sont entrés dedans et ont sorti 12 fells dont 2 sous-chefs et 1 aspi (qui est mort suite aux gaz). Toutes les armes ont été récupérées, tu vois ça c'est du boulot. À part cela je peux te dire qu'il y a une semaine lors d'un décrochage, il y a eu 4 tirailleurs tués et 5 blessés, du côté fells ouallou." Vergès, Oussedik, and Benabdallah, *Nuremberg pour l'Algérie*, first section.

64. Fanon, *Les damnés de la terre*, 82.

65. See Djebar's reconstruction of the enfumade in *L'amour, la fantasia* (Paris: Éditions J. C. Lattès, 1985), discussed in my introduction.

66. "Des répercussions fâcheuses sur leur état d'esprit et sur le moral des corps et services dont ils font partie." Halimi and Beauvoir, *Djamila Boupacha*, 195, 201.

67. "Un certain désarroi et un long silence accueillirent, au Ministère de la Justice, ce dépôt de plainte. . . . La France est-elle devenue un pays *sans justice*?" Halimi and Beauvoir, *Djamila Boupacha*, 203.

68. All three painters created visual works informed by accounts of torture and resistance in Algeria, copies of which are included in the fly pages of *Djamila Boupacha*.

69. "J'écrivais, deux heures durant, sur la petite table de bois blanc de ce parloir de Barberousse. Djamila répondait à mes questions; elle s'épuisait dans la recherche des précisions que j'exigeais d'elle; elle s'interrompait, elle reprenait le cours de son récit. À un moment, elle dégrafa sa blouse: sur sa poitrine, jusqu'à hauteur de son sein droit, il y avait un chapelet de traces minuscules, comme des confetti bruns. Ils avaient appuyé, par touches rapides, leurs cigarettes allumées sur sa peau. Sur sa cuisse droite, le bout incandescent de la cigarette avait sans doute été écrasé plus fort: le cercle était plus foncé, plus épanoui. Je reprenais mon papier. J'avais chaud, j'avais peur de mal noter le nombre de cicatrices, la durée de la détention, le nom de l'officier. *L'accumulation des détails était notre seule chance.*" Halimi and Beauvoir, *Djamila Boupacha*, 22; emphasis added.

70. Halimi and Beauvoir, *Djamila Boupacha*, 14–15.

71. "*Séquestration s'étant poursuivie pendant plus d'un mois et ayant été accompagnée de tortures corporelles.*" Halimi and Beauvoir, *Djamila Boupacha*, 219; emphasis in original.

72. "Dans ces conditions, j'ai l'honneur, Monsieur le Juge d'Instruction, de déposer entre vos mains une plainte pour les crimes sus-énoncés, en me constituant partie civile." Halimi and Beauvoir, *Djamila Boupacha*, 219.

73. "Je demande à être examinée par un médecin. J'ai été torturée." Halimi and Beauvoir, *Djamila Boupacha*, 19.

74. "Le juge dicte. La machine du greffier crépite." Halimi and Beauvoir, *Djamila Boupacha*, 39.

75. "Les policiers sont derrière la porte: de sa déclaration dépend la destination de son retour." Halimi and Beauvoir, *Djamila Boupacha*, 39.

76. Halimi and Beauvoir, *Djamila Boupacha*, 39.

77. "À ce moment, Djamila a envie de hurler. Les policiers sont toujours là. Tant pis, tant pis. / Elle veut le dire. / Elle crie presque: /—Oui. Inscrivez que j'ai été torturée à Hussein Dey... oui, que j'ai souffert beaucoup.../ Et soudain brisée: /—Je vous en prie... *Il faut me faire voir...*" Halimi and Beauvoir, *Djamila Boupacha*, 39.

78. Maurice Blanchot and Jacques Derrida, *The Instant of My Death, Demeure: Fiction and Testimony*, trans. Elizabeth Rottenberg (Stanford, CA: Stanford University Press, 2000), 76.

79. Halimi and Beauvoir, *Djamila Boupacha*, 22.

80. Blanchot and Derrida, *Instant of My Death*, 75.

81. Halimi and Beauvoir, *Djamila Boupacha*, 15–16.

82. Halimi and Beauvoir, *Djamila Boupacha*, 43.

83. "Troubles des règles qui sont de nature constitutionnelle." Halimi and Beauvoir, *Djamila Boupacha*, 116.

84. "Cette pseudo-délicatesse n'explique rien. S'il n'a pas examiné Djamila, si elle n'a pas fait allusion à ces sévices particuliers, comment pouvait-il savoir qu'elle souffrait de troubles constitutionnels des règles?" Halimi and Beauvoir, *Djamila Boupacha*, 49.

85. Halimi and Beauvoir, *Djamila Boupacha*, 49.

86. "OUI, BOUPACHA DJAMILA A PU SUBIR L'INTRODUCTION D'UN GOULOT DE BOUTEILLE DANS LE VAGIN . . . PEUT-ÊTRE EN FAVEUR D'UNE DEFLORATION TRAUMATIQUE." Halimi and Beauvoir, *Djamila Boupacha*, 140.

87. Halimi and Beauvoir, *Djamila Boupacha*, 186.

88. "C'est possible. Je ne m'en souviens plus. . . . Je ne sais pas si Djamila avait des traces de torture sur le corps: je ne l'ai pas examinée nue." Halimi and Beauvoir, *Djamila Boupacha*, 187.

89. "—Alors, dites-nous? Vous avez déjà vu ça? Le juge insistait. Alors Djamila se leva brusquement et cria:—C'est la gégène ça! C'est la gégène!" Halimi and Beauvoir, *Djamila Boupacha*, 167.

90. "Ses déclarations *peuvent* correspondre à la vérité, mais je n'en ai pas conservé le souvenir. Depuis février 1960 j'ai vu beaucoup de choses et tout ce qui s'est passé à cette époque n'est pas resté dans ma mémoire." Halimi and Beauvoir, *Djamila Boupacha*, 189.

91. "Quelle meilleure preuve Djamila pouvait-elle donner de la force de ses souvenirs et de ses possibilités de nous dévoiler à tous le visage de ses tortionnaires?" Halimi and Beauvoir, *Djamila Boupacha*, 191.

92. "Il s'agit là de séquelles de la vérole, du totalitarisme nazi." Lindon, *La gangrène*, 7.

93. "Ces documents ne peuvent être produits que par l'autorité militaire. Or ce sont les deux chefs de cette autorité qui ont pris, d'un commun accord, la décision de refus." Halimi and Beauvoir, *Djamila Boupacha*, 203.

94. "Existe-t-il un droit civique plus élémentaire que celui d'obtenir justice quand on a été victime d'un crime? Existe-t-il un principe constitutionnel plus élémentaire que celui de la séparation des pouvoirs?" Halimi and Beauvoir, *Djamila Boupacha*, 204.

95. Halimi and Beauvoir, *Djamila Boupacha*, 208, 213.

96. Critical rumination on Nazi violence and on the great post-Holocaust legal trials of the last century generated much of this scholarship. In her "Trauma Theory: Contexts, Politics, Ethics" (*Paragraph* 30, no. 1 [March 2007]: 9–29), Susannah Radstone situates the rise and institutionalization of "trauma studies" in a cultural moment defined by a sense of coming "after" the Shoah and received in a cultural context abruptly transformed by September 11, 2001: "Trauma theory," she writes, "arguably constitutes one attempt by history to think itself 'through' a post-Auschwitz world" (21). Cathy Caruth's *Unclaimed Experience: Trauma, Narrative, and History* (Baltimore: Johns Hopkins University Press, 1996) was the first to use the term *trauma theory*; this was indebted to Shoshana Felman and Dori Laub's earlier *Testimony: Crises of Witnessing in Literature, Psychoanalysis, and History* (New York: Routledge, 1992). Other work of the moment includes Geoffrey Hartman, "On Traumatic Knowledge and Literary Study," *New Literary History* 26, no. 3 (1995): 537–63; Geoffrey Hartman, *The Longest Shadow: In the Aftermath of the Holocaust* (Bloomington: Indiana University Press, 1996); Dominick La Capra, *Representing the Holocaust: History, Theory, Trauma* (Ithaca, NY: Cornell University Press, 1996); Dominick La Capra, *Writing History, Writing Trauma* (Baltimore: Johns Hopkins University Press, 2000); Marianne Hirsch, *Family Frames: Photography, Narrative, and Postmemory* (Cambridge, MA: Harvard University Press, 1997); Allan Young's ethnography of PTSD in *Harmony of Illusions: Inventing Post-Traumatic Stress Disorder* (Princeton, NJ: Princeton University Press, 1995); and Shoshana Felman's *The*

Juridical Unconscious: Trails and Traumas of the Twentieth Century (Cambridge, MA: Harvard University Press, 2002). Felman's study includes a substantial reflection on the Eichmann trial in Jerusalem in 1961, as do other influential studies of testimony that emerged in this period, such as Annette Wieviorka's *The Era of the Witness*; and Agamben's *Remnants of Auschwitz: The Witness and the Archive*, trans. Daniel Heller-Roazen (New York: Zone Books, [1998] 1999), but they do not consider the contemporaneous failed trials at the heart of my reflections here.

97. Halimi and Beauvoir, *Djamila Boupacha*, 227.

98. Halimi and Beauvoir, *Djamila Boupacha*, 225.

99. Halimi and Beauvoir, *Djamila Boupacha*, 226.

100. "Depuis février 1960 j'ai vu beaucoup de choses et tout ce qui s'est passé à cette époque n'est pas resté dans ma mémoire." Halimi and Beauvoir, *Djamila Boupacha*, 189.

101. Halimi and Beauvoir, *Djamila Boupacha*, 227; emphasis added.

102. "Mme. B était habillée et coiffée à la mode arabe, avec un grand safsari qu'elle enroulait autour de ses vêtements." Halimi and Beauvoir, *Djamila Boupacha*, 47.

103. "Mais aussi, avec une précision qui m'émerveillait, elle répondait à mes questions, et dépassant le cas de Djamila, elle me disait comment les militaires arrêtaient, torturaient, pillaient. Elle me donnait des noms d'Algériens disparus, des dates..." Halimi and Beauvoir, *Djamila Boupacha*, 47.

104. "Quand Mme Boupacha fut à hauteur du portail, elle se retourna brusquement et me cria: 'N'oublie pas... mes yeux, je te les donnerai pour Djamila!'" Halimi and Beauvoir, *Djamila Boupacha*, 47–48.

3. MOURNING REVOLT

Epigraphs: Yamina Mechakra, quoted in Rachid Mokhtari, *Yamina Mechakra: Entretiens et lectures* (Algiers: Chihab International, 1999), 87; Kateb Yacine, *Les ancêtres redoublent de férocité*, in *Le cercle des représailles* (Paris: Éditions du seuil, 1959), 149.

1. This changed in 2019 with the completion of the Jāmiʿ al-Jazāʾir, a new mosque that is widely regarded as a symbol of the reign (or a monument to the megalomania) of President Abdelaziz Bouteflika.

2. This information is from a private interview with Dr. Mohamed Tedjiza, director of psychiatry at Drid Hocine Hospital, conducted on the grounds of the hospital in June 2014. In 1999, on the occasion of the publication of Mechakra's novel *Arris*, Rachid Mokhtari interviewed Mechakra in her house on the hospital grounds. Their conversation was recorded on cassette tapes, not found until after her death in 2013, then given by Mechakra's sister to Mokhtari, who transcribed and published them as *Yamina Mechakra: Entretiens et lectures*. As far as I know, this interview is the most comprehensive detail about Mechakra's life that exists in print.

3. Marcel Bois, Kateb Yacine, and Rachid Boudjedra helped to get Mechakra's first novel published. Marcel Bois, who died in June 2018, was a Catholic priest and the preeminent translator of Algerian Arabic literature into French. He worked as a reader at the state publishing house SNED in the 1970s. He had known Mechakra since she

was a student; the boarding house where she lived was also on the grounds of his own church and residence in Kouba. Marcel Bois selected the manuscript and worked with Mechakra to edit it. These details are from a private interview with Marcel Bois conducted at his church and residence at Kouba, in Algiers, June 2014.

4. For further information on this prize, consult news about it in the Algerian press: see Sarah Haider, "Création du prix Yamina Mechakra," *Le soir d'Algerie*, September 2, 2018, https://www.lesoirdalgerie.com/culture/creation-du-prix-yamina-mechakra-10475; "Lancement du prix Yamina Mechakra pour la fin de l'année," *Algérie Presse Service*, September 1, 2018, http://www.aps.dz/culture/78032-lancement-du-prix-yamina-mechakra-pour-la-fin-de-l-annee.

5. Yamina Mechakra, "L'éveil du mont," *El Moudjahid culturel* 196, no. 2111 (October 1976): 8–9.

6. The original edition was published by SNED in 1979, and the following three editions were published by ENAL (1986 and 1991) and ENAG (2000).

7. For Mechakra's story about meeting Kateb Yacine for the first time (including her claim that she had no idea who he was and had never read his writing), see her account in Mokhtari, *Yamina Mechakra*, 62.

8. I do not cite in my main text the now-iconic closing line from Kateb Yacine's preface to Mechakra's novel, because so many works of academic criticism that discuss Mechakra's *La grotte éclatée*—as well as most references to her in the Algerian press—introduce Mechakra this way. The statement reads: "À l'heure actuelle, dans notre pays, une femme qui écrit vaut son pesant de poudre." (In our country at the present moment, a woman who writes is worth her weight in gunpowder.) Among scholarly works that introduce Mechakra by way of this sentence or her association with Kateb Yacine: Benjamin Stora, "Women's Writing between Two Algerian Wars," *Research in African Literatures* 30, no. 3 (1999): 78–94; Marie-Blanche Tahon and Ruthmarie H. Mitsch, "Women Novelists and Women in the Struggle for Algeria's National Liberation (1957–1980)," in "North African Literature," special issue, *Research in African Literatures* 23, no. 2 (summer 1992): 39–50; Danielle Marx-Scouras, "Muffled Screams/Stifled Voices," in "Post/Colonial Conditions: Exiles, Migrations, and Nomadisms," special issue, *Yale French Studies* 82, no. 1 (1993): 172–82; Valerie Orlando, "War, Revolution, and Family Matters," in *Of Suffocated Hearts and Tortured Souls* (Washington, DC: Lexington Books, 2003), 147–64; and Orlando's chapter on Mechakra in *The New Algerian Novel: The Poetics of a Modern Nation, 1950–1979* (Charlottesville: University of Virginia Press, 2017), which includes brief discussion of the Issiakhem painting that features prominently in my own work on Mechakra, 257–58.

9. Eileen Julien, "The Extroverted African Novel," in *The Novel: History, Geography and Culture, Vol. 1*, ed. Franco Moretti (Princeton, NJ: Princeton University Press, 2006), 667–702.

10. "Il dérangeait la politique de l'époque." For her discussion of this, see Mokhtari, *Yamina Mechakra*, 64.

11. "Trois grands mondes où je n'avais pas de frontière: celui de Moïse, celui de Jésus, et celui de Sidna Mohamed." Yamina Mechakra, *La grotte éclatée* (Algiers: SNED, 1979), 33.

12. "Sans fiche d'état civil, sans nom, sans prénom... une *hors-la-loi*." Mechakra, *La grotte éclatée*, 34.

13. Yamina Mechakra, *La grotte éclatée: al-Maghāra al-Mutafajjira*, trans. Aïda Bamia (Algiers: ENAL, 1989).

14. These details from a private interview with Lamis Saïdi in Algiers, June 2014. In a more recent conversation in October 2018, Saïdi reports that she decided to set aside her translation of *La grotte* in order to work on an Arabic translation of *Arris* instead, both because she learned of the existing Arabic translation by Bamia and because she finds the latter novel even more iconoclastic and surprising than the first, and therefore a more interesting candidate for translation.

15. "Je m'en allais vers ARRIS[(1)]"; "[(1)] ARRIS: petite ville de l'Aurès." Mechakra, *La grotte éclatée*, 14.

16. In the preface that he wrote for *La grotte éclatée*, Kateb Yacine advocated for it precisely because of this generic and temporal torque: "Ce n'est pas un roman, et c'est beaucoup mieux: un long poème en prose qui peut se lire comme un roman" (This is not a novel, but something much better: a long poem in prose than can be read as a novel). Kateb Yacine, preface to Mechakra, *La grotte éclatée*, 7.

17. Mechakra, *La grotte éclatée*, 175.

18. In his introduction to *Les lieux de mémoire de la guerre d'indépendance algérienne* (Paris: Éditions Karthala, 2017), Emmanuel Alcaraz discusses this, and also comments insightfully on the multivalent sense and orthography of the word *moudjahid*. See especially 17–18.

19. "La mère ferme les mains en coquille autour de la bouche d'Arris. Recueille le vomi bilieux qu'elle verse dans un vieux chiffon qui lui sert de serviette. Le petit se remet à somnoler." Yamina Mechakra, *Arris* (Algiers: Marsa, 1999), 7.

20. "Un monde coupé du reste des mondes." Mechakra, *Arris*, 8.

21. "Cet Aurès qui défie le temps." Mechakra, *Arris*, 45.

22. "—Arris est revenu, il n'y a plus de veuve! Et tout le peuple dit:—Amin! Amin! Amin!" Mechakra, *Arris*, 91.

23. Notable exceptions include Rachid Mokhtari and Afifa Bererhi. Mokhtari includes an essay on *Arris* in his *La graphie de l'horreur* (Algiers: Chihab, 2003). See also his *Le nouveau souffle du roman algérien* (Algiers: Chihab, 2006), which includes a chapter on Mechakra. It was Afifa Bererhi who first alerted me to these other texts, and who generously loaned me her copies of both *Arris* and "L'éveil du mont" in Algiers in 2014.

24. In the interview with Mokhtari, Mechakra underscores this continuity between her novels. Asked about the twenty years of silence between the two publications, she insists that she was in fact writing the entire time: "Les gens s'imaginent que je me suis tue. Or, je n'ai pas cessé d'écrire, mais j'écris et je perds mes textes" (People imagine that I have fallen silent. And yet, I haven't stopped writing—but I write and I lose my texts). Mokhtari, *Yamina Mechakra*, 73. Mechakra also claims that she wrote many texts before and after both novels: in 1990, she says, she wrote at least ten stories for *El Moudjahid* that she wishes to recuperate (she lists their titles in the interview, but I have found only one of these in print). She also lists what she calls her *textes transhumants*, a lost archive of drafts; she claims that the novel *Arris* itself is just a tenth of the full manuscript, and

that what was eventually published as *La grotte* was the third version of an original manuscript.

25. "À la fois... l'arc de triomphe,... la tombe du soldat inconnu, et... la crypte du Panthéon." Emmanuel Alcaraz, "La mise en scène de la mémoire nationale: De la guerre d'indépendance algérienne au *maqam al-chahid* d'Alger," in *Autour de Morts de Guerre*, ed. Raphaëlle Branche, Nadine Picaudou, and Pierre Vermeren (Paris: Éditions de la Sorbonne, 2013), 21–45. Quoted material from paragraph 12 in the open source version of the essay. Alcaraz also published a book-length study, *Les lieux de mémoire de la guerre d'indépendance algérienne* (Paris: Éditions Karthala, 2017).

26. "Un projet esthétique, à la fois politique et littéraire, basé sur ce jeu de forces qui transforment la réalité bien qu'ils la représentent." Pierre Nora, "Entre mémoire et histoire," in *Les lieux de mémoire*, vol. 1: *La République* (Paris: Gallimard, 1984).

27. The constitution's Article 62, on civic duties, includes this point: "(3) The State guarantees the respect of the symbols of the Revolution, the memory of the 'shuhadā" and the dignity of the rightful heirs, and the 'mujāhidīn.'" For the full text of the 1976 constitution, see *Journal Officiel de la République Algérienne* 15, no. 94 (1976).

28. Alcaraz notes that the museum was initially called the Musée du Jihad, and was meant to be housed in the former Serkadji/Barberousse prison, but was moved to the Maqām al-shahīd and renamed in 1993. More recently there has been discussion of transforming the prison into a memorial site as well. See the chapter on Serkadji prison in Alcaraz, *Les lieux*, 83–121, titled "Le premier projet de Musée national du mujāhid sous Ben Bella et sous Boumédiène dans un lieu de souffrance devenu un symbole national."

29. Both Alcaraz and Malika Rahal detail these omissions. Alcaraz notes that nowhere does Messali Hadj, the Union Démocratique du Manifeste Algérien (UDMA), or the Parti Communiste Algérien (PCA) appear, nor does any acknowledgment that detracts from the discourse of total national unity and the primacy of the FLN: "Le mythe de l'unanimité du peuple algérien permet ainsi d'effacer le pluralisme du mouvement national" (The myth of the unanimity of the Algerian people allows for the national movement's pluralism to be glossed over). Alcaraz, "La mise en scène," 42. See also Malika Rahal, "Fused Together and Torn Apart: Stories and Violence in Contemporary Algeria," *History and Memory* 24, no. 1 (spring/summer 2012): 118–51.

30. Rahal, "Fused Together and Torn Apart," 125.

31. These three points, materialized by the Maqām al-shahīd complex, are also the explicit content of the first three articles of Algeria's 1976 constitution, as follows: (1) Algeria is a People's Democratic Republic. It is one and indivisible. (2) Islam is the state religion. (3) Arabic is the national and official language. For the full text of the 1976 constitution, see *Journal Officiel de la République Algérienne* 15, no. 94 (1976).

32. Notably, the first radical critiques of the Algerian state as an institution came from Islamists, which also partly explains why the monument itself was a target for attack. It was in the name of protecting the state that progressivists opposed Islamists during the 1990s; these debates rest on the ideological content of the nation, and manifest in struggles for narrative control over the present and future meaning of the national war for independence.

33. The Maqām al-shahīd's direct association of *shahīd* with sacrifice and martyrdom corresponds to the usual translation of the word in European-language media and scholarship; the word is also often associated with Islamist violence in general and suicide bombers in particular. The Arabic word *shahīd* has been naturalized in English and can be found in the *Oxford English Dictionary*, which defines it as "Muslim martyr" based on cases of use in British-colonized South Asia beginning in 1881 ("the Musalman name shahid"; "The martyrs of the new Indian religion, known by the Musalman name shahid, were to have their own exceeding great reward in a future state") and on entries from the 1934 *Encyclopedia of Islam* ("the muslim who falls on the battlefield is called Shahid, 'witness,' 'martyr'").

34. The call to prayer begins: "Allāhu akbar, *ashhadu* an lā ilāha illā llāh, ashhadu anna Muḥammadan rasūlu llāh ..." Note that this use is the same imperative verb form that appears in the national anthem.

35. "L'architecte de l'État algérien." This description of Boumédiène is from Alcaraz, "Les monuments aux martyrs de la guerre d'indépendance algérienne: Monumentalité, enjeux de mémoire et commémorations," in *Guerres mondiales et conflits contemporains*, January 2010, no. 237: 125–46. Quoted material from 126.

36. Rahal, "Fused Together and Torn Apart," 119.

37. Rahal, "Fused Together and Torn Apart," 120.

38. Rahal, "Fused Together and Torn Apart," 125.

39. See James McDougall, "Savage Wars? Codes of Violence in Algeria, 1830s–1990s," in "The Politics of Naming: Rebels, Terrorists, Criminals, Bandits and Subversives," special issue, *Third World Quarterly* 26, no. 1 (2005): 124.

40. My argument concerning the production of archival silences/silencings and the fictional processes of historiography draws on Michel-Rolph Trouillot's *Silencing the Past: Power and the Production of History* (Boston: Beacon Press, 1995), as well as on Ariella Azoulay's essay "Potential History: Thinking through Violence," *Critical Inquiry* 39, no. 3 (spring 2013): 548–74.

41. For sustained critical reflection on the relationship between law-preserving/colonial and law-making/revolutionary violence, see Fanon's warnings in *Les damnés de la terre* (Paris: La Découverte, [1961] 2014), especially the chapter "Mésaventures de la conscience nationale," 145–93; Walter Benjamin's "Critique of Violence," in *Walter Benjamin: Selected Writings, Vol. 1: 1913–1926*, ed. Marcus Bullock and Michael Jennings (Cambridge, MA: Harvard University Press, 1996); and Jacques Derrida's "Force of Law: The Mystical Foundation of Authority," in *Acts of Religion: Jacques Derrida*, ed. Gil Anidjar (New York: Routledge, 2001), 230–98. For an anthropologist's reflection on the force of law and state repression in 1990s Algeria, see Abderrahmane Moussaoui, *De la violence en Algérie: Les lois du chaos* (Arles: Actes Sud, 2006). Moussaoui observes the fragile equilibrium, after the 1999 and 2005 amnesties, between "oubli pathologique et exaltation maladive de la mémoire" (pathological forgetting and unhealthy exaltation of memory) (411).

42. Natalya Vince and Walid Benkhaled, "Performing Algerianness: The National and Transnational Construction of Algeria's 'Culture Wars,'" in *Algeria, Nation, Culture, and Transnationalism 1988–2015*, ed. Patrick Crowley (Liverpool: Liverpool University Press, 2017), 243–69.

43. Quoted in Rahal, "Fused Together and Torn Apart," 143.

44. On the archive as performance of state power, see two chapters in Carolyn Hamilton et al., eds., *Refiguring the Archive* (Dordrecht: Kluwer Academic Publishers, 2002): Ann Laura Stoler, "Colonial Archives and the Arts of Governance: On the Content in the Form," 83–102, and Achille Mbembe, "The Power of the Archive and Its Limits," 19–27. On the battle over archives in the specific context of Algerian decolonization, see Todd Shepard, "'Of Sovereignty': Disputed Archives, 'Wholly Modern' Archives, and the Post-Decolonization French and Algerian Republics, 1962–2012," *American Historical Review* 120, no. 3 (June 2015): 869–83.

45. Rahal, "Fused Together and Torn Apart," 142.

46. Rahal, "Fused Together and Torn Apart," 127.

47. Also called "la Toussaint Rouge," this was the date of a series of armed attacks in Algiers and in the Aurès, and of the FLN's first written declaration to the Algerian people calling on them to revolt against the French in the struggle for North Africa's liberation. A full transcription of the "Déclaration du 1er novembre" is on display at the Musée du moudjahid. It is also available online: "Déclaration du 1er novembre 1954," Wikisource, last updated March 8, 2020, https://fr.wikisource.org/wiki/D%C3%A9claration_du_1er_novembre_1954.

48. "Au rhythme de cannonades futures." Mechakra, "L'éveil du mont," unnumbered page.

49. These details are from Benjamin Stora, "Boumédiène, the State, and the Institutions," in *Algeria 1830–2000: A Short History*, trans. Jane Marie Todd (Ithaca, NY: Cornell University Press, 2004), 143–50.

50. Quoted in Stora, "Boumédiène, the State, and the Institutions," 147.

51. Stora, "Boumédiène, the State, and the Institutions," 147.

52. Quoted in Stora, "Boumédiène, the State, and the Institutions," 148.

53. "Des processions avançaient, se confondaient. La terre se mit à trembler. Le tonnerre grondait." Mechakra, "L'éveil du mont," unnumbered page.

54. Mechakra, "L'éveil du mont," unnumbered page.

55. "Des héros transformés en chair pourrie"; "gisaient sous les dégâts de bombes, oubliés de tous sauf peut-être de quelque ami lointain." Mechakra, *La grotte éclatée*, 101.

56. "Pour Tunis ces hommes n'avaient jamais existé. Sur ces hommes que j'avais aimés, l'oubli était retombé lourdement." Mechakra, *La grotte éclatée*, 100–101.

57. "Là-bas, à quelques centaines de kilomètres, ce soleil si bienfaisant à Tunis transforme mes frères en charognes puantes." Mechakra, *La grotte éclatée*, 116.

58. "On me promut lieutenant. Deux étoiles sur mon épaule sans bras. C'était le prix de mon handicap.... À Tunis, on me regardait comme une héroïne." Mechakra, *La grotte éclatée*, 100.

59. "Le F.L.N. décida la circoncision de tous les fils de chouhada. On offrit à Arris une gandourah blanche et un tarbouche rouge." Mechakra, *La grotte éclatée*, 104.

60. "On me ramena le corps de mon fils: / Age: deux mois. / Victime du napalm. / Mon fils vivant, aveugle et sans jambes. Mon fils brûlé." Mechakra, *La grotte éclatée*, 96.

61. "Mon fils, visage sans yeux tués par le napalm, mon fils bambin aux jambes assassinées"; "Mon fils mutilé par le feu"; "Enfant aux jambes martyres." Mechakra, *La grotte éclatée*, 101, 102.

62. "J'irai retrouver ma rivière et, de la main qui me reste, je frotterai mes seins et mon ventre de bâtarde d'un sang jeune qui chante, qu'on a arraché des entrailles bouillonnantes d'amour de milliers de mères, penchées sur un enfant qui n'existe plus. / Comme elles, je suis penchée sur mon fils qui n'existe plus / Une grande ride sur le dos. / Comme elles, je tresse encore des couronnes sur le front de mon fils qui n'existe plus, une grande ride dans les yeux. / Comme elles, mes seins pleurent encore des larmes de lait. / Comme elles, mon ventre frémit encore sur un enfant / dont se souviennent mes entrailles. / Comme elles, ma mémoire vacille: mon fils que je vois n'est pas." Mechakra, *La grotte éclatée*, 142.

63. "Toute la nuit, au chevet de mon fils, à moitié consciente, / Je le suppliai de ne pas s'en aller. / Je lui disais les randonnées que nous ferions ensemble le / Long des sentiers de nos villages. / Je lui disais nos grands-mères cassées en deux, roulant / de leurs doigts d'artistes un fin couscous que nos infinis / champs de blé avaient mûri au soleil. / Je lui disais nos monts qu'une auréole de neige couron- / Nait toute l'année. / Je lui disais la quobba de Sidi Othman qui surplombe la / plaine de Meskiana, vers laquelle se levaient les regards / quand les cœurs réclamaient une aube paisible et de l'eau / pour nourrir la terre, remplir les greniers." Mechakra, *La grotte éclatée*, 105–6.

64. "Langage pétri dans les nattes tressées au feu de l'amour qui flambe depuis des siècles au cœur de mes ancêtres et dans mon cœur vers lequel je tends mon visage gelé et mon regard humide pour pouvoir sourire. Langage pétri dans les tapis, livres ouverts portant l'empreinte multicolore des femmes de mon pays qui, dès l'aube, se mettent à écrire le feu de leurs entrailles pour couvrir l'enfant le soir quand le ciel lui volera le soleil; dans les khalkhals d'argent, auréoles glacées aux fines chevilles, dont la musique rassure et réconforte celui qui dort près de l'âtre et déjà aime le pied de sa mère et la terre qu'elle foule." Mechakra, *La grotte éclatée*, 13.

65. "Je dis à mon fils Alger la languissante et blessée, trem- / blante pour l'indépendance. / Je dis à mon fils Constantine et Kef Chkara. / Je dis à mon fils La Kabylie et Amirouche, Tlemcen et / sa colère, Oran et sa revanche. / Je dis à mon fils les Aurès et ma peine. // Je me souviens des cieux de mon pays. / Je dis à mon fils le ciel moutonneux d'Alger, son soleil / debout sur la Casbah, sa capitale. / Je dis à mon fils le ciel propre et immense coiffant un / lointain soleil qui s'insinue dans les ruelles de Constantine la / secrète. / Je dis à mon fils le ciel sombre et envoûtant, casquant un / soleil jaune et ruisselant accroché aux rocs aurésiens encore / couverts de neige. / Je dis à mon fils le ciel horizontal et flottant, rafraîchis- / sant un soleil rouge et viril, de peur qu'il ne brûle Tlemcen / l'andalouse." Mechakra, *La grotte éclatée*, 118–19.

66. The title *La grotte éclatée* was Marcel Bois's suggestion; he worked with Mechakra on the entire manuscript. These details are from a private interview with Marcel Bois conducted in Algiers, June 2014.

67. "Là-bas, là-bas / Dans mes Aurès … / La grotte des peines, / Trois milles ans, quatre mille ans … / Et que mon âme apaisée / Y repose éternellement." Mechakra, *Arris*, 71.

68. Recall, in addition to the references to these caves in Kateb's preface, Assia Djebar's reconstruction of the enfumades in *L'amour, la fantasia* discussed in the introduction and the references to asphyxiation in Claude Copenal's letter in *Nuremberg pour l'Algérie* that I analyze in chapter 2. For an excellent study of the symbolic resonance of caves in Algerian history and cultural production, see Denise Brahimi, *Des refuges et des pièges: Grottes symboliques en Algérie coloniale* (Algiers: Casbah Éditions, 2011).

69. "5 JUILLET 1962 / Sur le chemin d'ARRIS, je rencontrai le regard indif- / férent de quelques rares voyageurs. / Le soleil se noyait de chaleur. / Je retrouvai un instant Constantine. / J'arrêtai mon regard sur les yeux de mon fils. / Arris, mon fils, tu étais ma révolte. / A toi, aujourd'hui, mon enfant, / Je dis ton père mort, sur ses lèvres mon amour. / Je dis ma maison tuée là-bas au pied d'un arbre qui / blasphème à la face du ciel. / Je dis mes amis écrasés d'oubli, mais vivants encore dans / la mémoire d'un vieux chacal; il vient chaque soir déchirer / la nuit de lents sanglots. / Je dis ma foi en demain, clouée sur ma poitrine. / Je dis ARRIS mon pays et ses moissons / ARRIS mes ancêtres et mon honneur / ARRIS mon amour et ma demeure. / Septembre 1973." Mechakra, *La grotte éclatée*, 175.

70. In the interview with Mokhtari, she reports that this is when she was in close communication with Kateb Yacine, who encouraged her to take her time with the new manuscript. See Mokhtari, *Yamina Mechakra*, 65.

71. "De cette scène est né *Arris* dans lequel je pose le statut de la fille-mère et des enfants abandonnés. Je suis restée six mois à Beni Messous mais j'ai toujours gardé cette image d'une mère adolescente de 17 ans qui m'a jeté dans les bras son nourrisson avant de tomber évanouie." Mokhtari, *Yamina Mechakra*, 74.

72. "C'est la première fois qu'elle vient au village." Mechakra, *Arris*, 8.

73. "Un monde coupé du reste des mondes." Mechakra, *Arris*, 8.

74. "Elle se retrouve dans une pièce étroite, sombre. Il lui faut un bon moment pour percevoir les objets. L'infirmier tire une fiche sur laquelle sont inscrites bon nombre de questions. /—Je sais seulement, dit la mère, qu'il s'appelle Arris et qu'il est âgé de quatre printemps. Il est né au début du printemps et il y a de cela quatre printemps. / L'infirmier renverse le petit, lui place un thermomètre dans l'orifice anal. La mère ne comprend rien et refuse, au fond d'elle-même, ce geste insolite. /—Il est fébrile; de quoi souffre-t-il? /—Le monstre. / Elle prend la main de l'infirmier et la pose sur la tumeur. Elle ramasse avec tendresse Arris contre sa poitrine." Mechakra, *Arris*, 10.

75. "La mère n'a jamais entendu parler de fiche d'état-civil ou d'extrait d'acte de naissance"; "Elle connaît seulement son prénom, le prénom du père, notés sur le dossier de l'enfant, les Ben du grand-père; de l'arrière-grand-père jusqu'à la 14ème génération." Mechakra, *Arris*, 14, 17.

76. "Araki la mère de tous"; "Là-bas, tu n'existes pas. Ils t'ont banni à jamais de leur cité." Mechakra, *Arris*, 14, 18.

77. "Laisserai-je donc la chair de ma chair dans une ville, un pays que je n'ai pas choisi?"; "A l'hôpital, la mère place ses empreintes digitales sur le cahier, faute de savoir signer." Mechakra, *Arris*, 18, 17.

78. "La mère pousse un cri de chacal; elle se vide du dernier cri qui lui reste. Ni femme, ni bête, ni femme, ni bête." Mechakra, *Arris*, 19.

79. "Je suis seule sur le terrain où il fut conçu et a grandi. On m'a promis, à l'hôpital, de me le restituer une fois guéri ou mort. / Douleur, ô ma douleur / De quelle blessure béante / T'écoules-tu en sourdine / Je t'entends ô ma douleur…" Mechakra, *Arris*, 19.

80. For examples of this, see Mechakra, *Arris*, 44, 52, 53, 55, 68, 71; a verse repeats the line "les Aurès et ma peine" on page 72; a verse includes an epigraph from *La grotte*, "Je suis venu tête folle," on page 77.

81. "Coupé de mes racines, je me trouve dans un autre pays, qui n'est pas le mien et je te dis." Mechakra, *Arris*, 41.

82. "Ô Arris, Arris,… Mon amour… mon amour"; "Je t'aurais conté"; "Je te racontais des histoires"; "Je t'aurais légué toute ma mémoire en heritage." Mechakra, *Arris*, 50, 77, 78, 79.

83. "Ici même, dans ces lieux; dans cette ville qui, jadis, appartenait à Castellum, des murs entiers parlent de moi, de toi, ô de toi. Nos noms sont venus se superposer à ceux de millions d'autres." Mechakra, *Arris*, 43.

84. "Terre, quand tu me couvriras et que petit à petit tu m'assimileras jusqu'à ce que mon corps soit baptisé et que je devienne un élément semblable aux éléments qui te composent, je pousserai un hurlement qui déchirera l'espace et le temps jusqu'à parvenir aux oreilles de mon fils. Il viendra. L'appel de la terre, oui, cet appel terrible et qui vous prend aux tripes, existe. Il existe. Il viendra. Ce jour-là les chacals hurleront jusqu'à l'aube et nous entendrons le tonnerre gronder de la joie.… Arris est revenu." Mechakra, *Arris*, 49.

85. "La nuit, nous eûmes une visite des plus inattendues: des maquisards et deux prisonniers, un soldat français et un harki. Nous dûmes assister à deux brefs interrogatoires." Mechakra, *La grotte éclatée*, 55.

86. "Tu as tué *nos* enfants et violé *nos* femmes. Tu es Algérien pétri dans la chair algérienne; chacun de tes gènes porte en lui la lettre rouge de l'honneur frustré… ta femme est à l'abri; *nos* femmes sont violées. *Nos* fœtus servent de ballons aux légionnaires. Tes enfants vont à l'école, ils n'ont pas peur, ils n'ont pas faim, ils ont chaud en hiver. Regarde-le (et il montra Salah du doigt. L'enfant dans un geste de confusion chercha à cacher ses jambes). Il n'a point de jambes, ses mains sont sales, sa tête est surpeuplée de parasites indésirables, de poux. Il ne sait pas écrire, il ne se souvient pas d'avoir marché un jour, il a faim et froid. Il est seul. Ses parents tués. Voilà *nos* enfants." Mechakra, *La grotte éclatée*, 58–59; emphases added.

87. "—En 1914, nos pères sont morts pour permettre aux tiens alors au berceau de vivre. / Leurs os exilés cherchent une sépulture. / En 1939 nos frères sont morts pour te permettre à toi de pousser. En 1945 ton père a violé ma mère. / Aujourd'hui, fiston, tu es venu fouiner dans le ventre de ma femme et assassiner mon fils au berceau. / … Tu as fait l'accrochage de Djebel Boukhadra (Ouenza). Cent innocents sont morts. 'On vous monte comme des automates et on vous lâche sur des populations qui ne vous ont rien fait'* / A Mesloula (Ouenza) des femmes et des enfants réfugiés dans une grotte ont subi une enfumade à la Pélissier. / Vous incendiez nos forêts, vous incendiez nos douars. Saint-Arnaud se réjouit dans sa tombe." Mechakra, *La grotte éclatée*, 60.

88. Mechakra, *La grotte éclatée*, 61.

89. "Nous entendîmes un cri sauvage." Mechakra, *La grotte éclatée*, 59.

90. "Le lendemain, Kouider et moi fîmes une tournée dans le maquis. À quelques centaines de mètres de la grotte gisait un homme incomplètement brûlé. Nous l'enterrâmes avec les autres." Mechakra, *La grotte éclatée*, 62.

91. "Je toussotai et repris mon rôle d'Imam." Mechakra, *La grotte éclatée*, 44.

92. "Sa femme s'était déjà promis de donner son prénom à l'enfant qu'il allait naître." Mechakra, *La grotte éclatée*, 43.

93. "Je revis ses yeux puis j'imaginai les miens." Mechakra, *La grotte éclatée*, 44.

94. "L'un des blessés se vida d'un soupir. / Je m'approchai des victimes de la scie. Ils avaient tous de la fièvre; leur état n'était guère encourageant. / Une mère quelque part priait à genoux, les yeux levés vers le ciel. / Elle ne savait pas que son fils était sur le point de la quitter dans une grotte couverte de neige. / Elle aurait traversé la plaine et la montagne pour venir cueillir le dernier souffle de son enfant qui, avant de mourir, se mit à parler d'elle. / Son cœur avait battu à côté du sien; elle avait rajeuni pour lui permettre de grandir. Elle / aurait traversé la plaine et la montagne pour lui chuchoter une dernière fois des choses qu'elle ne disait qu'à lui et que personne ne connaît." Mechakra, *La grotte éclatée*, 39–40.

95. "Son front sillonné de rides, ses larges mains parcourues dans tous les sens de veines turgescentes parlaient pour lui, *témoins muets* de nombreuses années qui l'enveloppaient." Mechakra, *La grotte éclatée*, 45.

96. "Tu t'y tailleras une flûte, tu y souffleras ta musique; c'est une écriture qui parle. Elle a la force de plusieurs écritures." Mechakra, *La grotte éclatée*, 46.

97. "Il existe là, tout près, tout près, racontait le Patriarche, un charnier, béant, où des squelettes de nourrissons gisent dans un ghetto à la mesure de la colère de nos pères. Petites choses à la bouche encore ouverte sur le sein de la mère qui, malgré les clous incrustés dans ses os, les serrait encore. Page d'histoire qui vient se surajouter à bien d'autres pages de notre histoire, de l'histoire d'humanité. Les ghettos nazis, vietnamiens, palestiniens, sud-africains...! Nous faudra-t-il faire le procès de l'histoire tout court?" Mechakra, *Arris*, 70.

98. "Qu'as-tu compris, mon tout petit, lorsque le couteau de l'assassin te lacérait la poitrine et t'arrachait les yeux sous le regard figé de ta mère et de bien d'autres mères muettes de terreur?" Mechakra, *Arris*, 70.

99. "Qui te connaît, toi l'anonyme dont le nom ne figure même pas sur le registre des nouveaux-nés?" Mechakra, *Arris*, 70.

100. "Qui te connaît, toi la mère, ma mère qui tissait des années durant le tapis, tableau où toutes les couleurs s'élançaient, avec cette harmonie qui pleurait la flûte du fugitif?" Mechakra, *Arris*, 70.

101. "Surpris, ô fils de ma mère, ô fils de ma sœur, ô mon fils, on t'avait d'abord arraché les ongles, puis éventré. Surprise, ô ma sœur, ils ont violé ton corps et bu ton sang." Mechakra, *Arris*, 70.

102. "Qui, pour parler de toi et dresser, là où tu mourus, ton portrait?... Dans d'autres pays, des femmes te ressemblent. Quel historien, quel poète te dira un jour? Et toi, mon frère qu'on écorchait, puis qu'on crucifiait vivant. Les clous de l'assassin cognaient contre tes os et tu ne disais mot. A-t-on, aujourd'hui, érigé un mur là où tu mourus, un mur où viendrait pleurer le désemparé?" Mechakra, *Arris*, 70.

103. "—Octobre 1958—Mort des compagnons. Éclatement d'une grotte. /—Octobre 1958—je mourus. /—Octobre 1958—le napalm m'arracha Salah. /—Février 1958—Des petits écoliers assassinés n'avaient pas encore compris qu'ils étaient morts. /—Octobre 1958—Kouider sauva mon corps de l'oubli. /—Octobre 1958—Kouider sentait sa chair brûlée. /—Octobre 1958—j'avais souhaité perdre la mémoire." Mechakra, *La grotte éclatée*, 95.

104. "Je parcourus les premières lignes, je lus 'Sétif' 'Guelma.' Je reposai le journal. Je fermai les yeux." Mechakra, *La grotte éclatée*, 97.

105. "—Tu pleures? /—Non. /—Tu as lu le journal? /—Je ne sais pas. /—C'est un vieil article datant de 1945. /—Je n'y crois pas. Nous l'avons peut-être inventé. /—Mai 1945–1er Novembre 1954-Bugeaud-l'Emir Abdelkader. /—Inventé." Mechakra, *La grotte éclatée*, 97–98.

106. "—Ta main brûlée. /—Ma main a couronné d'une caresse d'adieu le front de mes fils, souvenir ensoleillé de Sakiet. Elle m'a gardé le chant d'une enfant qui a marché sur les ronces et qu'ils ont aimée. J'ai vu les marguerites gémir dans l'aurore une chanson couverte de neige et de sable, j'ai vu les ronces rougir et j'ai aimé la petite fille." Mechakra, *La grotte éclatée*, 98.

107. "J'aimais une statue. Elle dominait le vide de Constantine. C'était ma liberté. Puis, un jour, on me l'a blessée; elle refusait le couvre-feu. Elle saignait, vous n'avez pas pu la sauver. Ma statue est morte. Son cadavre? Un caillou." "—Ta statue vole toujours au-dessus du vide de Constantine. /—Inventé." Mechakra, *La grotte éclatée*, 98.

108. Mechakra, *La grotte éclatée*, 98.

109. "On lui avait tiré une balle en plein poumon"; "A l'hôpital on lui découvrit une large blessure sur le crâne. Vous avez dit qu'elle datait des tranchées de 14–18." Mechakra, *La grotte éclatée*, 98.

110. Mechakra, *La grotte éclatée*, 98.

111. Mechakra, *La grotte éclatée*, 118.

112. These local legends are well known by residents of Constantine—beginning with Sophonisbe's suicide in 203 BC, but in particular the legendary execution of Saint Sidi Mhamed el Ghrab, who was put into a sack and thrown into the ravine by the soldiers of Salah Bey (*chkara* means "sack" and *kef* is a cliff or mountain). There is also a legend about women in Constantine throwing themselves into the ravine to avoid being raped at the moment of the French conquest of the city. The site also figures in French Orientalist accounts, which are unreliable but revealing; see Charles Feraud, "Visite au palais de Constantine," in Édouard Charton, ed., *Le tour du monde*, Vol. 33, 1877, which includes reference to Kef Chkara, and suggests that adulterous women were executed by being thrown into the ravine. Achille Robert's *L'arabe tel qu'il est: Études algériennes et tunisiennes* (Alger: Imprimerie Joseph Angelini, 1900) also refers to this history of punishing adulterous women, but the title of this book undermines its credibility. I thank Walid Bouchakour for his investigation into these details.

113. "Elle s'assit à même le sol. Je m'assis à côté d'elle. Elle porta ses mains à son visage et pleura doucement. Je dégageai la statue de l'étreinte de mon regard et partis. Dehors, des cloches tintaient. La nuit je rêvai que j'émergeais à la surface d'un monde plat et vide au bout duquel ma statue pleurait, la tête dans les mains. Et puis, un jour où Constantine

écoutait le vent jouer dans les arbres de sa brèche, puis couler entre ses gorges en faisant frémir ses ponts, un jour où Constantine semblait saupoudrée de verdure, on m'a tué ma statue." Mechakra, *La grotte éclatée*, 99.

114. "Mon corps est une autre ville. On dirait une ville surréaliste. La pierre que je suis, en s'insinuant dans la cité en prend la forme. Je deviens le reflet difforme d'une cité où l'architecte, épris de perfection, va jusqu'à calculer la hauteur des murs au millimètre près, pour qu'une pierre ne dépasse pas l'autre. Sans aucun doute. Il suffit d'un premier coup d'œil pour en saisir toute la beauté. Je regarde avec courage mes difformités et je leur trouve une beauté singulière. La ville me dévore jusqu'à l'anéantissement de tout mon être..." Mechakra, *Arris*, 59.

115. "Je ressemble encore à la pierre d'où je viens. Je ressemble à ces sculptures incomplètes, celles qu'on ne saurait encore définir, qu'on aimerait arracher au créateur pour en faire quelque chose..." Mechakra, *Arris*, 60.

116. "Délire de pierre fait par l'homme pour canaliser son angoisse, face à sa vulnérabilité"; "Un jour, quelque chose de terrible s'éveille en moi, prend naissance. La révolte." Mechakra, *Arris*, 59.

117. "Je hais la ville dont j'ai pris la forme et qui me rejette indéfiniment." Mechakra, *Arris*, 82.

118. "Ma mère d'adoption m'a indiqué le pays et l'hôpital où je fus vendu." Mechakra, *Arris*, 87.

119. "Je feuillette le dossier dans un bureau aussi poussiéreux que les archives. Je retrouve l'empreinte du doigt de ma mère." Mechakra, *Arris*, 87.

120. "Là, je ne trouve pas âme qui vive. Quelques murs sont encore debout; le reste est effondré et couvert de poussière." Mechakra, *Arris*, 88.

121. "Je retrouve, à l'aide de mon guide, un squelette couvert d'une longue chevelure blanche et un métier à tisser." Mechakra, *Arris*, 88.

122. "Ils sont tous partis. Il ne restait que la mère d'Arris qui l'attendait." Mechakra, *Arris*, 88.

123. "Pour sortir le cimetière de l'oubli." Mechakra, *Arris*, 88.

124. "Avec une infinie douceur, j'enterre ma mère.... J'hésite longtemps avant de me décider à couvrir le corps de Petite mère. Je retire la chevelure blanche et accepte, selon le rituel, de l'enterrer complètement." Mechakra, *Arris*, 89.

125. "Il regarde les paysans qui l'entourent, aussi silencieux que la mort.... Il essaie de reconstituer les contes de sa mère.... Il prend sa tête entre ses mains et ferme les yeux. Il ne prend pas la peine de dégager son visage de la poussière mêlée à la sueur et aux larmes." Mechakra, *Arris*, 91.

126. "Le silence est rompu par le centenaire: /—Arris est revenu, il n'y a pas de veuve! Et tout le peuple dit: /—Amin! Amin! Amin!" Mechakra, *Arris*, 91.

127. "Comment, dans Alger, ville noire, s'est opérée la passation entre bourreaux d'hier et ceux d'aujourd'hui?" Assia Djebar, *Le blanc de l'Algérie* (Paris: Albin Michel, 1995), 220–21.

128. "Le F.L.N. décida la circoncision de tous les fils de chouhada." Mechakra, *La grotte éclatée*, 104.

129. "Gris étincelant des instruments métalliques." Djebar, *Le blanc de l'Algérie*, 216.

130. "Le tribut en cadavres chauds de l'Algérie qui renaît, pantelante, tout en transes, scintillera-t-il dans ce soleil: les *chahids* ou les *chouhadas*, disait-on, c'est-à-dire littéralement 'les martyrs au nom de dieu'? Pourquoi pas les *abtals*, héros de la guerre, les volontaires, qui ont offert d'emblée leur vie, leur ardeur, pourquoi déjà cette hyperbole et dans un consensus suspect? Fanon nous a manqué, pour protester sémantiquement: lui, plus que tout autre, prêt à sortir le scalpel de sa lucidité!" Djebar, *Le blanc de l'Algérie*, 111. Note that Djebar assimilates the Arabic words into her French spelling and grammar ("les chouhadas" and "les abtals" are, for instance, twice pluralized).

131. I drafted an early version of this analysis of Issiakhem's painting and its haunting significance on the cover of Mechakra's novel, which I delivered as a talk entitled "Amnesty/Amnesia/Arris: Yamina Mechakra's Fictions of Justice," at the Middle East Studies Association conference in Washington, DC, November 2014. This was for a panel that I coorganized with Brahim El Guabli called "Writing Revolution: Literature and State Violence in the Postcolonial Maghreb," with Aomar Boum as discussant and Valerie Orlando as panel chair.

132. Yamina Mechakra, preface to *La grotte éclatée* (Algiers: ENAG, 2000), 1.

133. "Un jour viendra où j'écrirais ce témoignage resté intact." Mechakra, preface to *La grotte éclatée*, 1.

134. "Je croyais aux héros. Aujourd'hui, je sais. Il n'y a pas de héros qui ne soit martyr. Chacun de nous l'est à sa manière. Esclave ou libre." Mechakra, *Arris*, 55.

4. OPEN ELEGY

This chapter is significantly revised from a previously published article: "Lines of Flight: Laredj and Djaout beyond the Fiction of Terror," *Expressions maghrébines*, special issue on Tahar Djaout, 17, no. 1 (summer 2018): 83–101.

Epigraphs: Fadhma Aïth Mansour Amrouche, *Histoire de ma vie* (Paris: F. Maspero, 1968), 213; Mahmoud Darwish, in an interview with Randa Abou-Bakr, *The Conflict of Voices in the Poetry of Dennis Butrus and Mahmud Darwish* (Berlin: Reichert, 2004), 206.

1. "Le récit d'un destin brisé par le fanatisme religieux." Waciny Laredj, *Les ailes de la reine*, trans. Marcel Bois (Arles: Actes Sud, 2009), back cover.

2. Benjamin Stora opens *La guerre invisible: Algérie, années 90* (Paris: Les presses de Sciences Po, 2001) by pointing out that the different ways in which the war has been named signal the unresolved antagonisms and uncertainties about what actually happened: "'Guerre de civilisation' entre partisans de la 'modernité républicaine' et adeptes d'un 'fanatisme intégriste,' entre ténèbres de l'obscurantisme et lumières de la raison?" (A "clash of civilizations" between partisans of "Republican modernity" and followers of "fundamentalism fanaticism," between obscurantist shadows and enlightenment reason?); "Le conflit meurtrier qui oppose le gouvernement algérien à des groupes armées depuis 1992 est-il alors une guerre civile? . . . Au-delà de cette querelle sémantique, le fait est que ce conflit a causé la mort de plus de 100 000 personnes et en cela, il s'agit bien d'une 'guerre *contre* les civils'?" (Is the murderous conflict which has since 1992 positioned the Algerian government against armed groups a civil war? Beyond this semantic quarrel, the fact is that the conflict has killed more than 100,000 people, and

is thus a "war against civilians"). Stora, *La guerre invisible*, 13, 14–15. Natalya Vince and Walid Benkhaled note that the FIS was an extension of the FLN and thus "disagree with labelling the 1990s a 'civil war,' preferring instead to use the term 'war against civilians' as more accurately reflecting the lack of clear ideological dividing lines." Natalya Vince and Walid Benkhaled, "Performing Algerianness: The National and Transnational Construction of Algeria's 'Culture Wars,'" in *Algeria: Nation, Culture, and Transnationalism*, ed. Patrick Crowley (Liverpool: Liverpool University Press, 2017), 250. For these reasons, I use the term *war against civilians*.

3. The full quotation from the translated book's back cover: "Récit d'un destin brisé par le fanatisme religieux, *Les Ailes de la reine* est aussi, et peut-être surtout, une leçon de courage. Celui des hommes et des femmes qui savent, comme Miryam—et qui en tirent toutes les conséquences, au péril de leur vie—, que la culture est le dernier rempart contre la barbarie." Laredj, *Les ailes de la reine*, back cover.

4. This framing is clear in the heavy-handed French paratext that invites reading the novel as an enlightened weapon in a civilizational war against Islamist barbarity. Antiterror discourse is strong in Algeria, as well, yet closer reading reveals Laredj's multivalent critique. For example, the headline for an interview with Laredj by Rachid Mokhtari reads: "L'art est notre dernier rempart pour faire face à l'islamisme" (Art is our last defense against Islamism). However, Laredj's actual statement in the text of this interview reads quite differently: "L'art est notre dernier rempart pour faire face *non seulement à l'islamisme mais aussi à toutes les expressions totalitaires*" (Art is our last defense against *not only Islamism but also all forms of totalitarianism*). "Waciny Laredj: 'L'art est notre dernier rempart pour faire face à l'islamisme.'" *Le matin d'Algérie*, November 18, 2011, https://www.lematindz.net/news/6279-waciny-laredj-lart-est-notre-dernier-rempart-pour-faire-face-non-seulement-lintegrisme-mais-aussi-a-toutes-les-expressions-totalitaires-lire-lentretien.html.

5. On this, see Stora, *La guerre invisible*, 15, and the collection of interviews by Sid Ahmed Semiane, *Octobre, ils parlent* (Algiers: Le matin, 1998).

6. "Un vendredi 7 octobre de l'automne 1988." Laredj, *Les ailes de la reine*, 12. In this chapter, all citations are drawn from Marcel Bois's French translation, which he did in close collaboration with Waciny Laredj, and which I discussed with Bois during conversations with him in Kouba, Algiers, during the spring of 2014 and again in June 2015. The English translations in the chapter are my own, done in comparison to Laredj's Arabic text.

7. Laredj, *Les ailes de la reine*, 11.

8. "Onze chapitres, sur le point d'être achevés." Laredj, *Les ailes de la reine*, 241.

9. "La balle sort d'un pistolet, et le tireur, à son insu, provoque un désastre irréparable. Peut-être un des passants que je croise chaque jour dans les rues, un jeune homme à peine libéré du service national ou antinational. Qui sait? Hélas!... Un militaire, c'est un militaire." Laredj, *Les ailes de la reine*, 12.

10. "Le choix entre une démocratie anarchique et des 'Inquisiteurs'! Tu parles d'une situation!" Laredj, *Les ailes de la reine*, 46.

11. In a private conversation, this association to the monument was drawn immediately by Marcel Bois in his first comment on the Arabic title—you know, he said, like *the "maqām."* Private interview, Kouba, Algiers, June 10, 2015.

12. During a conference session called "Cartographie urbaine du Hirak" held at the University of Algiers in July 2019, for instance, the urban sociologist Madani Safar Zitoun underlined the significance of *ḥūma* in his talk. Mustapha Benfodil, "Regards croisés sur le 'Hirak,'" *El Watan*, June 30, 2019, https://www.elwatan.com/edition/actualite/regards-croises-sur-le-mouvement-du-22-fevrier-a-luniversite-alger-2-cartographie-urbaine-du-hirak-01-07-2019.

13. See *Encyclopedia of Islam*, s.v. "marthīyā," accessed June 1, 2020, https://referenceworks.brillonline.com/browse/encyclopaedia-of-islam-2.

14. See Rebecca Dyer, "Poetry of Politics and Mourning: Mahmoud Darwish's Genre-Transforming Tribute to Edward W. Said," *PMLA* 122, no. 5 (2007): 1447–62; her discussion of the neoclassical genre and its nationalist function in early twentieth-century Egypt is on 1453–54.

15. Judith Butler, *Antigone's Claim* (New York: Columbia University Press, 2002), 33. For Butler's further reflection on such questions, see *Precarious Life: The Powers of Mourning and Violence* (New York: Verso Books, 2004) and *Frames of War: When Is Life Grievable?* (New York: Verso Books, 2009).

16. ".... L'armée nationale [prend] position contre la nation." Laredj, *Les ailes de la reine*, 133. The rupture generated by the shock of October 1988 has been discussed by many, including Abed Charef, *Octobre* (Algiers: Laphomic, 1989) and "Les émeutes d'octobre 1988: une crise fondatrice?," in *Algérie, 30 ans, les enfants de l'indépendance*, ed. Merzak Allouache and Vincent Colonna (Paris: Autrement 1992), 76–85; Hafid Gafaïti, "Culture and Violence: The Algerian Intelligentsia between Two Political Illegitimacies," in "Translating Algeria," special issue, *Parallax* 4, no. 2 (1998): 71–77; Zineb Ali-Benali, Najib Redouane, and Yamina Mokaddem, *1989 en Algérie: Rupture tragique ou rupture féconde* (Toronto: La source, 1999); Mahfoud Bennoune, *The Making of Contemporary Algeria, 1830–1987* (Cambridge: Cambridge University Press, 2002); Rabah Soukehal, *L'écrivain de langue française et les pouvoirs en Algérie* (Paris: L'Harmattan, 1998); Benjamin Stora, *La guerre invisible: Algérie, années 90* (Paris: Presses de Sciences Po, 2003); and a number of writers of homages included in Amin Khan's collection, *Présence de Tahar Djaout, poète* (Algiers: Barzakh, 2013).

17. Anne-Emmanuelle Berger, in *Algeria in Others' Languages* (Ithaca, NY: Cornell University Press, 2002), warns against a too tidy linguistic schema (arabophone/francophone/berberophone) often used to describe the radicalization of linguistic difference in 1990s Algeria, to point out that linguistic practices, identifications, and polemics among Algerians are far more intricate and nuanced. Rabah Soukehal, in *L'écrivain de langue française et les pouvoirs en Algérie*, is more vehement on this point: "La querelle linguistique apparaît beaucoup plus comme un faux débat ou d'une absurdité déconcertante que comme une profonde réflexion sur l'avenir linguistique de l'Algérie.... [L]'affrontement idéologique (politique) autour de cette question linguistique est absurde." (The linguistic quarrel seems much more like a false debate or disconcerting nonsense than a deep reflection on the linguistic future of Algeria.... [T]he ideological [political] confrontation around this linguistic question is absurd.) Rabah Soukehal, *L'écrivain de langue française*, 109, 115.

18. Video of the full speech is available online: AlgerianMedia, "خطاب بوتفليقة كاملا سطيف" Algerie Discours de Bouteflika Setif Complet [HD] 2012," YouTube video, 41:58, May 10, 2012, https://www.youtube.com/watch?v=aoTGwf9uYcA. A French transcript is available online: "Discours intégral de Bouteflika à Sétif," in *Algérie Focus*, May 8, 2012; https://www.algerie-focus.com/2012/05/discours-integral-de-bouteflika-a-setif/. See also the article "Cinq ans après avoir lancé 'Tab jnanou', Bouteflika s'accroche au pouvoir," a discussion of the speech by Achira Mammeri published on the TSA Algérie site, May 8, 2017, https://www.tsa-algerie.com/cinq-ans-apres-avoir-lance-tab-jnanou-bouteflika-saccroche-toujours-au-pouvoir/.

19. On which, see John P. Entelis's 2016 article in the *Washington Post*, which argues that the redraft of the constitution in 2016 "served to reinforce the authority of the state at the expense of civil society" and that "constitutional engineering in Algeria is but another instrument by which an embedded military industrial complex constructs a legal scaffold to maintain and perpetuate the authority of the state." John P. Entelis, "What Does an Amended Constitution Really Change about Algeria?," *Washington Post*, January 19, 2016, https://www.washingtonpost.com/news/monkey-cage/wp/2016/01/19/what-does-an-amended-constitution-really-change-about-algeria/?noredirect=on&utm_term=3e2f223764e7.

20. "Je m'adresse à vous dépositaires du legs du chouhada." Citations from Bouteflika's speech are drawn from the French transcript, with reference to the filmed version of the speech, which was delivered in Arabic.

21. "Ces élections seront exceptionnelles au regard des nombreuses garanties que nous avons mises en place, elles seront propres et transparentes à la hauteur des attentes de notre peuple."

22. "De Sétif, ville séculaire et symbole, nous commémorons aujourd'hui l'anniversaire tragique du 8 mai 1945 dans un une atmosphère de recueillement à la mémoire des martyrs, femmes, hommes, et enfants sans défense, qui ont été massacrés dans de nombreuses régions du pays, notamment à Sétif, Guelma, et Kherrata, alors qu'ils étaient sortis pacifiquement, les drapeaux à la main, à l'instar des peuples qui ont vaincu le nazisme et le fascisme, pour célébrer la fin de la guerre mondiale à laquelle leur peuple a pris part, avec l'espoir d'obtenir leur droit légitime à la liberté et à la dignité."

23. "Une nouvelle étape ... d'évolution démocratique dans votre pays"; "le seuil d'une étape cruciale"; "notre nation arabo-musulmane"; "l'État de droit et de démocratie auquel nous aspirons."

24. "Tous les chouhada du 8 mai 1945"; "ceux enfermés dans des cellules obscures ou dans des camps funestes, brûlés dans des grottes oubliées ou enterrés dans des fosses communes, sans nom aucun"; "les ennemis du pays"; "instigateurs de la Fitna."

25. "Les éléments de l'Armée nationale populaire et de tous les corps de sécurité qui ont fait face à la machine de la mort et du terrorisme abject pour que la République demeure debout unifiée et réconciliée, digne, fière et rayonnante."

26. "Vous qui avez l'esprit accablé par les affres du colonialisme et de la fitna, qui êtes conscients des dangers complexes qui guettent le pays dans un espace géographique en proie aux bouleversements ... vous montrerez au monde le visage reluisant d'Algérie d'aujourd'hui et celle de demain."

27. "La liberté et la souveraineté nationale ont été recouvrées au prix d'énormes sacrifices. Un tribut tout aussi lourd a été versé pour préserver l'unité du pays et le régime républicain et consacrer la sécurité, la paix et la réconciliation."

28. Nasséra Dutour, "Algérie: De la Concorde civile à la Charte pour la paix et la réconciliation nationale: Amnistie, amnésie, impunité," in "Mouvements," special issue, *La découverte* 53, no. 1 (2008): 146. The first sentences of her article read: "Si les autorités imposent des lois d'amnistie, c'est pour oublier... si elles veulent effacer les mémoires, c'est forcément qu'elles se sont rendues coupables d'actes condamnables qui les couvrent de honte. Ce qui me réconforte, c'est que nous, victimes, sommes toujours debout face à eux et déterminées à ce qu'ils disent la verité." (If the authorities impose amnesty laws, it is in order to forget... if they want to erase memories, it is inevitably because they are guilty of wrongful acts which cover them in shame. What comforts me is that we, the victims, are still standing before them, determined that they will speak the truth.) Dutour, "Algérie," 144.

29. "Algeria: New Amnesty Law Will Ensure Atrocities Go Unpunished, Muzzles Discussion of Civil Conflict," *Human Rights Watch* news release, February 28, 2006. hrw.org/news/2006/02/28/algeria-new-amnesty-law-will-ensure-atrocities-go-unpunished.

30. "C'est ainsi que la machine politique a réglé le dossier. Aujourd'hui, il n'y a ni réparation, ni justice, juste l'amnistie et l'amnésie." Dutour, "Algérie," 148.

31. For a detailed report, see the Ligue algérienne de défense des droits de l'homme document *La répression du printemps noir April 2001–April 2002* (Algiers: Ligue algérienne de defense des droits de l'homme, 2002), issued as a corrective to an existing government-sponsored report.

32. Vince and Benkhaled, "Performing Algerianness."

33. Vince and Benkhaled, "Performing Algerianness," 254.

34. "Un texte qui sommeille en moi depuis ma tendre enfance... ma référence inévitable." In Katia Ghosn, "Waciny Laredj, un pont entre deux rives," *L'Orient Littéraire*, December 2010, http://lorientlitteraire.com/article_details.php?cid=33&nid=3315.

35. The novel explicitly establishes a metatextual commentary on the precarity of aesthetic performance under threat of annihilation that casts Laredj's own act of writing in this light: "Dans ce pays," asserts the narrator (also a novelist), "nous n'avons pas d'autre choix que d'écrire. Je me suis rappelé ses derniers mots: À un de ces jours! Quand on écrit, la première phrase est la plus difficile: on a toujours l'impression de se trouver face au danger, à l'abîme, à l'impossible." (In this country... we have no other choice but to write. I remember his last words: Til one of these days! When we write, it's the first sentence that is the hardest: we always have the impression of finding ourselves confronted by danger, by the abyss, by the impossible.) Laredj, *Les ailes de la reine*, 73.

36. This point builds on Nasrin Qader's reflections on the *Nights* in the introduction to her *Narratives of Catastrophe* (New York: Fordham University Press, 2009), 15. Qader writes: "With storytelling, Shahrazad interrupts the repetitive economy of death, while she is still threatened by this economy. So long as there is the story, the menace of death, though abated temporarily, looms large on the horizon. The reprieve every night, as she faces the king and tells her tale, remains uncertain and threatened.... This fragile

dynamic of Shahrazad's survival constitutes the condition of singularity of narration, each and every time."

37. ".... les dernières paroles de Miryam, avant que le médecin palestinien ne retire les tuyaux de son nez, de sa bouche, de sa tête, quand soudainement son cœur s'est arrêté, en plein récit de la dernière nuit dans la salle de danse: elle se laisse emporter par sa passion pour le ballet de Rimski Korsakov et elle, Schéhérazade, affronte le tyran frustré qui avait juré de la décapiter. *Dieu te maudisse, Chahriyar!*" (.... Miryam's last words, before the Palestinian doctor removed the tubes from her nose, from her mouth, from her head, when suddenly her heart stopped, in the middle of an account of the last night in the dance hall: she lets herself be carried away by her passion for Rimsky Korsakov's ballet and she, Scheherazade, confronts the frustrated tyrant who had sworn to behead her. May God damn you, Chahriyar!) Laredj, *Les ailes de la reine*, 13.

38. "Criminels prédateurs, criminels oppresseurs, criminels prévaricateurs..." Laredj, *Les ailes de la reine*, 244.

39. For a history of *Alf layla* and its multitude of translations and transmissions, see Daniel Heller-Roazen's introduction to a Norton critical edition that he edited, *The Arabian Nights* (New York: Norton, 2009). The collection of criticism in this volume is illuminating, in particular the essays by Jorge Luis Borges, Andras Hamori, and Abdelfattah Kilito. *Alf layla* has long been an important intertext for Maghrebi novelists; Nasrin Qader's *Narratives of Catastrophe* is especially illuminating on this. Notably, Laredj has published another novel, *Raml al-Māya: Fājiʿat al-layla al-sābiʿa baʿd al-alf*, whose subtitle might be translated as *The Catastrophe of the Thousand and Seventh Night* (the title *Raml al-Māya* names a genre of Andalucian music devoted to songs of love and intoxication).

40. Michael Wood, "The Last Night of All," in "Remapping Genre," special issue, PMLA 1122, no. 5 (October 2007): 1394–402. Wood calls the *Nights* "the genre of the unfinishable work, as distinct from works that are unfinished or open-ended—the work whose themes and style involve what comes last and then what comes after that, if there is anything after that" (1394).

41. "En étant dans les deux langues je suis dans deux traditions d'écriture très différentes et j'ai souvent ce sentiment d'être bicéphale." In Ghosn, "Waciny Laredj."

42. "Mon lien à la langue arabe fut d'abord affectif. Ma grand-mère, pour qui l'islam est inséparable de la langue, m'a poussé vers l'arabe. Apprendre l'arabe est un geste d'amour pour cette femme qui a incarné pour moi les images absentes du père et de la mère." In Ghosn, "Waciny Laredj."

43. "À l'école coranique, placé sur le même rayon que les livres saints, je tombe sur un exemplaire des Mille et une Nuits que je vole et lis en secret. Le fait d'écrire a été déterminé par cet acte illicite. Je garde toujours d'ailleurs cet exemplaire avec moi. La lecture des Nuits m'a fait définitivement sortir du sacré." In Ghosn, "Waciny Laredj."

44. Eileen Julien, "The Extroverted African Novel," in *The Novel: History, Geography and Culture, Vol. 1*, ed. Franco Moretti (Princeton, NJ: Princeton University Press, 2006), 679.

45. Qader, *Narratives of Catastrophe*, 15.

46. Laredj, *Les ailes de la reine*, 149.

47. As the narrator walks the streets of Algiers on his last night, he communicates in direct address to his dead lover: "Ah! Miryam... Toi, abécédaire effacé, la danse interrompue, le chant étouffé dans la gorge. Laisse-moi m'endormir, laisse-moi dévaler vers la cité du désespoir." (Ah! Miryam... you, primer erased, dance interrupted, song smothered in throat. Let me sleep, let me rush towards the city of despair.) Laredj, *Les ailes de la reine*, 13–14. Entire passages are given over to abrupt citation, at times with quotation marks (23) and at times without (26) so that the two splice indistinguishably together: "Une sorte d'osmose entre ton visage et le mien. Ton visage s'insinue en moi comme un nuage mauve" (A sort of osmosis between your face and mine. Your face creeps into me like a mauvish cloud) (27). In passages narrated by Miryam, only subtle cues help to distinguish her perspective, which gives way imperceptibly to her mother's voice (56, 77).

48. Laredj, *Les ailes de la reine*, 68.

49. See Laredj, *Les ailes de la reine*, 149–55.

50. "Honte à toi, pays qui oublie ses amoureux et ses martyrs: le matin tu les vénères et le soir tu les condamnes. Je vous souhaite la mort, nouveaux criminels!" Laredj, *Les ailes de la reine*, 156.

51. He discusses this in the interview with Katia Ghosn, "Waciny Laredj."

52. For Fayrouz's lyrics, see Laredj, *Les ailes de la reine*, 241. Iguerbouchène integrated elements from Kabyle and Arabic Andalusian music in his orchestral pieces. He was fluent in eighteen languages (including Russian, Japanese, Tamahaq, Tachawit, Tashelhit) and studied music in Manchester and Vienna before collaborating on scores for films such as *Pepe le Moko* (1937) and *Algiers* (1938), which launched his career as film score composer; it happens that in 1945 he also wrote about a hundred songs based on Rabindranath Tagore's *Thousand Nights*. See Mouloud Oumnoughene, *Mohamed Iguerbouchene, une œuvre intemporelle* (Algiers: Dar Khettab, 2015).

53. A recording is available online: Da Boudj, "Abdelmadjid Meskoud 'El Assima,'" YouTube video, 6:21, April 20, 2009, https://www.youtube.com/watch?v=CoW2dKrvmIc.

54. "Un des plus beaux textes écrits sur cette ville au moment où elle s'effondre et tombe en ruine." Laredj, *Les ailes de la reine*, 179. Recall that the Hebrew book of Lamentations is a collection of poetic laments for the destruction of the city of Jerusalem by Babylon.

55. "Alger ma belle, / Submergé de tous côtés, / Tu as perdu le goût de la vie. De tous côtés on fait irruption. / Où sont passés les tailleurs de caftans, / Les artisans de medjboud? Disparus, les brodeurs sur soie, / Et les brodeurs sur cuir! / Où sont les dinandiers, les artisans selliers, / Et les artistes peintres? / Dites-moi, vous qui m'écoutez..." Laredj, *Les ailes de la reine*, 180.

56. "Qui va t'entendre, Abdelmajid mon frère?" Laredj, *Les ailes de la reine*, 180.

57. A recording is available online: MrLeMaure—Andalous & Chaabi, "El Hadj El Ghaffour مريم ولفي," YouTube video, 16:45, December 5, 2014, https://www.youtube.com/watch?v=FMAt7tCFYLM.

58. "Arrivé au portail que franchissent les ambulances, j'ai songé à mon amie, la poétesse Safia Kettou, que la ville avait tuée. Elle s'était jetée du haut du pont de Telemly qui relie la ville basse à ses hauteurs. Sans me livrer à de grandes réflexions, j'ai laissé

mon corps déambuler à travers les rues où les flaques d'eau s'étaient multipliées et j'ai tendu l'oreille à la voix de Ghaffour qui s'élevait du café-bar voisin de l'hôpital; une voix triste et funèbre... / Ton absence m'est brûlure, Miryam, tendre compagne! / Qu'es-tu devenue, ma toute belle? /... Et ton regard, chargé de promesses? Salue-moi de là-bas, / Miryam, ma tendre compagne." Laredj, *Les ailes de la reine*, 225.

59. "Qui, pour parler de toi et dresser, là où tu mourus, ton portrait? Dans d'autres pays, des femmes te ressemblent. Quel historien, quel poète te dira un jour?" Yamina Mechakra, *Arris* (Algiers: Marsa, 1999), 70.

60. It is not possible to know why Safia Kettou jumped from Telemly Bridge in January 1989, but in *Le blanc de l'Algérie* (1995) Assia Djebar speculates about why her own friend Josie Fanon committed suicide by jumping from the fifth-story window of her apartment in El Biar—a neighborhood adjacent to Telemly—a few months later, on July 13, 1989. In August 1988, Josie Fanon and Assia Djebar had spent a month together in a coastal village near Algiers, and then returned in September to their separate residences in the capital. Djebar recounts what happened just before her friend's suicide: "Les premiers jours d'octobre 88, Alger s'enfiévra; sous le balcon de Josie, à El Biar, des adolescents révoltés brûlèrent, les premiers, des voitures de police. Le lendemain, les jours suivants, cette fois en plein cœur d'Alger, l'armée investit la capitale et, face à des manifestations pacifiques, tire: six cents jeunes furent abattus. D'un bout à l'autre de la ville en émeute, ne pouvant pas nous rejoindre, nous nous parlions au téléphone: j'entends encore aujourd'hui la voix de Josie, rageuse, sans fin commenter les scènes de violence qu'elle avait vues ou qu'on lui avait rapportées. *A nouveau, ô Frantz, les damnés de la terre'!*" (The first days of October of '88, Algiers became feverish; beneath Josie's balcony, in El Biar, rebellious adolescents were the first to set fire to police cars. The next day, the following days, this time in the middle of Algiers, the army invaded the capital and, faced with peaceful protests, opened fire: six hundred youths were gunned down. With the city in riots from one end to the other, we spoke on the telephone, not being able to meet each other in person: to this day, I hear Josie's voice, full of rage, describing the scenes of violence that she had witnessed or that others had reported to her. Once more, oh Frantz, the "wretched of the earth"!) Assia Djebar, *Le blanc de l'Algérie* (Paris: Albin Michel, 1995), 98–99.

61. "Criminels prédateurs, criminels oppresseurs, criminels prévaricateurs, criminels mauvais pasteurs. / Criminels dans le ciel, criminels sur la terre, criminels entre ciel et terre. / Criminels dans les airs, criminels sur les eaux, criminels vociférant, criminels agissant en silence. / Criminels en plein jour, criminels dans la nuit noire, criminels entre chien et loup. Criminels sanguinaires, criminels tortionnaires, assassins de la mémoire. / Cri... mi... nels des derniers soupirs que brise l'épouvante dans ce désert sauvage." Laredj, *Les ailes de la reine*, 244.

62. "Sous le choc des premiers témoignages le 17 octobre 1988." Comité national contre la torture, *Cahier noir d'octobre* (Algiers: Comité national contre la torture, 1989), http://ettahaddi.net/sites/default/files/asset/document/Cahier-Noir-D-Octobre.pdf, 11.

63. See Laredj, *Les ailes de la reine*, 39, 42–43.

64. "Écoutons-les car tout torturé a d'abord besoin de notre écoute; écoutons-les pour eux mais aussi pour nous-mêmes, pour savoir l'atrocité de la torture, écoutons-les pour

prémunir notre société de funestes avenirs car leurs paroles ont la force de '*la mémoire contre l'oubli.*'" Comité national contre la torture, *Cahier noir d'octobre*, 7.

65. "Un crime impuni d'abord, la torture. Puis des victimes suppliciées qui souffrent encore dans leurs âmes, et, pour beaucoup, dans leurs corps. Enfin des tortionnaires d'État impunis et confortés dans leurs pratiques. Ce constat est amer. Pour que la victoire des tortionnaires ne soit pas complète en Algérie, il faut lui opposer sans cesse la parole des victimes, à défaut de justice." Anouar Benmalek, new preface to *Cahier noir d'octobre*, by Comité national contre la torture, unnumbered page.

66. "Ce fut un moment terrible d'émotion car, pour la première fois depuis l'indépendance du pays, des citoyens algériens avaient pu témoigner de la torture que leur avaient infligée les forces de l'ordre pendant leur arrestation." Comité national contre la torture, *Cahier noir d'octobre*, 135.

67. "La main du crime est guidée par des commanditaires et justifiée par la raison d'Etat." Comité national contre la torture, *Cahier noir d'octobre*, 9.

68. "Et pourtant 'on' tortura encore et encore et la liste serait bien longue de tous les crimes perpétrés au nom de la raison de l'état. PRS, FPS, ORP, PAGS, intégristes, benbellistes, divers opposants ou victimes des luttes d'appareils—à chaque 'affaire' de répression politique et policière cette pratique revient et parfois les torturés d'hier—ou leurs exécutants—torturent, ou se taisent, *au nom du pouvoir*. À chaque 'affaire,' les récits hallucinatoires devant une justice impuissante ou lâchement complice." Comité national contre la torture, *Cahier noir d'octobre*, 8.

69. "JUSTICE DANS NOTRE PAYS"; "jugement des tortionnaires conformément à la constitution et à la loi." Comité national contre la torture, *Cahier noir d'octobre*, 10, 11.

70. "Pour que: La torture soit définitivement bannie; L'armée ne tire jamais sur le peuple; Justice se fasse." Comité national contre la torture, *Cahier noir d'octobre*, 106.

71. "*Qui* a peur de la mobilisation contre la torture?" Comité national contre la torture, *Cahier noir d'octobre*, 103.

72. "Une salle publique pour la tenue du tribunal populaire contre la torture." Comité national contre la torture, *Cahier noir d'octobre*, 104.

73. Laredj, *Les ailes de la reine*, 42.

74. Laredj, *Les ailes de la reine*, 42.

75. "Je témoignerai devant la Ligue des droits de l'homme, devant le Comité contre la torture. Je dirai qu'ils ont utilisé des balles explosives. Ils nous ont forcés de rendre les corps à leurs familles. Ils nous ont forcés d'écrire des noms sur des cercueils bourrés de coton et de membres en lambeaux non-identifiés. Je raconterai l'histoire de cette mère qui a insisté pour voir le visage de son fils, victime des événements..." Laredj, *Les ailes de la reine*, 42.

76. "Presque aveugle, elle lui caressait le visage.... Elle a éclaté en sanglots et elle s'en est allée comme un nuage d'été." Laredj, *Les ailes de la reine*, 43.

77. "Nos détresses se multipliaient comme des grains de sable, et l'on palabrait, on grinçait les dents. Ne fallait-il pas chercher autre chose?!" Laredj, *Les ailes de la reine*, 39. In 2008, the CFDA had eight thousand dossiers of the disappeared (Dutour, "Algérie," 145), indeed multiplied like grains of sand. This is surely a fraction; most testimonies have not been recorded. The CFDA is driven by the engine of grief, especially of women. See the

CFDA memorial site for a visual illustration of "grains of sand": Mémorials des disparus en Algérie, http://www.memorial-algerie.org/?q=fr/node/3309/retratos/all/all/all/.

78. "Les disparus ne sont pas dans mes poches.... Vous me faites honte dans le monde comme des pleureuses, avec vos photos." Dutour, "Algérie," 147.

79. "Je te salue Fadhma, jeune fille de ma tribu, pour nous tu n'es pas morte! On te lira dans les douars, on te lira dans les lycées, nous ferons tout pour qu'on te lise!" Kateb Yacine, preface to *Histoire de ma vie*, by Fadhma Aïth Mansour Amrouche (Paris: F. Maspero, 1968).

80. "Un sentiment profond commence à me dévorer: chaque fois que je répète *La Berbère*, je ressens une douleur poignante. Je l'ai dans le sang. Je sais la souffrance de ne pas connaître son père. Je me retrouve en elle: son présent, son passé, son exil." Laredj, *Les ailes de la reine*, 61.

81. "Une voix blanche et presque sans timbre, infiniment fragile et proche de la brisure." Kateb, preface to *Histoire de ma vie*, 11.

82. "Une tribu plurielle et pourtant singulière." Kateb, preface to *Histoire de ma vie*, 11.

83. "La première fois qu'une femme d'Algérie ose écrire ce qu'elle a vécu." Kateb, preface to *Histoire de ma vie*, 11.

84. "Cette histoire est vraie, pas un épisode n'en a été inventé, tout ce qui est arrivé avant ma naissance m'a été raconté par ma mère." Fadhma Aïth Mansour Amrouche, letter to Jean Amrouche dated August 1946 in *Histoire de ma vie* (Paris: F. Maspero, 1968), 15.

85. "La nuit de ma naissance, ma mère était couchée seule, avec ses deux petits; personne auprès d'elle pour l'assister ou lui porter secours: elle se délivra seule, et coupa le cordon ombilical avec ses dents." Fadhma Aït Mansour Amrouche, *Histoire de ma vie* (Paris: F. Maspero, 1968), 25.

86. "Ma mère était une courageuse. Elle avait coutume de dire: 'Tichert-iou khir t'mira guergazen!'—'le tatouage que j'ai au menton vaut mieux que la barbe des hommes'!" Amrouche, *Histoire de ma vie*, 29.

87. "Elle fut enceinte, et l'homme nia être le père de l'enfant. Les mœurs Kabyles sont terribles. Quand une femme a fauté, il faut qu'elle disparaisse, qu'on ne la voie plus, que la honte n'entache pas sa famille. Avant la domination française la justice était expéditive; les parents menaient la fautive dans un champ où ils l'abattaient. Et ils l'enterraient sous un talus.... Mais en ce temps-là, la justice française luttait contre les mœurs trop rudes. Et ma mère eut recours à elle." Amrouche, *Histoire de ma vie*, 25.

88. "Je n'en mourus pas." Amrouche, *Histoire de ma vie*, 25.

89. "Le monde est méchant, et c'est 'l'enfant de la faute' qui devient le martyr de l'Algérie, surtout en Kabylie." Amrouche, *Histoire de ma vie*, 26.

90. "Pour les Kabyles, nous étions des Roumis, des renégats; pour l'armée, nous étions des bicots commes les autres." Amrouche, *Histoire de ma vie*, 203.

91. "Nous vécûmes de mars 1957 à octobre 1958 dans les transes de la guerre; la population était en butte aux mauvais traitements de l'armée; les maquisards faisaient des sabotages, la nuit, le matin, l'armée forçait les populations à les réparer. Il y avait du malheur chez les civils des deux camps, et mon mari maigrissait à vue d'œil.... C'est dire combien l'ambiance était sinistre! Toute la nuit nous tremblions dès que nous entendions

un bruit. Malgré la serrure et les verrous, nous avions peur de tout et de l'inconnu." Amrouche, *Histoire de ma vie*, 203, 205.

92. "Octobre 1958, Henri; janvier 1959, son père; avril 1962, c'est Jean. Depuis août 1939, cela fait cinq de mes fils, et leur père: six deuils me frappent, et je survis à tous ces malheurs. Parfois je me demande quel genre de mort je pourrais choisir pour disparaître sans souffrance, sans me voir mourir par étapes comme les paralysés." Amrouche, *Histoire de ma vie*, 208.

93. "Les hommes de chez nous sont si endurants au malheur, si dociles à la volonté de Dieu, mais on ne le comprend vraiment que si on entre dans cette langue qui me fut un réconfort tout au long de mes exils." Amrouche, *Histoire de ma vie*, 208.

94. "Je suis comme l'aigle blessé / L'aigle blessé entre les ailes. / Tous ses enfants se sont envolés / Et lui ne cesse de pleurer. / Pitié, ô maître des vents, / Venez en aide à ceux qui souffrent. // Je suis comme l'aigle des montagnes, / Sur la roche la plus haut dressée. / Il passe ses nuits à observer le ciel / Espérant découvrir, parmi les étoiles, / Le visage de ceux qui se sont envolés." Amrouche, *Histoire de ma vie*, 213.

95. "Mais ce livre est aussi, dans son humilité, un implacable réquisitoire." Kateb, preface to *Histoire de ma vie*, 14.

96. "Algériennes, Algériens, témoignez pour vous-mêmes! N'acceptez pas d'être des objets, prenez vous-mêmes la plume, avant qu'on se saisisse de votre propre drame, pour le tourner contre vous!" Kateb, preface to *Histoire de ma vie*, 15.

CONCLUSION. PRISONS WITHOUT WALLS
This conclusion includes a significantly revised version of a previously published article. "Subterranean Musics: Reading Samira Negrouche," *Yale French Studies*, 'North African Poetry in French,' ed. Thomas Connolly, nos. 137–38 (forthcoming), 231–47.
Epigraphs: Assia Djebar, *Vaste est la prison* (Paris: Albin Michel, 1995), 346; Assia Djebar, *Le blanc de l'Algérie* (Paris: Albin Michel, 1995), 56; Françoise Vergès, *Le ventre des femmes: Capitalisme, racialisation, féminisme* (Paris: Albin Michel, 2017), 21.

1. Soolking's music video was also a YouTube viral sensation, which is available at Soolking Officiel, "Soolking feat. Ouled El Bahdja—Liberté [Clip Officiel] Prod by Katakuree," YouTube video, 4:50, March 14, 2019, https://www.youtube.com/watch?v=CTAH-AqYm48. For a video of the song being played on the streets of Algiers during the Hirak protests in March 2019, see La Joie Du Bled, "Soolking Ouled El Bahdja—La Liberté—Manifestation 22 Mars 2019," YouTube video, 4:42, April 25, 2019, https://www.youtube.com/watch?v=jbm6F2ktczk.

2. The feminine singular "rahi" and "marhuma" here suggest that it may be "al-hurrīya" or "la liberté" itself that has been taken hostage and killed.

3. For a good working sense of key terms in this vernacular lexicon, see the "Hirak Glossary" that is currently being compiled by Muriam Haleh Davis, Hiyem Cheurfa, and Thomas Serres. "A Hirak Glossary: Terms from Algeria and Morocco," *Jadaliyya*, June 13, 2019, https://www.jadaliyya.com/Details/38734.

4. On this, see also Ghaliya N. Djelloul and Aniss M. Mezoued's essay "Les ressorts spatiaux de la mobilisation révolutionnare à Alger," *Forum Vies Mobiles*, June 1,

2019, https://fr.forumviesmobiles.org/2019/06/28/ressorts-spatiaux-mobilisation-revolutionnaire-alger-12995?utm_source=metropolitiques&utm_medium=breve&utm_campaign=2019_07_05. They write: "Les slogans 'Yetne7aw ga3! Yet7asbou ga3! Netrabaw ga3!' ('Qu'ils partent tous! Qu'ils soient tous jugés! Que nous nous éduquions tous!') expriment bien la volonté de rupture, mais également d'évolution vers une nouvelle forme de vivre-ensemble, où la non-violence, qui semble aujourd'hui former une nouvelle forme de 'thérapie collective' (Carlier 1995), garantirait enfin l'existence d'un lien civil." (The slogans "Yetne7aw ga3! Yet7asbou ga3! Netrabaw ga3!" [Let them all go! Let them all be judged! Let us all educate ourselves!] clearly express the desire for rupture, but also for progress toward a new form of living together, where nonviolence, which today seems to form a new form of "collective therapy" (Carlier 1995), would finally guarantee the existence of a civil bond.)

5. See Ziad Bentahar, "'Ytnahaw ga'!: Algeria's Cultural Revolution and the Role of Language in the Early Stages of the Spring 2019 Hirak," in *Journal of African Cultural Studies* online, July 2020, 4, https://doi.org/10.1080/13696815.2020.1788517. Bentahar provides a transcription and translation of the televised interview (6), arguing astutely that "it is the very language used in the short exchange that made it iconic, and the linguistic dynamics at play that struck a charge with people" (7).

6. A description of the conference published in *El Watan* outlines talks on subjects such as sociolinguistic analysis of slogans and chants, the function of Facebook in vetting and revising slogans before they hit the streets, and the semiotic analysis of the graffiti that appear in plurilingual scripts across the city's walls (Fuṣḥa, Darija, French, Kabyle in a single tag). For details, see Mustapha Benfodil, "Des universitaires décryptent le mouvement du 22 février: Regards croisés sur le Hirak," in *El Watan* online, June 30, 2019, https://www.elwatan.com/edition/actualite/regards-croises-sur-le-hirak-30-06-2019.

7. A series of different essays was published on *Jadaliyya* and *Africa Is a Country* in the weeks immediately after the protests got underway, including Muriam Haleh Davis, "Quick Thoughts: Historical Memory in Algeria's Current Protests," *Jadaliyya*, March 7, 2019, https://www.jadaliyya.com/Details/38442; Thomas Serres, "Quick Thoughts on Algeria's Protests," *Jadaliyya*, March 2, 2019, https://www.jadaliyya.com/Details/38428; Thomas Serres, "Algeria, Where Is Your African Revolution?," *Jadaliyya*, March 13, 2019, https://www.jadaliyya.com/Details/38467; Brahim Rouabah, "Reclaiming the Narrative of Algeria's Revolt," *Africa Is a Country*, April 26, 2019, https://africasacountry.com/author/brahim-roubah. Davis and Serres also compiled a list of "Essential Readings: The Hirak (Algerian Uprisings 2019)," on *Jadaliyya*, December 16, 2020, https://www.jadaliyya.com/Details/42148?fbclid=IwAR2-wAQK3AMP_231XSP6AosBioUdvZDwMgXT7JgAoHMMigyMk-UtEkrsli4.

8. In the essay cited in the previous note, Rouabah comments on the specificity of Algerian justice demands. Rouabah, "Reclaiming the Narrative of Algeria's Revolt."

9. A petition in Arabic, French, and English calling for solidarity with the popular revolt in Algeria circulated online in early September 2019. It begins: "The Algerian anti-colonial revolution was a catalyst for liberation struggles around the world. Algeria has strayed far from that historic mission and the people's independence was confiscated by a military-oligarchic elite that, for decades, has dispossessed, pauperized, and

stifled Algerians and Algerian political life.... The people's demands—for full sovereignty, social justice, demilitarization of political life, civilian democratic rule, an end to subservience to imperialist and neocolonial designs in African and elsewhere—have so far fallen on deaf ears." The petition lists these demands in full. Its first signatories are: the Malcolm X Grassroots Movement (USA), the Frantz Fanon Foundation and the Parti des indigènes de la République (France), the National Lawyers Guild (USA), and the Red Nation (USA).

10. Maytha Alhassen, "Please Reconsider the Term 'Arab Spring,'" *HuffPost*, February 10, 2012, https://www.huffpost.com/entry/please- reconsider-arab-sp_b_1268971.

11. Rouabah, "Reclaiming the Narrative of Algeria's Revolt."

12. "En 1988, le régime a donc eu peur de son peuple, dont une partie avait voté pour les islamistes du Front islamique du salut. La punition fut terrible: dix ans de guerre civile dont on a fait porter la responsabilité au peuple qui avait mal voté, qui s'était fait manipuler." Thomas Serres, interviewed by Catherine Calvet, "Thomas Serres: 'La révolution symbolique a déjà eu lieu,'" *Libération*, March 24, 2019, https://www.liberation.fr/planete/2019/03/24/thomas-serres-la-revolution-symbolique-a-deja-eu-lieu_1716884.

13. See, e.g., Abed Charef, *Octobre* (Alger: Laphomic, 1990); and Abed Charef, "Les émeutes d'octobre 1988: Une crise fondatrice?," in *Algérie, 30 ans, les enfants de l'indépendance*, ed. Merzak Allouache and Vincent Colonna (Paris: Autrement, 1992), 16–85; Hafid Gafaïti, "Culture and Violence: The Algerian Intelligentsia between Two Political Illegitimacies," in "Translating Algeria," special issue, *Parallax* 4, no. 2 (1998): 71–77; Zineb Ali-Benali, Najib Redouane, and Yamina Mokaddem, *1989 en Algérie: Rupture tragique ou rupture féconde* (Toronto: La source, 1999); Rabah Soukehal, *L'écrivain de langue française et les pouvoirs en Algérie* (Paris: L'Harmattan, 1998); and Benjamin Stora, *La guerre invisible* (Paris: Presses de Sciences Po, 2001). Tristan Leperlier devotes considerable and nuanced attention to October 1988 in his *Algérie, les écrivains dans la décennie noire* (Paris: CNRS, 2018), esp. the chapter "Du silence à l'âge d'or: Les écrivains algériens face à la libéralisation du régime," 39–72.

14. Clarisse Zimra, "'When the Past Answers Our Present': Assia Djebar Talks about Loin de Médine," *Callaloo* 16, no. 1 (winter 1993): 122.

15. "C'est une irruption, je dirais presque une cassure dans mon œuvre—qui a été écrite d'un coup, pour participer à un débat précis: c'est une œuvre de circonstance." In Clarisse Zimra, "Not So Far from Medina: Assia Djebar Charts Islam's 'Insupportable Feminist Revolution,'" *World Literature Today* 70, no. 4 (autumn 1996): 823–34. See 832n2; last interpolation in Zimra's translation.

16. Reports of the details of these massacres are available online from organizations such as Amnesty International, Human Rights Watch, the UN Office of the High Commissioner of Human Rights, and the US Department of State. Also available on YouTube are video footage and news report interviews with survivors, including a forty-five-minute television piece that aired on French television in 1999 called "Bentalha: Autopsie d'un massacre." For a short Amnesty International report on this period, see "Algeria: Civilian Population Caught in a Spiral of Violence," Amnesty International, 1997, https://www.amnesty.org/en/documents/MDE28/023/1997/en/. In *La guerre invisible* (1999), Benjamin Stora analyzes the widespread uncertainty concerning the

identities of perpetrators behind many such crimes during the civil war; consider in particular his succinct and cautious discussion of the enigmas surrounding the massacre at Bentalha (32–35, 40–45). See also Abed Charef's *Algérie, autopsie d'un massacre* (La Tour d'Aigues: L'Aube, 1998).

17. Of course, this remains a highly controversial topic. On this unresolved matter, see, in addition to previously cited reports from Amnesty International, Human Rights Watch, and Benjamin Stora's *La guerre invisible*, the report entitled "Les massacres en Algérie, 1992–2004" that was compiled by the Comité justice pour l'Algérie in preparation for an independent People's Tribunal that was held in Paris in 2004 with the collaboration of human rights organizations in Algeria, France, and the international community. It is available online at Comité justice pour l'Algérie, "32e session du Tribunal permanent des peuples," https://www.algerie-tpp.org/tpp/presentation_courte.htm.

18. "Écrire, ce serait tuer la voix, l'épuiser, ce serait l'exposer, la brûler pour atteindre ses os invisibles, ses nerfs arachés, son acier étincelant." Assia Djebar, "Raïs, Bentalha … un an après," *Ces voix qui m'assiègent* (Paris: Albin Michel, 1999), 254–58. Citation from stanza I.

19. "Écrire la voix des autres, de la mère orpheline qui clame le deuil infini." Djebar, "Raïs, Bentalha," II. *Ces voix qui m'assiègent*, the collection in which this poem appears, also includes an essay about Amrouche, "D'un silence l'autre," which confirms the implicit reference here to Fadhma Aïth Mansour Amrouche. Assia Djebar, "D'un silence l'autre," in *Ces voix qui m'assiègent*, 116.

20. "Au cœur du hameau détruit, Raïs, Bentalha, ô Mitidja de l'enfance souillée." Djebar, "Raïs, Bentalha," II.

21. This tribunal was conducted as a collaboration between multiple human rights groups in Algeria, France, and the international community, outside the aegis of any state's authority. For a description of its objectives and organization, see Comité Justice pour l'Algérie, "32e session du Tribunal permanent des peuples," which also includes a list of all of the other dossiers that were presented to the Tribunal permanent des peuples (TPP), and are available in PDF form on the site.

22. "Dans ces conditions, seule une commission d'enquête internationale et impartiale, peut disposer du crédit moral nécessaire pour faire la lumière sur ce qui se passe en Algérie." Comité justice pour l'Algérie, "32e session du Tribunal permanent des peuples," Dossier no. 2, "Les massacres en Algérie, 1992–2004," compiled by Salima Mellah, May 2004, 76, https://www.algerie-tpp.org/tpp/pdf/dossier_2_massacres.pdf.

23. "Les attentats et les massacres n'ont jamais cessé à ce jour, même s'ils ne font plus l'objet que de minuscules entrefilets dans les journaux occidentaux. Cette 'banalisation du crime' permet depuis le début des années 2000 de montrer une image de l'Algérie pacifique, contrôlée, sécurisée. Il est vrai que depuis que Abdelaziz Bouteflika est président (avril 1999), leur nombre a baissé; en revanche, la confusion et l'opacité qui les entourent se sont intensifiées et *les rendent encore plus difficilement déchiffrables que dans la période qui précédait son premier mandat*. Ce qu'il est important de relever, c'est que *toutes les structures qui ont permis, d'une part, de commettre ces crimes et, de l'autre, d'instaurer l'impunité, sont toujours en place, de sorte que la machine peut à tout moment s'emballer à nouveau*." "Les massacres en Algérie, 1992–2004," 5; emphasis added.

24. "Corps mêlés les uns aux autres." Djebar, "Raïs, Bentalha," IV.

25. Assia Djebar, *L'amour la fantasia* (Paris: Éditions J. C. Lattès, 1985), 255.

26. Djebar, "Raïs, Bentalha," IV.

27. Avery Gordon, *Ghostly Matters: Haunting and the Sociological Imagination* (Minneapolis: University of Minnesota Press, 1997), xvi.

28. These details are from a talk and discussion given by Negrouche at NYU in Florence in September 2018. The event can be viewed online at NYU Florence, "Tea with Poet Samira Negrouche," YouTube video, 1:04:50, October 15, 2018, https://wwwyoutube.com/watch?v=joxIXiKV3aQ.

29. On the history of Éditions Barzakh, see Alice Kaplan's essay "Algeria's New Imprint," *The Nation*, April 3, 2017, https://www.thenation.com/article/algerias-new-imprint/.

30. Negrouche's published collections to date: *Faiblesse n'est pas de dire* (Algiers: Barzakh, 2001); *L'opéra cosmique* (Bordj El Kiffan: Éditions Ikhtilef, 2003); *À l'ombre de Grenade* (Toulouse: Éditions A. P. l'étoile, 2003); *Iridienne* (Saint-Génis-des-Fontaines: Éditions Color Gang, 2005); *A chacun sa révolution* (Naples: La stanza del poeta, 2006); *Le jazz des oliviers* (Blida: Éditions du Tell, 2010); *Six arbres de fortune autour de ma baignoire* (Plaisir: Éditions Mazette, 2017); and *Quai 2 / 1, partition à trois axes* (Plaisir: Éditions Mazette, 2019).

31. Among Negrouche's early publications are her French translations of Arabic works, including Inaâm Bioud's poetry collection *Poste restante* (Algiers: Barzakh, 2003) and Yasmina Salah's novel *Les vagues du silence* (Algiers: El-Ikhtilef, 2003); more recently, she translated Mazen Maarouf's *Un ange sur une corde à linge* (Paris: Éditions de l'Amandier, 2013).

32. Samira Negrouche, ed., *Quand l'amandier refleurira: Anthologie de poètes algériens de langue française* (Paris: Éditions de l'Amandier 2012); and Samira Negrouche, ed., *Triangle: Anthologie de sept poètes internationaux traduits dans trois langues—tamazight, arabe, français* (Algiers: Éditions Alpha, 2008).

33. References to conversations with Negrouche in this essay are from a telephone interview and follow-up emails that we exchanged in early January 2019.

34. From "Qui parle," translated by Marilyn Hacker as "Who is speaking," originally published in French in *Po&sie* (March 2016): 153–54, https://www.cairn.info/revue-poesie-2015-3-page-210.htm. English translation published in *World Literature Today* in March 2018, https://www.worldliteraturetoday.org/2018/march/who-speaking-samira-negrouche.

35. Assia Djebar, *Le blanc de l'Algérie* (Paris: Albin Michel, 1995), 56.

36. Yousef Sebti, "Balles / Nuit / 27/28 / Décembre / 1993"; Tahar Djaout, "Balles / 25 ans / 26 Mai / 1993"; and Jean Sénac, "Arme / Blanche / Cave / Été / Août." There is a second date written on the bottom of the Djaout poster, with a question mark between the dates: 1975–?–1993. The year 1975 is not the year in which Djaout was born, but rather the year that he published his first collection of poems, *Solstice Barbelé* (Québec: Editions Naaman, 1975). Thus it appears that the "25 ans" does not refer to Djaout's lifespan, but to the years that he published. The question mark further signals the fact that his last work was an unfinished novel, published posthumously six years after his murder interrupted the completion of this manuscript (*Le dernier été de la raison* [Paris, Seuil, 1999]).

37. Amrouche, "accablé"; Dib, "exilé"; Djaffar, "disloqué"; Gréki, "sacrifice"; Amrani, "Torturé / de l'os au conjonctif / Témoin / Témoin de tout."

38. From a talk that she delivered in Johannesburg on November 19, 2011, entitled "Redécouvrir le petit sentier vers soi-même." Unpublished text provided by Samira Negrouche; translation mine.

39. From the introduction to Negrouche, *Quand l'amandier refleurira*; translation mine.

40. This line may be from Myriam Ben, *Le soleil assassiné* (Paris: L'Harmattan, 2002).

41. "La poétesse algérienne de demain." From "Redécouvrir le petit sentier vers soi-même," a talk delivered in Johannesburg on November 19, 2011. Unpublished text provided by Samira Negrouche; translation mine.

42. "Camarades, il faut faire peau neuve, développer une pensée neuve." Frantz Fanon, *Les damnés de la terre* (Paris: La Découverte, [1961] 2014). I have translated literally the expression "faire peau neuve" to highlight the shared metaphor that links Negrouche's text to Fanon's.

43. In a clarification during a private conversation via email in April 2020, Negrouche explained that this aphorism comes from a verse by the Kabyle singer Lounis Aït Menguellet and that it expresses a sentiment profoundly anchored in Kabyle culture. She remembers hearing her own grandmother say this, speaking with a sense of loss and tragedy about fields and paths around her village where people no longer went and that the grass had grown over, "car la terre et ce qui vient des ancêtres est sacré, le moins qu'one puisse faire, c'est d'y aller pour que le chemin ne se perde pas" (for the earth and all that comes from the ancestors is sacred; the least we can do is to walk on the paths so that they aren't lost). On Aït Menguellet, see Tassadit Yacine's *Aït Menguellet Chante . . . Chansons berbères contemporains* (Paris: La Découverte, 1989).

44. For more on this reclaiming of public space, see Ghaliya N. Djelloul and Aniss M. Mezoued, "Les ressorts spatiaux de la mobilisation révolutionnaire à Alger," *Forum vies mobiles*, July 1, 2019, http://fr.forumviesmobiles.org/printfvm/12995. It is too soon to comment on the impact of the Covid-19 confinement on this transformation.

45. Samira Negrouche, "Poémes," *Po&sie* 148, no. 2 (2014): 24–35, https://www.cairn.info/revue-poesie-2014-2-page-24.htm. Marilyn Hacker's translation, "Seven Little Jasmine Monologues," in *ArabLit*, July 11, 2017, is available online at https://arablit.org/2017/07/11/samira-negrouches-seven-little-jasmine-monologues/.

46. The English translations of Negrouche's poem in my text here are Marilyn Hacker's.

Bibliography

Agamben, Giorgio. *Homo Sacer: Sovereign Power and Bare Life*. Translated by Daniel Heller-Roazen. Stanford, CA: Stanford University Press, [1995] 1998.

Agamben, Giorgio. *Quel che resta di Auschwitz: L'archivo e il testimone*. Turin: Bollati Boringhieri, 1998.

Agamben, Giorgio. *Remnants of Auschwitz: The Witness and the Archive*. Translated by Daniel Heller-Roazen. New York: Zone Books, [1998] 1999.

Agamben, Giorgio. "What Is a Camp?" In *Means without End: Notes on Politics*, 37–48. Translated by Vincenzo Binetti and Cesare Casarino. Minneapolis: University of Minnesota Press, 2000.

Aïth Mansour Amrouche, Fadhma. *Histoire de ma vie*. Paris: F. Maspero, 1968.

Alcaraz, Emmanuel. *Les lieux de mémoire de la guerre d'indépendance algérienne*. Paris: Éditions Karthala, 2017.

Alcaraz, Emmanuel. "Les monuments aux martyrs de la guerre d'indépendance algérienne: Monumentalité, enjeux de mémoire et commémorations." *Guerres mondiales et conflits contemporains* 237, no. 1 (2010): 125–46.

"Algeria: Civilian Population Caught in a Spiral of Violence." Amnesty International. 1997. https://www.amnesty.org/en/documents/MDE28/023/1997/en/.

"Algeria: New Amnesty Law Will Ensure Atrocities Go Unpunished." Human Rights Watch, February 28, 2006. hrw.org/news/2006/02/28/algeria-new-amnesty-law-will-ensure-atrocities-go-unpunished.

Alhassan, Maytha. "Please Reconsider the Term 'Arab Spring.'" *Huffington Post*, February 10, 2012. https://www.huffpost.com/entry/please-reconsider-arab-sp_b_1268971.

Ali-Benali, Zineb, Najib Redouane, and Yamina Mokaddem. *1989 en Algérie: Rupture tragique ou rupture féconde*. Toronto: La Source, 1999.

Allal, Amin, Youcef Chekkar, Lalia Chenoufi, François Gèze, Nacira Guénif, and Farida Souiah, eds. "Hirak, Algérie en révolution(s)." *Mouvements*, no. 102 (summer 2020).

Alleg, Henri. *La question*. Paris: Éditions de Minuit, 1957.

Amrani, Djamal. *Le témoin*. Paris: Éditions de Minuit, 1960.

Anidjar, Gil. *The Jew, the Arab: A History of the Enemy*. Stanford, CA: Stanford University Press, 2003.

Arendt, Hannah. *Eichmann in Jerusalem: A Report on the Banality of Evil*. New York: Viking Press, 1963.

Arnaud, Georges, and Jacques Vergès. *Pour Djamila Bouhired*. Paris: Éditions de Minuit, 1961.

Arthur, Paige. *Unfinished Projects: Decolonization and the Philosophy of Jean-Paul Sartre*. New York: Verso Books, 2010.

Asseraf, Arthur. "Between the World and Algeria: International Histories of the Algerian War of Independence." *Arab Studies Journal* (spring 2017): 198–201.

Atkinson, David. "Encountering Bare Life in Italian Libya and Colonial Amnesia in Agamben." In *Agamben and Colonialism*, ed. Marcelo Svirsky and Simone Bignall, 155–77. Edinburgh: Edinburgh University Press, 2012.

Azoulay, Ariella. "Potential History: Thinking through Violence." *Critical Inquiry* 39, no. 3 (spring 2013): 548–74.

Barkat, Sidi Mohammed. *Le corps d'exception: Les artifices du pouvoir colonial et la destruction de la vie*. Paris: Amsterdam, 2005.

Barrat, Denise. *Espoir et parole*. Paris: Seghers, 1963.

Beauvoir, Simone de. *La force des choses*. Paris: Gallimard, 1963.

Bediya, Bachir. *L'oued en crue*. Paris: Éditions du Centenaire, 1979.

Ben, Myriam. *Ainsi naquit un homme*. Algiers: Maison des livres, 1982.

Ben, Myriam. *Le soleil assassiné*. Paris: L'Harmattan, 2002.

Bencheikh, Jamel-Eddine, and Jacqueline Lévi-Valens, eds. *Diwan algérien: La poésie algérienne d'expression française de 1945 à 1965, étude critique et choix de textes*. Algiers: Société d'édition et de diffusion, 1967.

Benfodil, Mustapha. "Regards croisés sur le 'Hirak.'" *El Watan*, June 30, 2019. https://www.elwatan.com/edition/actualite/regards-croises-sur-le-hirak-30-06-2019.

Benjamin, Walter. "Critique of Violence." In *Walter Benjamin: Selected Writings, Vol. 1, 1913–1926*. Edited by Marcus Bullock and Michael Jennings. Cambridge, MA: Harvard University Press, 1996.

Bennoune, Mahfoud. *The Making of Contemporary Algeria, 1830–1987*. Cambridge: Cambridge University Press, 2002.

Benslama, Fethi. "La représentation et l'impossible." *Évolution psychiatrique* 66, no. 3 (2001): 448–66.

Bensmaïl, Malek. *La bataille d'Alger: Un film dans l'histoire*. Hikayet Flims, 2018.

Bentahar, Ziad. "'Ytnahaw ga'!: Algeria's Cultural Revolution and the Role of Language in the Early Stages of the Spring 2019 Hirak." In *Journal of African Cultural Studies*. July 2020. https://doi.org/10.1080/13696815.2020.1788517.

Berger, Anne-Emmanuelle. *Algeria in Others' Languages*. Ithaca, NY: Cornell University Press, 2002.

Bherer, Marc-Olivier. "Macron en Algérie: La définition juridique du crime contre l'humanité ne peut s'appliquer à la colonisation." *Le Monde*, February 16, 2017.

Bioud, Inaâm. *Poste restante*. Translated by Samira Negrouche. Algiers: Barzakh, 2003.

Blais, Hélène. *Mirages de la carte: L'invention de l'Algérie coloniale*. Paris: Fayard, 2014.

Blanchot, Maurice, and Jacques Derrida. *The Instant of My Death, Demeure: Fiction and Testimony*. Translated by Elizabeth Rottenberg. Stanford, CA: Stanford University Press, 2000.

Blévis, Laure. "Droit colonial algérien de la citoyenneté: Conciliation entre des principes républicains et une logique d'occupation coloniale 1865–1947." In *La guerre d'Algérie au miroir des décolonisations françaises: Actes du colloque en l'honneur de Charles-*

Robert Ageron, Sorbonne, Novembre 2000, edited by Daniel Lefeuvre, 87–103. Paris: Société française d'histoire d'outre-mer, 2000.

Brahimi, Denise. *Des refuges et des pièges: Grottes symboliques en Algérie coloniale*. Algiers: Casbah Éditions, 2011.

British Pathé. "Concentration Camp Footage 1945." Video, 3:19. Accessed June 2020. http://www.britishpathe.com/video/concentration-camp-footage.

Brower, Benjamin. *A Desert Called Peace: The Violence of France's Empire in the Algerian Sahara*. New York: Columbia University Press, 2009.

Brozgal, Lia. *Absent the Archive: Cultural Traces of a Massacre in Paris, 17 October 1961*. Liverpool: Liverpool University Press, 2020.

Brozgal, Lia. *Against Autobiography: Albert Memmi and the Production of Theory*. Lincoln: University of Nebraska Press, 2013.

Brozgal, Lia. "In the Absence of the Archive (Paris, October 17, 1961)." *South Central Review* 31, no. 1 (2014): 34–54.

Butler, Judith. *Antigone's Claim*. New York: Columbia University Press, 2002.

Butler, Judith. *Frames of War: When Is Life Grievable?* New York: Verso Books, 2009.

Butler, Judith. "Hannah Arendt's Death Sentences." In "Trials of Trauma." Special issue, *Comparative Literature Studies* 48, no. 3 (2011): 280–95.

Butler, Judith. *Precarious Life: The Powers of Mourning and Violence*. New York: Verso Books, 2004.

Byrne, Jeffrey James. *Mecca of Revolution: Algeria, Decolonization, and the Third World Order*. Oxford Studies in International History. Oxford: Oxford University Press, 2016.

Camp, Juan Eduardo. *Encyclopedia of Islam*. Boston: Credo Reference, 2019.

Camus, Albert. *Chroniques algériennes, 1939–1958*. Paris: Gallimard, 1958.

Canetti, Elias. *Les voix de Marrakech*. Translated by François Ponthier. Paris: Albin Michel, 1980.

Caruth, Cathy. *Unclaimed Experience: Trauma, Narrative, and History*. Baltimore: Johns Hopkins University Press, 1996.

Casta, Ange, and Igor Barrère. *L'Algérie dix ans après: Partie 1, L'Algérie des Algériens*. INA 1972. https://madelen.ina.fr/programme/lalgerie-dix-ans-apres-1-lalgerie-des-algeriens.

Césaire, Aimé. *Discours sur le colonialisme*. Paris: Présence Africaine, 1955.

Charef, Abed. *Algérie, autopsie d'un massacre*. La Tour d'Aigues: L'Aube, 1998.

Charef, Abed. "Les émeutes d'octobre 1988: Une crise fondatrice?" In *Algérie, 30 ans, les enfants de l'indépendance*, edited by Merzak Allouache and Vincent Colonna, 16–85. Paris: Autrement, 1982.

Charef, Abed. *Octobre*. Algiers: Laphomic, 1990.

Chaulet-Achour, Christiane. "La torture et la guerre: Mémoires en décalage." *Diacritik*, September 28, 2018. https://diacritik.com/2018/09/28/la-torture-et-la-guerre-memoires-en-decalage-france-algerie/.

Cixous, Hélène. "Lettre à Zohra Drif." *Leggendaria* 14 (April 1999): 4–9.

Comité Justice pour l'Algérie. "Les massacres en Algérie, 1992–2004." Paris: Comité Justice pour l'Algérie, 2004. https://www.algerie-tpp.org/tpp/presentation_courte.htm.

Comité national contre la torture. *Cahier noir d'octobre.* Algiers: Comité national contre la torture, 1989. http://ettahaddi.net/sites/default/files/asset/document/Cahier-Noir-D-Octobre.pdf.

Comité résistance spirituelle. *Des rappelés témoignent.* Paris: Comité résistance spirituelle, 1957.

Crowley, Patrick, ed. *Algeria: Nation, Culture and Transnationalism, 1988–2013.* Liverpool: Liverpool University Press, 2017.

Davis, Muriam Haleh. "Quick Thoughts: Historical Memory in Algeria's Current Protests." *Jadaliyya,* March 7, 2019. https://www.jadaliyya.com/Details/38442.

Davis, Muriam Haleh, and James McDougall, eds. "The Afterlives of the Algerian Revolution." *JADMAG* 2, no. 1, June 2014.

Davis, Muriam Haleh, and Thomas Serres. "Essential Readings: The Hirak (Algerian Uprisings 2019)." Jadaliyya, December 16, 2020. https://www.jadaliyya.com/Details/42148?fbclid=IwAR2-wAQK3AMP_231XSP6AosBioUdvZDwMgXT7JgAoHMMigyMk-UtEkrsli4. Davis, Muriam Haleh, and Thomas Serres. "Essential Readings: The Hirak (Algerian Uprisings 2019)." Jadaliyya, December 16, 2020. https://www.jadaliyya.com/Details/42148?fbclid=IwAR2-wAQK3AMP_231XSP6AosBioUdvZDwMgXT7JgAoHMMigyMk-UtEkrsli4.

Davis, Muriam Haleh, Thomas Serres, and Hiyem Cheurfa. "A Hirak Glossary: Terms from Algeria and Morocco." *Jadaliyya,* June 13, 2019. https://www.jadaliyya.com/Details/38734.

"Déclaration du président de la République sur la mort de Maurice Audin." Élysée website, September 13, 2018. https://www.elysee.fr/emmanuel-macron/2018/09/13/declaration-du-president-de-la-republique-sur-la-mort-de-maurice-audin.

Derrida, Jacques. "Force of Law: The Mythical Foundation of Authority." In *Acts of Religion: Jacques Derrida,* edited by Gil Anidjar, 230–98. New York: Routledge, 2001.

Derrida, Jacques. *Le monolinguisme de l'autre, ou, La prothèse d'origine.* Translated by Patrick Mensah. Paris: Galilée, 1996.

Derrida, Jacques. "Politics and Poetics of Witnessing." In *Sovereignties in Question: The Poetics of Paul Celan,* edited by Thomas Dutoit and Outi Pasanen, 65–96. New York: Fordham University Press, 2005.

Djaout, Tahar. *Solstice Barbelé.* Québec: Editions Naaman, 1975.

Djebar, Assia. *Ces voix qui m'assiègent.* Paris: Albin Michel, 1999.

Djebar, Assia. *L'amour, la fantasia.* Paris: Éditions J. C. Lattès, 1985.

Djebar, Assia. *Le blanc d'Algérie.* Paris: Albin Michel, 1995.

Djebar, Assia. *Loin de Médine.* Algiers: Albin Michel, 1991.

Djebar, Assia. *Vaste est la prison.* Paris: Albin Michel, 1995.

Djelloul, Ghaliya N., and Aniss M. Mezoued. "Les ressorts spatiaux de la mobilisation révolutionnaire à Alger." *Forum Vies Mobiles,* July 1, 2019. https://fr.forumviesmobiles.org/2019/06/28/ressorts-spatiaux-mobilisation-revolutionnaire-alger-12995?utm_source=metropolitiques&utm_medium=breve&utm_campaign=2019_07_05.

Dutour, Nasséra. "Algérie: De la Concorde civile à la Charte pour la paix et la réconciliation nationale: Amnistie, amnésie, impunité." In "Mouvements." Special issue, *La découverte* 53, no. 1 (2008): 144–49.

Dyer, Rebecca. "Poetry of Politics and Mourning: Mahmoud Darwish's Genre-Transforming Tribute to Edward W. Said." *PMLA* 122, no. 5 (2007): 1447–62.
EichmannTrialEN. "Eichmann Trial—Session No. 68, 69." March 9, 2011. YouTube video, 52:15. https://www.youtube.com/watch?v=m3-tXyYhd5U.
Einaudi, Jean-Luc. *La bataille de Paris—17 octobre 1961*. Paris: Seuil, 1991.
Elhariry, Yasser. *Pacifist Invasions: Arabic, Translation, and the Postfrancophone Lyric*. Liverpool: Liverpool University Press, 2017.
El Shakry, Hoda. *The Literary Qur'an: Narrative Ethics in the Maghreb*. New York: Fordham University Press, 2020.
Entelis, John P. "What Does an Amended Constitution Really Change about Algeria?" *Washington Post*, January 19, 2016. https://www.washingtonpost.com/news/monkey-cage/wp/2016/01/19/what-does-an-amended-constitution-really-change-about-algeria/.
Esmeir, Samera. *Juridical Humanity: A Colonial History*. Stanford, CA: Stanford University Press, 2012.
Fanon, Frantz. *Les damnés de la terre*. Paris: La Découverte, [1961] 2014.
Fanon, Frantz. "Lettre à un Français." In *Pour la révolution africaine: Écrits politiques*, 55–58. Paris: La Découverte, 2001.
Fanon, Frantz. *Peau noire, masques blancs*. Paris: Seuil, 1952.
Fanon, Frantz. "Le 'syndrome nord-africain.'" *Esprit* 187, no. 2 (February 1952): 237–48.
Farès, Nabile. *Mémoire de l'Absent*. Paris: Seuil, 1974.
Feldman, Hannah. *From a Nation Torn: Decolonizing Art and Representation in France, 1945–1962*. Durham, NC: Duke University Press, 2014.
Felman, Shoshana. *The Juridical Unconscious: Trails and Traumas of the Twentieth Century*. Cambridge, MA: Harvard University Press, 2002.
Felman, Shoshana, and Dori Laub. *Testimony: Crises of Witnessing in Literature, Psychoanalysis, and History*. New York: Routledge, 1992.
Feraud, Charles. "Visite au Palais du Bey." In *Le tour du monde*, vol. 33, edited by Édouard Charton, 225–56. Paris: Libraire de L. Hachette, 1877.
Fraser, Nancy. "Abnormal Justice." *Critical Inquiry* 34, no. 3 (spring 2008): 393–422.
Fraser, Nancy. "Reframing Justice: In a Globalizing World." *New Left Review* 11 (November–December 2005): 69–88.
Gafaïti, Hafid. "Culture and Violence: The Algerian Intelligentsia between Two Political Illegitimacies." In "Translating Algeria." Special issue, *Parallax* 4, no. 2 (1998): 71–77.
Ghosn, Katia. "Waciny Laredj, un Pont Entre Deux Rives." *L'Orient Littéraire*, November 9, 2018. http://lorientlitteraire.com/article_details.php?cid=33&nid=3315.
Gikandi, Simon. "Poststructuralism and Postcolonial Discourse." In *The Cambridge Companion to Postcolonial Literary Studies*, edited by Neil Lazarus, 97–119. Cambridge: Cambridge University Press, 2004.
Gordon, Avery. *Ghostly Matters: Haunting and the Sociological Imagination*. Minneapolis: University of Minnesota Press, 1997.
Grandmaison, Olivier Le Cour. *De l'indigénat. Anatomie d'un "monstre" juridique: Du droit colonial en Algérie et dans l'empire français*. Paris: Zones/La Découverte, 2010.

Guha, Ranajit. "On Some Aspects of the History of Colonial India." In *Selected Subaltern Studies*, edited by Ranajit Guha, 37–44. Oxford: Oxford University Press, 1995.

Guha, Ranajit. "The Prose of Counter-insurgency." In *Selected Subaltern Studies*, edited by Ranajit Guha, 45–88. Oxford: Oxford University Press, 1995.

Hadj Ali, Bachir. *L'arbitraire*. Paris: Éditions de Minuit, 1966.

Halimi, Gisèle. "D'Henri Alleg à Djamila Boupacha." *Les temps modernes* (June 1960): 1822–1832.

Halimi, Gisèle, and Simone de Beauvoir. *Djamila Boupacha*. Paris: Gallimard, 1962.

Hannoum, Abdelmajid. *Violent Modernity: France in Algeria*. Cambridge, MA: Harvard University Press, 2010.

Hartman, Geoffrey. *The Longest Shadow: In the Aftermath of the Holocaust*. Bloomington: Indiana University Press, 1996.

Hartman, Geoffrey. "On Traumatic Knowledge and Literary Study." *New Literary History* 26, no. 3 (1995): 537–63.

Heller-Roazen, Daniel, ed. *The Arabian Nights*. New York: Norton Critical Editions, 2009.

Hirsch, Marianne. *Family Frames: Photography, Narrative, and Postmemory*. Cambridge, MA: Harvard University Press, 1997.

Hochberg, Gil. *In Spite of Partition: Jews, Arabs, and the Limits of Separatist Imagination*. Princeton, NJ: Princeton University Press, 2008.

Julien, Eileen. "The Extroverted African Novel." In *The Novel: History, Geography and Culture, Vol. 1*, edited by Franco Moretti, 667–702. Princeton, NJ: Princeton University Press, 2006.

Kaplan, Alice. "Algeria's New Imprint." *The Nation*, April 3, 2017. https://www.thenation.com/article/algerias-new-imprint/.

Kateb, Kamel. *Européens, "Indigènes" et Juifs en Algérie, 1830–1962: Représentations et réalités des populations*. Paris: Institut national d'études démographiques, 2001.

Kateb, Kamel. "Le bilan démographique de la conquête de l'Algérie (1830–1880)." In *Histoire de l'Algérie à la période coloniale (1830–1962)*, edited by Abderrahmane Bouchène, Jean-Pierre Peyroulou, Ouanassa Siari Tengour, and Sylvie Thénaut, 82–88. Paris: La Découverte, 2014.

Kateb, Yacine. *Les ancêtres redoublent de férocité*, in *Le cercle des représailles*. Paris: Éditions du seuil, 1959.

Kateb, Yacine. Preface to *La grotte éclatée*, by Yamina Mechakra, 7–8. Algiers: SNED, 1979.

Ka-Tzetnik. *Moni: A Novel of Auschwitz*. Translated by Moshe Kohn. Secaucus, NJ: Citadel Press, [1961] 1963.

Keneally, Thomas. *Schindler's Ark*. London: Coronet, 1983.

Khan, Amin. *Présence de Tahar Djaout, poète*. Algiers: Barzakh, 2013.

Khanna, Ranjana. *Algeria Cuts: Women and Representation, 1830 to the Present*. Stanford, CA: Stanford University Press, 2008.

La Capra, Dominick. *Representing the Holocaust: History, Theory, Trauma*. Ithaca, NY: Cornell University Press, 1996.

La Capra, Dominick. *Writing History, Writing Trauma*. Baltimore: Johns Hopkins University Press, 2000.

Laredj, Waciny. *Les ailes de la reine*. Translated by Marcel Bois. Arles: Actes Sud, 2009.

Lazali, Karima. *Le trauma colonial: Une enquête sur les effets psychiques et politiques contemporains de l'oppression coloniale en Algérie.* Paris: La Découverte, 2018.

Lazreg, Marnia. *Torture and the Twilight of Empire: From Algiers to Baghdad.* Princeton, NJ: Princeton University Press, 2008. http://catdir.loc.gov/catdir/toc/ecip0715/2007014846.html.

Lemire, Vincent, and Yann Potin. "Ici on noie les Algériens: Fabriques documentaires, avatars politiques et mémoires partagées d'une icône militante (1961–2011)." *Genèses* 49, no. 4 (2002): 140–62.

Leperlier, Tristan. *Algérie: Les écrivains dans la décennie noire.* Paris: CNRS, 2018.

Leuvrey, Elisabeth, dir. *At(h)ome.* Les écrans du large, 2013.

Levi, Primo. *The Drowned and the Saved.* Translated by Raymond Rosenthal. New York: Random House, [1986] 1989.

Levi, Primo. *Se questo è un uomo.* Turin: De Silva, 1947.

Levi, Primo. *Si c'est un homme.* Translated by Martine Schruoffeneger. Paris: Julliard, 1987.

Levi, Primo. *I sommersi e i Salvati.* Turin: Einaudi, 1986.

Levi, Primo. *Survival in Auschwitz.* Translated by Stuart Woolf. New York: Crane Books, [1947] 2012.

Lewis, Mary Anne. "The Maghreb Goes Abroad: The 'Worlding' of Postcolonial North African Francophone Literature and Film in a Global Market." Unpublished dissertation, Yale University, 2013.

Lindon, Jérôme, ed. *La gangrène.* Paris: Éditions de Minuit, 1959.

Maarouf, Mazen. *Un ange sur une corde à linge.* Paris: Éditions de l'Amandier, 2013.

Macey, David. *Frantz Fanon: A Life.* London: Granta, 2000.

MacMaster, Neil, and Jim House. *Paris 1961: Algerians, State Terror, and Memory.* Oxford: Oxford University Press, 2006. http://site.ebrary.com/lib/yale/Doc?id=10271661.

Mammeri, Achira. "Cinq ans après avoir lancé 'Tab Jnanou,' Bouteflika s'accroche au pouvoir." *TSA*, May 8, 2017. https://www.tsa-algerie.com/cinq-ans-apres-avoir-lance-tab-jnanou-bouteflika-saccroche-toujours-au-pouvoir/.

Marx-Scouras, Danielle. "Muffled Screams/Stifled Voices." In "Post/Colonial Conditions: Exiles, Migrations, and Nomadism." Special issue, *Yale French Studies* 82, no. 1 (1993): 172–82.

Mattei, Georges-Mathieu. "Jours kabyles." *Les temps modernes*, May 1957.

Mbembe, Achille. "Necropolitics." Translated by Libby Meintjes. *Public Culture* 15, no. 1 (2003): 11–40.

Mbembe, Achille. *Politiques de l'inimitié.* Paris: La Découverte, 2016.

Mbembe, Achille. "The Power of the Archive and Its Limits." In *Refiguring the Archive*, edited by Carolyn Hamilton et al., 19–27. Norwell, MA: Kluwer Academic Publishers, 2002.

McDougall, James. *A History of Algeria.* Cambridge: Cambridge University Press, 2017.

McDougall, James. "Savage Wars? Codes of Violence in Algeria, 1830s–1990s." In "The Politics of Naming: Rebels, Terrorists, Criminals, Bandits and Subversives." Special issue, *Third World Quarterly* 26, no. 1 (2005): 117–31.

Mechakra, Yamina. *Arris.* Algiers: Marsa, 1999.

Mechakra, Yamina. *La grotte éclatée.* Algiers: SNED, 1979.

Mechakra, Yamina. *La grotte éclatée: Al-maghāra al-mutafajjira.* Translated by Aïda Bamia. Algiers: ENAL, 1989.

Mechakra, Yamina. "L'éveil du mont." *El Moudjahid culturel* 196, no. 2111 (October 1976): 8–9.
Meddeb, Abdelwahab. *Histoire des relations entre juifs et musulmans des origines à nos jours*. Paris: Albin Michel, 2013.
Mokhtari, Rachid. *La graphie de l'horreur*. Algiers: Chihab, 2003.
Mokhtari, Rachid. *Le nouveau souffle du roman algérien*. Algiers: Chihab, 2006.
Mokhtari, Rachid. *Yamina Mechakra: Entretiens et lectures*. Algiers: Chihab, 2015.
Mokhtefi, Elaine. *Algiers: Third World Capital*. New York: Verso Books, 2018.
Moussaoui, Abderrahmane. *De la violence en Algérie: Les lois du chaos*. Arles: Actes Sud, 2006.
Murphy, Andrew, ed. *The Go-To How-To Book of Anarchiving*. Montreal: The SenseLab, 2016.
Negrouche, Samira. *À chacun sa révolution*. Naples: La stanza del poeta, 2006.
Negrouche, Samira. *À l'ombre de Grenade*. Toulouse: Éditions A. P. l'étoile, 2003.
Negrouche, Samira. *Faiblesse n'est pas de dire*. Algiers: Barzakh, 2001.
Negrouche, Samira. *Iridienne*. Saint-Génis-des-Fontaines: Éditions Color Gang, 2005.
Negrouche, Samira. *Le jazz des oliviers*. Blida: Éditions du Tell, 2010.
Negrouche, Samira. *L'opéra cosmique*. Bordj El Kiffan: Éditions Ikhtilef, 2003.
Negrouche, Samira. "Poèmes." *Po&sie* 148, no. 2 (2014): 24–35.
Negrouche, Samira. *Quai 2/1, partition à trois axes*. Plaisir: Éditions Mazette, 2019.
Negrouche, Samira, ed. *Quand l'amandier refleurira: Une anthologie de poètes algériens contemporains de langue française*. Paris: L'Amandier, 2012.
Negrouche, Samira. "Seven Little Jasmine Monologues." Translated by Marilyn Hacker. *ArabLit*, July 11, 2017. https://arablit.org/2017/07/11/samira-negrouches-seven-little-jasmine-monologues.
Negrouche, Samira. *Six arbres de fortune autour de ma baignoire*. Plaisir: Éditions Mazette, 2017.
Negrouche, Samira, ed. *Triangle: Anthologie de sept poètes internationaux traduits dans trois langues—tamazight, arabe, français*. Algiers: Éditions Alpha, 2008.
Nora, Pierre. "Entre mémoire et histoire." In *Les lieux de mémoire*, vol. 1, *La République*. Paris: Gallimard, 1984.
Orlando, Valerie. *The New Algerian Novel: The Poetics of a Modern Nation, 1950–1979*. Charlottesville: University of Virginia Press, 2017.
Orlando, Valerie. "War, Revolution, and Family Matters." In *Of Suffocated Hearts and Tortured Souls*, 147–64. Washington, DC: Lexington Books, 2003.
Oumnoughene, Mouloud. *Mohamed Iguerbouchene, une œuvre intemporelle*. Algiers: Dar Khettab, 2015.
Panchasi, Roxanne. "'No Hiroshima in Africa': The Algerian War and the Question of French Nuclear Tests in the Sahara." *History of the Present* 9, no. 1 (spring 2019): 84–112.
Patterson, Orlando. *Slavery and Social Death*. Cambridge, MA: Harvard University Press, 1985.
Péju, Marcel, and Paulette Péju. *Le 17 octobre des Algériens, suivi de Gilles Manceron, la triple occultation d'un massacre*. Paris: La Découverte, 2012.

Puar, Jasbir. "The 'Right' to Maim: Disablement and Inhumanist Biopolitics in Palestine." *Borderlands* 14, no. 1 (2015): 1–27.
Qader, Nasrin. *Narratives of Catastrophe.* New York: Fordham University Press, 2009.
Radstone, Susannah. "Trauma Theory: Contexts, Politics, Ethics." *Paragraph* 30, no. 1 (March 2007): 9–29.
Rahal, Malika. "Fused Together and Torn Apart: Stories and Violence in Contemporary Algeria." *History and Memory* 24, no. 1 (spring/summer 2012): 118–51.
Rahmani, Zahia. *France: Récit d'une enfance.* Paris: Sabine Wespieser, 2006.
Rahmani, Zahia. *Moze.* Paris: Sabine Wespieser, 2003.
Rahmani, Zahia. *"Muslim": A Novel.* Translated by Matt Reeck. Dallas: Deep Vellum, 2019.
Rahmani, Zahia. *"Musulman" roman.* Paris: Sabine Wespieser, 2005.
La répression du printemps noir avril 2001–avril 2002. Algiers: Ligue algérienne de défense des droits de l'homme, 2002.
Robert, Achille. *L'arabe tel qu'il est: Études algériennes et tunisiennes.* Algiers: Imprimerie Joseph Angelini, 1900.
Rosello, Mireille. *The Reparative in Narratives: Works of Mourning in Progress.* Liverpool: Liverpool University Press, 2010.
Rosnoblet, Jean-François, and Mathieu Rosemain. "France's Macron Seeks to End Controversy over Algeria Comments." Reuters, February 18, 2017. https://www.reuters.com/article/us-france-election-idUSKBN15X0QP.
Ross, Alison, ed. "The Agamben Effect." Special issue, *South Atlantic Quarterly* 107, no. 1 (winter 2008).
Ross, Kristin. *Fast Cars, Clean Bodies: Decolonization and the Reordering of French Culture.* Cambridge, MA: MIT Press, 1996.
Ross, Kristin. *May '68 and Its Afterlives.* Chicago: Chicago University Press, 2002.
Rothberg, Michael. *Multidirectional Memory: Remembering the Holocaust in the Age of Decolonization.* Stanford, CA: Stanford University Press, 2009.
Rouabah, Brahim. "Reclaiming the Narrative of the Algerian Revolt." *Africa Is a Country*, April 26, 2019. https://africasacountry.com/author/brahim-roubah.
Saada, Emmanuelle. "Une nationalité par degrés: Civilité et citoyenneté en situation coloniale." In *L'esclavage, la colonisation, et après: France, États-Unis, Grande-Bretagne*, edited by Patrick Weil and Stéphane Dufoix, 193–227. Paris: Puf, 2005.
Sakthivel, Vish. "Algeria's Hirak: A Political Opportunity in COVID-19?" *Middle East Institute.* April 1, 2020. https://www.mei.edu/publications/algerias-hirak-political-opportunity-covid-19.
Salah, Yasmina. *Les vagues du silence.* Translated by Samira Negrouche. Algiers: El-Ikhtilef, 2003.
Salama, Mohamed Ben. *Alger: La Mecque des révolutionnaires (1962–1974).* Paris: Arte, 2014.
Sanyal, Debarati. *Memory and Complicity: Migrations of Holocaust Remembrance.* New York: Fordham University Press, 2015.
Sanyal, Debarati, Michael Rothberg, and Max Silverman, eds. "Nœuds de Mémoire: Multidirectional Memory in Postwar French and Francophone Culture." Special issue, *Yale French Studies* 118–19 (2010).

Scarry, Elaine. *The Body in Pain: The Making and Unmaking of the World.* New York: Oxford University Press, 1985.

Schreier, Joshua. *Arabs of the Jewish Faith: The Civilizing Mission in Colonial Algeria.* New Brunswick, NJ: Rutgers University Press, 2010.

Semiane, Sid Ahmed. *Octobre ils parlent.* Algiers: Le matin, 1998.

Serres, Thomas. "Algeria, Where Is Your African Revolution?" *Jadaliyya*, May 13, 2019. https://www.jadaliyya.com/Details/38467.

Serres, Thomas. "Quick Thoughts on Algeria's Protests." *Jadaliyya*, March 2, 2019. https://www.jadaliyya.com/Details/38428.

Shatz, Adam. 2002. "The Torture of Algiers." *New York Review of Books*, November 21, 2002. https://www.nybooks.com/articles/2002/11/21/the-torture-of-algiers/.

Shepard, Todd. *The Invention of Decolonization: The Algerian War and the Remaking of France.* Ithaca, NY: Cornell University Press, 2006.

Shepard, Todd. "'Of Sovereignty': Disputed Archives, 'Wholly Modern' Archives, and the Post-Decolonization French and Algerian Republics, 1962–2012." *American History Review* 120, no. 3 (June 2015): 869–83.

Silverman, Max. *Palimpsestic Memory: The Holocaust and Colonialism in French and Francophone Fiction and Film.* New York: Berghahn Books, 2013.

Simon, Pierre Henri. *Contre la torture.* Paris: Éditions du Seuil, 1957.

Skinner, Rob. "Bombs and Border Crossings: Peace Activist Networks and the Post-Colonial State in Africa, 1959–62." *Journal of Contemporary History* 50, no. 3 (2015): 418–38.

Slaughter, Joseph. "Narration in International Human Rights Law." *CLCWeb: Comparative Literature and Culture* 9, no. 1 (2007). https://doi.org/10.7771/1481-4374.1031.

Soukehal, Rabah. *L'écrivain de langue française et les pouvoirs en Algérie.* Paris: L'Harmattan, 1998.

Spivak, Gayatri Chakravorty. "Assia Djebar (1936–2015)." *Frontier*, November 11, 2015, 14.

Spivak, Gayatri Chakravorty. "Can the Subaltern Speak?" In *Marxism and the Interpretation of Culture*, edited by Cary Nelson and Lawrence Grossberg, 271–313. Urbana: University of Illinois Press, 1988.

Spivak, Gayatri Chakravorty. "Scattered Speculations on the Subaltern and the Popular." *Postcolonial Studies* 8, no. 4 (2005): 475–86.

Stein, Sarah Abrevaya. "Dividing South from North: French Colonialism, Jews, and the Algerian Sahara." *Journal of North African Studies* 7, no. 5 (2012): 773–92.

Stoler, Ann Laura. "Colonial Archive and the Arts of Governance: On the Content in the Form." In *Refiguring the Archive*, edited by Carolyn Hamilton et al., 83–102. Norwell, MA: Kluwer Academic Publishers, 2002.

Stora, Benjamin. "Boumédiène, the State, and the Institutions." In *Algeria 1830–2000: A Short History*, 143–50. Ithaca, NY: Cornell University Press, 2004.

Stora, Benjamin. *Juifs, musulmans: Chronique d'une rupture.* Paris: L'esprit du temps, 2017.

Stora, Benjamin. *La gangrène et l'oubli: La mémoire de la guerre d'Algérie.* Paris: La Découverte, 1991.

Stora, Benjamin. *La guerre invisible: Algérie, années 90.* Paris: Presses de Sciences Po, 2001.

Stora, Benjamin. *Le livre, mémoire de l'histoire: Réflexions sur le livre et la guerre d'Algérie*. Paris: Éditions le Préau des collines, 2005.

Stora, Benjamin. *Les mots de la guerre d'Algérie*. Toulouse: Presses universitaires du Mirail, 2005.

Stora, Benjamin. "Women's Writing between Two Algerian Wars." *Research in African Literatures* 30, no. 3 (1999): 78–94.

Stora, Benjamin, and Abdelwahab Meddeb. *Histoire des relations entre juifs et musulmans*. Paris: Albin Michel, 2013.

Tahon, Marie-Blanche, and Ruthmarie H. Mitsch. "Women Novelists and Women in the Struggle for Algeria's National Liberation (1957–1980)." In "North African Literature." Special issue, *Research in African Literatures* 23, no. 3 (summer 1992): 39–50.

"The Trial of Adolf Eichmann: Record of Proceedings in the District Court of Jerusalem." Jerusalem: State of Israel Ministry of Justice, 1992.

Thénault, Sylvie. "À quoi va servir la reconnaissance de l'implication de l'État dans la mort de Maurice Audin." *The Conversation*, September 13, 2018. https://theconversation.com/a-quoi-va-servir-la-reconnaissance-de-limplication-de-letat-dans-la-mort-de-maurice-audin-103144.

Thénault, Sylvie. *Une drôle de justice: Les magistrats dans la guerre d'Algérie*. Paris: La Découverte, 2001.

Thénault, Sylvie. *Violence ordinaire dans l'Algérie coloniale: Camps, internements, assignations à résidence*. Constantine: Saïd Hannachi, Editions Média-Plus, 2012.

Thornber, Laura. *Empire of Texts in Motion: Chinese, Korean, and Taiwanese Transculturations of Japanese Literature*. Cambridge, MA: Harvard University Press, 2009.

Tristan, Anne. *Le silence du fleuve: Ce crime que nous n'avons toujours pas nommé*. Bezons: Au nom de la mémoire, 1991.

Trouillot, Michel-Rolph. *Silencing the Past: Power and the Production of History*. Boston: Beacon Press, 1995.

Tuck, Eve, and K. Wayne Yang. "Decolonization Is Not a Metaphor." *Decolonization: Indigeneity, Education, and Society* 1, no. 1 (2010): 1–40.

Vergès, Françoise. *Le ventre des femmes: Capitalisme, racialisation, féminisme*. Paris: Albin Michel, 2017.

Vergès, Jacques. *De la stratégie judiciaire*. Paris: Les Éditions de Minuit, 1968.

Vergès, Jacques, Mourad Oussedik, and Abdessamad Benabdallah. *Nuremberg pour l'Algérie*. Paris: Maspero, 1961.

Vergès, Jacques, Michel Zavrian, and Maurice Courrège. *Les disparus: Le cahier vert*. Paris: Éditions de Minuit, 1959.

Vidal-Naquet, Pierre. *La torture dans la République*. Paris: Éditions de Minuit, 1972.

Vince, Natalya. *Our Fighting Sisters: Nation, Memory, and Gender in Algeria, 1954–1962*. Manchester, UK: Manchester University Press, 2015.

Vince, Natalya, and Walid Benkhaled. "Performing Algerianness: The National and Transnational Construction of Algeria's 'Culture Wars.'" In *Algeria: Nation, Culture, and Transnationalism*, edited by Patrick Crowley, 243–69. Liverpool: Liverpool University Press, 2017.

"Waciny Laredj: 'L'art est notre dernier rempart pour faire face à l'islamisme.'" *Le matin d'Algérie*, November 18, 2011. https://www.lematindz.net/news/6279-waciny-laredj-lart-est-notre-dernier-rempart-pour-faire-face-non-seulement-lintegrisme-mais-aussi-a-toutes-les-expressions-totalitaires-lire-lentretien.html.

Weil, Patrick. *How to Be French: Nationality in the Making since 1789*. Durham, NC: Duke University Press, 2008.

Weil, Patrick. "Le statut des musulmans en Algérie coloniale: Une nationalité française dénaturée." *Histoire de la justice* 16 (2005): 93–109.

Wiesel, Elie. *La Nuit*. Paris: Éditions de Minuit, 1958.

Wieviorka, Annette. *The Era of the Witness*. Translated by Jared Stark. Ithaca, NY: Cornell University Press, [1998] 2006.

Wieviorka, Annette. "L'expression 'camp de concentration' au 20e siècle." *Vingtième siècle: Revue d'histoire* 54 (April 1997): 4–12.

Wilder, Gary. *The French Imperial Nation State: Negritude and Colonial Humanism between the Two World Wars*. Chicago: University of Chicago Press, 2005.

Willis, Michael. *The Islamist Challenge in Algeria: A Political History*. New York: New York University Press, 1997.

Wood, Michael. "The Last Night of All." In "Remapping Genre." Special issue, *PMLA* 122, no. 5 (2007): 1394–402.

Yacine, Tassadit. *Aït Menguellet Chante... Chansons berbères contemporaines*. Paris: La Découverte, 1989.

Young, Allan. *The Harmony of Illusions: Inventing Post-Traumatic Stress Disorder*. Princeton, NJ: Princeton University Press, 1995.

Young, Robert J. C. *White Mythologies: Writing History and the West*. New York: Routledge, 1999.

Zimra, Clarisse. "Not So Far from Medina: Assia Djebar Charts Islam's 'Insupportable Feminist Revolution.'" *World Literature Today* 70, no. 4 (autumn 1996): 823–34.

Zimra, Clarisse. "'When the Past Answers Our Present': Assia Djebar Talks about Loin de Médine." *Callaloo* 16, no. 1 (winter 1993): 116–31.

Index

Page numbers followed by f indicate figures.

Abraham (biblical figure), 61
Agamben, Giorgio: contrast with Zahia Rahmani, 32–33, 49–51, 52–53, 212n47; *Homo Sacer: Sovereign Power and Bare Life*, 27, 29; *musulman* (*Muselmann*), 23, 27, 29–30, 39–40, 41–43, 45–46, 47, 208n8, 209n15; and Primo Levi, 27, 29–30, 33, 35–38; *Remnants of Auschwitz*, 29, 31–32, 33–41, 43–44, 51, 211n42
Ailleret, General Charles, 87, 93
Aït Djaffer, Ismail, 183
Al Anka, M'hamed, 156, 194, 195
Alcarez, Emmanuel, 105–6
Alf layla wa-layla (*The Thousand and One Nights*), 147, 152–54
Algerian civil war (1988–99): connected to recent protests, 173; literature about, 15, 173; naming of (*décennie noire*, "uncivil war"), 10, 143, 238–39n2
Algerian independence war (1954–62): Évian Accords, 24, 67, 68; French language and, 186; French recognition of, 10–11; literature about, 15, 102–3, 165; narrative of, 9, 112, 136, 229n32; violence of, 14
Algiers: 1988 protests, 9, 25, 76, 150, 161; 2019–20 protests, 172–73; as capital of Third World, 9
Alhassan, Maytha, 172
Ali, Bachir Hadj, 183
Alleg, Henri, 65, 86, 88
Améry, Jean, 41
Amnesty International, 137, 250n16
amnesty laws, 24, 68, 137, 147, 150, 160, 176, 179
Amrani, Djamel, 183
Amrouche, Fadhma Aïth Mansour, 142f; Arabic language, 164; artistic process, 163; biographical information, 162–63, 164, 165, 176; French language, 164, 165; *Histoire de ma vie*, 142f, 147, 155, 162–67; Kabyle language, 164, 165–66; in Waciny Laredj's work, 163, 164, 166; writing as testimony, 163–64, 165
Amrouche, Jean, 162, 163, 183
Amrouche, Taos, 162, 163, 165–66
anarchive: defined, 3–4, 199n9; literature as, 15, 32, 124; of October 1988, 147; oral histories as, 110–11; in Samira Negrouche's work, 186–87. *See also* Brozgal, Lia
Anidjar, Gil, 30
Antigone, 54, 101, 105, 127, 146
Arabic language: as Algerian national language, 107, 109, 112, 126, 178; blending with French language, 170, 205n63, 238n130; formal, 145, 171, 186; and Islam, 152, 153; literature written in, 60, 69, 146, 152, 163, 178; translation to/from French, 20, 83, 96, 100, 132, 141, 143, 145, 180, 207n86, 226–27n3. *See also* Darija (colloquial Arabic)
"Arab Spring," 10, 172
Arendt, Hannah, 29, 30, 32, 34
Armée islamique du salut (AIS), 137
Arnaud, Georges, 65
Arris (town), 102
Audin, Maurice, 65, 69, 86, 88
Aurès mountains, 102, 104, 110, 111, 113, 118–19, 123, 128, 130, 134, 139
Auschwitz: *musulman* (*Muselmann*), 29, 30, 31, 34, 40–41, 50, 208n8, 211n42; physical remnants, 37; satellite camps (lagers), 35–37
Azzegagh, Ahmed, 183

Bamia, Aïda, 101
Belhadj, Abdelkader, 71, 74
Ben, Myriam (Marylise Ben Haïm), 183, 186
Benabdallah, Abdessamad, 78. See also *Nuremberg pour l'algérie*
Ben Bouali, Hassiba, 172
Ben Haïm, Marylise (Myriam Ben), 183, 186
Ben Jelloun, Tahar, 153
Benkhaled, Walid, 14, 110, 151
Benmalek, Anouar, 159
Ben M'hidi, Larbi, 65, 172
Bentahar, Ziad, 171
Bentalha massacre, 25, 173–75, 176, 177
Bergen-Belsen, 33, 34, 36, 37, 51
Black Panthers, 9, 202n40
Bois, Marcel, 24, 100, 141, 145, 226–27n3, 232n66, 239n11
Bouabdellah, Abdelkader, 81
Boucebci, Mahfoud, 138
Boudiaf, Mohamed, 172
Bouhired, Djamila, 65, 172
Boumaza, Béchir, 71–72, 74–76, 82, 111
Boumédiène, Houari, 1965 coup, 112, 187; historical narratives of regime, 108, 109; nationalism, 107, 108
Boumendjel, Ali, 65
Boupacha, Abdelaziz (father of Djamila), 93–96
Boupacha, Djamila, 64f, 86f; arrest and torture, 63–64, 66, 69, 85–86, 89; legal case, 65, 67, 85, 87, 90–93; release from prison, 68, 93; as symbol, 67, 172
Boupacha, Madame (mother of Djamila), 96
Boupacha, Nefissa, 96
Bouteflika, Abdelaziz, 226n1; 2012 speech at Sétif, 147–51; amnesty laws, 137, 150; candidacy for fifth term, 172, 177, 181, 192; end of Algerian civil war, 10, 137, 176–77; removal from office, 171, 192; resistance against regime of, 10
Brozgal, Lia, 3–4, 46–47, 110. See also anarchive
Buchenwald, 40
burial: and mourning process, 105, 127; of murder victims, 127, 137, 149, 164; rights to, 54; rites of, 105, 124, 135
Butler, Judith, 147

Cahier noir d'octobre, 137, 157–62
Carpi, Aldo, 28f, 33, 34, 41, 209n20

Celan, Paul, 70
Cervantes, Miguel de, 154
Cesaire, Aimé, 13–14
Chaâbi music, 155, 195
Chaouia language, 24, 101, 102, 110–11, 117, 118, 135
Chaulet-Achour, Christiane, 69–70
Chausserie-Laprée, Philippe, 87
Chenoua language, 117
Chenu, R. P., 88
Cixous, Hélène, 4–5
Code de l'indigénat, 5
Collectif des familles des disparus en Algérie (CFDA), 137, 149, 179, 246n77
Comité Justice pour l'Algérie, 176, 251n17
concentration camps: in Algeria, 5, 47, 48, 52, 65; colonial history of, 18, 42; firsthand accounts, 17–18, 35; footage of, 33–34, 50; liberation, 31; survivors of Nazi camps, 17–18, 27, 28f, 63. See also Auschwitz; Bergen-Belsen; Dachau; Majdanek; Ravensbrück
Copenal, Claude, 82–85
Crémieux Decree, 4

Dachau, 40, 65, 221n35
Dali, Salvador, 154
Dalsace, Dr. Jean, 88
Darija (colloquial Arabic), examples of use: 106, 145, 146, 207n87; in literature, 20; in music, 170; in opposition to formal Arabic, 171; relationship to French language, 186
Davis, Muriam Haleh, 14, 172
de Beauvoir, Simone, 65–66, 87, 88, 218n17
de Bollardière, General, 88
de Gaulle, Charles, 65
décennie noire, 10, 143. See also Algerian civil war (1988–99)
decolonial justice, 6, 97
decolonization: and amnesia, 12; centering of French perspectives, 12; defined by author, 14; effects on popular memory, 12, 14–15; failures of, 10; as a French invention, 9, 12; and justice, 93–94, 97; literature as tool for, 173; literature's role in, 173, 179–80; political action, 172, 192. See also Algerian independence war (1954–62); Évian Accords
Delacroix, Eugène, 154

demonstrations, 45–46, 136, 158, 159, 160, 168–72, 169f, 179. *See also* Hirāk (present-day demonstrations); protestors, violence against
Derradji, Abderraouf (Soolking), 169–70, 172, 177, 248n1
Derrida, Jacques, 4, 70–71, 90, 91
Dib, Mohammed, 183, 184–85
Dinur, Yechiel (Ka-Tzetnik), 30, 44
Diop, Boubacar Boris, 153
"direct translation" protocol, 82, 89
Djamila Boupacha, 64f, 86f; account of Boupacha's father, 94–96; account of Boupacha's mother, 96; publication, 66, 85, 87, 218n17; as testimony, 91, 93–94, 96–97, 160; writing style, 87, 88, 89–90. *See also* Boupacha, Djamila; de Beauvoir, Simone; Halimi, Gisèle
Djaout, Tahar, 138, 183, 186, 252n36, 253–53n38
Djebar, Assia: biographical information, 174, 245n60; *L'amour, la fantasia*, 16, 19–23, 84, 174, 175; *Le blanc de l'Algérie*, 138, 182; multilingual writing, 178; politics of testimony, 178; on state violence, 136–37, 174–80, 245n60
Djelloul, Galiya, 193
Drid Hocine Hospital, 100, 104, 138, 226n2
Drif, Zohra, 4, 172
Dutour, Nasséra, 149–50

Eichmann, Adolf, 35, 44, 63, 217n10
El-Biar detention center, 64, 86, 92, 93, 95, 96
elections in Algeria: 1991–92 (canceled), 10, 48, 148; 2012, 148, 149; 2014, 147–48; 2019, 148, 172, 177, 181, 187, 192
El Ghaffour, Mohamed, 156
Esmeir, Samera, 32
Évian Accords, 24, 67, 68, 93, 197n1
Ezzerhouni, Khaddour Benachour, 156

Fanon, Frantz: on anti-Muslim racism, 17; on concentration camps, 17–18; death, 191; on decolonization, 7, 136–37, 191–92; linguistic choices, 201n27; on state violence, 5–6, 8–9, 16–17, 66, 84
Farès, Nabile, 1–2, 183
Fédération euro-méditerranéenne contre les disparitions forcées (FEMED), 149
Feldman, Hannah, 13, 31, 208–9n12
Felman, Shoshana, 44
Fonlupt-Esperaber, J., 88

Francis, Mustapha, 71–72, 74
French language: and Algerian independence war, 186; as an Algerian language, 13, 15, 171, 180–81, 183, 186; Algerian literature written in, 117, 121, 180–81, 183, 220n27; blending with Arabic language, 170, 205n63, 238n130; and legal system, 2–3, 4, 8, 51–52, 68, 78, 93, 158; role in decolonization, 13; translation to/from Arabic, 20, 83, 96, 100, 132, 141, 143, 145, 180, 207n86, 226–27n3
Fromentin, Eugène, 20, 22
Front de libération nationale (FLN): 1991 elections, 10; heroic narratives, 140; in literature, 114–17, 124–26, 128, 129; news organ, 46, 111, 112; regime in Algeria, 11, 105, 107, 109, 110, 140, 229n29, 238–39n2
Front islamique du salut (FIS), 10, 148, 173, 238–39n2

genocide: in Algeria, 11, 16, 78; legal framework, 78, 80, 85, 94; by Nazis, 42, 50; in Rwanda, 3
Gestapo, 73–74, 75
gharnāṭī music, 156
ghosts: Frantz Fanon on, 7; as literary characters, 115, 138, 139; made visible by literature, 15, 21, 25, 173; *musulmans* as, 23, 34, 48, 52; in Nazi camps, 36, 37; as symbols of French violence, 84, 85, 102, 111, 173, 179
Gordon, Avery, 19, 179
Grandmaison, Olivier Le Cour, 5
Gréki, Anna, 183, 186
grief: collective, 76, 77, 116; and linguistic choices, 166; maternal, 104, 122, 127–28, 161, 165, 166, 176, 246n77; poetics of, 123, 146; public expressions of, 128–29, 146
Guelma massacre, 13, 75, 131, 149. *See also* May 8, 1945

Hadj, Ali, 72
Hagar (biblical figure), 61
Halimi, Gisèle, 64–65, 78, 85, 87–88, 88–89
Hamdani, Adda, 81
Hannoum, Abdelmajid, 31
Hanouz family, 76–77
Hirāk (present-day demonstrations in Algeria), 10, 171–72, 173, 188
Hitler, Adolf, 42
Holocaust survivors, 17–18, 27, 28f, 63

House, Jim, 14, 47
Human Rights Watch, 137, 150

Ibrahimi, Khaoula Taleb, 171
Iguerbouchène, Mohamed, 155
imperialism: Arab, 119; French, 5, 12, 20, 30, 45, 249n9; of the Global North, 169; neoimperialism, 173; Roman, 119; in work of Giorgio Agamben, 53
Indigènes, 4, 6, 8, 17, 52, 57, 63, 210n24; *indigène musulman* (juridical status), 4, 16, 17, 33, 52, 55, 76, 199n13; *indigènes israélites*, 4
Ishmael (biblical figure), 61
Islam: as Algerian state religion, 229n31; and Arabic language, 152, 153; fundamentalist interpretations, 174; rituals, 41, 49
Islamists: and modernity, 10; criticism of Algerian state, 11, 107, 229n32; fundamentalist, 145; and political violence, 110, 144, 148, 150, 151, 159, 176, 179, 239n4. *See also* Front islamique du salut (FIS)
Islamophobia, 17, 40, 60
Issiakhem, M'hamed, 99f, 138–39, 183

Jews: citizenship in Algeria, 4–5, 23, 33, 34, 57, 199n14; categorized as *musulman* or *Muselmann*, 29, 32, 40, 47, shared history with Muslims, 33, 50, 57, 61, 209n15; in Vichy-era Paris, 65, 71, 73–74, 212n50. *See also* concentration camps
Julien, Eileen, 101, 153
juridical personhood, 2, 4, 29, 31–32, 42, 45, 47, 62, 199n13
justice: abnormal, 220n28; amnesty laws, 24, 68, 137, 147, 150, 160, 176, 179, 137, 150; extrajudicial, 160; linguistic barriers to, 78; literature as, 24, 57–58, 62, 71, 94, 158, 167

Kabyle culture, 110–11, 164, 244n52, 253n45
Kabyle language, 23, 24, 60, 110–11, 117, 155, 163, 165–66, 193
Kabylie region, 42, 110–11, 150
Kateb, Yacine: friendship with Yamina Mechakra, 100, 138–39, 227n7; writing, 119, 163, 166–67, 182–83, 185, 186
Ka-Tzetnik (Yechiel Dinur), 30, 44
Kef Chkara, 132–33, 133f, 164
Keneally, Thomas, 41–42

Kettou, Safia (Zohra Rabhi), 156–57, 158, 245n60
Khadda, Mohamed, 154
Khatibi, Abdelkébir, 153
Khebaili, Moussa, 72, 74
Kherrata massacre, 13, 75–77, 149
Kłodziński, Stanisław, 41

La gangrène, 24, 71–78, 72f, 160
Lagers (satellite camps), 35–37, 210n26
la Pointe, Ali, 172
Lapoujade, Robert, 88
Laredj, Waciny: biographical information, 148; *Histoire de ma vie*, 162–63; *Sayyidat al-maqām, Marthīyāt al-yawm al-ḥazīn*, 141, 143–47, 151–54, 155–58, 160–62, 166; *The Thousand and One Nights* as intertext, 151–54, 243n39; translation into French, 141, 143, 145, 239n6; use of Arabic language, 143, 145–46, 152, 153, 158, 166; writing as testimony, 143, 154, 158, 160, 161
Lazali, Karima, 3, 9, 15, 18–19
Lazreg, Marnia, 14
Leperlier, Tristan, 15
Levi, Primo: biographical information, 35; *The Drowned and the Saved*, 35–36, 37, in Giorgio Agamben's work, 27, 33, 35–39, 51; *musulman* (*Muselmann*), 27, 29–30, 33–34, 35, 41, 208n8, 210n26; *Survival in Auschwitz*, 35; in Zahia Rahmani's work, 50, 51
Levy-Leroy, Dr., 91, 92
"Liberté" (Soolking song), 169–70, 172, 177, 248n1
lieux de mémoire, 12, 105–6, 109–10, 133
Ligue des droits de l'homme, 65
Ligue islamique pour la dawa et le djihad [LIDD], 137
Lindon, Jérôme, 68, 71, 72
literature: about Algerian independence war, 15, 102–3, 165; role in mourning, 76, 103, 120, 134, 136, 162; as supplement to legal justice, 24, 57–58, 62, 71, 94, 160; as tool for decolonization, 173, 179; written in Arabic, 60, 69, 146, 152, 163, 178; written in French, 117, 121, 180–81, 183, 220n27; written in Kabyle, 23, 24, 155, 163, 165–66
Lounès, Matoub, 192–93

MacMaster, Neil, 14, 47
Macron, Emmanuel, 11, 24, 69, 219n21
Maghreb region, 60, 118, 153

Majdanek, 50
Mallet-Joris, Françoise, 88
Malraux, André, 65
Maqām al-shahīd (monument), 98, 105–6, 107, 126
marthīyā (literary genre), 146–47, 162
Maspero (publisher), 65, 78, 79f
Matta, Roberto, 88
Mauriac, François, 65
Mauthausen-Gusen, 40
May 8, 1945, 13, 31, 75, 148–50, 185. *See also* Sétif massacre; Guelma massacre
Mayer, Daniel, 65, 88
McDougall, James, 14, 109, 110, 200n18
Mechakra, Yamina: *Arris*, 101–2, 103–5, 108, 119, 121–24, 132, 139–40, 157; biographical information, 98, 100, 104, 121, 138, 226n2; friendship with Kateb Yacine, 100, 119, 138–39, 227n7, 233n70; *La grotte éclatée*, 100, 101–3, 104, 105, 108, 114–21, 124–28, 130–34, 138–40; "L'éveil du mont," 100, 111–14, 119; *musulman (Muselmann)*, 113; publication process, 101, 138, 226–27n3, 228–29n24; use of Arabic language, 108, 114; use of French language, 102, 108, 117–18, 121, 125–26; writing as testimony, 24, 120, 128, 129–30, 139
memory studies, 12–13, 30
Meskoud, Abdelmajid, 155–56
Messmer, Pierre, 87, 93
Mezoued, Aniss, 193
Michelet, Edmond, 65, 73, 93, 221n35
Minuit (publisher), 65, 71, 72f, 73
Mokhtari, Rachid, 101, 121, 226n2, 228n23
monuments, 98, 105–8, 109, 112, 132, 134, 145, 164
mourning: and burial, 127; collective, 76, 103; Islamic rituals, 49; legal restrictions, 105, 147; literature's role in, 76, 103, 120, 134, 136, 162; professional mourners, 146; public, 105, 136, 137, 146, 147, 162, 182, 192–93; rituals, 49, 146. *See also* Antigone; burial; grief; marthīyā
Mozabite language/culture, 101, 117
Muslims: anti-Muslim racism, 17, 40, 54–55, 57; citizenship in Algeria, 4; as majority population of Algeria, 107, 109, 112, 126; fundamentalist, 179; shared history with Jews, 33, 50, 57, 61, 209n15; violence against, 54–55, 57, 151. *See also* Islam; Islamists; *musulman (Muselmann)*

musulman (Muselmann): in Auschwitz, 29, 30, 31, 34, 40–41, 50, 208n8, 211n42; in Giorgio Agamben's work, 23, 27, 29–30, 39–40, 41–43, 45–46, 47, 208n8, 209n15; *indigène musulman* juridical status, 4, 16, 17, 33, 55, 76, 199n13; origin and interpretation, 33, 36, 39–40, 41, 208n7; in Primo Levi's work, 27, 29–30, 33–34, 35–36, 41, 208n8, 210n26; typographic treatment of term, 35, 38, 43, 48; in Yemina Mechakra's work, 113; in Zahia Rahmani's work, 48, 50, 51–52, 53, 54, 55, 59–60, 175, 212n47. *See also* Muslims

national charters: 1964, 112; 1976, 108–9, 112; 2005, 137, 150
Nazism: and colonization, 18, 31, 47, 101, 128; jargon, 42–43; linked to French state violence, 73; as precedent for French state violence, 71, 73, 74, 77, 93; trials, 43–44, 57, 68, 85; in Vichy-era Paris, 71, 75–76. *See also* concentration camps
Negrouche, Samira: "2×2", 187–192; artistic installations, 181–91, 182f, 184f, 185f; "Bâton/Totem," 182–83; biographical information, 180, 192–93; publications, 180; *Quand l'amandier refleurira (When the Almond Tree Reblooms)*, 180; *Six arbres de fortune autour de ma baignoire*, 193–95; *Triangle*, 180; use of Kabyle language, 193; work as translator, 180; writing as testimony, 25, 173–74; "XIII planches/poètes (a genealogy a constellation)," 174, 181–82, 183–87
noncitizen subjects (*sujets*), 2, 4. *See also indigènes*
Nora, Pierre, 12, 106. *See also lieux de mémoire*
Nuremberg pour l'algérie, 79f; description of contents, 80–85; publication, 67–68; as testimony, 24, 78, 160
Nuremberg trials, 35, 43–44

October 17, 1961 (police massacre in Paris), 12, 45–47, 76. *See also* protestors, violence against; racism; state violence
octobre noir (October 1988 violence in Algiers): government silence about, 150–51, 158–59; relationship to other movements, 9–10, 150–51, 173; role in literature, 25, 136–37, 143–44, 147, 148, 158, 161, 174, 180, 194. See also *Cahier noir d'octobre*

Organisation armée secrète (OAS), 87
Orientalism, 40, 41, 53, 60, 100, 110, 132, 236n112
Ould Aoudia, Amokrane, 80
Oussedik, Mourad, 78. See also *Nuremberg pour l'algérie*

Palestine, 101, 128, 204n51
Panijel, Jacques, 46
Papon, Maurice, 45–46
Pélissier, General Aimable, 19, 21, 125
Philip, André, 88
Picasso, Pablo, 88, 154
poetry: in Arabic, 69, 146–47; in French, 180–81, 252n36; in Kabyle, 163, 165–66; lack of popular recognition, 69; *marthīyā* genre, 146–47, 162; as political, 141; as testimony, 176–78. See also Djebar, Assia; Kateb, Yacine; Negrouche, Samira
police violence. *See* October 17, 1961 (police massacre in Paris); *octobre noir* (October 1988 violence in Algiers); protestors, violence against; state violence
prisons: in Algeria, 47, 48, 52–53, 59; colonial context, 5, 55
protestors, violence against: 1945 (Sétif, Guelma, Kherrata), 13, 31; 1961 (Paris), 12, 45–47, 76; 1980 (Berber Spring), 150; 2001 (Kabylie), 150; 2019–20 (Algiers), 172–73. See also *octobre noir* (October 1988 violence in Algiers); state violence
public spaces: Algerians restricted from, 45, 146; art in, 174, 181–86, 192; corpses displayed in, 45, 174–75; counternarratives in, 151; mourning in, 105, 137, 146; reclamation by protestors, 168, 179, 192, 193

Qader, Nasrin, 153, 242n36

Rabhi, Zohra (Safia Kettou), 156–57, 158, 245n60
racism: of Algerian state, 57; anti-Algerian, 96; anti-Muslim, 17, 40; in France, 7, 14, 45; of French state, 12, 57, 66, 78
Rahal, Malika, 14, 107, 108–9, 110–11
Rahmani, Zahia: biographical information, 48; *France, récit d'une enfance*, 49; *Moze*, 49–50, 51–52, 53–59; *"Musulman" roman*, 32–33, 47–49, 50, 51, 52–53, 59–62; and work of Giorgio Agamben, 32–33, 49–51, 52–53,

212n47; writing about torture, 52, 57; writing as testimony, 23, 57, 61–62, 129
Raïs massacre, 25, 173, 174–75, 176, 177, 178, 179
rape: in literature, 22, 113, 125, 129, 152, 157; by state agents, 64, 66, 74, 82–83, 86, 93, 166
Ravensbrück, 37, 40, 210n26
Resnais, Alain, 50, 212n50
Revel, J. F., 88
Rezaiguia, Ryma, 187–88, 190, 192
Rihani, Lazhari, 171
Rothberg, Michael, 12, 27, 204n54, 217n10
Rouabah, Brahim, 172–73
Roucolle, Colonel, 81
Roy, Jules, 88
Rwandan genocide, 3
Ryn, Zdzisław, 41, 53

Sagan, Françoise, 88, 218n17
Saïdi, Lamis, 100, 101, 228n14
Saint-Arnaud, General Armand-Jacques Leroy, 18, 19, 125
Sakiet Sidi Yousef, 130, 131
Sakri, Lamine, 187–88, 190, 192
Sanyal, Debarati, 12
Sebti, Yousef, 183
Seghir, Khider, 72
Sénac, Jean, 183, 187
September 11 attacks, 9, 14, 48, 131, 147
Serres, Thomas, 172, 173
Sétif massacre, 13, 31, 75, 81, 131, 149. See also May 8, 1945
Seuil (publisher), 65
shahīd/shuhadā' (martyr, witness), 102, 106, 107–8, 111, 114, 120, 136, 137, 210n25, 230n33
Shahrazād, 153–54, 242–43n36
Shepard, Todd, 3, 9, 12, 13–14, 199n14
Silem, Ali, 182, 183
Silverman, Max, 12
Simon, Pierre Henri, 65
slavery, 12, 37, 55, 60–61, 215–16n103
Sofsky, Wolfgang, 41
Soolking (Abderraouf Derradji), 169–70, 172, 177, 248n1
Souami, Benaïssa, 71–72, 74
South Africa, 3, 101, 128
Spivak, Gayatri, 16, 19, 207n84
state violence, counting Algerian victims of, 3, 84; in France, 14; French attitudes toward,

66; historical context, 18, 31, 73–74, 75–76, 211n39, 218n16; invisibility of, 12, 46, 66, 75, 140, 179, 211n39; legal consequences of, 94; resistance to, 172; and testimony, 29, 47, 74. *See also* demonstrations; protestors, violence against; torture

Stora, Benjamin, 10, 11, 216n7, 238–39n2, 250n16

Tamasheq language, 60, 117

Tamazight language, 15, 20, 24, 166, 180, 186

testimony: alternative forms, 24–25; and anarchive, 3–4; Arabic etymology, 107–8; in Assia Djebar's work, 178; *Djamila Boupacha*, 90–91, 93–94, 96–97, 160; Fadhma Aïth Mansour Amrouche's writing as, 163–64, 165; issues in translating, 71; as literary genre, 15–16, 47, 70–71, 102, 117; in Nazi trials, 39, 44–45, 63, 94, 217n10; *Nuremburg pour l'algérie* as, 24, 78, 160; of perpetrators, 82; in poetry, 176–78; in Primo Levi's work, 35; relationship to law, 4, 24; Samira Negrouche's writing as, 25, 173–74, 181–82; under state violence, 29–30, 47, 74; by torture survivors, 71–78, 84, 91, 93–94, 96–97, 137, 158–60, 176, 216n7; in Waciny Laredj's work, 143, 154, 158, 160, 161; Yamina Mechakra's writing as, 24, 120, 128, 129–30, 139, 102–3, 105, 108, 111; Zahia Rahmani's writing as, 23, 47, 52, 56–59, 61–62

Texier, Jean, 44f, 45

Thénault, Sylvie, 3, 5, 14, 27, 81–82, 210n24

Third Reich, 36, 37, 44, 81. *See also* Nazism

torture: in Algerian literature, 69–70; amnesty laws, 24, 68, 137, 147, 150, 160, 176, 179; of Djamila Boupacha, 63–64, 66, 69, 85–86, 89; French popular awareness of, 11–12, 66, 77, 220n27; French state acknowledgment of, 10–11, 24; methods, 83, 86, 89, 91, 92; testimony by survivors, 65, 71–78, 84, 91, 93–94, 96–97, 137, 158-160, 176, 216n7; in Waciny Laredj's work, 161–62; in Zahia Rahmani's work, 52, 57. *See also* protestors, violence against; state violence

Tristan, Anne, 45

Vergès, Françoise, 3, 12–13, 168

Vergès, Jacques, 65, 78. See also *Nuremberg pour l'algérie*

Vince, Natalya, 14, 110, 151, 239n2

"war on terror," 10, 14, 48, 160

Wiesel, Elie, 17, 41, 53, 65

Wieviorka, Annette, 44, 217n10

Wilder, Gary, 12

xenophobia, 14. *See also* racism

Yacine, Kateb. *See* Kateb, Yacine

Zéroual, Liamine, 176

www.ingramcontent.com/pod-product-compliance
Lightning Source LLC
Chambersburg PA
CBHW050210240426
43671CB00013B/2286